ANTHROPOLOGICAL DEMOGRAPHY

POPULATION AND DEVELOPMENT
A series edited by Richard A. Easterlin

Previously published:

Fertility Change in Contemporary Japan
Robert W. Hodge and Naohiro Ogawa

Social Change and the Family in Taiwan
Arland Thornton and Hui-Sheng Lin

Swing Low, Sweet Chariot:
The Mortality Cost of Colonizing Liberia
in the Nineteenth Century
Antonio McDaniel

From Parent to Child: Intrahousehold Allocations
and Intergenerational Relations in the
United States
Jere R. Behrman, Robert A. Pollak,
and Paul Tawbman

ANTHROPOLOGICAL DEMOGRAPHY

Toward a New Synthesis

Edited by David I. Kertzer *and* Tom Fricke

The University of Chicago Press   *Chicago & London*

DAVID I. KERTZER is Paul Dupee University Professor of Social
Science and professor of anthropology and history at Brown
University. TOM FRICKE is associate professor of anthropology
and associate chair of the Department of Anthropology at the
University of Michigan.

The University of Chicago Press, Chicago 60637
The University of Chicago Press, Ltd., London

© 1997 by The University of Chicago
All rights reserved. Published 1997

Printed in the United States of America

06 05 04 03 02 01 00 99 98 97   1 2 3 4 5

ISBN: 0-226-43195-9 (cloth)
ISBN: 0-226-43196-7 (paper)

Library of Congress Cataloging-in-Publication Data

Anthropological demography : toward a new synthesis / edited by David
I. Kertzer and Tom Fricke.
    p. cm. — (Population and development)
  "Revised versions of papers originally presented at the Brown
University Conference on Anthropological Demography, November 3–5,
1994."
  Includes bibliographical references and index.
  ISBN 0-226-43195-9 (cloth : alk. paper). —ISBN 0-226-43196-7
(pbk. : alk. paper)
  1. Demographic anthropology—Congresses.   2. Demography—
Congresses.   I. Kertzer, David I., 1948– .   II. Fricke, Thomas
E. (Thomas Earl), 1954– .   III. Conference on Anthropological
Demography (1994 : Brown University)   IV. Series: Population and
development (Chicago, Ill.)
GN33.5.A57   1997
304.6—dc21   96-46664
                                                                    CIP

∞ The paper used in this publication meets the minimum requirements of the
American National Standard for Information Sciences—Permanence of Paper for
Printed Library Materials, ANSI Z39.48-1984.

In memory of Robert McC. Netting
anthropologist, demographer, and friend

Contents

Acknowledgments

The chapters in this volume are substantially revised versions of papers originally presented at the Brown University Conference on Anthropological Demography, November 3–5, 1994. This conference was organized by the editors, who gratefully acknowledge conference support provided by the National Institute of Child Health and Human Development and the National Institute on Aging (Grant no. R13 HD31811), the Mellon Foundation, and the Brown University Population Studies and Training Center.

An interdisciplinary conference of this kind requires the special dedication of many people. We would especially like to acknowledge the conference efforts of several graduate assistants in the Anthropological Demography program at Brown University: Steven Lubkemann, Fallon Moursund, Rebecca Upton, and Danyu Wang. Our gratitude to the conference coordinator, Carol Walker, for her overall behind-the-scenes attention to detail, is great.

We also need to thank the many discussants and session organizers whose contributions were far from silent and yet whose names do not appear among the list of authors here. Each of these chapters bears the imprint of probing remarks from Bill Axinn, Candice Bradley, Stanley Brandes, Tony Carter, John Casterline, Anastasia Gage, Dennis Hogan, Marida Hollos, Ron Lesthaeghe, Geoff McNicoll, Emily Martin, Dominique Meekers, Phil Morgan, Bob Netting, Lucille Newman, Biju Rao, Harry Sanabria, Jane Schneider, Peter Schneider, Arland Thornton, and Susan Watkins.

Additional editorial support for this volume has been provided by our respective academic homes, including (for David Kertzer) Brown University's Department of Anthropology and its Population Studies and Training Center and (for Tom Fricke) the University of Michigan's Department of Anthropology, Institute for Social Research, and Population Studies Center. We also thank University of Chicago Press editor Geoffrey Huck for his support for and help with this volume and production editor Leslie Keros and copyeditor Gayle Boyer for their superb attention to detail.

Our final thanks go to Bob Netting. Little did we know that his witty and elegant participation as a discussant at the Brown Conference would be among his last contributions to the union of anthropological and demographic inquiry that he inspired for many of us. His death in the early months of 1995 is a loss of an unparalleled combination of human warmth, humanistic spirit, and scientific rigor. We dedicate this volume to his memory.

Chapter One

Toward an Anthropological Demography

David I. Kertzer and Tom Fricke

The relationship between sociocultural anthropology and demography has been long, tortured, often ambivalent, sometimes passionate. Its ebbs and flows follow the dual paths of the two fields, where changes in research problems, methods, epistemologies, and populations of special interest have produced periods of keen hope for the virtues of collaboration interspersed with times of mutual indifference bordering on reciprocal disdain. Some of this uneven history originates in the usual lag of conceptual and methodological development in the crossing of disciplinary boundaries; other sources reflect more fundamental differences in disciplinary worldviews.

Within both demography and anthropology[1] recent years have been marked by great theoretical and methodological ferment. Demography for its part has been thriving—the recipient of research funding from a variety of governmental and nongovernmental sources at levels that make many anthropologists envious and, often, suspicious. The political and policy relevance of demographic research could hardly be more apparent, as Americans and populations of other richer countries worry about the high levels of fertility and consequent emigration from poorer parts of the world and about the consequences of low fertility, illegitimacy, and an aging population in their own countries.

Driven by a combination of such policy concerns, the funding that flows from them, and their early disciplinary experience with quantified data in Euro-American contexts, demographers have linked themselves to a positivist epistemology and a can-do attitude toward pragmatic social research. By emphasizing particular types of methodological development within a relatively closed sphere of pragmatic issues, demography has fashioned the self-image of a discipline whose practitioners are able to apply their standard toolkits to the explanation of demographic behavior anywhere in the world. Much demographic training still consists of an emphasis on a small number of common dependent variables, outcome measures largely unchanged since well before Alfred Lotka's watershed work (1907), and a few statistical techniques for ferreting out relationships among variables. At the center of data collection for this research paradigm is the social and demographic survey, aimed at reducing social life and demographic behavior to a series of discrete, measurable variables whose relationships can be modeled mathematically.

Given this picture of demography, there would seem to be little basis for a renewed excitement about the possibilities for a productive union of demography and anthropology. A parallel thumbnail sketch of sociocultural anthropology could be taken for a study in contrasts. It would likely emphasize the movement in the past two decades away from positivist epistemologies, an erosion of the status of quantification, and political as well as epistemological objections to research that treats the people being studied as objects whose behavior is rendered into the western observer's already existing categories.[2]

Yet, despite these superficially disparate characterizations, the basis for a highly productive and influential union of demography and sociocultural anthropology is now being crafted by scholars from various fields.[3] The chapters in this book indicate many of the theoretical and practical contours of this development and we sketch some of these out in this introduction. Although we need to acknowledge forces in both fields working against this new synthesis, we nevertheless believe that the intellectual forces propelling it can overcome these impediments.

Curiously, the primary incentives for this most recent rapprochement come from within demography itself. Dissatisfactions arising over the past two decades in demography have diluted some of the self-assurance of the reigning paradigm. One of the most notable outcomes of this dissatisfaction has been the insistent call to incorporate more anthropological insights into the study of population processes (Caldwell, Caldwell, and Caldwell 1987; Caldwell, Hill, and Hull 1988). This call has had two related motivations, one more obviously technical and the other touching on theoretical issues. First has been a growing recognition of the limitations of survey modes of data collection for gathering accurate, fully textured, and nuanced data at multiple levels of social reality and a consequent interest in the contributions that anthropology can make through its intensive fieldwork methodology (Caldwell 1985; Axinn, Fricke, and Thornton 1991). Indeed, for some demographers, "anthropological" demography refers to these methodological borrowings and little else. In this limited view, anthropology's only demographic contributions of value are intensive fieldwork methods giving rise to the various forms of microdemography.

The second motivation, however, arises from demographic researchers who are themselves dissatisfied with the state of demographic theory, and offers more complex, interesting, and potentially transformative possibilities of intellectual sharing. These motivations grow out of the increasing recognition of a role for culture in the satisfactory understanding of demographic behavior (Anderson 1986; Lesthaeghe and Surkyn 1988; Caldwell, Caldwell, and Caldwell 1987). Paradoxically, given that this most recent call originates internally, the implications of this rethinking may be more troubling to the current demographic enterprise, since this is not simply a matter of add-fieldwork-and-stir. Rather, long-standing demographic models, both explicit and implied, of human behavior and of social explanation are placed at risk by the quest for a more sophisticated social and cultural theory.

Before analyzing the current state of relations between anthropology and demography, however, we would like to review the roller-coaster history of the work done at the intersection of these two fields. We then examine the forces within each field that today stand in the way of progress in bringing anthropology and demography together, and suggest how and why they should be overcome. Finally, we take a look at the topics discussed in the various chapters, before concluding with a query regarding demography's disciplinary status.

Anthropology and Demography—A Brief History

The sources of contemporary obstructions to a full synthesis lie in the history of the relationship between demography and anthropology. That history reveals that British, rather than American, anthropologists originally showed the greater interest in demography. Similarly, early demographers tended to be drawn to fieldwork firmly within the classical tradition of British social anthropology. The logic at work here was neither sinister nor conspiratorial.[4] The British fieldwork tradition stressed social structure and kinship over the cultural reconstruction approach which marked much American anthropology. Such an emphasis lent itself well to the demographic quest to embed population processes within kin and family contexts. At the same time, notions of culture in demography imported all the implications for contemporary theoretical development of the more jural, rule-oriented style of British structural anthropology from which they were drawn.

Precursors to Contemporary Interest

In reconstructing the history of the relations between sociocultural anthropology and demography, we might begin with its prehistory. In this epoch, before today's disciplinary boundaries were firmly drawn, anthropologists went about demographic research on their own. Indeed, as modern fieldwork methods began to develop, even before their apotheosis with Malinowski stranded on the Trobriand Islands in World War I, demographic data occupied a central place. That well-worn British guide to anthropological fieldwork of the latter nineteenth and twentieth century, *Notes and Queries in Anthropology*, established census-taking as one of the first steps of fieldwork, constructing a framework on which all further social research would rest.[5]

Even before Malinowski made it to the Trobriands, his future nemesis, Andrew Brown (later to become A. R. Radcliffe-Brown), was engaged in fieldwork in the Andaman Islands off the Burma coast. Following a verandah-based fieldwork style soon to be superseded, Brown found it necessary to begin his classic monograph, *The Andaman Islanders* (1964),[6] by providing

basic population estimates for the various islands, including a critical evaluation of the 1901 Indian census results. He went on to trace the decline of
the population of the various islands, discussing the different European-
introduced diseases responsible for heightened mortality, and discussing as
well the decline in fertility. The social impact of this population decline also
drew his attention. His approach followed a well-established pattern of anthropological research.

The generation of British anthropologists who followed Radcliffe-Brown,
and who were to become the major figures in the heyday of British anthropology in the postwar years, further developed these demographic interests;
driven by an underlying Durkheimian model of social morphology, demographic data were considered fundamental to good anthropological fieldwork, and relations between various social and cultural elements and features
of population attracted attention. This succeeding generation also made the
first anthropological forays into adopting demographic methods, especially
life tables, to anthropological data.

Raymond Firth and Meyer Fortes, two of the most influential students of
Malinowski, exemplify the main thrust of this demographic development in
social anthropology.[7] Both came upon population issues primarily through a
focus on analyzing kinship systems, which by the 1930s had become the major
emphasis of British anthropology. In Firth's classic study of the Polynesian
island of Tikopia ([1936] 1968), an entire chapter is devoted to "A Modern
Population Problem." This chapter indeed signals a shift in Firth's interests
from kinship per se to issues of economic organization. The population "problem" in question is that of balancing land and population on a small island.
Firth critiques the deficiencies of earlier European population data on Tikopia, and points to the unfortunate impact that European contact had on
the previous cultural mechanisms supporting population-land equilibrium.
Christian missionaries are taken to task for their ethnocentric opposition to
the traditional population-regulating mechanisms of abortion and infanticide
(1968:374–76).

Even more influential than Firth in emphasizing the central role to be
played by demographic data was Meyer Fortes. Fortes begins a 1943 article,
for example, by declaring: "Anthropologists have begun to realize the importance of demographic data for their inquiries. . . ." He goes on to say, "our
knowledge of primitive population structures is most inadequate. In the case
of Africa, official statistics are of little help." He concludes by observing
that "anthropologists have had to be their own demographers, in however a
rough-and-ready fashion." Fortes then discusses the defects of the demographic data that anthropologists have produced, and presents the results of
his fertility analysis of the West African Tallensi, based on his surveys of men
and women.

One interesting eddy within the broader current of British social anthro-

pology is associated with Max Gluckman[8] and the department he started at the University of Manchester in 1949, and was unique for its emphasis on standardization and training in methods (Epstein 1967), including life table analysis (Barnes 1949). The work of Gluckman's colleagues and students was concerned with social change and its impact on kinship and family systems in Africa. As something of a precursor to today's applied anthropology, this group went as far as any in making use of the tools and concepts of other disciplines, especially sociology, in their investigations of central demographic processes such as marriage, divorce, and fertility (Richards 1940; Mitchell 1949; Barnes 1951; Schapera 1955; Colson 1958; Ardener 1962). While their demographic methods appear crude by the standards of today's demography, they were an important exception to the general lack of quantitative sophistication among most anthropologists of the time. One unfortunate outcome of the Manchester School's inability to bring these methods to bear on their motivating questions about marriage and social structure, however, was that its technical recommendations remained marginal to the wider anthropological community.

Demography Reaches Out

This early work of anthropologists on demographic topics did not go unnoticed by the emerging field of demography. Even in the proto-demography of early British administrative efforts, the boundaries between strictly demographic and ethnographic interests were elided as British censuses strove to identify the social diversity of colonized populations along with their numbers. The 1901 Indian census referred to by Radcliffe-Brown, for example, based many of its enumeration categories on earlier attempts to define every caste and ethnic group in the subcontinent (see chapter 6 in this volume). Nevertheless, the end of World War II ushered in a boom period for demography, especially in directing attention to population "problems" affecting nonwestern countries. Here anthropologists were deemed potentially useful experts on the social practices that lay behind demographic behavior in nonwestern settings. It is probably no accident that the turn toward anthropology was mostly directed toward the British structural-functionalist school. First, their focus on kinship systems and culture defined largely in terms of jural norms of behavior lent itself well to embedding the more proximate determinants of population processes into social systems. A second relevant factor was that many of the newly independent states were former British colonies and British anthropologists were the primary fieldworkers studying these populations.

A major achievement in this plumbing of anthropology for demographic purposes came in 1951 when the International Union for the Scientific Study of Population established the grandly titled Committee on Population Problems of Countries in Process of Industrialization (following the orthodoxies of modernization theory, this category included any place that was not already industrialized). What was regarded as the major population "problem" was not high mortality but rather high fertility and consequent population growth in the poorer countries. Chaired by demographer Frank Notestein—famous for his formulation of demographic transition theory—the committee also counted Raymond Firth as one of its most active members. UNESCO offered the Committee funds for a study of "social and cultural conditions affecting fertility in nonindustrial societies," and the demographer Frank Lorimer was selected to undertake a grand synthesis of what was then known. His treatise consists almost entirely of a survey of the anthropological literature.

The highly influential result of this project was the volume *Culture and Human Fertility,* published in 1954, which contained not only a 250-page section on "General Theory" by Lorimer, but studies by Africanist anthropologists Meyer Fortes, Audrey Richards, and Priscilla Reining as well. In many ways this work set the terms of the subsequent debate on the role of culture in demographic behavior, especially fertility, and on the contribution that anthropology had to make to demography. The functionalist assumptions of this work are only now beginning to be questioned.

Two of the elements of this paradigm that merit mention are (1) the structural-functional approach; and (2) an emphasis on the interpretation of cultural mechanisms producing homeostasis between population and resources.

On the first point, Lorimer provides, for example, a chapter titled "The Relation of Kinship Systems to Fertility." The notion is that various social institutions must fit together well enough to provide social stability, and that change in any one of them is likely to reverberate (negatively) through the whole social system. Lorimer's hypothesis that "there is some functional relation between corporate kinship structure . . . and high fertility" (1954:98) has itself produced something of a cottage industry in subsequent decades as anthropologists and anthropologically informed demographers examined lineage systems and their consequences for fertility.[9]

The other niche provided for anthropologists in this demographic paradigm was that of determining fertility-reducing practices in small-scale (or nonliterate) societies. Lorimer pointed to Carr-Saunders's earlier claim that cultural evolution had resulted in "a universal tendency toward the maintenance of an 'optimum population' appropriate to the resources of each area and the economic technology of its occupants." Such cultural measures ranged from the indirect—prolonged lactation and child neglect among them—to the direct: prolonged abstention from intercourse, abortion, and infanticide. A process of natural selection, operating at the cultural level, assured that those societies having cultural elements leading to population stability would survive while others would die out (Lorimer 1954:15).

To this theory Lorimer contrasted that advanced by some prominent American demographers, including the IUSSP committee chair, Frank Notestein, whose words he quoted: "Any society having to face the heavy mortality characteristic of the premodern era must have high fertility to survive. All such societies are therefore ingeniously arranged to obtain the required births. Their religious doctrines, moral codes, laws, education, community customs, marriage habits, and family organization are all focused toward maintaining high fertility."[10] Just what such religious doctrines, codes, customs, marriage habits, family organization, etc. consisted of in these societies was a matter left to the professional anthropologists to discover. A prominent example of this came in 1966, when British anthropologist Mary Douglas authored a study of "Population Control in Primitive Groups," based on published anthropological research from four different societies. In keeping with Carr-Saunders's and Wynne-Edwards's theses, she concluded that "population homeostasis does occur in human groups," although she phrased this not in terms of competition for limited physical resources so much as for limited "social advantage" (Douglas 1966:272).

Douglas concluded her article by arguing that "there is a message here for countries whose prosperity is threatened by uncontrolled population increase" (1966:273). Fear of such uncontrolled population growth, which provided much of the fuel for the growth of demography in the 1960s, had its impact on anthropology as well, although feeble in comparison.

Anthropological Demography Redux

A new phase of anthropological interest in demography opened with new theoretical developments tied to the breakdown of the functionalist paradigm and a more general attempt to connect social behavior to wider systems. Renewed attention to the transformation of social systems through time—motivated in part by the fears of population growth—led to an interest in causal analysis, but a widespread inability to resolve the relationships between individual behavior and larger social processes stymied some of the promising new directions found within this work.

In 1968, British social anthropologist and historian Alan Macfarlane harshly criticized his anthropological colleagues for paying so little heed to the impending population crisis. His basic message is evident in his title, "Population Crisis: Anthropology's Failure," while the doomsday tone is evident in the first sentence: "We are rapidly moving towards a population catastrophe which will make past plagues and two world wars seem insignificant by comparison." He excoriates both his British colleagues (specifically excepting Mary Douglas) and American anthropologists for their failure to collect and examine data relevant to demographic behavior (Macfarlane 1968: 519).[11] Macfarlane went on to produce his own ethnographic (1976) and historical (1986) examinations of social and demographic interactions. In addition to his ringing statement of social engagement, Macfarlane's earlier training in history provides one key to his critique of anthropology, which is simultaneously phrased as a critique of static functionalist models and a denunciation of the failure to examine population pressure as a source of social change: "It is one of the most revealing indications of the blinding effects of a theoretical system that fieldworkers should have almost entirely managed to miss the most important social change that was occurring in the society around them. . . . Any contributions which can be made to mitigate this disaster would be acceptable; it is too late completely to avoid it" (1976:2).

However, concern with the "population bomb" did spur a significant development in American anthropology in the later 1960s and into the 1970s. Identified with such figures as Steven Polgar (who had earlier worked for a family planning research organization and consulted with the World Health Organization) and Moni Nag (who had spent seventeen years with the Anthropological Survey of India before moving to the United States in 1965), this movement involved a flurry of organizational and scholarly activities aimed at involving anthropologists in research on fertility in Third World settings and in promoting the need for anthropological research as part of the demographic study of high fertility societies (see, for example, Polgar ed. 1971; Polgar 1972, 1975; Nag 1972, 1975).

Anthropological interest in demography in the early 1970s was also fueled by continuing concern for the question of population homeostasis and the relationship between environmental resources and human population. One notable conference sponsored by the Wenner-Gren Foundation brought together an interdisciplinary group of biological and social anthropologists, geneticists, and demographers in 1970. Its product was a book explicitly intended to break down the barriers between social and natural scientists by defining the entire array of dimensions relevant to human population structure (Harrison and Boyce 1972). The heavy representation of biological anthropologists and geneticists, however, seems to have kept it from the curricula of most sociocultural anthropologists in the United States.

Much earlier, Julian Steward's watershed exposition of the relation between population density and the social organization of foragers had given population a crucial place in the link between environment and human systems, but Steward never elaborated on population processes themselves (1936). Renewed interest in this question came in part as a result of the 1965 publication of economist Ester Boserup's book, *The Conditions of Agricultural Growth: The Economics of Agrarian Change under Population Pressure*. Her thesis—suggesting that it was population growth that led to the adoption of agriculture and sedentism, rather than the other way around—hit at a classic issue in anthropological archaeology, and one that brought both archaeologists and sociocultural anthropologists of a cultural ecological bent into the debate. A conference on the topic held at the University of Pennsylvania in 1970 led to the publication of an influential volume, *Population Growth: An-*

thropological Implications (Spooner ed. 1972), and the issue surfaced again at the Ninth International Congress of Anthropological and Ethnological Sciences in 1974.[12]

Within sociocultural anthropology, cultural ecological work—prominent in the late 1960s and early 1970s—provided a natural bridge for anthropologists to focus on population issues. From Roy Rappaport's now classic work on the link between a Melanesian society's ritual system and the balance of people, pigs, and natural resources (1967) to Marvin Harris's call for a "cultural materialist" approach (1966, 1979; Harris and Ross 1987), this variegated tradition focused anthropologists' attention on the balance of population and resources. As central as the population and resource equation was for works in this tradition, however, such works are widely characterized by a notable lack of familiarity with demographic methods and the general demographic literature.[13]

A final development of the late 1960s and early 1970s that contributed to anthropological interest in demography came from a renewed emphasis on the earlier Stewardian focus on the study of small-scale, foraging (or hunting/gathering) societies. Nancy Howell, whose studies of the !Kung of Botswana were important exceptions to the lack of methodological sophistication noted above, contributed importantly to this development (Howell 1979). She refers to this as a move toward demographic "microanalysis," meaning "the study of particular populations of a group of locally bounded people, defined as small enough that they can be studied by one or a few investigators over a period of a few months to a few years" (Howell 1986:226). In addition to her own work and that of Richard Lee (1979) on the !Kung, she cites Napoleon Chagnon's work on the Yanomamo (1975, 1979) as especially influential. A somewhat different example is provided by Robert Netting (1981), whose microdemographic study of a Swiss mountain community examined a lengthy series of historical records to reconstruct population dynamics in a small, highly circumscribed population. Other works in this tradition of intensive demographic description based on accurate data among nonliterate populations include Macfarlane's (1976) and Fricke's (1994) community studies from Nepal.

The book that drew the most attention to the importance of demographic microanalysis within anthropology was the 1968 volume *Man the Hunter*, edited by Richard Lee and Irven DeVore. Generating quite a bit of controversy, not least over its title, the book focused on the often unacknowledged impact of demographic variables on marriage practices. Anthropologists' long fascination with complex marriage systems had led, the authors argued, to misleading and incomplete understandings of how the selection of marriage partners actually works in a small-scale society. The prototypical case was provided in essays by Mervyn Meggitt and Aram Yengoyan on the Australian aborigines, who had long provided anthropologists with the raw material for generating highly complex structural models of marriage systems.

Meggitt (1968) argued that data on marriage practices in central Australia showed that demographic factors exerted considerable influence on actual patterns of marriage, even though the structural system itself—that is, the official norms regarding who fell into what marriage category—remained unaffected by them. Yengoyan (1968) specifically called for a cultural ecological model emphasizing demographic factors in the study of small-scale societies, and he too pointed out that in small and dwindling populations the marriage rules found in societies such as that of the Australian aborigines could not in fact be followed. The implications of this work for anthropology were great, though perhaps not fully appreciated in all sectors of the anthropological community. It would not be enough to focus on cultural systems to provide an accurate understanding of such classic anthropological topics as marriage, nor would it be enough to supplement such cultural models with a later focus on individual "agency." Rather, unless demographic variables were taken into account, even basic ethnography would be misleading and inadequate.

There were, then, several streams of anthropological research in the 1960s and 1970s drawing attention to the importance of demographic variables and topics. They might roughly be divided into those that contributed to the principal agenda of the demographic community (concerned with the population explosion in nonwestern societies) and those that contributed to traditional anthropological topics (marriage systems, the rise of agriculture, etc.) by paying more serious and systematic attention to demographic forces. Whereas the former, by its nature, involved anthropologists in working with demographers and often reading their work, the latter—with a few exceptions—did not.

More Recent Trends in Demography

Some important developments within demography, however, were at the same time leading a growing number of demographers to anthropology, directly or indirectly. Perhaps the most surprising of these came from an ambitious research project that began at Princeton in 1963, led by economic demographer Ansley Coale, who was ultimately joined by a dozen or so collaborators. The intellectual history of the project could be traced back to an earlier director of Princeton's Office of Population Research, Frank Notestein (chair, as we saw, of the early 1950s committee that led to the Lorimer volume). Coale set about testing the by then dominant paradigm identified with Notestein, demographic transition theory, by undertaking the imposing task of collecting comparable provincial-level demographic and related social and economic data for all of western Europe for a period of more than a hundred years.

This is a surprising impetus for anthropological demography because the rather large group of Princeton researchers included no anthropologists and because Coale himself was a pillar of mainstream demography. Yet the pri-

mary finding of the two-decade research project was that demography's dominant paradigm did not hold. The classic predictor variables of demographic
transition theory—urbanization, literacy, infant and child mortality, and
industrialization—failed to account for the historic decline in fertility.[14] The
result was some serious rethinking of fertility decline and, more generally, of
approaches to understanding demographic behavior.

One of the major elements of this rethinking involved the championing of
cultural factors as an alternative, or at least supplementary, set of explanatory
forces. Two of the core members of the Princeton project summarized the
project's findings as follows: "Cultural setting influenced the onset and spread
of fertility decline independently of socioeconomic conditions. Proximate
areas with similar socioeconomic conditions entered the transition period at
different times, whereas areas differing in the level of socioeconomic development but with similar cultures entered the transition at similar times" (Knodel
and van de Walle 1986:412). Taking up this theme and pointing not only to
the Princeton project's results for Europe but also the World Fertility Survey
results for the contemporary high fertility societies, demographers John Cleland and Christopher Wilson similarly noted that "the most striking feature
of the onset of transition is its relationship to broad cultural groupings. . . .
The spread of knowledge and ideas seems to offer a better explanation for the
observed pattern than structural determinism" (1987:20). All this, of course,
led demography straight to anthropology, the presumed repository of wisdom
on the nature of culture.

A second impetus arising within demography, moving it closer to anthropology, came from methodological rather than theoretical concerns. For a variety of reasons, the sample survey had become, by the 1970s, the method of
choice for demography.[15] With the boom in research on the problem of fertility in poorer countries, the large-scale survey seemed to offer the ideal
method for collecting a large amount of data on national populations around
the world. The demographer could study a society without (at least from an
anthropologist's point of view) knowing much of anything about it: no need
to speak the language, or even to ever meet a non-Ph.D.-holding native. Visits
to the country, if required at all, could be confined to short stays in western
luxury hotels. Data came in categories provided by the demographer rather
than by the local people so there was no problem understanding them, and
having the data in this form also permitted straightforward computer manipulation and cross-national comparison.

While the majority of demographers continue to find the survey research
paradigm satisfactory, some influential voices of concern began to be raised in
the 1970s and continue to reverberate today. Geoffrey McNicoll put the matter this way: "For a number of years . . . survey research on demographic
behavior has been experiencing diminishing returns. We learn the same kinds
of things about more and more societies, while important and interesting

questions on the theoretical frontier remain out of reach—lying, so to speak, below the focal length of this instrument" (1988:10). He went on to point to "micro-approaches" as providing a potential way out of this impasse.

But the leading voice in this call from within demography for more anthropological methods has been that of the Australian demographer Jack Caldwell. Caldwell's own transformation from a traditional demographer to an internal critic grew out of his exposure to village studies and the reading of ethnographic literature, largely from the British tradition, in West Africa:

> Most demographers work on large data sets, often with little contact with the people whom the statistics describe. Fortunately, in early 1962 it became clear that the 1960 Ghana Census was not going to yield material quickly enough to absorb my time. We [Jack Caldwell and his wife, Pat] thereupon used our limited funds for cheap and relatively small scale investigations which meant borrowing methodology from the anthropologists (and reading them) and becoming intimately acquainted with each village and its families in turn. For a demographer with traditional training, the experience was illuminating—so illuminating that we have attempted to use similar methods ever since. (1982:4)

Later, writing with demographer Allan Hill (see chapter 9), he lamented the fact that demographic research was "surprisingly deficient in theory," attributing this both to an (understandable) obsession with measurement issues and "the reluctance of demographers to engage in research whose methods are unconventional and whose output cannot be measured in numerical terms" (Caldwell and Hill 1988:1). Surveys are not only limited in the nature of the data they collect, but the data themselves are of questionable validity, for "the tendency is to obtain normative responses or reflections of the rules, particularly on sensitive topics" (1988:4). To rectify this problem, they called for the adoption of a "micro-level" or "anthropological" approach, in order to "encourage a more holistic view" (1988:2). One important institutional expression of this movement has been the establishment of a Committee on Anthropological Demography by the International Union for the Scientific Study of Population.

The "anthropological demography" of this committee essentially refers to microdemography incorporating a fieldwork element. Within this rather broad umbrella are a wide range of methodological styles illustrated by the contributions in the Caldwell, Hill, and Hull volume mentioned above, Caldwell's work in South India (Caldwell, Reddy, and Caldwell 1988), numerous contributions from Africa (Bledsoe et al. 1994; Renne 1995), and work in Nepal (Axinn, Fricke, and Thornton 1991; Niraula 1994). These research strategies share a focus on community studies as well as some combination of survey and more typical forms of ethnographic field inquiry, but differ in the extent to which, for example, the principal investigators are full-time residents of study communities or even speak the local languages. Tellingly, these micro-demographic projects have spawned some of the more successful collaborations between anthropological and sociological demographers.[16]

Over the past decade, then, the move from within demography toward anthropology has been driven primarily by two catalysts: first, the perceived insufficiency of traditional demographic methodology, with the call for employing anthropological methods to supplement and enrich these methods; and second, the perceived insufficiency of the theoretical explanatory models employed by demographers. The first of these is especially identified with the work of Jack Caldwell, as discussed above, and the second can be seen as the legacy of the Princeton European Fertility project, though it has roots in contemporary Third World demographic studies as well.

No one is more identified with this second movement than Belgian demographer Ron Lesthaeghe, a core member of the Princeton project. In work on both contemporary Africa and contemporary and historical Europe, he has sought to broaden the range of variables employed in demographic research. His goal has been to pay more serious attention to culture and particularly social organization by operationalizing them in ways that are suitable to more traditional demographic survey methods. For example, collaborating with anthropologist Georgia Kaufmann and others, Lesthaeghe has attempted to employ anthropological insights into sub-Saharan African kinship systems to more creatively infuse social analyses into the World Fertility Survey data (Lesthaeghe 1989; Lesthaeghe et al. 1994).[17] In the historical and contemporary European context, he has emphasized ideational and institutional features associated with religion and secularization (Lesthaeghe 1983, 1991, 1992; Lesthaeghe and Wilson 1986).

If demographers have been drawn to anthropology in part via the burgeoning demographic interest in Third World societies traditionally studied by anthropologists, the two fields have also been drawn together by their parallel move into history. Of course, both anthropology and demography have been interested in historical questions from their origins, but these were initially of a more speculative and theoretical sort.[18] Empirical historical study began to gain prominence in demography in France in the late 1950s and by the 1960s—with the Princeton project in the United States, major reconstitution studies underway in France, and the launching of historical household study by the Cambridge Group in Britain—historical research came fully into the demographic limelight.

It remains a curious, and thus far not fully examined, fact that much of the most influential demographic work by American anthropologists has focused not on contemporary Third World societies but on historical Europe and East Asia. For example, Laslett and Wall's landmark volume *Household and Family in Past Time* (1972), which launched historical demographic household study, contains chapters on Serbian household organization from the sixteenth to the nineteenth centuries by anthropologists Eugene Hammel (1972) and Joel Halpern (1972), and a chapter on pre-modern Japan by Robert J. Smith (1972). Other Europeanist anthropologists produced historical demographic work through the 1980s and into the early 1990s on Portugal (Brettell 1986), Switzerland (Netting 1981), Italy (Schneider and Schneider 1984; Douglass 1980, 1984; Kertzer 1984, Kertzer and Hogan 1989); France (Segalen 1984); and Turkey (Duben and Behar 1991). East Asian studies included work on Taiwan (Wolf 1984; Wolf and Huang 1980) and Japan (Skinner 1988, 1993; Hanley and Wolf 1985). All of these settings were characterized by the historical presence of ecclesiastical or state apparatuses which collected and stored data more amenable to sophisticated demographic analyses than that of many other world societies.

Historical demography as done by anthropologists, as opposed to demographers, was marked by a greater focus on the social system. Whereas much historical demography focused on the demographic data and had an inductive, empiricist cast (Kertzer 1985), work by anthropologists tended to focus on family and kinship systems, gender relations, inheritance norms and practices, and land tenure systems. For anthropologists, historical demographic sources offered, above all, a privileged vantage point for investigating relatively long-term processes of change in peasant societies. The organizing paradigm was much in the British social anthropological tradition, with its focus on social organization and, in particular, domestic group processes. Once again, the communion between the British tradition and demography was fostered by the availability of data receptive to its analytic categories. At the same time, efforts to provide a more thorough cultural analysis were occasionally made possible through other archival documents, including those of government origin, newspapers and the popular press, letters, and even field interviews with survivors from the later periods of historical interest (Kertzer and Hogan 1989; Duben and Behar 1991; Kertzer 1993).

New Anthropological Agendas

If up to this point our review suggests a good deal of convergence in anthropological and demographic interests, it is because it has largely focused on the shared research problems of the two traditions as they converge on the explanation of population dynamics. It is not that demography has set the agenda, but rather that the anthropological agenda encompasses much that is straightforwardly demographic even when it brings a unique set of techniques and concepts into the framing of these questions. Along with this convergent stream, however, anthropologists have long recognized another current more directly connected to the motivating questions of their own discipline. As Fortes wrote some twenty years ago, "From a strictly demographic point of view it is of no significance that some of these constraints [on natural fertility] may be of cultural origin. . . . From an anthropologist's point of view, by contrast, it is the qualities and incidence of such constraints, and of their counterparts, the institutions and ideals that distort natural fertility that are crucial" (1978:122).

Thus, where the demographer begins the analysis from the starting point of the demographic process of interest, those constraining factors are for anthropologists subjects of study in their own right. Demographic anthropologists are still anthropologists and, as such, involved in the central issues of social theory that have come to concern anthropologists more generally since the early 1980s. The ferment characterizing the broader discipline of anthropology in areas ranging from developments in the relationship between political economy, history, and culture (Wolf 1982; Sahlins 1981, Ortner 1984; Roseberry 1989) to the intersection of gender, culture, and social life (Yanagisako 1979; Collier and Yanagisako 1987) have, since the early 1980s, increasingly found their way into the analyses of demographic anthropologists and many of the later works cited above were influenced by these developments.

Much of this new ferment relates to a reevaluation of the theoretical significance of culture in a late twentieth-century world of globalized linkages and permeable boundaries. This complexity has forced anthropologists to conceptualize culture in more dynamic terms and to draw out implications for demographic analysis in the process. One early work in this new agenda, for example, criticized mainstream demography for its tendency to treat culture as yet another independent variable in multivariate models instead of as a dynamic and changing set of interpretive and motivational resources available to specific actors (Greenhalgh 1988). Other work increasingly draws new insights from the political economy of state and local relations, local contexts of power, and historical relationships between real actors into their analyses (Scheper-Hughes 1992; Greenhalgh 1995; Kertzer 1995; Fricke 1995). And more recently, anthropologists have turned to the literature on gendered social reproduction to inform critiques of applied demography (Ginsburg and Rapp 1995). The nondemographic origin of many of the questions informing these new inquiries is a key to some of the tension in the current relationship between demography and anthropology; at the same time, it is a potential source of revitalization of demographic inquiry itself.

Steps Toward a New Synthesis

Our condensed history of the highlights from demography's and anthropology's long courtship overlaps with this most recent rocky phase. Although many of the same actors and issues encountered in our summary continue to leave their mark (and this volume's contributors are central players in the new agenda), the structure of contemporary anthropological demography nevertheless differs in important ways from that of the past. Much of this structural transformation is rooted in the extraordinary openness that many of our demographic colleagues have shown to the insights of anthropologists, an openness leading to a new institutionalization of anthropology within the demographic community.

Interest in attracting more anthropological attention to demographic research is also reflected among those responsible for funding such work. This is evident in the interest expressed by such federal agencies as the National Institute for Child Health and Human Development, the National Institute on Aging, and the National Science Foundation, as well as such private organizations as the Mellon and MacArthur Foundations (all of which were represented at the Conference on Anthropological Demography from which this book springs). The Mellon Foundation in particular has had a major impact by developing new programs for enhancing the cross-fertilization between demography and anthropology.

In the United States today more anthropologists are getting graduate and postdoctoral training in demography than ever before, and a small band of anthropologists can now be seen regularly at meetings of the Population Association of America, the primary organization of demographers in the United States. While a number of the country's major population research centers still have no anthropologists among their senior staff, even this is beginning to change.[19]

Despite these enhanced conditions for a new synthesis of demography and anthropology, impediments to a companionate marriage continue to create misperceptions and difficulties. The foundation of many of these has to do with the fundamental assumptions framing research questions and motivating data collection strategies in the two fields. We have frequently noted in our historical sketch, for example, the tendency of anthropologists to pursue analyses relating to structural relationships and we have contrasted this with the positivist, survey-oriented approaches of the reigning demographic paradigm. We quoted Caldwell and Hill's association of anthropological approaches with a more "holistic view" (1988:2). These strains of holism in anthropology, far from being accidental, at least partly inform the basic worldview of nearly all anthropologists and emerge in any treatment of meaning or any consideration of the individual actor in social and cultural context. At some level, anthropology's perennial concern with culturally relevant categories for variables ("on the ground") and local knowledge ("the native's point of view"; Geertz 1983) derives from a predisposition toward the more interpretive as opposed to the empiricist, generalizing tradition of demography. The two traditions do not always mix well. As Taylor writes in his useful discussion of interpretive approaches, "In general, the empiricist orientation must be hostile to a conduct of enquiry which is based on interpretation. . . . This cannot meet the requirements of inter-subjective, non-arbitrary verification which it considers essential to science. And along with this epistemological stance goes the ontological belief that reality must be susceptible to understanding and explanation by science so understood. From this follows a certain set of notions of what the sciences must be" (1985:20–21).[20]

Not that there is a scarcity of strong disagreement on these issues from within the anthropological tradition. Even among this volume's contributors, it would be difficult to reach consensus on the relative admissibility of the various forms of both data and analysis. Although few among demographic anthropologists would be willing to toss away the entire legacy of the structuralist emphasis on kinship and features of social organization, they vary considerably in their approaches to culture, meaning, and motivation. Some of these debates turn on the relative autonomy of culture and the admissibility of symbolic analysis in discerning motivation (Hammel 1990; Kertzer 1995, in press; Fricke, chapter 10 of this volume, in press); others on the possibilities for common measures subject to reasonable cross-societal comparisons (Scheper-Hughes, chapter 8 of this volume). These differences in part constitute continuations of long-standing arguments over the relative role of structure and agency in social action (Alexander 1988).

Nevertheless, unlike non-anthropological demographers who can slip into professional training in demography early in their graduate careers, anthropologists cannot easily evade these debates on interpretation in their professional training since the holistic perspective continues to permeate anthropological training. Their familiarity with the interpretive tradition creates an at least diffuse appreciation for viewing human behavior as contextualized at levels beyond the individual. Despite growing recognition of the importance of social and institutional contexts to demographic phenomena by both the more theoretically inclined and the more empiricist members of the demographic community (McNicoll 1980, 1994; Entwisle, Casterline, and Sayed 1989), few have extended dynamic notions of context to the ideational realm. This different orientation has given rise to at least three sets of impediments to the new synthesis.

One set has to do with the tendency of some demographers to confine anthropology's contribution to the narrower methodological tricks of microdemography. From this point of view, it is the anthropologist's role to contribute a multitude of highly nuanced community studies from which, however, no scientifically valid generalizations can be made. Rather, these ethnographies gain their demographic value by stimulating the construction, by demographers, of a series of novel variables suitable for testing via subsequent demographic surveys. A corollary of this viewpoint is that the value of an anthropological study is a direct function of the size of the population to which it can be (through subsequent surveys) generalized; in this view, studies of Han Chinese trump studies of the Yanomamo.

Anthropologists see the value of such ethnographic work quite differently.[21] The value of individual community studies need not be limited to their suitability for statistical generalization if they allow researchers to bring to bear a more extensive and highly variable range of data on the understanding of population processes. Within anthropology and demography, too, the power of community studies is reflected in their numerous contributions to testable social theory (Caldwell 1982; Caldwell, Reddy, and Caldwell 1988; Cain 1977; Greenhalgh 1994; Kertzer and Hogan 1989).

A second set of impediments relates to the very issues of meaning that have motivated much demographic interest in anthropological concepts to begin with. While the turn to anthropology was, in part, intended to allow demography to make use of the culture concept, the notion of culture with which most demographers were familiar was considered outmoded by anthropologists (Greenhalgh 1996). Not only has there been a tendency for some demographers to misconstrue culture as kinship structure alone (Kertzer 1995) but, as Hammel notes with his customary pungency:

> Without putting too fine a point on it, the use of "culture" in demography seems mired in structural-functional concepts that are about 40 years old, hardening rapidly, and showing every sign of fossilization. . . .
> Over the last 40 years, anthropological theory has moved away from the institutional, structural-functionalist approach it has long presented to its sister social sciences, toward the elucidation of local, culture-specific rationalities, in the building of which actors are important perceiving, interpreting, and constructing agents. (1990:456)

Contemporary cultural theories, in other words, treat culture as an environment, or context, that influences and is influenced by human action. This suggests a very different view than the old structural-functionalist models that treat culture as much less flexible.

More controversially, the rigidity of these older notions of culture may, in combination with the reliance on the social survey form of data collection, encourage demographers' penchant for confining their search for cultural meaning to the individual level. While it is undeniable that meanings must exist for individuals, anthropology has long carried with it a tradition of cultural analysis that located other senses of meaning at levels transcending the individual (Ortner 1984; Wuthnow 1987). Taylor refers to this kind of meaning as "common and inter-subjective" and suggests that such meanings "fall through the net of mainstream social science" (1985:40); they cannot be captured by the social survey. Yet much of the ideational work in demography is dependent on attitude and value surveys (Arnold et al. 1975; Lesthaeghe and Surkyn 1988; Mason and Taj 1987).

Again, it is not that research in this tradition has no contribution to make, but rather that it often proceeds without an awareness of its limitations. Caldwell's sense of illumination in his turn to anthropological techniques stemmed from this encounter with data that the survey missed. A further heartening development in the linking of intersubjective and individual realms of meaning lies in the recent work of cultural psychologists who have begun to develop plausible mechanisms for linking individual motivation and larger cultural patterns (D'Andrade and Strauss 1992). Such theoretical developments promise to make such linkages less abstract and more acceptable to the healthy empiricist impulses of demography.

The third set of impediments has to do with the mutual unfamiliarity of disciplinary practitioners with the traditions and methods of their counterparts. Demographers, on their part, are often ignorant of the full range of traditions within anthropological theory, of which the British structural functionalists are but one skein. It comes as something of a shock to most demographers to realize that opening the doors to anthropological research entails opening them to the full range of political-economic and revisionist traditions as well. Many of these traditions are pointedly critical of the social intervention research that has been the bread and butter of much demographic work. Mamdani's controversial criticism of the Khanna Study in India is an early example of this debunking impulse in anthropology (1972).[22]

The critical impulse lives on in explicit and implicit forms in later anthropological demography formulated out of political economic perspectives (Greenhalgh 1990, 1995). Some of the most sophisticated recent anthropological treatments merge this tradition with feminist anthropology to frame a critically engaged version of the culture theories mentioned above (Greenhalgh 1994; Ginsburg and Rapp 1991, 1995; Nancy Riley, chapter 5 in this volume). Much of this tradition proceeds from an inherent distrust of politically dominant groups; demography's close alliance with government policy and its prized position with respect to research funding certainly place it close to the seats of power (Greenhalgh 1996). Demographic reaction to this blunt, politically edged critique is often one of incomprehension and defensiveness (see the Lauman et al. and Lewontin exchange cited in note 20).

On the other hand, the critiques themselves sometimes fail to acknowledge the real complexity of motivations and theoretical positions of the researchers they attack. Moreover, an initial distrust of quantification based on reasonable wariness with past uses of survey data (already criticized by demographers themselves) has unnecessarily shielded many anthropologists from important advances in statistical methodology, such as event history modeling, which allow for dynamic and life course-based analyses that converge on the newly dynamic theories relating individual and culture.

The danger at both extremes is to turn these debates into Manichean struggles of light against darkness, as the overheated rhetoric of some past debates within anthropology itself tended to do (e.g., Harris 1979). More productive and creative in this moment of great synthetic potential is the process of re-examining fundamentals, defining areas of agreement, and arguing over ways to resolve areas of disagreement. This is what the contributors to this volume do. The solution will not always lie somewhere between positions—either one considers cultural levels as context or one doesn't—but the return to the sometimes philosophical sources of disagreement is a sign of health.

This volume is motivated by a sense that the time is ripe for a reconsideration and renewal of past achievements together with the development of a new synthesis in the relationship between anthropology and demography. The contributors actively participate in that process. As a group they represent the wide range of contributions that anthropology stands to make to a new engagement of research traditions. While the scope of contributions encompasses both the familiar and trusted and the novel and disturbing, all are parts of an ongoing dialogue rather than a final word.

The contributions take various and not always reconcilable points of view. The opening chapters, for example, illustrate that the foundations of demographic engagement with anthropology in issues of kinship, social organization, and the formation of domestic groups are as alive and valid today as in the past. Subsequent chapters expand on standard demographic concepts by demonstrating the role of anthropology in rethinking their cross-cultural validity. Some chapters more critically evaluate the relationship between demography and anthropology with reference to their epistemological roots, while others apply specific frameworks from the general anthropological and theoretical literature to demographic issues.

The Chapters
Kinship Systems and Demographic Regimes

Monica Das Gupta, extending the tradition with which demographers have long felt comfortable, expands on recent attempts to reinvigorate demographic analysis through the application of anthropological kinship theory. Her chapter reviews earlier attempts to link kinship and fertility regimes and criticizes these attempts for ignoring the relationship between kinship systems and fertility regimes as a whole. She develops extended examples of the relationship between kinship and health and kinship and old age support, contrasting Northern Europe and South Asia. The chapter focuses especially on the demographic implications of kin systems as explicated by demographers to show how more intensive use of anthropological insights can enlarge the contextual understanding of population processes as a social subsystem.

Family Systems and Demographic Processes

G. William Skinner's chapter, again within the tradition that looks to the intersection of social structures and organizations and demographic processes, is concerned with the causal pathways by which family systems shape demographic processes. It sets out some of the analytical dimensions of family systems and then turns to their impact on particular population processes, beginning with nuptiality. The core argument enlarges on how parents develop strategies that will give them offspring sets that conform with family system norms in light of empirical contexts which produce particular infant mortality regimes. Skinner argues that demographic processes are unintelligible without attention to the normative contexts of family systems and their implications for individual strategic behaviors.

An Anthropological Approach to the Concept of Fertility: Parenthood, Fertility, and Social Reproduction

Nicholas Townsend argues that the picture of reproduction in demography is essentially a biological one in which children are attributed uncritically to the women who gave them birth. Such a view contrasts with anthropological theory in which the emphasis is on the social reproduction of structures of relationship and social positions rather than of actual individuals. While demography's traditional approach is adequate to the modeling of population dynamics as strictly biological phenomena, the recent turn toward social theory necessitates a rethinking of fundamental concepts such as fertility. The chapter examines features of social parenthood cross-culturally and contributes to the enrichment of demography by showing how anthropology can go beyond mere contribution to the study of the determinants of fertility by redefining the very concept of fertility itself.

Similarities and Differences: Anthropological and Demographic Perspectives on Gender

Nancy Riley examines the different ways that anthropology and demography have approached the study of gender. Her chapter looks at the reasons why the study of gender has found a more attentive and comfortable home within anthropology, and discusses the importance of the theoretical, epistemological, substantive, and political "scaffolding" which is more readily available in anthropology than in demography. Especially important in the differences between the two fields is the easy recognition within anthropology of the cultural construction of gender, and the development of theoretical and research agendas that make this notion a central concern. Because of both the nature of anthropology in general and the development of feminist work within the field, feminist anthropologists have been more actively engaged in and notable contributors to important debates within the field of feminist scholarship. Particularly important has been anthropology's contributions to one of the most active debates in feminist scholarship in recent years, the notion of differences—differences between women and men, and differences among women. Riley closes with a discussion of how demography could benefit from the debates and research on gender within anthropology and, in turn, contribute to them.

Population and Identity

Philip Kreager contrasts the quite different conceptualizations of culture in demography and anthropology. He recommends that demographic anthropologists give greater credence to the focus on identity that constitutes the demographic emphasis, but that they do so by emphasizing the process of identity construction itself. In exploring the uses of identity as a fulcrum uniting the differing emphases of anthropological and demographic thinking, Kreager notes that a focus on identity construction provides working solutions to the enduring problems of incorporating human agency into culture. Importantly, the focus on identity also allows for the integration of contemporary notions of culture into new and theoretically more sophisticated analyses of existing demographic data sets. Finally, Kreager's chapter shows the close relationship between divergent disciplinary perspectives in the social sciences and the twentieth-century efforts of the state to articulate its relationship with increasingly varied constituent subpopulations. He illustrates these points by examining British efforts in India at the beginning of the twentieth century.

Anthropology and Demography: Marriage, Liaison, or Encounter?

Eugene A. Hammel and Diana Friou examine the relationship between anthropology and demography, focusing on the historical differences between the two disciplines, on the nature and utility of culture and symbolic utterances as indicators of motivation, on alternatives to considering motivation, and on two problems in the use of ethnographic data for demographic research. The first problem deals with social behavior that directly affects demographic outcomes; the second deals with social behavior that affects our ability to observe demographic outcomes. Hammel and Friou suggest that demographers are at their best in analyzing aggregates, while anthropologists are best at analyzing individual behavior. Obscure behaviors may have marked results on demographic events, and social conventions may greatly confound the ability of demographers to count events of interest; nevertheless, they suggest that an alliance between the disciplines seems not only useful but necessary.

Demography without Numbers

Nancy Scheper-Hughes's provocative argument is the clearest representative of the critical tradition applied to demography. She argues for a particular qualitative methodology for anthropological demography which she calls a "critical interpretive approach." Her chapter argues against a model of demographic research based on the search for quantitatively measured "facts" and suggests that one must begin with the very definition of what is to count as facts. Such a critical interpretive approach includes an analysis of the data-gathering process itself and requires a special sensitivity to the interests served outside of the academy. Scheper-Hughes argues that the critical interpretive approach is meaning-centered and inherently better suited to capturing the meaning of demographic events in the lives of the subjects of study themselves. Her examples are derived from research into child mortality in a Brazilian shantytown.

"Truth Lies in the Eye of the Beholder": The Nature of Evidence in Demography and Anthropology

Allan Hill follows Scheper-Hughes's chapter with a more sympathetic critique from within the demographic profession. He explores the question of whether the differences between demographers and anthropologists are merely technical or more fundamentally rooted in differing epistemologies and suggests that, indeed, the differences between the two fields are deep enough to make a simple merger problematic. A fundamental distinction has to do with what counts as evidence and this, he argues, determines methodological approaches and theoretical constructs. A further difference grows out of the different goals of theory-building and theory-testing that characterize the two disciplines. The chapter explores specific examples of the different sources of "proof" in anthropology and demography through materials from an ongoing collaborative study by demographers and anthropologists on the motivations for breastfeeding in West Africa. In concluding remarks, Hill recommends a broader and more theoretically sensitive demography able to make use of a variety of methods and wider insights from allied social science disciplines.

Culture Theory and Population Process: Toward a Thicker Demography

Tom Fricke expands on current arguments that the explanation and understanding of demographic variation must give attention to culture as a distinct analytic level. While non-anthropological demographers have long recognized and been receptive to methods intended to capture information at this level, they have been less likely to follow conceptual debates on the nature of culture. The predictable outcome is the antique feel of the culture concepts used by many contemporary demographers. More seriously, an inadequate definition of culture and its relationship to other levels of social analysis hinders research into the very motivational contexts of demographic behavior found to be so important. Fricke characterizes demography's current situation as one of "epistemological crisis" that requires rethinking fundamentals. He suggests some of the methodological implications of a view of social reality that joins the three levels of culture, society, and the individual and provides examples from research in Nepal.

A Concluding Query

A final issue relevant to the development of a new synthesis between anthropology and demography is the question of demography's disciplinary status. We began this chapter by granting equal disciplinary status to the two enterprises but quickly switched to circumlocutions such as "field" or "research tradition." In closing our review, we raise the issue of whether the disciplinary autonomy of demography is itself an impediment to theoretical development. The issue is not trivial since autonomy affords a greater luxury of choice in deciding the relative merits of interdisciplinary borrowing. As members of a discipline, demographers can afford to ignore the more arcane readings of culture theory while absorbing the more immediately useful notions of kinship or household structure in comfortably piecemeal fashion. If, on the other hand, demography defines a problem area within the social sciences more broadly, then its specialized boundaries are more permeable to the larger developments of social and cultural theory that have stirred anthropology (and sociology) in recent decades. Demographers are already long-standing members of the economic and sociological communities and most doctorates in demography are granted within these disciplines. Is an anthropological demography to be developed along these lines or will contemporary developments foment an even larger ecumenicalism?

In his introduction to an edited volume with the provocative title *Demography as an Interdiscipline,* J. Mayone Stycos suggested that "demographers in the earlier part of the twentieth century tended to eschew theory" but that "the demographers of the 1980s seem a new breed, with concerns for models and conceptual schemes as elegant and empirically based as any seen in the social sciences" (1989:viii). He went on to write that "the success of the new theorizing lies in the willingness of the demographer to venture into a variety of other disciplines." One could ask for a convergent movement by anthropologists. Susan Greenhalgh, for example, identifies "the association of demography with quantification and manipulation of numbers" as a major stumbling block to anthropological engagement in demographic research (1990:100). Perhaps the fuller engagement of demographic research in social theory will help convince anthropologists that there is a pay-off to being able to read the demographic literature, offering them an incentive to learn the necessary statistical methods so that they can do so.

The contributions to this volume suggest that such a convergence is not only desirable and possible, but also likely. We argue that demographic inquiry is continuing its steady movement toward new streams of sociocultural theory, and that this movement has been progressively toward greater contextualization of the brute demographic events of birth and death about which Lotka developed mathematical models. Early steps in the process brought large gains for demography. The potential gains for anthropology are equally great, promising a refreshing enlargement of the discipline's relevance and theoretical power. The following chapters, from a variety of occasionally contentious points of view, are united in their examination of demography and anthropology from the perspective of their roots in larger theoretical issues and point toward the construction of a truly anthropological demography.

NOTES

We acknowledge the very helpful comments of Susan Greenhalgh, Eugene Hammel, Philip Kreager, Nancy Riley, and Arland Thornton on earlier drafts of this introduction.

1. We are concerned in this chapter, as in this book, with the relationship between demography and *sociocultural* anthropology. We use the term "anthropology" here as a convenient abbreviation for sociocultural anthropology. It must be recognized, however, that there are important relationships between two other major anthropological subfields—biological and archaeological anthropology—and demography. The history and current status of those relationships, however, are quite different from those involving sociocultural anthropology. Interested readers can find useful guides to these literatures in Swedlund 1978, Wood 1990, Weiss 1976, and Ellison 1994 for biological anthropology, and Hassan 1979, Brinkman 1984, and Willey 1992 for archaeological anthropology.

2. A still excellent review of theoretical developments in anthropology is in Ortner 1984. One useful representation and review of the ethical engagement of anthropology is in Marcus and Fischer 1986. The debate about objectivity vs. morality in anthropology is well illustrated in a recent exchange between D'Andrade (1995) and Scheper-Hughes (1995).

3. A recent collection of theoretically driven empirical papers that are explicitly directed toward a critical consolidation of anthropological and demographic perspectives is Susan Greenhalgh's edited volume (ed. 1995). Greenhalgh's comprehensive and provocative statements concerning an "anthropologized" demography are found in her article in *Population and Development Review* (1990) and in the introduction to the edited volume (1995).

4. While it is fashionable to note the consonance of British structural-functionalist interests with the needs of British colonial administration (Kuklick 1991), this was probably a secondary motivation at best for structural anthropology's concern with census taking. See Goody 1995 for a more complex view of the relation between colonialism and British field anthropology. A more recent argument for the strong connection between demography and the politics of the world system may be found in Riedmann's very critical evaluation of Caldwell's early work in Africa (1993).

5. The original edition, entitled *Notes and Queries on Anthropology, for the Use of Travellers and Residents in Uncivilized Lands,* was published in 1874 by a committee charged with enhancing the quality of data coming from "travellers, ethnologists and other anthropological observers" in the far reaches of the British Empire (Stocking 1987:258–61). Wildly successful as a guide for ethnographic tyros and experts alike, it went through numerous new editions. Even now, in an age when the accusation of being a "Notes and Queries anthropologist" constitutes a rebuke, the sanctity of initial census-taking in community ethnography lives on (Barnard and Good 1984; Bernard 1988).

6. The monograph was initially drafted in 1908–9 but was not published until 1922.

7. Firth would take over Malinowski's chair at LSE. Fortes was to become Professor and chair of social anthropology at Cambridge. It is tempting to mention here as well Daryll Forde, who took over anthropology at University College London. Forde, interested in environmental issues, was very much concerned with demographic matters in the 1930s. His work on Kako villages in eastern Nigeria pays a great deal of attention to generating more accurate population statistics than are provided by government censuses (Forde [1937] 1964).

8. Gluckman was himself firmly within the Radcliffe-Brown camp of British social anthropology, although he left South Africa to study at Oxford in 1936 before Radcliffe-Brown got there and commuted to LSE to attend Malinowski's seminars. He and Fortes were very close personal friends, possibly because of their shared Russian Jewish and South African backgrounds. Leach, his implacable scholarly enemy, writes that "like Fortes, he ended up with an irrational devotion to stable systems in general and to Oxford in particular" (1984). His agenda of extending the methodology of social anthropology into more quantitative, survey-oriented studies was fostered during his directorship of the Rhodes-Livingstone Institute in Africa.

9. Some of these intellectual interests, albeit transformed, live on in various contemporary versions of human sociobiology. See Betzig, Mulder, and Turke 1988 for a useful collection.

10. Frank Notestein, "Population—The Long View," in Food for the World, ed. Theodore Schulz (Chicago: University of Chicago Press, 1945), 39, quoted in Lorimer 1954:17.

11. It is interesting that the early 1960s in some ways parallel the early 1990s as a time when demographers appeared more interested in involving anthropologists in their research than vice versa. Symptomatic, perhaps, was the invitation to prominent American anthropologist Cora Du Bois to speak on the sociocultural aspects of population growth at a conference on "human fertility and population problems" in 1963. The desperation behind this request is painfully clear from Du Bois' all too appropriate prefatory remarks to her contribution: when she was approached by the conference organizer she assured him "that I know nothing about population growth." She then went on to dredge up some nuggets from the ethnographic literature.

12. From the Spooner volume, see especially Spooner's preface (ed. 1972) and chapters by Carneiro (1972), Netting (1972), and Spooner himself (1972). For the ninth ICAES conference, see the volume edited by Polgar (ed. 1975), especially the chapters by archaeologists Hassan (1975) and Cohen (1975) and the sociocultural anthropologist Harner (1975).

13. Indeed, in Harris's well-developed materialist framework (1979), the Marxist view of infrastructure is inadequate precisely because it fails to note the centrality of each society's mode of reproduction. Similarly, Rappaport's paradigm-defining classic appears at times to be more concerned with the social repercussions of the fertility of pigs than people.

14. For the capstone summary volume of the Princeton project, see Coale and Watkins 1986.

15. See Converse 1987 for the larger story of the rise of survey research as the dominant mode of investigation in the social sciences. See Greenhalgh 1996 for a capsule history and discussion of the intellectual trends motivating demography's explicit scientism.

16. Among the fieldwork collaborations between anthropologists and others are the Bledsoe-Hill team in West Africa, Axinn-Fricke-Thornton and Morgan-Niraula in Nepal, and Knodel-Podhisita in Thailand. Many microdemographic practitioners, of course, work more or less singly in the field, too.

17. This use of existing ethnographies to cast light on separately collected survey or other statistical data is an under-explored technique in the merger of anthropology and demography. Apart from Lesthaeghe's work, other examples include Dyson and Moore's (1983) comparison of North and South Indian kin systems and their implications for demographic processes; Fricke, Syed, and Smith's (1986) use of Punjabi ethnographies to develop multivariate analyses of marriage strategies; and Thornton and Lin's comprehensive treatment of twentieth century family and social change in Taiwan (1994).

18. Again, note we refer here only to *sociocultural* anthropology.

19. The presence of anthropology in the demographic world is also evident in the major demographic journals, such as *Demography* (e.g., Fricke and Teachman 1993; Hogan and Kertzer 1985), *Population Studies* (e.g., Clark et al. 1995; Kreager 1993), and, especially, *Population and Development Review* (e.g., Bledsoe et al. 1994; Das Gupta 1987; Greenhalgh 1990; Hammel 1991; Kreager 1982, 1991).

20. For interesting examples that turn on this issue while also demonstrating that even scientists can disagree on how much interpretation is allowable in studies of humanity, see the recent autobiography of Paul Feyerabend (1995) and the exchange in the *New York Review of Books* between a geneticist and social scientists (Lewontin 1995a, 1995b; Lauman et al. 1995).

21. See, for example, Mitchell 1983. For a collection addressing the relative merits of single case studies and quantitative studies including many cases, see the volume edited by Charles Ragin and Howard Becker (1992).

22. But see the follow-up study by Nag and Kak (1984) for a criticism of Mamdani based on research in the same fieldsite. That this tension between applied and scientific anthropological work has been long-standing is illustrated by Jack Goody's account of the early years of the British structural functionalists themselves (1995).

REFERENCES

Alexander, Jeffrey. 1988. *Action and Its Environments: Toward a New Synthesis*. New York: Columbia University Press.

Anderson, Barbara A. 1986. "Regional and Cultural Factors in the Decline of Marital Fertility in Europe." In *The Decline of Fertility in Europe*, ed. Ansley Coale and Susan Watkins, 293–313. Princeton: Princeton University Press.

Ardener, Edwin. 1962. *Divorce and Fertility: An African Study*. Oxford: Oxford University Press for Nigerian Institute of Social and Economic Research.

Arnold, Fred, Rodolfo Bulatao, Chalio Buripakdi, Betty Jamie Chung, James T. Fawcett, Toshio Iritani, Sung Jin Lee, and Tsong-Shien Wu. 1975. *The Value of Children: A Cross-National Study*. Honolulu: East-West Population Institute.

Axinn, William G., Tom Fricke, and Arland Thornton. 1991. "The Microdemographic Community Study Approach: Improving Data Quality by Integrating the Ethnographic Method." *Sociological Methods and Research* 20(2): 187–217.

Barnard, Alan, and Anthony Good. 1984. *Research Practices in the Study of Kinship*. Orlando, Fla.: Academic Press.

Barnes, John A. 1949. "Measures of Divorce Frequency in Simple Societies." *Journal of the Royal Anthropological Institute* 79: 37–62.

————. 1951. *Marriage in a Changing Society: A Study in Structural Change among the Fort Jameson Ngoni.* Papers of the Rhodes-Livingstone Institute, No. 20.

Bernard, H. Russell. 1988. *Research Methods in Cultural Anthropology.* Newbury Park, Cal.: Sage Publications.

Betzig, Laura, Monique Borgerhoff Mulder, and Paul Turke, eds. 1988. *Human Reproductive Behavior: A Darwinian Perspective.* Cambridge: Cambridge University Press.

Bledsoe, Caroline H., Allan G. Hill, Umberto D'Alessandro, and Patricia Langerock. 1994. "Constructing Natural Fertility: The Use of Western Contraceptive Technologies in Rural Gambia." *Population and Development Review* 20(1): 81–113.

Boserup, Ester. 1965. *The Conditions of Agricultural Growth: The Economics of Agrarian Change under Population Pressure.* Chicago: Aldine.

Brettell, Caroline B. 1986. *Men Who Migrate, Women Who Wait.* Princeton: Princeton University Press.

Brinkman, John A. 1984. "Settlement Surveys and Documentary Evidence: Regional Variation and Secular Trend in Mesopotamian Demography." *Journal of Near Eastern Studies* 43: 169–80.

Cain, Mead. 1977. "The Economic Activities of Children in a Village in Bangladesh." *Population and Development Review* 3(3): 201–27.

Caldwell, John C. 1982. *Theory of Fertility Decline.* New York: Academic Press.

————. 1985. "Strengths and Limitations of the Survey Approach for Measuring and Understanding Fertility Change: Alternative Possibilities." In *Reproductive Change in Developing Countries: Insights from the World Fertility Surveys,* ed. John Cleland and John Hobcraft, 45–63. London: Oxford University Press.

Caldwell, John C., Bruce Caldwell, and Pat Caldwell. 1987. "Anthropology and Demography: The Mutual Reinforcement of Speculation and Research." *Current Anthropology* 28: 25–34.

Caldwell, John C., and Allan Hill. 1988. "Recent Developments Using Micro-Approaches to Demographic Research." In *Micro-Approaches to Demographic Research,* ed. John Caldwell, Allan Hill, and Valerie Hull, 1–9. London: Kegan Paul.

Caldwell, John C., Allan G. Hill, and Valerie J. Hull, eds. 1988. *Micro-Approaches to Demographic Research.* London: Kegan Paul International.

Caldwell, John C., P. H. Reddy, and Pat Caldwell. 1988. *The Causes of Demographic Change: Experimental Research in South India.* Madison: University of Wisconsin Press.

Carneiro, Robert L. 1972. "From Autonomous Villages to the State, a Numerical Estimation." In *Population Growth: Anthropological Implications,* ed. Brian Spooner, 64–77. Cambridge: MIT Press.

Chagnon, Napoleon. 1975. "Genealogy, Solidarity and Relatedness: Limits to Local Group Size and Patterns of Fissioning in an Expanding Population." *Yearbook of Physical Anthropology* 19: 95–110.

————. 1979. "Mate Competition Favoring Close Kin, and Village Fissioning among the Yanomamo Indians." In *Evolutionary Biology and Human Social Behavior,* ed. Napoleon Chagnon and William Irons, 86–131. North Scituate, Mass.: Duxbury Press.

Cleland, John, and Christopher Wilson. 1987. "Demand Theories of the Fertility Transition: An Iconoclastic View." *Population Studies* 41: 5–30.

Clark, Sam, Elizabeth Colson, James Lee, and Thayer Scudder. 1995. "Ten Thousand

Tonga: A Longitudinal Anthropological Study from Southern Zambia, 1956–1991. *Population Studies* 49(1):91–109.

Coale, Ansley J., and Susan C. Watkins, eds. 1986. *The Decline of Fertility in Europe.* Princeton: Princeton University Press.

Cohen, Mark A. 1975. "Population Pressure and the Origins of Agriculture: An Archaeological Example from the Coast of Peru." In *Population, Ecology, and Social Evolution,* ed. Steven Polgar, 79–121. The Hague: Mouton.

Collier, Jane F., and Sylvia J. Yanagisako, eds. 1987. *Gender and Kinship: Essays Toward a Unified Analysis.* Stanford: Stanford University Press.

Colson, Elizabeth M. 1958. *Marriage and Family among the Plateau Tonga of Northern Rhodesia.* Manchester: Manchester University Press.

Converse, Jean M. 1987. *Survey Research in the United States: Roots and Emergence, 1890–1960.* Berkeley: University of California Press.

D'Andrade, Roy. 1995. "Moral Models in Anthropology." *Current Anthropology* 36(3):399–408.

D'Andrade, Roy, and Claudia Strauss, eds. 1992. *Human Motives and Cultural Models.* Cambridge: Cambridge University Press.

Das Gupta, Monica. 1987. "Selective Discrimination against Female Children in Rural Punjab, India. *Population and Development Review* 13(1):77–100.

Douglas, Mary. 1966. "Population Control in Primitive Groups." *British Journal of Sociology* 17:263–73.

Douglass, William A. 1980. "The South Italian Family: A Critique." *Journal of Family History* 5:338–59.

———. 1984. *Emigration in a South Italian Town.* New Brunswick, N.J.: Rutgers University Press.

Duben, Alan, and Cem Behar. 1991. *Istanbul Households: Marriage, Family, and Fertility, 1880–1940.* Cambridge: Cambridge University Press.

Du Bois, Cora A. 1963. "Sociocultural Aspects of Population Growth." In *Human Fertility and Population Problems,* ed. Roy O. Greep, 247–65. Cambridge: Schenkman.

Dyson, Tim, and Mick Moore. 1983. "On Kinship Structure, Female Autonomy, and Demographic Behavior in India." *Population and Development Review* 9(1): 35–60.

Ellison, Peter T. 1994. "Advances in Human Reproductive Ecology." *Annual Review of Anthropology* 23:255–75.

Entwisle, Barbara, John B. Casterline, and Hussein A.-A. Sayed. 1989. "Villages as Contexts for Contraceptive Behavior in Rural Egypt." *American Sociological Review* 54(6):1019–34.

Epstein, Arnold L., ed. 1967. *The Craft of Social Anthropology.* London: Tavistock.

Feyerabend, Paul K. 1995. *Killing Time.* Chicago: University of Chicago Press.

Firth, Raymond. [1936] 1968. *We, the Tikopia: Kinship in Primitive Polynesia.* 3d ed. Boston: Beacon Press.

Forde, Daryll. [1937] 1964. "Land and Labour." *Geographical Journal* 90. Reprinted in Daryll Forde, *Yako Studies,* 1–30. London: Oxford University Press.

Fortes, Meyer. 1943. "A Note on Fertility among the Tallensi of the Gold Coast." *Sociological Review* 35(4,5)99–113.

———. 1954. "A Demographic Field Study in Ashanti." In *Culture and Human Fertility,* ed. Frank Lorimer et al., 253–340. Paris: UNESCO.

————. 1978. "Parenthood, Marriage, and Fertility in West Africa." In *Population and Development,* ed. Geoffrey Hawthorne, 121–49. London: Frank Cass.

Fricke, Tom. 1994. *Himalayan Households: Tamang Demography and Domestic Processes.* Enlarged Edition. New York: Columbia University Press.

————. 1995. "History, Marriage Politics, and Demographic Events in the Central Himalaya." In *Situating Fertility: Anthropology and Demographic Inquiry,* ed. Susan Greenhalgh, 202–24. Cambridge: Cambridge University Press.

————. In press. "Marriage Change as Moral Change: Culture, Virtue, and Demographic Transition." In *The Continuing Demographic Transition,* ed. Gavin W. Jones, John C. Caldwell, Robert M. Douglas, and Rennie D'Souza. London: Oxford University Press.

Fricke, Tom, Sabiha H. Syed, and Peter C. Smith. 1986. "Rural Punjabi Social Organization and Marriage Timing Strategies in Pakistan." *Demography* 23(4): 489–508.

Fricke, Tom, and Jay D. Teachman. 1993. "Writing the Names: Marriage Style, Living Arrangements, and Family Building in a Nepali Society." *Demography* 30(2): 175–88.

Geertz, Clifford. 1983. *Local Knowledge: Further Essays in Interpretive Anthropology.* New York: Basic Books.

Ginsburg, Faye, and Rayna Rapp. 1991. "The Politics of Reproduction." *Annual Review of Anthropology* 20:311–43.

————, eds. 1995. *Conceiving the New World Order: The Global Politics of Reproduction.* Berkeley: University of California Press.

Goody, Jack. 1995. *The Expansive Moment: Anthropology in Britain and Africa, 1918–1970.* Cambridge: Cambridge University Press.

Greenhalgh, Susan. 1988. "Fertility as Mobility: Sinic Transitions." *Population and Development Review* 14(4):629–74.

————. 1990. "Toward a Political Economy of Fertility: Anthropological Contributions." *Population and Development Review* 16(1):85–106.

————. 1994. "Controlling Births and Bodies in Village China." *American Ethnologist* 21(1):3–30.

————. 1995. "Anthropology Theorizes Reproduction: Integrating Practice, Political Economic, and Feminist Perspectives." In *Situating Fertility: Anthropology and Demographic Inquiry,* ed. Susan Greenhalgh, 2–28. Cambridge: Cambridge University Press.

————. 1996. "The Social Construction of Population Science: An Intellectual, Institutional, and Political History of Twentieth-Century Demography." *Comparative Studies in Society and History* 38(1):26–66.

————, ed. 1995. *Situating Fertility: Anthropology and Demographic Inquiry.* Cambridge: Cambridge University Press.

Halpern, Joel M. 1972. "Town and Countryside in Serbia in the Nineteenth Century." In *Household and Family in Past Time,* ed. Peter Laslett and Richard Wall, 401–27. Cambridge: Cambridge University Press.

Hammel, Eugene A. 1972. "The Zadruga as Process." In *Household and Family in Past Time,* ed. Peter Laslett and Richard Wall, 335–73. Cambridge: Cambridge University Press.

————. 1990. "A Theory of Culture for Demography." *Population and Development Review* 16(3):455–85.

Hammel, Eugene A., and Nancy Howell. 1987. "Research in Population and Culture: An Evolutionary Framework." *Current Anthropology* 28(2)141–60.

Hanley, Susan B., and Arthur P. Wolf, eds. 1985. *Family and Population in East Asian History*. Stanford: Stanford University Press.

Harner, Michael J. 1975. "Scarcity, the Factors of Production, and Social Evolution." In *Population, Ecology, and Social Evolution*, ed. Steven Polgar, 123–38. The Hague: Mouton.

Harris, Marvin. 1966. "The Cultural Ecology of India's Sacred Cattle." *Current Anthropology* 7:51–59.

———. 1979. *Cultural Materialism*. New York: Random House.

Harris, Marvin, and Eric B. Ross. 1987. *Death, Sex and Fertility*. New York: Columbia U. P.

Harrison, Geoffrey A., and Anthony J. Boyce, eds. 1972. *The Structure of Human Populations*. Oxford: Oxford University Press.

Hassan, Fekri A. 1975. "Determination of the Size, Density, and Growth Rate of Hunting-Gathering Populations." In *Population, Ecology, and Social Evolution*, ed. Steven Polgar, 27–52. The Hague: Mouton.

———. 1979. "Demography and Archaeology." *Annual Review of Anthropology* 8: 137–60.

Hogan, Dennis P., and David I. Kertzer. 1985. "Migration Patterns during Italian Urbanization." *Demography* 22(3):309–25.

Howell, Nancy. 1979. *Demography of the Dobe !Kung*. New York: Academic Press.

———. 1986. "Demographic Anthropology." *Annual Review of Anthropology* 15: 219–46.

Kertzer, David I. 1984. *Family Life in Central Italy*. New Brunswick, N.J.: Rutgers University Press.

———. 1985. "Future Directions in Historical Household Studies." *Journal of Family History* 10:98–107.

———. 1993. *Sacrificed for Honor: Italian Infant Abandonment and the Politics of Reproductive Control*. Boston: Beacon Press.

———. 1995. "Political-economic and Cultural Explanations of Demographic Behavior." In *Situating Fertility: Anthropology and Demographic Inquiry*, ed. Susan Greenhalgh, 29–52. Cambridge: Cambridge University Press.

———. In press. "The Proper Role of Culture in Demographic Explanation." In *The Continuing Demographic Transition*, ed. Gavin W. Jones, John C. Caldwell, Robert M. Douglas, and Rennie D'Souza. London: Oxford University Press.

Kertzer, David I., and Dennis P. Hogan. 1989. *Family, Political Economy, and Demographic Change*. Madison: University of Wisconsin Press.

Knodel, John, Aphichat Chamratrithirong, and Nibhon Debavalya. 1987. *Thailand's Reproductive Revolution: Rapid Fertility Decline in a Third World Setting*. Madison: University of Wisconsin Press.

Knodel, John, and Etienne van de Walle. 1986. "Lessons from the Past: Policy Implications of Historical Fertility Studies." In *The Decline of Fertility in Europe*, ed. Ansley J. Coale and Susan C. Watkins, 420–49. Princeton: Princeton University Press.

Kreager, Philip. 1982. "Demography *In Situ*." *Population and Development Review* 8(2):237–66.

———. 1991. "Early Modern Population Theory: A Reassessment." *Population and Development Review* 17(2):207–27.

————. 1993. "Histories of Demography." *Population Studies* 47(3):519–39.

Kuklick, Henrika. 1991. *The Savage Within: The History of British Anthropology, 1885–1945.* Cambridge: Cambridge University Press.

Laslett, Peter, and Richard Wall. 1972. *Household and Family in Past Time.* Cambridge: Cambridge University Press.

Lauman, Edward O., John H. Gagnon, Robert T. Michael, and Stuart Michaels. 1995. "Reply to Lewontin." *New York Review of Books,* May 25, 43.

Leach, Edmund R. 1984. "Glimpses of the Unmentionable in the History of British Social Anthropology." *Annual Review of Anthropology* 13:1–23.

Lee, Richard B. 1979. *The !Kung San.* Cambridge University Press.

Lee, Richard B., and Irven DeVore, eds. 1968. *Man the Hunter.* Chicago: Aldine.

Lesthaeghe, Ron. 1983. "A Century of Demographic and Cultural Change in Western Europe." *Population and Development Review* 9:411–35.

————. 1991. "Moral Control, Secularization, and Reproduction in Belgium (1600–1900)." In *Historiens et Populations,* ed. Société belge de démographie, 259–79. Louvain-la Neuve: Eds. Académia.

————. 1992. "Beyond Economic Reductionism: The Transformation of the Reproductive Regimes in France and Belgium in the Eighteenth and Nineteenth Centuries." In *Fertility Transitions, Family Structure, and Population Policy,* ed. Calvin Goldscheider, 21–44. Boulder, Colo.: Westview Press.

————, ed. 1989. *Reproduction and Social Organization in Sub-Saharan Africa.* Berkeley: University of California Press.

Lesthaeghe, Ron, Georgia Kaufmann, Dominique Meekers, and Johan Surkyn. 1994. "Post-Partum Abstinence, Polygyny, and Age at Marriage: A Macro-Level Analysis of Sub-Saharan Societies." In *Nuptiality in Sub-Saharan Africa,* ed. Caroline Bledsoe and Gilles Pison, 25–54. Oxford: Clarendon.

Lesthaeghe, Ron, and Johan Surkyn. 1988. "Cultural Dynamics and Economic Theories of Fertility Change." *Population and Development Review* 14(1):1–45.

Lesthaeghe, Ron, and Chris Wilson. 1986. "Modes of Production, Secularization, and the Pace of the Fertility Decline in Western Europe, 1870–1930." In *The Decline of Fertility in Europe,* ed. Ansley J. Coale and Susan C. Watkins, 261–92. Princeton: Princeton University Press.

Lewontin, Richard. 1995a. "Sex, Lies, and Social Science." *New York Review of Books,* April 20, 24–29.

————. 1995b. "Reply to Lauman, et al." *New York Review of Books,* 25 May, 43–44.

Lorimer, Frank. 1954. "General Theory." In *Culture and Human Fertility,* ed. Frank Lorimer, 13–251. Paris: UNESCO.

————, ed. 1954. *Culture and Human Fertility.* Paris: UNESCO.

Lotka, Alfred J. 1907. "Relation Between Birth Rates and Death Rates." *Science* 26:21–22.

Macfarlane, Alan. 1968. "Population Crisis: Anthropology's Failure." *New Society,* 10 Oct., 519–21.

————. 1976. *Resources and Population: A Study of the Gurungs of Nepal.* Cambridge: Cambridge University Press.

————. 1986. *Marriage and Love in England: Modes of Reproduction 1300–1840.* Oxford: Basil Blackwell.

McNicoll, Geoffrey. 1980. "Institutional Determinants of Fertility Change." *Population and Development Review* 6:441–62.

―――. 1988. "On the Local Context of Demographic Change." In *Micro-Approaches to Demographic Research,* ed. John Caldwell, Allan Hill, and Valerie Hull, 10–24. London: Kegan Paul.

―――. 1994. "Institutional Analysis of Fertility." In *Population, Economic Development and the Environment,* ed. Kerstin Lindahl-Kiessling and Hans Landberg, 199–230. Oxford: Oxford University Press.

Mamdani, Mahmood. 1972. *The Myth of Population Control: Family, Caste, and Class in an Indian Village.* New York: Monthly Review Press.

Marcus, George E., and Michael M. J. Fischer. 1986. *Anthropology as Cultural Critique.* Chicago: University of Chicago Press.

Mason, Karen Oppenheim, and Anju M. Taj. 1987. "Differences between Women's and Men's Reproductive Goals in Developing Countries." *Population and Development Review* 13(4):611–38.

Meggitt, Mervyn. J. 1968. "'Marriage Classes' and Demography in Central Australia." In *Man the Hunter,* ed. Richard B. Lee and Irven DeVore, 176–84. Chicago: Aldine.

Mitchell, J. Clyde. 1949. "An Estimate of Fertility in Some Yao Hamlets in Liwonde District of Southern Nyasaland. *Africa* 19:293–308.

―――. 1983. "Case and Situation Analysis." *Sociological Review* 31(2):187–211.

Nag, Moni. 1962. *Factors Affecting Human Fertility in Nonindustrial Societies.* New Haven, Conn.: Human Relations Area Files Press.

―――. 1972. "Sex, Culture, and Human Fertility: India and the United States." *Current Anthropology* 13:231–37.

―――, ed. 1975. *Population and Social Organization.* The Hague: Mouton.

Nag, Moni, and Neeraj Kak. 1984. "Demographic Transition in a Punjab Village." *Population and Development Review* 10(4):661–78.

Netting, Robert M. 1972. "Sacred Power and Centralization: Aspects of Political Adaptation in Africa." In *Population Growth: Anthropological Implications,* ed. Brian Spooner, 219–44. Cambridge: MIT Press.

―――. 1981. *Balancing on an Alp.* New York: Cambridge University Press.

Niraula, Bhanu B. 1994. "Marriage Changes in the Central Nepali Hills." *Journal of the Association for Asian Studies* 29(1-2):91–109.

Ortner, Sherry B. 1984. "Theory in Anthropology Since the Sixties." *Comparative Studies in Society and History* 26(1):126–66.

Polgar, Steven. 1972. "Population History and Population Policies from an Anthropological Perspective." *Current Anthropology* 13:203–11.

―――. 1975. "Population, Evolution, and Theoretical Paradigm." In *Population, Ecology, and Social Evolution,* ed. Steven Polgar, 1–25. The Hague: Mouton.

―――, ed. 1971. *Culture and Population.* Cambridge: Schenkman.

―――, ed. 1975. *Population, Ecology, and Social Evolution.* The Hague: Mouton.

Radcliffe-Brown, A. R. 1964. *The Andaman Islanders.* Glencoe, Ill.: Free Press.

Rappaport, Roy. 1967. *Pigs for the Ancestors.* New Haven, Conn.: Yale University Press.

Ragin, Charles C., and Howard S. Becker, eds. 1992. *What is a Case? Exploring the Foundations of Social Inquiry.* Cambridge: Cambridge University Press.

Renne, Elisha P. 1995. "Houses, Fertility, and the Nigerian Land Use Act." *Population and Development Review* 21(1):113–26.

Richards, Audrey I. 1940. *Bemba Marriage and Present Economic Conditions.* Papers of the Rhodes-Livingstone Institute, No. 4.

Richards, Audrey I., and Priscilla Reining. 1954. "Report on Fertility Surveys in Buganda and Buhaya, 1952." In *Culture and Human Fertility,* ed. Frank Lorimer et al., 351–403. Paris: UNESCO.

Riedmann, Agnes. 1993. *Science That Colonizes: A Critique of Fertility Studies in Africa.* Philadelphia: Temple University Press.

Roseberry, William. 1989. *Anthropologies and Histories: Essays in Culture, History, and Political Economy.* New Brunswick, N.J.: Rutgers University Press.

Royal Anthropological Institute. 1899. *Notes and Queries on Anthropology.* 3d edition. London: Royal Anthropological Institute.

Sahlins, Marshall. 1981. *Historical Metaphors and Mythical Realities: Structure in the Early History of the Sandwich Islands Kingdom.* Ann Arbor: University of Michigan Press.

Schapera, Isaac. 1955. "An Anthropologist's Approach to Population Growth: Studies in the Bechuanaland Protectorate." In *The Numbers of Men and Animals,* ed. J. B. Cragg and Norman W. Pirie, 23–29. Edinburgh: Oliver and Boyd.

Scheper-Hughes, Nancy. 1992. *Death Without Weeping: The Violence of Everyday Life in Brazil.* Berkeley: University of California Press.

———. 1995. "The Primacy of the Ethical: Propositions for a Militant Anthropology." *Current Anthropology* 36(3):409–20.

Schneider, Jane, and Peter Schneider. 1984. "Demographic Transitions in a Sicilian Town." *Journal of Family History* 9(3):245–73.

Segalen, Martine. 1984. "Nuclear is Not Independent: Organization of the Household in the Pays Bigouden Sud in the Nineteenth and Twentieth Centuries." In *Households: Comparative and Historical Studies of the Domestic Group,* ed. Robert Netting, Richard Wilk, and Eric Arnould, 163–86. Berkeley: University of California Press.

Skinner, G. William. 1988. "Reproductive Strategies, the Domestic Cycle and Fertility among Japanese Villagers, 1717–1869." Paper presented at the Workshop on Women's Status in Relation to Fertility and Mortality, Bellagio, Italy, June 6–10.

———. 1993. "Conjugal Power in Tokugawa Japanese Families: A Matter of Life or Death." In *Sex and Gender Hierarchies,* ed. Barbara Miller, 236–70. Cambridge: Cambridge University Press.

Smith, Robert J. 1972. "Small Families, Small Households, and Residential Instability: Town and City in 'Pre-Modern' Japan." In *Household and Family in Past Time,* ed. Peter Laslett and Richard Wall, 429–72. Cambridge: Cambridge University Press.

Spooner, Brian. 1972. "The Iranian Deserts." In *Population Growth: Anthropological Implications,* ed. Brian Spooner, 245–68. Cambridge: MIT Press.

———, ed. 1972. *Population Growth: Anthropological Implications.* Cambridge: MIT Press.

Steward, Julian H. 1936. "The Economic and Social Basis of Primitive Bands." In *Essays in Honor of A. L. Kroeber,* ed. R. L. Lowie, 331–50. Berkeley: University of California Press.

Stocking, George W., Jr. 1987. *Victorian Anthropology.* New York: Free Press.

Stycos, J. Mayone, ed. 1989. *Demography as an Interdiscipline.* New Brunswick, N.J.: Transaction Publishers.

Swedlund, Alan C. 1978. "Historical Demography as Population Ecology." *Annual Review of Anthropology* 7:137–73.

Taylor, Charles. 1985. "Interpretation and the Sciences of Man." In *Philosophy and the Human Sciences,* 15–57. Cambridge: Cambridge University Press.

Thornton, Arland, and Hui-Sheng Lin. 1994. *Social Change and the Family in Taiwan.* Chicago: University of Chicago Press.

——. 1976. "Demographic Theory and Anthropological Inference." *Annual Review of Anthropology* 5:351–81.

Willey, Gordon. 1992. "Precolumbian Population History in the Maya Lowlands." *Journal of Field Archaeology* 19:527–30.

Wolf, Arthur P. 1984. "Family Life and the Life Cycle in Rural China." In *Households: Comparative and Historical Studies of the Domestic Group,* ed. Robert Netting, Richard Wilk, and Eric Arnould, 279–98. Berkeley: University of California Press.

Wolf, Arthur P., and Chieh-shan Huang. 1980. *Marriage and Adoption in China, 1845–1945.* Stanford: Stanford University Press.

Wolf, Eric R. 1982. *Europe and the People without History.* Berkeley: University of California Press.

Wood, James W. 1990. "Fertility in Anthropological Populations." *Annual Review of Anthropology* 19:211–42.

Wuthnow, Robert. 1987. *Meaning and Moral Order: Explorations in Cultural Analysis.* Berkeley: University of California Press.

Yanagisako, Sylvia Junko. 1979. "Family and Household: The Analysis of Domestic Groups." *Annual Review of Anthropology* 8:161–205.

Yengoyan, Aram A. 1968. "Demographic and Ecological Influences on Aboriginal Australian Marriage Sections." In *Man the Hunter,* ed. Richard B. Lee and Irven DeVore, 185–99. Chicago: Aldine.

Chapter Two

Kinship Systems and Demographic Regimes

Monica Das Gupta

The study of kinship systems and their interaction with demographic outcomes is one of the richest areas for substantive and theoretical work in
anthropological-demographic research. It is also an obvious one, since most
of demographers' concerns pertain to events that take place at the level of the
household.

Nothing is ever so simple in real life. The interest of demographers in
studying kinship has grown almost simultaneously with the decline of interest
in kinship studies amongst anthropologists. Indeed, many anthropologists
view it as an obsolete area of study. This makes it important to examine exactly *what* is seen as obsolete. Anthropologists have turned away from their
erstwhile consuming interest in the study of the formal rules of marriage and
descent, and of kinship terminology. Much of the traditional anthropological
work on kinship was based on the theoretical framework of structural functionalism, in which social institutions are perceived as a set of structures that
have identifiable functions in sustaining the social order. Anthropologists have
turned away from this intrinsically static analytical approach.

Since Barth's classic study of the Swat Pathans (1965), there has been a
shift of interest away from structural-functional or structural analytical approaches, and toward focusing on people's negotiations with one another. This
approach does not deny that there exist some overall institutional frameworks
within which people conduct their negotiations, and which they manipulate
for purposes of negotiating with others. To borrow Viazzo's (in press) terminology, the institutional framework provides a set of long-term strategies
(such as the goal of keeping the estate undivided) which will be internalized as
a norm, while there will also be a set of shorter-term individual strategies
whereby people will maneuver around this norm to achieve ends such as trying to give something to other children, delaying transfer of the property, etc.
Thus a turning away from older, more static theories in anthropology does
not preclude the study of kinship systems (Goody and Goody 1969; Goody
1973, 1975; Collier and Yanagisako 1987).

Many aspects of kinship systems—notably the forms of marriage, inheritance and household formation—have a considerable bearing on demographic
outcomes. This is reflected in the life course of individuals through the structuring of marriage and reproduction. It is also reflected in the interactions
between individuals and groups, through the structuring of intragenerational,
intergenerational and interhousehold relationships, all of which influence

health and fertility regimes. Yet our understanding of these issues is still in fledgling form (Laslett 1972).

This chapter attempts to push forward the analysis of kinship systems to develop our theoretical understanding of demographic processes. It begins by reviewing some of the existing theories linking kinship systems with fertility, and moves on to the curiously neglected field of the relationship between kinship systems and demographic regimes viewed as a whole. Building on earlier work (Das Gupta 1995a, 1995b), I sketch out some examples of how we might study the interactions between kinship systems and fertility, health and mortality, as well as the implications for old age support and policies for providing such support. I focus throughout on the demographic literature and on the concerns of demographers; the rich anthropological literature on these subjects would have to form the subject of another paper.

Some Major Theories Relating Kinship to Demographic Outcomes

Much of the existing work in this field focuses on how kinship systems influence fertility behavior, a question which permeates the demographic literature.[1] The interest in this goes back at least as far as Malthus, with his discussion of the west European "nuptiality valve" regulating the growth of population in response to available resources. Malthus might well be horrified to be perceived as an anthropological demographer, and he does not explicitly address the question of kinship systems as such. Nevertheless, his discussion of the "nuptiality valve" of course subsumes a particular system of marriage, inheritance, and control of access to resources.

Contrasts between European and Asian Kinship Systems

The clearest formulation of a theoretical model of kinship systems and their implications for fertility behavior was that put forward by Kingsley Davis (1955). In this article, which was especially remarkable for having being written long before others showed interest in this field, Davis contrasts the kinship and marriage systems of Europe with those of South and East Asia to show how the logic of the joint family system would make for higher fertility than the European system.

In particular, he pointed out that in the joint family system marriage tends to be early and universal; the couple is absorbed into the larger economic unit of the joint family and is thus not expected to be economically self-sufficient, while childbearing helps the couple to establish themselves as social adults and gain power in the household. Thus, he emphasizes, the costs of childbearing are spread out over the entire household and there are powerful incentives at work to make for high fertility. By contrast, the European system required that a couple be economically in a position to raise a family before they could marry, and the fact of marriage established the couple's social adulthood. This would make for smaller family size than the joint family system, both because of the older age at marriage and because the couple would have to bear all the costs of childbearing themselves.

This was and continues to be an enormously influential article, whose ideas have been incorporated directly and indirectly into the demographic literature on fertility behavior. The themes of the low costs of childbearing in joint families, the role of elders and the lack of independence of the couple in making fertility decisions, and the need to have several children in order to establish oneself in the household, have come to be so commonly addressed in the literature that some of those writing about this today may not even be aware of the intellectual influence of Davis's work.

Hajnal (1982) developed the contrast between the kinship and demographic regimes of preindustrial northern European households and the joint household systems of India, China, and Tuscany. He focused on how these two contrasting systems resulted in very different composition of households. In northern Europe, the great majority of households consisted of one couple with some children and some unrelated people who were servants in the household. The age at marriage was high, and the great majority of married people were in charge of their own household. The aged tended to live separately from their married children. It was also common for children not to live with their parents, but to live and work in other households under the system of "circulation of servants." By contrast, in Indian households, children live with their parents, and aged parents live mostly with their children. There are few non-relatives, the age at marriage is younger, and it is common for married sons not to be in charge of the household but to live with their parents or brothers.

These contrasts are brimming with demographic implications, but these are not developed much in Hajnal's article. The only direct link drawn between these systems of household formation and demographic regimes is the implication the system of circulation of servants had for fertility. Hajnal discusses the system of "life cycle service," whereby people would try to save up enough money to marry. This obviously made for an older average age at marriage and lower fertility. Hajnal goes further to suggest that "the institution of service was probably an essential part of the mechanism by which marriage could be delayed, with the result that population growth was under partial control. Populations with joint household systems lack that mechanism" (1982:481). He does not discuss one implication of his findings, which is that northern European peasants may have had less incentive for childbearing than Indian households, insofar as the household labor force can be maintained through hiring other people's children, rather than through bearing the next generation of the household.

There is reason to believe that Davis and Hajnal were wrong to conclude that joint family systems necessarily exhibit universal early marriage and lack a "nuptiality valve" to help balance household numbers with available resources. While it is obviously possible within a joint family system to incorporate married couples into an existing household, there is no reason in principle why the household would not respond to threats to its continued economic viability by regulating marriage and reproduction.

Davis's and Hajnal's argument rests on the assumption that since the costs of childbearing in a joint family are borne by the household and not by the couple, there are few constraints on high fertility. It is certainly true that the *couple* may be able to spread the costs of childbearing, but they overlook the possibility that the *household* may want to regulate the number of new members born into it. If a joint family household is in a position to make effective *joint* decisions about fertility, Davis's and Hajnal's assumption may not be valid. One way to make joint decisions about fertility is for other household members to make inputs into young couples' childbearing decisions, and this is a feature of joint families that is widely noted in India and in South Asia as a whole. Another way to regulate fertility at the household level is to regulate marriage.

To elaborate further on this point, consider the following two examples from joint family kinship systems in India and Italy. In both these settings, there is evidence that marriage was regulated in response to changes in the resource base. Moreover, a detailed look at communities in these regions shows that richer and poorer subgroups in these communities responded differently to the fact of changes in the resource base, depending on the exigencies of their situations.

In a study of a district in Punjab in northern India, Das Gupta found high proportions of men who never married (1995b). Moreover, this proportion rose as population pressure increased. For example, 13 percent of landowner caste men aged forty and above were unmarried in 1921. By 1969—that is, when the effects of mortality decline created increased pressure on resources— the proportion of men who never married rose to 23 percent. It is clear from the genealogies that families with several sons surviving to adulthood were most likely to discourage their marrying, especially if they already had a small landholding.

By contrast, the proportion of agricultural laborer caste men remaining unmarried in both 1921 and 1969 remained around 5 percent. The more strenuous efforts of the landowning caste to regulate population growth in their households can be attributed to the fact that they had clearly defined property which subdivided visibly if marriage was not regulated. For the agricultural laborers, the perception of population pressure was diffused because they did not own specific productive resources and depended instead on the generalized security of patron-client relations for their livelihood.

A similar pattern of marriage regulation has been found in Italy. In a study of peasant families in Casalecchio in north-central Italy between 1861 and 1921, Kertzer (1991) notes that as many as 16 percent of males among the sharecroppers in 1871 had never married. Whether or not a man remained unmarried depended on how many brothers there were in the family: men with no brothers would be encouraged to marry, but those with several brothers would be discouraged from marrying, "since a point could be reached where the number of family members would become too great for the farm to support" (1991:42). A far lower proportion (6 percent) of agricultural laborers were unmarried. Kertzer attributes this to the fact that the sharecroppers had complex households which could provide satisfactory living and economic conditions for their unmarried men, while the agricultural laborer households were typically nuclear, so unmarried men would be likely to be left on their own once their parents died.

West African Kinship Systems

West African kinship systems have also been studied in terms of their implications for fertility behavior. In particular, Caldwell developed his influential "wealth flows" theory of fertility, which hinges around a theory of kinship relations, in the context of fieldwork in Nigeria (Caldwell 1976, 1978).

Caldwell argues that there are two types of societies: one in which it is rational for people to have as many children as possible, and the other in which it is rational to have no children at all. High fertility is enjoined by the familial mode of production, which is associated with peasant economies, hunting and gathering, shifting cultivation, and nomadic herding. Under the familial mode of production, the head of the family can benefit from exploiting the labor of other family members, and thereby stands to gain from ensuring high fertility within the family. When the capitalist mode of production has been firmly established in these societies, however, the family has to invest in the offspring to make them productive members of the new economy; this reverses the intergenerational flow of wealth from going up the age hierarchy to down the age hierarchy. At this point, the society turns around completely, and childbearing is no longer economically beneficial.

This theory is clearly formulated for a society in which the children born into a household continue to live and work in that household. Where it is common for children to circulate, as in northern Europe or the regions of west Africa with matrifocal families, the potential benefits (as well as the costs) of childbearing are spread over a network of households and do not necessarily devolve to the head of the household in which the children were born. The economic rationale for childbearing has to be quite different in these societies, even if they belong to a non-capitalist mode of production.

Potential for Further Work on Kinship Systems and Demographic Regimes

Compared to the volume of work relating kinship and fertility, there is relatively little which relates the logic of kinship systems to health and mortality, and thereby to demographic regimes as a whole. In the context of work on developing countries, this can be understood as resulting from the greater stress until recently on analyzing fertility behavior. It is less easy to understand this gap in the case of historical work on preindustrial Europe, where much work has been done on the effects of the kinship and inheritance systems on fertility, but little relating these to the discussion of the health and mortality conditions found in these societies.

Hajnal's work (1982) is a good example of this puzzling lack of explication of the totality of the demographic regime. He develops a complete model of two kinds of kinship and inheritance systems, but seems almost to restrain himself from developing the demographic implications further. In particular, he does not begin to address the implications for health and mortality.

Some work relating kinship systems to health and demographic regimes has emanated from the study of the position of women in South Asia. For example, Dyson and Moore (1983) explain the long-standing contrast between the demographic regimes of northern and southern India in terms of differences in their kinship systems. The north has been characterized by higher fertility, higher child mortality, and more masculine sex ratios than the south. This is attributed to the stricter working of the rules of patrilineal descent and exogamy in marriage in the north. Cain's work on the vulnerability of widows in Bangladesh (1981, 1986) and Das Gupta's work on selective discrimination against female children (Das Gupta 1987) and on female autonomy over the life cycle (Das Gupta 1995a) are examples of research attributing negative health outcomes for females to the workings of the kinship system.

There is considerable scope for developing models of kinship and demographic processes which help to identify (1) the incentives for childbearing and (2) the groups whose position in the social structure exposes them to elevated risks of ill-health and mortality. This section sketches out some examples of this approach.

Northern Europe and Northern India

A comparison of the kinship and inheritance systems of peasant societies in northern Europe and northern India suggests that there is a clear logic making not only for differences in fertility behavior, as put forward by Davis (1955) and Hajnal (1982), but also for differences in the vulnerability of different groups to poor health and mortality (Das Gupta 1995a). To describe this, it is necessary to summarize briefly the way the inheritance and household formation systems worked in these two settings.

The discussion of preindustrial northern Europe is based on studies of eighteenth-century Austria (Berkner 1972); nineteenth-century Austria (Sieder and Mitterauer 1983); and nineteenth-century Scandinavia (Gaunt 1983, 1987; Plakans 1989; Sorensen 1989). These were characterized by impartible inheritance and nuclear or stem families. The discussion of northern India is based largely on studies of contemporary rural northern India, which is characterized by partible inheritance and joint families.

In the northern European societies, the rules of inheritance and household formation enabled one couple to take over the farm when the parents aged. Typically, a retirement contract was drawn up, stipulating how much food and other support the aged parents would receive from the young couple. The aged parents would then hand over the management of the farm to the new couple. The children who did not inherit the farm would have limited or no claims on the resources of the farm in which they were born. They would go to make a living elsewhere, most frequently by working as agricultural laborers. They might be able to save enough money to marry, but their standard of living would be far lower than that of their sibling on the farm. It was common for the farming couple to send their children out to live and work on other farms if their labor was not required on their own farm, so the non-inheriting children may well have been living as agricultural laborers for some time already before the transfer of ownership of their parents' farm.

This system operated on a "lifeboat ethic," whereby the social and economic position of the farming family was effectively maintained by removing the potential claims of other kin to support from the household. The couple owning the farm were little encumbered by claims other than their own. One exception to this was their own aged parents, whose claims were acknowledged, though frequently deeply resented (Gaunt 1983). Siblings typically moved down the class hierarchy, where they were exposed to far greater vulnerability to ill-health and mortality than the class into which they had been born. Children were also not necessarily perceived as having an intrinsic right to be maintained by their household of birth, and in being sent off as laborers elsewhere must often have received less care and protection against ill-health than if they had remained in their parental household.

The north Indian joint family system, on the other hand, operates on a completely different logic. All members of the household are perceived as having a claim to household resources. Of course there are inequities in the operation of these claims, as is well-documented in the case of differences between the position of men and women in the household, but these inequalities pale when compared to those of the stem family. The joint family system is the diametric opposite of the "lifeboat ethic," which maintains the position of some at the cost of worse conditions of health and mortality for others within each generation. Intergenerationally, the sharing of poverty within the joint family system has the potential to lead to a diminution of resources per capita and thereby lead to increased ill-health and mortality.

Where the average wealth of households was not low, the joint family system would tend to make for lower overall levels of mortality than the stem family system. It is harder to hypothesize the relative levels of mortality in the two systems under conditions of sustained poverty, but it should be possible to model this.

While much of the above discussion pertains to the situation of people related to each other by birth, the situation of those marrying into the family in the two kinship systems complicates the picture. Both societies are patrilineal in inheritance and patrilocal in residence, so typically it is women who marry into the peasant household. The position of these in-marrying women differs in important ways between these two systems (Das Gupta 1995a).

In the northern European peasant household, the critical economic and social unit is the team formed by the farming couple. Much emphasis is thus placed on the strength of the conjugal bond, while intergenerational and other intragenerational bonds are relatively weak. Moreover, the couple had their independent economic base, with the right to decide how best to use their resources. This meant that the woman had considerable autonomy and power in domestic decisions, and could use this to protect her own and her children's health as seemed best to her. The only person above her in the family decision-making hierarchy was her husband.

In the north Indian joint family system, there are strong intergenerational and intragenerational bonds between household members related to each other by blood. Concomitantly, the development of a strong conjugal bond is discouraged. This means that the woman marrying into the household is in a very weak position in terms of making decisions to protect her own and her children's health. Layers of people are above her in the household hierarchy of status and authority, beginning with all the adult males, and continuing through all the women older than her. Autonomy and power rise as a woman ages and bears children, thereby establishing her position in the household.

The stage of being a young married woman overlaps with the peak childbearing years, resulting in a situation in which the woman is most lacking in autonomy at the time when her own health is under the stresses of reproduction and she is responsible for the health of young children at the most vulnerable stage of their life. Her constraints in making and implementing decisions to protect her own health and that of her young children make for elevated rates of maternal mortality and child mortality (Das Gupta 1995a). By the time the double burden of being young and female is lightened, the peak childbearing years are also over, so it is likely to be too late for the woman's newly acquired autonomy to reflect itself in more positive demographic outcomes.

There are obvious pronatalist implications of having one's status related to success in childbearing. Besides, the constraints on husband-wife communication and the authority over family decisions wielded by senior members of the household are also potential complications in the effective regulation of fertility. There is also a powerful stimulus to exhibit a preference for sons. Since sons are critical to ensuring the woman's future well-being in the household, there is an inbuilt preference for bearing sons and developing close emotional bonds with them. Daughters are discriminated against by the mother and the rest of the household, a fact that is reflected in substantially higher child mortality levels for girls than for boys.

The logic of these kinship and inheritance systems would suggest that we should expect to find heightened mortality in early childhood (for both sexes, and with an additional stress amongst female children) and amongst women of reproductive age in northern India. These outcomes are found, as hypothesized, in India (Das Gupta 1995a). By contrast, in northern Europe the categories of people suffering from heightened mortality would be older children (many of whom would be sent to live in other households as servants), noninheriting adults, and older people. Narrower hypotheses can also be generated—for example, that the relative vulnerability of two siblings to ill-health over their life cycle may be very different in a stem family vs. a joint family system.

West Africa

It is also possible to put together some of the diverse work on west African societies to arrive at the beginnings of an integrated view of the interaction between these systems of marriage and household formation on the one hand and the demographic regime on the other.

One body of literature pertains to those west African societies characterized by matrifocal households. The gradual and easily reversible process of marrying in these societies (Meekers 1992) increases the probability of a woman having several partners over her lifetime. Along with the pressure to bear children in each consecutive relationship, this is likely to make it difficult for a woman to take an overall view of how many children she would like to have, and at what stage of her life she would like to have them. At the same time, the fact that there is considerable flexibility in who actually raises the child means that women do not necessarily have to bear all the costs of child-rearing: these may be borne by "grannies" and other types of foster parents (Goody and Goody 1969; Goody 1973; Isiugo-Abanihe 1985; Bledsoe 1990). This cost-spreading can help sustain high fertility.

This system of household formation has implications not only for fertility, but also for health. One implication of child fostering, for example, is that the children who are fostered out may be less well cared for than those who remain with their mothers, resulting in higher rates of ill-health and mortality (Bledsoe et al. 1988). It is interesting to note that similar patterns of marriage and fostering are found in the matrifocal societies of the Caribbean and result in similar neglect of foster children's health (Rawson and Berggren 1973; Desai 1992). Since Goody and Goody suggest that fostering is not common in west African societies with unilineal descent systems (1969), it is possible to hypothesize that, other things being equal, children's health is better protected in these societies.

Literature from other west African societies gives us a more hierarchical and structured picture of kinship and fertility. For example, there is considerable discussion of the long postpartum taboo on sexual relations, which is too frequently recounted as an exotic feature of these societies. Following Saucier (1972), both Lesthaeghe (1980) and Caldwell and Caldwell (1981) remove this from exotica and place it in the context of the kinship system by attributing it to the desire of the elders of the lineage to prevent the formation of a close conjugal bond amongst their youth:

> In the traditional African context, control of the reproductive pool and of female and child labor are only two among many elements of an overall pattern of gerontocratic control over people in lineages and crops on lineage land. . . . The prevention of close husband-wife solidarity through the long postpartum taboo in particular and through the maintenance of physical and psychological distance in general, also ensures lineage dominance. (Lesthaeghe 1980:530)

This would suggest that we should not expect to find this long postpartum taboo in African societies without unilineal descent systems; for example, where the matrifocal family predominates. Here we have a testable hypothesis.

Caldwell and Lesthaeghe are clearly referring to societies with unilineal descent systems, characterized by considerable parental authority over the couple's behavior, fairly stable marriages, and incorporation of the children of a marriage into the household and the lineage. The logic of these kinship systems is quite different from that of other systems, such as that of the west African or Caribbean matrifocal family or the northern European stem family.

Familial Support for the Aged

The living arrangements and care of the aged are profoundly influenced by kinship systems and patterns of inheritance. This is evident when we contrast the northern European stem family and the north Indian joint family. As already mentioned, retirement under this form of the stem family system involved transferring ownership and managerial authority to the younger couple (Berkner 1972; Gaunt 1983, 1987; Plakans 1989; Sorensen 1989). This was accompanied by a sudden loss of power and status for the older couple. The aged couple would subsequently be dependent on the younger couple to fulfill their contractual obligation to provide them with food and shelter.

This highly discontinuous transfer of power made for considerable tension between the generations. The older generation could have an incentive to delay relinquishing control of the farm, while the younger generation could resent having to wait for their turn to manage the farm. After retirement, the resentment at having to support the aged couple could result in neglect, "especially when they have reached the age when they can no longer work; then it is no longer hidden that the young wish them a quick departure" (Gaunt 1983:262, quoting from a contemporary observer in eighteenth century Sweden). Plakans summarizes the literature on the treatment of the old: "there is now something like a consensus that the treatment of the old was harsh and decidedly pragmatic. Dislike and suspicion, it is said, characterized the attitudes of both sides" (1989:177).

By contrast, in the north Indian system, managerial authority is transferred gradually from father to son as the son(s) get older. The actual transfer of ownership comes much later, ideally after the father's death. This more gradual transfer of power makes for smoother intergenerational relations. Unlike the retired couple's loss of power in northern Europe, in this system status and autonomy *rise* with age, for both men and women. Also, the parental couple is far less likely to be perceived as constituting a burden on the household. On the contrary, they not only have a legitimate claim to a share of the household's resources, but a claim which is buttressed by their process of aging and concomitant rise in status.

The differences in the nature of intergenerational relations engendered by these different systems of kinship and inheritance are reflected in the arrangements made for the care of the aged. Laslett (1985) argues that it was common for the elderly in northern Europe to live on their own, a view which is quite widely held by historians working on Europe. Kertzer (1995) has questioned the validity of this view, pointing to studies by Wall (1995), Robin (1984), and Sieder and Mitterauer (1983) which find that it was not uncommon for the aged to live with their children in England and Austria.

This helps to redress the perspective on the living arrangements of the aged in preindustrial Europe, but it does not detract from the starkness of the contrast between these societies and South Asia. For example, from a South Asian perspective it is not impressive to learn that more than half of the aged with surviving children lived with their children in an English village in 1851–71 (Robin 1984). In contemporary India more than 80 percent of the aged live with their children. It is the exception for people *not* to live with their children. (This is true even of those who do not have surviving children of their own: they live with close relatives in a familial situation.) Far higher proportions of the Indian elderly live with their children than in the mid-nineteenth-century English village held up as an example of high levels of coresidence between parents and their children. This is despite the fact that contemporary India has experienced the forces of industrialization and urbanization, which are believed to place stresses on family systems.

Another important question hinges around what is *meant* by coresidence with children, in terms of the living conditions of the aged. Gaunt (1983, 1987) describes a variety of arrangements for living with one's children, none of which suggest any of the entitlements that the aged in India normally have. Some parents would be shifted at retirement to a separate cottage, where specified amounts of food, fuel, etc. would be delivered to them. Others would continue to live in the main homestead, but their retirement contracts would specify which room they would occupy and whether they were allowed to do things such as sit by the fire. Sometimes the room they were given had clear symbolic connotations of the aged being on their way out of this life, such as "the west room." Other parents circulated amongst their children, living for some duration with each in turn.

Indian parents living with their children typically exercise a considerable degree of autonomy in their access to the household's resources. They expect to be central members of the household, and to participate in household affairs with confidence. The description of the living arrangements of the aged in northern Europe suggests that they were viewed as a burden on the young. It does not suggest that they could expect the same level of physical and emotional support from children and grandchildren as in contemporary India.

Casterline et al. (1993) present evidence that familial support persists for the aged in Southeast and East Asia by showing that metropolitan areas differ little from rural areas in the proportion of the aged living with their children. Moreover, they show that high proportions of the aged in East Asia coreside with more than one child in the classic joint family tradition. They also find that parents have a high intensity of contact with non-resident children. These high levels of physical and emotional support for the elderly contrast sharply with the descriptions of conflict and neglect of the aged in preindustrial northern Europe (Gaunt 1983, 1987; Sorensen 1989). This would make for poorer levels of health and mortality, *ceteris paribus*, amongst the aged in northern Europe.

The persistence of kinship systems is not simply a question of whether the old typically live with their children, but extends to the question of which children they typically live with. Casterline, Chang, and Domingo (1993) point out that because of the strongly patrilineal Chinese joint family system, Taiwanese parents have a strong aversion to living with married daughters and an overwhelming tendency to live with married sons. This contrasts with their findings for the Philippines, which is characterized by a bilateral family system, and parents coreside equally with sons and daughters.

There seems to be a striking continuity between the forms of familial support and living arrangements for the aged in the kinship systems of the preindustrial precursors of contemporary societies, and those of today. For example, 80–85 percent of the aged in India in 1987–88[2] and Sri Lanka in 1975 lived with their children regardless of whether they were currently married, while only 14–20 percent of the aged in Denmark in 1963 and the United States in 1975 did so (De Vos and Holden 1988:696–97; Hashimoto 1991:369).

Those societies in which intergenerational relations were characterized by conflict show lower proportions of the elderly living with their children, in both preindustrial and contemporary times. The lack of support must have made for poorer health and mortality than would be expected on the basis of the disease environment alone. By contrast, in societies which were characterized by smoother intergenerational relations, the aged tend to live with their children and receive much more physical and emotional support from their children.

This supports the view that the forces of industrialization and urbanization have a very attenuated impact on the predisposition of societies to provide familial support to their elderly. Asia as a whole shows very high proportions of the elderly living with their children compared to Europe. Even in Japan, with its high level of industrialization and urbanization (as well as constraints on living space), around 80 percent of the elderly lived with their children in 1973 (De Vos and Holden 1988:696–97). A similar pattern prevails in South Korea.

There is little evidence, then, of the quick convergence to the western conjugal family system, which is often expected to accompany the process of industrialization and urbanization. This has important implications for policy-making with regard to old age support in these societies. Instead of preparing for an impending destruction of familial support systems, there seems to be more need to provide support to families in caring for their aged.

Conclusions

Most of the work linking kinship systems with demographic outcomes has concerned itself largely with understanding fertility behavior. The implications that kinship systems have for health have been relatively neglected in the literature so far. This chapter shows how kinship systems are logically interlinked with demographic regimes as a whole, including not only fertility but also health and mortality. It shows how the health of individuals is encouraged to prosper or fail depending on where they fit in the organization of the family and the household.

It may well be that kinship systems have a more pervasive and persistent impact on health and mortality than they do on fertility. The relative evaluation of different individuals within a family or a household is far more deeply embedded in a society's cultural constructs than the pros and cons of different family sizes. Besides, fertility behavior is subject to conscious evaluation and can therefore change in response to altered circumstances. By contrast, norms regarding the treatment of different categories of individuals are upheld by ideas of which we are not always even aware, let alone in a position to re-assess.

Nor do the values and constructs of a kinship system change rapidly, even in the face of the forces of industrialization and urbanization. Abundant evidence can be found in Asia of high levels of familial support for the elderly, even in highly industrialized countries such as Japan and South Korea. There seem to be large and persistent differences between societies in the extent to which the aged receive physical and emotional support from their children: differences which seem to be closely related to the way in which intergenerational relations were structured in the preindustrial precursors to the present-day societies.

The apparent persistence of levels of familial support for the elderly over time suggests that policy-making for old-age support can reasonably plan around the expectation that current patterns of familial support are likely to continue into at least the near and middle future. Further study of kinship systems and demographic regimes have considerable potential for developing theoretical and analytical approaches in anthropological demography, as well as for inputs to policy-making.

There is a need for more work along the lines of Kingsley Davis's thesis, explicitly comparing different models of kinship and spelling out how the logic of these systems relates to demographic regimes. The comparative approach has the advantage of illuminating issues which are not necessarily apparent in the context of studying any one society. The study of kinship systems is rich with potential for theory-building and understanding the deeper forces underlying demographic outcomes.

NOTES

This research was supported by funding from the Mellon Foundation grant to the Population Studies and Training Center, Brown University, and a Visiting Fellowship at the Institut d'Estudis Demografics, Universitat Autonoma de Barcelona. I am grateful for discussions with Debraj Ray in formulating this paper. The chapter has also benefited from comments from David Kertzer and Tom Fricke.

1. A vast literature also exists on the household economy and how it influences fertility through the costs and benefits of childbearing. This ranges from the purely theoretical (for example, Becker 1960; Leibenstein 1957), to the empirical (for example, Cain 1977; Mamdani 1972; Nag, White, and Peet 1978). While it is based on assumptions or observation of how different members of the family interact in the household economy, this literature is not discussed here because it does not explicitly consider the functioning of the kinship system.

2. These are figures for the percentage of the elderly living in multigenerational households in India, and not strictly those living with their children. However, the two are largely synonymous, with a few exceptions in the form of people with no children.

REFERENCES

Barth, Fredrik. 1965. *Political Leadership among Swat Pathan.* London: Athlone Press.

Becker, Gary S. 1960. "An Economic Analysis of Fertility." In *Demographic and Economic Change in Developed Countries,* ed. Ansley J. Coale, 209–31. Princeton: Princeton University Press.

Berkner, Lutz K. 1972. "The Stem Family and the Developmental Cycle of the Peasant Household: An Eighteenth-Century Austrian Example." *American Historical Review* 77:398–418.

Bledsoe, Caroline. 1990. "The Politics of Children: Fosterage and the Social Management of Fertility among the Mende of Sierra Leone." In *Births and Power: Social Change and the Politics of Reproduction,* ed. W. Penn Handwerker, 81–100. Boulder, Colo.: Westview Press.

Bledsoe, Caroline et al. 1988. "The Effect of Child Fostering on Feeding Practices and Access to Health Services in Rural Sierra Leone." *Social Science and Medicine* 27(6):627–36.

Cain, Mead. 1977. "The Economic Activities of Children in a Village in Bangladesh." *Population and Development Review* 3(3):201–27.

———. 1981. "Risk and Insurance: Perspectives on Fertility and Agrarian Change in India and Bangladesh." *Population and Development Review* 7(3):435–74.

———. 1986. "The Consequences of Reproductive Failure: Dependence, Mobility, and Mortality among the Elderly of Rural South Asia." *Population Studies* 40(3): 375–88.

Caldwell, John C. 1976. "Towards a Restatement of Demographic Transition Theory." *Population and Development Review* 2(3–4):321–66.

———. 1978. "A Theory of Fertility: From High Plateau to Destabilization." In *Population and Development Review* 4(4): 553–77.

Caldwell, Patricia, and John C. Caldwell. 1981. "The Function of Childspacing in Traditional Societies and the Direction of Change." In *Childspacing in Tropical Africa: Traditions and Change,* ed. Hilary J. Page and Ron Lesthaeghe, 73–92. New York: Academic Press.

Casterline, John B., Ming-Cheng Chang, Napaporn Chayouan, and Lita Domingo. 1993. "The Density of Parent-Child Co-residence in East and Southeast Asia." Paper presented at the Population Association of America meeting, Cincinnati, April 1–3.

Casterline, John B., Ming-Cheng Chang, and Lita Domingo. 1993. "Which Children Co-reside with Elderly Parents? A Comparative Analysis of the Philippines and Taiwan." Paper presented at the Gerontological Society of America meeting, New Orleans, November 19–23.

Collier, Jane, and Sylvia J. Yanagisako. 1987. Introduction to *Gender and Kinship: Towards a Unified Analysis,* ed. Jane Collier and Sylvia J. Yanagisako, 1–13. Stanford: Stanford University Press.

Das Gupta, Monica. 1987. "Selective Discrimination against Female Children in Rural Punjab, India." *Population and Development Review* 13(1):77–100.

———. 1995a. "Lifecourse Perspectives on Women's Autonomy and Health Outcomes." *American Anthropologist* 97(3):481–91.

———. 1995b. "Fertility Decline in Punjab, India: Parallels with Historical Europe." *Population Studies* 49(3):481–500.

Davis, Kingsley. 1955. "Institutional Patterns Favouring High Fertility in Underdeveloped Areas." *Eugenics Quarterly* 2:33–39.

De Vos, Susan, and Karen Holden. 1988. "Measures Comparing Living Arrangements of the Elderly: An Assessment." *Population and Development Review* 14(4): 688–704.

Desai, Sonalde. 1992. "Children at Risk: The Role of Family Structure in Latin America and West Africa." *Population and Development Review* 18(4):689–717.

Dyson, Tim, and Mick Moore. 1983. "On Kinship Structure, Female Autonomy and Demographic Behavior in India." *Population and Development Review* 9(1):35–60.

Gaunt, David. 1983. "The Property and Kin Relationships of Retired Farmers in Northern and Central Europe." In *Family Forms in Historic Europe,* ed. Richard

Wall, Jean Robin, and Peter Laslett, 249–80. Cambridge: Cambridge University Press.

———. 1987. "Rural Household Organization and Inheritance in Northern Europe." In *Family History at the Crossroads*, ed. Tamara Hareven and Andrejs Plakans, 121–41. Princeton: Princeton University Press.

Goody, Esther. 1973. *Contexts of Kinship: An Essay on the Family Sociology of the Gonja of Northern Ghana*. Cambridge: Cambridge University Press.

———. 1975. "Delegation of Parental Roles in West Africa and the West Indies." In *Changing Social Structure in Ghana: Essays on the Comparative Sociology of a New State and an Old Tradition*, ed. Jack Goody. London: International African Institute.

Goody, Jack, and Esther Goody. 1969. "The Circulation of Women and Children in Northern Ghana." In *Comparative Studies in Kinship*, ed. Jack Goody, 184–215. Stanford: Stanford University Press.

Hajnal, John. 1982. "Two Kinds of Preindustrial Household Formation System." *Population and Development Review* 8(3):449–94.

Hashimoto, Akiko. 1991. "Living Arrangements of the Aged in Seven Developing Countries: A Preliminary Analysis." *Journal of Cross-Cultural Gerontology* 6: 359–81.

Isiugo-Abanihe, Uche. 1985. "Child Fosterage in West Africa." *Population and Development Review* 11(1):53–73.

Kertzer, David I. 1991. "Reflections on the European Marriage Pattern: Sharecropping and Proletarianization in Casalecchio, Italy, 1861–1921." *Journal of Family History* 16(1):31–45.

———. 1995. "Toward a Historical Demography of Aging." In *Aging in the Past*, ed. David Kertzer and Peter Laslett, 363–83. Berkeley: University of California Press.

Laslett, Peter. 1972. Introduction to *Household and Family in Past Time*, ed. Peter Laslett and Richard Wall, 1–90. Cambridge: Cambridge University Press.

———. 1985. "Societal Development and Aging." In *Handbook of Aging and the Social Sciences*, ed. Robert H. Binstock and Ethel Shanas, 87–116. New York: Van Nostrand Reinhold.

Leibenstein, Harvey. 1957. *Economic Backwardness and Economic Growth: Studies in the Theory of Economic Development*. New York: Wiley.

Lesthaeghe, Ron. 1980. "On the Social Control of Human Reproduction." *Population and Development Review* 6(4):527–48.

Mamdani, Mahmood. 1972. *The Myth of Population Control* New York: Monthly Review Press.

Meekers, Dominique. 1992. "The Process of Marriage in African Societies: A Multiple Indicator Approach." *Population and Development Review* 18(1):61–78.

Nag, Moni, Benjamin N. F. White, and Richard Creighton Peet. 1978. "An Anthropological Approach to the Study of the Economic Value of Children in Java and Nepal." *Current Anthropology* 19(2):293–306.

Plakans, Andrejs. 1989. "Stepping Down in Former Times: A Comparative Assessment of 'Retirement' in Traditional Europe." In *Age Structuring in Comparative Perspective*, ed. David I. Kertzer and Klaus Warner Schaie, 175–95. Hillsdale, N.J.: Lawrence Erlbaum Associates.

Rawson, I., and G. Berggren. 1973. "Family Structure, Child Location, and Nutritional Disease in Rural Haiti." *Environmental Child Health* 19(4):288–98.

Robin, Jean. 1984. "Family Care of the Elderly in a Nineteenth-Century Devonshire Parish." *Ageing and Society* 4:505–16.

Saucier, Jean F. 1972. "Correlates of the Long Postpartum Taboo: A Cross Cultural Study." *Current Anthropology* 23(2): 238–49.

Sieder, Reinhard, and Michael Mitterauer. 1983. "The Reconstruction of the Family Life Course: Theoretical Problems and Empirical Results." In *Family Forms in Historic Europe,* ed. Richard Wall, Jean Robin, and Peter Laslett, 309–46. Cambridge: Cambridge University Press.

Sorensen, Aage B. 1989. "Old Age, Retirement, and Inheritance." In *Age Structuring in Comparative Perspective,* ed. David I. Kertzer and Klaus Warner Schaie, 197–214. Hillsdale, N.J.: Lawrence Erlbaum Associates.

Viazzo, Pier Paolo. In press. "Anthropology, Family History and the Concept of 'Strategy.'" In *Economic and Social Aspects of the Family Life cycle, Europe and Japan, Traditional and Modern,* ed. Richard Wall and Osamu Saito. Cambridge: Cambridge University Press.

Wall, Richard. 1995. "Elderly Persons and Members of Their Households in England and Wales from Preindustrial Times to the Present." In *Aging in the Past: Demography, Society, and Old Age,* ed. David I. Kertzer and Peter Laslett, 81–106. Berkeley: University of California Press.

Chapter Three

Family Systems and Demographic Processes

G. William Skinner

In this chapter I consider the ways in which family systems shape demographic processes. Decisions about marriage, reproduction, and migration are, more often than not, made in the context of families and in relation to family strategies. Decisions by family members may also affect the probability of death at various stages in the life course. And quite apart from conscious decision-making, structural features of family systems directly affect demographic processes, often in ways not recognized by family members. I argue here that the cluster of norms informing family processes may be usefully viewed as a system and that differently configured family systems affect fertility, mortality, and migration in distinctive ways.

Familial and demographic processes are, in fact, so closely intertwined that they may be treated as a single system for certain purposes. Just as the family system shapes demographic process, so the demographic regime constrains family system norms. Nonetheless, for heuristic and expository reasons, I focus narrowly on the pathways from family system to demographic process, largely ignoring reverse causal flows. But this is only the first of four radical simplifications adopted here: Second, even though family systems and demographic regimes are both in continual flux, for the most part I pretend they are not. Third, despite the fact that family systems are everywhere embedded in more inclusive normative systems, not to mention political economies, they are here treated, if not wrenched, out of context. And fourth, family systems are taken as given and unexplained. Although much of the intellectual excitement in the field of family and kinship revolves around the problems of where family systems come from and what causes them to change, I resist the temptation to explore these questions here. This blinkered stance is adopted in the interests of pursuing a single-minded goal, namely, to show why sound demographic analysis must attend to the peculiarities of family systems.

My plan is as follows. I first set out some of the analytical dimensions of family systems and then turn to their impact on particular demographic processes, beginning with nuptiality. While this is a logical place to begin, it is also awkward because of the inherent tautology (how family systems, which include marriage customs, affect nuptiality is, after all, a pretty silly question). After this stumbling start, I move on to consider how couples (with or without the help of senior adults) seek to shape their offspring sets in accordance with family system norms. For reasons that will become apparent below, this section addresses the impact of family systems not only on fertility but also on infant and child mortality. The next two sections consider the impact family systems have on adult mortality and on migration, respectively. In a brief final section I address a couple of issues that sprawl across all terms of the demographic equation.

Varieties of Family Systems

As used here, family system refers to the customary, normative manner in which family processes unfold—that is, the usual, preferred pattern of family practices and household dynamics. It incorporates marriage form(s) and preferences, succession, the transmission of property, the normal sequence of co-residential arrangements, the normative roles associated with family statuses and relationships, and the customary bias by gender and relative age that informs the system as a whole. The term family *system* is used because these various elements of customary family life are contingently related such that a given family system can be modeled as a single process. Family system norms shape but do not control behavior. The sense in which I think family system should be understood is neatly captured in the following passage from Susan Rogers's ethnography of a rural community in southern France (the "ostal" system refers to the locality's stem family system in which continuity of the "house" is a central theme):

> Ste Foyans do not talk in terms of "structure," nor do they refer to an "ostal system" per se, but they do reiterate and explain the various rules defining it, using these frequently and explicitly as a way to guide and interpret behavior. Sometimes they lay out rules in a very straightforward manner. More often, these are presented as the moral of stories—many undoubtedly apocryphal—about persons and events past or present. . . . Ste Foyans certainly recognize that its rules may be more or less closely followed by particular individuals, under special circumstances, or at different moments in time. . . . But they take the rules themselves as absolutes, standing above shifting circumstances. . . . Although . . . there is ample room for conflict over interpretations of these rules in practice, there exists considerable consensus about what they are in principle, and about their legitimacy as a standard of behavior. (Rogers 1991:74–75)

Back when anthropologists focused their research primarily on small populations with relatively homogeneous cultures, limited inequality, and rudimentary political institutions, it was not wholly egregious to describe family systems in unitary fashion for a given society. Today, in the wake of a generation of research on agrarian and modern industrial societies, anthropologists generally recognize that within any "society" (and, a fortiori, any country) family systems may be expected to vary by class, ethnicity, and region, to mention only the major dimensions of differentiation. My own preferred research design investigates the manner in which and the degree to which various familial and demographic features co-vary by ethnicity and class and through regional space and historical time. This is not the approach adopted here. Instead, I cite as examples the family systems of populations that have been so circumscribed as to finesse issues of internal differentiation: the stem family system of owner-cultivators in Spanish Basque villages, say, rather than the Basque family system; the family system of nineteenth-century peasants in the Pearl River Delta rather than *the* Chinese family system. It will be understood that in a more abstract but very real sense a "Chinese family system" exists, incorporating the invariant principles underlying its many specific variants. But I avoid use of the term in this latter, abstracted sense.

I limit this discussion to the range of family systems found in the agrarian societies that rim Eurasia from Iceland, the British Isles, and Scandinavia in the northwest to Korea and Japan in the northeast, including insular Southeast Asia and North Africa.[1] I have no command of the literature on family and kinship in the rest of the world, and embrace any excuse for not confronting some of the excruciatingly complex family systems found there.

With respect to the sequence of coresidential arrangements, here referred to as the domestic cycle,[2] we may distinguish three broad classes of family systems: conjugal, stem, and joint. Conjugal family systems are characterized by neolocal marriage (both bride and groom leaving their natal household on marriage to establish a new family); by equal inheritance among offspring (or, rarely, among offspring of one or the other gender) and an absence of succession per se; and by a usual sequence of coresidential arrangements in which an extended phase of the fully-fleshed-out conjugal family is preceded by an initial phase when the young couple is childless and followed by the empty-nest phase when all offspring have departed. It is characteristic of conjugal family systems that family formation is equated with marriage, and family extinction with the death of the married partners. Since families do not persist beyond the lives of those who found them, they are not corporations, and the domestic cycle is a rather simple transformation of the life courses of its members.

Stem and joint family systems are distinguished from conjugal family systems, in the first instance, by the fact that a spouse is brought into the family for at least one of the offspring in each generation. It follows directly that in such systems households are potentially corporate—that is, they may persist indefinitely irrespective of the life spans of particular members—and that at least a portion of the domestic cycle will be characterized by a family structure comprising two or more conjugal units. Within the more inclusive category of potentially corporate family systems, stem family systems may be distinguished as follows: a spouse is brought in for only one of the offspring in each generation; succession is to the child who was married within the household or to the married couple; inheritance, which is unequal, favors the single successor/heir; and the domestic cycle is characterized by an alternation between a conjugal phase and a stem phase in which the junior and senior conjugal units coreside.

In joint family systems, spouses are brought in not for a single heir but for all of a category of offspring (usually those of one gender); inheritance is partible and equal among those within the favored category; succession is absent, variable, or fudged; and the domestic cycle is characterized by conjugal, stem, and joint phases. Joint family systems necessarily provide for family division: in the usual case, in which at least two conjugal units are formed in the junior generation, the family eventually fissions into two or more separate families. The new families formed through division are normally conjugal in structure, but when division is delayed until marriages occur in the next generation, the newly separated families may be stem or even joint.

It is necessary at this point to clarify terminology and specify my approach to classifying family structures. I take "family" to refer to coresiding kin who participate in a single domestic economy.[3] In my view, it is important to avoid using "family" to refer to what are merely subsystems of the family as defined. It is all too common in the literature to find conjugal units within a stem or joint family referred to as "conjugal or nuclear families" or "family units" or "component families"; particular conjugal units are singled out as "the young families," "the senior family," or "the eldest son's family." Confusion is avoided if these component subsystems are referred to consistently as conjugal units. The phrase "uterine family" has been introduced as the technical term for the subsystem (of a conjugal unit within a joint family) consisting of a mother and her children (Wolf 1972), once again misleading the unwary. The most widely used scheme for classifying family types refers to families consisting of more than one conjugal unit as "multiple family households"[4] or "multiple family units" (Hammel and Laslett 1974; cf. Kertzer 1989). But a family qua coresiding kin with a single domestic economy by definition cannot encompass other families that have separate domestic economies. These sloppy terminological practices, which conflate the family and its subsystems, are to be eschewed as confusing and often misleading.

My approach to classifying family structural types takes conjugal units as the basic building blocks.[5] The three elements of an intact conjugal unit are, of course, husband/father, wife/mother, and child(ren), and, in the usage advocated here, the analyst counts as a conjugal unit (CU) any coresiding two of these three elements. Thus, a childless couple, a mother and her children, and a father and his children all count as CUs. With this crucial point clarified, the basic family structures may be defined as follows. A conjugal family[6] contains one and only one CU. A stem family contains two or more CUs, but with no more than one per generation.[7] A joint family contains two or more CUs, at least two of which are in the same generation.[8] These definitions do not accord with the scheme set out by Hammel and Laslett some twenty years ago (1974), and in this regard I think Hammel was sold a bill of goods by his collaborator.

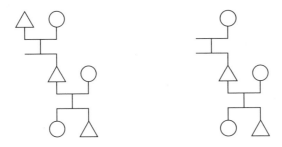

Consider the cases shown in the figure above. Hammel and Laslett count the domestic group on the left as a stem family (i.e., a "multiple family household" with the "secondary unit" lineal rather than lateral, whereas that on the right is classified as an "extended family household," the widow being seen as an "upward extension" of a "simple household." By my definition, both are stem families, being differentiated by the composition of the senior conjugal unit—intact on the left and mother-headed on the right. In populations with stem family systems, the family process leading to the structure on the right would, with few exceptions, have involved creation of the junior conjugal unit through in-marriage of the daughter-in-law and the subsequent death of the senior husband/father. In populations with conjugal family systems, the arrangement shown on the right would be less common and the process involved quite different: In all probability the senior woman would have joined her son's family on the death of her husband, yielding a family structure that could justifiably be classified as an extended conjugal family but might better be specified as a "reconstructed" stem family (see Kertzer 1991:168 for a discussion of the frequency of this arrangement in premodern Western European populations with conjugal family systems). The widespread adoption of the Hammel-Laslett conventions as the standard for cross-societal comparison has served to minimize the count of stem families as against conjugal (and of lineal joint families as against sibling joint families, etc.) and thereby provided unwarranted support for Laslett's argument (1972, since modified) that families everywhere tend to be small and uncomplex.[9]

The three family types just defined in terms of CUs—conjugal families, stem families, and joint families—provide a scheme for classifying the structure of particular families at a moment in time. *Family types,* it must be emphasized, are not *family systems.* The former constitute a typology of synchronic structures, the latter a typology of family processes. It is indeed the case that in societies with conjugal family systems the great majority of family types at any point in time will necessarily be conjugal in structure. But it does not follow—and it is normally not true—that societies with stem family systems are numerically dominated by stem families or that societies with joint family systems are numerically dominated by joint families. What is not always understood is that in the *normal* course of the domestic cycle, stem family systems yield conjugal as well as stem families on the ground (Berkner 1972) and joint family systems yield conjugal and stem as well as joint families. A snapshot or census-type record of family types in a community with a joint family system might well show a majority of all families in the conjugal phase; 15 percent joint, 30 percent stem and 55 percent conjugal is typical and wholly compatible with a dynamic whereby every person spends at least part of her life in a joint family (cf. Harrell and Pullum 1995). Similarly a census of a community with a stem family system might show only 30 percent stem families (and 70 percent conjugal) even though everyone spent a good portion of his life in a stem family.

In a stem family system the frequency of stem and conjugal families—or, to rephrase, the relative duration of the stem and conjugal phases of the domestic cycle—is a simple function of demographic rates. A rise in age at marriage delays the transition from the conjugal to the stem phase of the domestic cycle, and a rise in the mortality of mature adults accelerates the transition from the stem to the conjugal phase. Thus, in bad times the proportion of families in the stem phase may be very small indeed; in the wake of the Tempo Famine (in the 1830s) in Japan, for instance, the proportion of families in the stem phase fell to one-sixth in one of the Nôbi-region villages I studied. In a joint family system, the frequency of conjugal, stem, and joint families is a function not only of demographic rates but also of the timing of family division, which, however, is not entirely independent of adult mortality. When infant and child mortality are high (so that the proportion of families with only one or no surviving son is high) and adult mortality is high (so that more patriarchs die young, thereby precipitating early family division), the proportion of all families in the joint phase may fall as low as 10 percent. Whether because they are innocent of the domestic-cycle concept, because they fail to grasp the demographics of family structure in a processual model, or because they are classifying family structure according to a scheme that understates structural complexity, all too many scholars have misread joint family systems as stem or conjugal, and (with even greater frequency) stem family systems as conjugal family systems.

Gender bias informs these three types of family systems in contingent fashion. In general, structural bias is pronounced in joint family systems and minimal in conjugal family systems, with stem family systems intermediate. Patrilineal joint family systems, which obtain in one variant or another in a continuous belt of agrarian societies stretching from China across South Asia and the Middle East into Eastern Europe and North Africa, present the ex-

treme examples of consistent, thoroughgoing male bias. They are characterized by patrilineally organized extrafamilial kin groups, by virilocal marital
residence (whereby the bride moves to the groom's household), by inheritance
norms favoring sons, by descent through the male line, and by kinship terminologies that distinguish agnates from other kinsmen at the same genealogical
distance. And the patriarchy of patrilineal joint family systems is normatively
stark, if only because of its reinforcement by every other structural feature of
the system. Moreover, in the East and South Asian societies where marriage is
exogamous, the bride moves not only to the groom's family but to another
village or town altogether, where she has no connections and her social
knowledge is no longer of use.

Matrilineal joint family systems are relatively rare in Eurasia, and it may
not be entirely coincidental that the cases of the classic form that have been
most thoroughly studied are Muslim societies: the Malays of Negri Sembilan
(Peletz 1988), the Minangkabau of Sumatra (Kahn 1980, Kato 1982, Errington 1984), the Mappillas of Kerala (Gough 1961), and the Tamils of Sri Lanka
(Yalman 1967, ch. 13). While matrilineal joint family systems are hardly mirror images of patrilineal systems, a consistent gender bias is no less apparent.
They are generally characterized by matrilineally organized extrafamilial kin
groups, by uxorilocal marital residence (whereby the groom moves to the
bride's household), by inheritance norms favoring daughters, by descent
through the female line, and by kinship terminologies that distinguish enates
from other kinsmen at the same genealogical distance.

Stem family systems present a very different picture, in that kinship is cognatic or bilateral and unilineal kin groups are normally absent. These structural features alone greatly restrict the scope for gender bias in comparison
with joint family systems. Whether in Western Europe, Southeast Asia, or Japan, the kinship terminologies associated with stem family systems group together relatives at the same genealogical distance without regard to patrilater-
ality or matrilaterality. In the absence of patrilineages or matrilineages, the
scope of unilineality is limited to the ongoing corporate family itself. And, in
fact, the gender bias of any stem family system is expressed with neat consistency in terms of marital residence and the lineality of the family stem. If the
preferred sex of the single heir is female, then marital residence is uxorilocal
(whereby the groom moves on marriage to the bride's household) and the
family stem is matrilineal. Systems of this kind obtain in particular areas of
both mainland and insular Southeast Asia. If the preferred sex of the single
heir is male, then marital residence is virilocal and the family stem is patrilineal. Such systems were widespread in early modern Western Europe and Tokugawa Japan. If the normative preference is indifferent as to sex (taking the
form, for instance, of primogeniture or ultimogeniture regardless of gender),
then marital residence is ambilocal and the family stem is ambilineal. Gender-
neutral heirship was the norm in local areas of Western Europe, Southeast

Asia, and Japan (Suenari 1972). The Iban of Borneo are a case in point (Free-man 1958). After careful genealogical research, the ethnographer found that 51 percent of all the heirs over several generations were female and 49 percent male. A well-documented European case is that of French Basques. Prior to the onset of significant long-range migration in the nineteenth century, the norm of primogeniture regardless of gender was realized in the great majority of families (Arrizabalaga 1994).

Surnames that pass down through the male line, of course, add a distinct element of male bias to cognatic systems, a point that has been brought home to many Americans in recent decades, but most Southeast Asian societies have never had surnames, and Japanese peasants did not use surnames prior to the late nineteenth century. While a degree of normative patriarchy may be pres-ent in any of these variants (cf. Rogers 1975), on first principles one expects male authority to be hedged if not mitigated by the absence of agnatic privi-lege and by the gender-balancing ideologies normally associated with cognatic kinship (Skinner 1993; cf. Errington 1990).

While conjugal family systems generally afford even less scope for gender bias, particular variants characterized by patronyms, property inheritance for sons only, and normative patriarchy may be quite similar in this regard to patrilineal stem family systems. As it happens,[10] conjugal family systems char-acterized by equal inheritance regardless of gender, an absence of surnames, and a relaxed gender ideology are quite rare. And I should state explicitly that, to my knowledge, the societies with the most egalitarian gender systems are characterized not by conjugal family systems but by matrilineal and ambili-neal stem family systems and matrilineal joint family systems. One might speculate that only when a female-centered tilt in the family system is present to counteract the usual male-centered biases in nonfamilial institutions can overall gender equality be realized.

Nuptiality is almost always shaped by cultural norms, manifested as shared views concerning the proper age at marriage for women and for men and suitable (and especially unsuitable) patterns of spousal age difference (Casterline, Williams, and McDonald 1986; cf. the French proverbs presented in Segalen 1983). Thus, nuptiality is properly included within normative family systems, and, indeed, a number of theorists (Davis 1955; Laslett 1983; Hajnal 1982) have posited contingencies with the three ideal types of family system characterized above in terms of the domestic cycle. In conjugal family systems, it is argued, marriage would be delayed while the groom (or the couple) mustered the resources needed to rear a family, whereas in joint family systems the in-marrying spouse (or the couple) would be incorporated into an ongoing domestic economy. With respect to stem family systems, most theor-ists have focused on the particular model whereby the heir marries only when the father retires or dies, consequently positing late marriage.

In fact, these contingencies are weak. It may well be that customs involving marriage before puberty are found only in joint family systems. Child marriage (i.e., the marriage of girls prior to menarche) was once customary in many parts of South Asia and the Middle East. Little-daughter-in-law marriage, whereby "brides" entered their future husband's homes as infants or toddlers, was widespread in pre-Communist China (Wolf and Huang 1980). But by no means do all joint family systems incorporate early marriage norms. Kertzer and colleagues have thoroughly documented and accounted for late-marriage norms in the patrilineal joint family system of sharecroppers in central and northern Italy (Kertzer 1984; Kertzer and Hogan 1989, 1991; Barbagli 1991). Wherever bridewealth is customary, as among poor Chinese peasants, the marriage of later-born sons is typically delayed while a minimal bridewealth is accumulated—a pattern at odds with the logic of the sweeping theories. As for stem family systems, the customary age at marriage of the heir hinges on whether or not marriage is keyed to succession, in which regard there is a wide range of variation in Western Europe alone. On first principles, moreover, marriage norms are unlikely to be the same for nonheirs as for heirs, and it is usually the case that nonheirs who remain in their natal family are enjoined to celibacy. With respect to conjugal family systems, Barbagli (1991) presents a telling contrast between Sardinia and Sicily in the nineteenth century. The conjugal family system of the former involved equal inheritance among all offspring regardless of gender; women as well as men were expected to accumulate on their own the resources needed for marriage, spousal ages were close together, and marriage was late. In the conjugal family system of Sicily, by contrast, sons alone inherited property, daughters were provided with a dowry, husbands were normatively significantly older than their wives, and marriage was relatively early, especially for women. It should be clear from these examples that distinct nuptiality norms may characterize family systems within each of three broad domestic-cycle types.

Before moving on, I must register some dissatisfaction with the conceptualization of nuptiality as a simple continuum from early to late. An analysis of World Fertility Survey data for twenty-nine developing countries reveals much greater variability in the timing of marriage for men than for women (Casterline, Williams, and McDonald 1986), a pattern also shown in my own analyses of historical populations in China and Japan. A sensitive measure of nuptiality patterns in various family systems should encompass not only the mean/median marriage age for each sex separately but also the shape of the distribution of spousal age differences. Conceived in this manner, nuptiality patterns do tend to reflect the gender bias of family systems. In societies with patrilineal joint family systems, norms often sanction marriages in which husbands are a decade or more older than wives, and in patrilineal stem family systems marriages in which the husband is older are also preferred but usually with less extreme differences in age. In such societies it is understood that younger daughters-in-law are more tractable, can more readily be socialized to the ways of their new family, and are less likely to resist the mother-in-law's authority. In cognatic stem and conjugal family systems, by comparison, the observed frequencies of marriages with small age differences and marriages in which the wife is older are typically considerably closer to the expected values, as calculated from the joint distribution of male and female marriage ages.[11]

To this point, I have discussed conjugal, stem, and joint family systems in ideal-typical fashion. Family systems that approximate these ideal types may be dubbed "classic," to distinguish them from intermediate variants. I wish now to make brief mention of important variants along this continuum. We may begin with the "launching-pad" family system (intermediate between classic conjugal and classic stem systems), in which the young couple takes up initial residence with one or the other set of parents, establishing an independent conjugal family only after the durability of the union and its economic viability have been secured. A system of this kind has been well described for Iceland (Rich 1978), and a less clearly institutionalized variant has been noted in central Spain (Reher 1990).

Departures from classic stem family systems are of two kinds—one pertaining to the inheritance status of nonheirs, the other involving a distinctive domestic cycle. In the classic system, parental investment is sharply focused on the heir or heiress and typically also on one offspring of the opposite sex destined to marry the heir or heiress of another family. Some stem systems make normative provision for the establishment of cadet households, endowed with fewer resources than the main household, to be sure, but still greatly favored over other nonheirs. In Tokugawa Japanese villages in which male primogeniture was customary, a cadet household (*bunke*) might be established for a second son, who would remain in the village while other sons departed. The claims of nonheirs on the resources of the family estate varied greatly among European stem systems, but typically the heir made some kind of settlement, often only token, with each out-migrating nonheir (cf. Zink 1993:115–21).

A common variant of the classic stem system may be characterized as "hiving off." A case in point is the matrilineal stem family system of northeastern Thailand (Keyes 1975). There, a son-in-law is brought in for each daughter in order of birth, but when the second daughter marries, the CU of the first secedes, establishing a separate household nearby. Similarly, when the third daughter marries, the CU of the second establishes an independent household. Thus, the family structure is stem throughout even though the junior CU changes; the CU of the youngest daughter inherits the house in addition to an equal share of landed property. While the system smacks of female ultimogeniture, in fact the youngest daughter who continues the "stem" is less an heiress than a successor. Most hiving-off stem systems may be seen as intermediate between classic stem and classic conjugal systems not only because conjugal families are generated for virtually all nonsuccessors but also because the social status of the independent conjugal families is not sharply differentiated from that of the continuing stem family and inheritance is more nearly equal.

Within the broad category of patrilineal joint family systems, the major departures from the classic type also involve distinctive inheritance norms and/or domestic cycles. Whereas the classic system calls for equal inheritance among all sons, some variants privilege one son over the others. Among Korean peasants, for instance, the eldest son gets a larger share of landed property; since it is he who typically remains in the parental household after family division, the system appears as intermediate between patrilineal joint and patrilineal stem systems. As for the domestic cycle, a hiving-off system is the most common variant. As in the classic patrilineal joint case, a daughter-in-law is brought in for each son in order of birth, but, unlike the classic case, the conjugal units of some sons may secede and establish independent households prior to family division. In certain versions, the sequence is quite regular: the CU of the eldest son secedes a few years after the second marries, the CU of the second son moves out a few years after the third marries, and in the end the CU of the youngest son remains in the parental home. A system of this kind has been adopted in many parts of rural China in the wake of collectivization (Potter and Potter 1990; Chan, Madsen, and Unger 1984; Selden 1993), and less regular variants are prevalent in southern India (Caldwell, Reddy, and Caldwell 1984).[12] Segalen (1992) documents a family system in Pays Bigouden (southwestern Brittany) in which a hiving-off ambilineal joint family system is coupled with equal inheritance regardless of gender.

Although this treatment of family systems is far from comprehensive, even with respect to the agrarian societies of Eurasia,[13] it must suffice for present purposes, namely, an exploration of how family system affects demographic processes.

Nuptiality

Demographers attend to age at first marriage because of its intimate link to the onset of childbearing, and they use marital status, inter alia, as a proxy for differential risk of conception. Major hypotheses about the population dynamics of Western Europe rest on the distinction between nuptiality constraints and fertility controls. Uncontrolled fertility coupled with late marriage is seen as the functional equivalent of early marriage coupled with controlled fertility. As these hypotheses are tested elsewhere in the world, it is of some importance to problematize the posited link between marriage and conception risks in different family systems. It will hardly be news to anyone that sexual congress is seldom limited to married couples in any society. The point I wish to make is that the very operation of certain family systems serves to decouple marriage and the onset of childbearing and/or to blur the distinction between legitimate and illegitimate fertility.

In many societies, including some in Western Europe, premarital sex was the norm and pregnancy typically triggered marriage, rather than the other way around (e.g., Smout 1980). In the Icelandic "launching-pad" conjugal family system already introduced, childbearing precedes marriage. In this system, cohabitation begins when the young couple takes up residence with one set of parents. At this stage they are betrothed but not married; marriage typically follows the establishment of an independent family, by which time the conjugal unit is likely to include one or more children (Rich 1978). Indeed, Tomasson has shown that among premodern Scandinavian peasants generally, childbearing began with betrothal rather than marriage, so that the great majority of first births were "illegitimate"; the proportion in Sweden as a whole was over 50 percent as late as the 1960s (Tomasson 1976:255). Not even the Lutheran clergy in these societies have fully accepted "Christian" teachings on sex and marriage: in Iceland, for example, over 40 percent of the male clergy from 1901 to 1931 conceived their first-born children "out of wedlock" (1976:261). In the patrilineal stem family system of rural Norway, a father normally selected the heir only after his sons were adults; sons who had formed stable sexual unions that had already produced male issue were favored over those who had not (Park 1962). Marriage was a payoff, as it were, for success in building a suitable offspring set.

I shall limit examples from outside Europe to two from China. In much of the North China Plain, well-off farmers pursued a form of marriage designed to speed up the arrival of grandsons. Boys were married before puberty, as young as eight years old, to older girls, typically fifteen or sixteen years of age (Gamble 1954). By the time the lad could perform his conjugal duties, his wife would be at peak fecundity and the ideal age for assuming the responsibilities of motherhood. In these populations, marriage predated the onset of childbearing by many years.[14] A customary marriage form found in many regions of South China has a similar effect (Stockard 1989). This family system follows the usual sequence of wedding rituals in the groom's household up to the ceremonial visit of the young couple to the bride's family on the third day, but at that point instead of returning with her husband to take up residence in his family, the bride remains in her natal family, thereafter visiting her husband's family only for the three major festivals of the year. While sexual relations are not proscribed, the normative expectation is that brides will attempt to avoid conception if at all possible so as to prolong their period of freedom and independence. It is deemed uncouth to conceive within the first year or two after marriage, and the bride moves permanently to her husband's family only after conception or the passage of several years.[15]

My first point, then, is simple enough: The extent to which marital status is linked to risk of pregnancy may be expected to vary in accordance with the workings of particular family systems. The interpretation of standard rates for nuptiality, marital fertility, and illegitimacy in cross-societal research is thus fraught with peril.[16]

My second point in this section is that the nuptiality norms of particular family systems may have significant consequences for mortality. It appears to be generally true that marriage confers beneficial effects (through a combination of social, psychological, and environmental factors) such that mortality risks are higher for those who never marry than for married people of the same ages.[17] So, for instance, the customary late age at marriage characteristic of many Western European family systems in the early modern period served to deny these benefits to a significant proportion of the adult population and thereby increased overall mortality.

My third and final point in this section is that age at marriage is likely to vary systematically by phase in the domestic cycle. This argument applies only to corporate family systems, and I take as a case in point patrilineal stem family systems. The cultural expectation in such systems is that the heir's marriage would be arranged by his parents while they are still vigorous, so that childbearing would begin in the context of an intact stem family headed by the groom's father. Any departure from this most auspicious circumstance suggested a degree of demographic or social impairment. A widow or widower was at some disadvantage in seeking a daughter-in-law for the heir-designate, while an orphaned young man was at a distinct disadvantage on the marriage market. Thus the quality of brides presumably varied across household types. In the case of Japanese villagers in the Nôbi Plain during the Tokugawa era (Skinner 1987), husbands on average were eight years older than their wives and women were somewhat longer-lived than men in any case; as a result, the expected and most common form of the domestic cycle proceeded from the intact stem phase to the grandmother-only stem phase to the conjugal phase. The mean ages of the incoming bride in these three family types, respectively, were 19.5, 20.4, and 22.2, suggesting that intact couples took their pick of young girls as they came on the marriage market, leaving the dregs for the orphaned men who would be forming conjugal households on marriage.[18]

The marriage age of heirs in such a family system may also be expected to vary systematically by household structure in the domestic cycle. If one of the parents is deceased prior to the marriage of the heir/successor, the marriage age of the latter is likely to vary sharply according to the gender configuration of the remaining parent and the heir/successor. In the case of virilocal marriage, the heir will be married at an early age if the family is headed by a widower but at a relatively late age if headed by a widow. And in the case of uxorilocal marriage (the fallback norm when no sons survive in virtually all preferential virilocal family systems), the heiress will be married at an early age if the family is headed by a widow but at a relatively late age if headed by a widower. These expectations follow from the gender division of labor, which generates an urgent need to bring a woman into a household consisting of a widower and his son and to bring a man into a household consisting of a widow and her daughter. On the other hand, the marriage of the heir/succes-sor is delayed when it would "disrupt" the gender balance of a widowed mother and her adult son or a widowed father and his adult daughter. (We might also surmise that a widow would like to keep her son for herself as long as possible, just as a widower might want to put off the day when a son-in-law would have to be brought in for his daughter—but this logic is not peculiar to unilineal stem family systems.) These expectations are all borne out in my study of Japanese peasants; on first principles they should hold for classic unilineal stem family systems generally.

Fertility and Early Mortality

Some scholars would have us believe that prior to the onset of "modernity" fertility was generally uncontrolled, that "traditional" populations took whatever God or fate gave them in the way of children. Demographic anthro-pologists generally demur, noting, in the premodern populations studied, widespread recourse to folk methods of contraception, stopping behavior, induced abortion, and infanticide. I argue here that family system norms imply, if not specify, the relative desirability of differently configured offspring sets and that, in many if not most populations, families did what they could (and do what they can) to shape the size and configuration of their progeny accordingly. Moreover, it is not unreasonable to suppose that at least some of the customs embedded in family systems evolved (or were selected for) pre-cisely because they assisted families in achieving offspring sets auspiciously configured in terms of family system norms. In consequence, while some fami-lies may consciously strategize, i.e., engage in family planning, others in the same population may simply follow customary practices that willy-nilly favor certain "family planning" objectives.

I treat neonatal and early childhood mortality together with fertility in this section precisely because the final size and configuration of offspring sets may be manipulated either through controlling fertility (*birth control*) or through controlling survivorship (*child control*) (Greenhalgh 1988). In fact, there is a third form of offspring-set manipulation (*child transfer*), namely, sending par-ticular living infants and children out of the family and/or bringing others in. In effect, this form means that early life-course in- and out-migration is also implicated in family planning. Family systems per se are silent concerning means; the overall objectives of family planning may be deduced from family system norms, but not the mechanisms for achieving them.

It is useful at this point to focus a bit more sharply on the range of available means. Prior to the recent onset of high-technology sex-selective abortion, birth control (induced abortion, contraception, and such "natural" methods as abstinence, withdrawal, oral sex, rhythm, etc.) was necessarily sex blind with respect to the birth averted (or not, as the case may be). It should be recognized, however, that birth control is not blind with respect to the sex of surviving offspring and thus may be used to delay the next birth or to stop child-bearing for reasons related to the gender configuration of existing offspring.

The great advantage of child control over birth control, of course, is that it permits selection on the basis of observable characteristics of the live infant(s). In many populations, weak, sickly, and deformed infants were routinely killed. Selection according to sex was (again, until very recently) possible only through infanticide. A major advantage of infanticide over abortion, then, is that it can be used both to improve the "quality" of progeny and to shape in some detail the gender configuration of the offspring set as well as its size and spacing. Indirect or deferred infanticide is a cover term for other kinds of child control, in particular post-neonatal deaths due to inadequate or withheld parental investment (Scrimshaw 1983; Miller 1981; Scheper-Hughes 1987).

Turning to child transfer, live infants and children may, inter alia, be placed in public institutions, adopted out, abandoned, or sold. In practice, abandonment ranges from unambiguous child transfer, when the infant is placed where it will be found by foundling-home personnel, to unambiguous child control, when the infant is placed in the wilderness where it will be found by wild animals. It should be clear that all forms of child control and child transfer may be employed to remove unwanted children from the configuration of existing offspring. And, of course, child transfer, typically adoption, may be used to add a child of a particular age and sex to flesh out an offspring set. Child transfer customs, while not themselves a dimension of family systems, inevitably interface closely with them. In nineteenth-century China, where foundling homes and orphanages were few and far between, child transfer was largely commercialized. The Chinese market in infants and children dealt, of course, overwhelmingly with females,[19] who were sold by their parents to be maid servants, indentured servants, and slaves (Watson 1980). As might be expected in a society with a perennial shortage of young women, many of the girls who were sold ended up as prostitutes, concubines, or secondary wives. Little-daughters-in-law, too, were usually sold, but typically without recourse to outside brokers. In Western Europe, by contrast, child transfer transactions involved boys as often as girls and took place primarily via public institutions (Tilly et al. 1992; Kertzer 1993; Fuchs 1984).

It should be clear from this discussion that one cannot deduce from fertility data alone the extent to which offspring sets are shaped in accordance with family system norms. The magnitude of family planning in historical and non-Western populations is underestimated by many demographers because of unwarranted assumptions. An influential school in demography (Coale and Watkins 1986) argues that couples control fertility solely or largely through stopping behavior and that they decide to stop or continue childbearing according to the numbers only; that is, couples have a target size and stop when they reach it. This view strikes me as parochial, dogmatic, and wrongheaded on every count. The model is based on an interpretation of fertility control in

historical populations of Western Europe, and yet research on English historical demography has demonstrated conclusively that spacing played a significant role in fertility decline (Crafts 1989; Landers 1990; Friedlander, Schellekens, and Ben-Moshe 1991; and cf. Knodel 1987). Moreover, it is arbitrary
to assume that stopping behavior is normally based on the number of offspring
alone, without reference to their gender configuration. Misled, perhaps, by the
cognatic nature of kinship in Western Europe, demographers specializing in
that region typically assume that family planning was indifferent to gender.
But this is untenable even for strictly sex-egalitarian family systems. Such systems are likely to have a clear preference for gender *balance*, and there is no a
priori reason for imagining that they would not attempt to shape their offspring sets accordingly. Many demographers seem to have bought the fairy
tale that family planning began in eighteenth-century France when coitus in-
terruptus was discovered and the condom invented. Nonsense. It is time to
discard these parochial notions and entertain the likelihood that family planning has been present in one form or another in most societies and throughout
human history. Once we recognize that child control and child transfer may
be used along with birth control in pursuit of the same family planning objectives—that stopping behavior is stopping whatever the means; that spacing
can be achieved not only via contraception but also through breastfeeding,
infanticide, abortion, adoption out, and abandonment; that sex-selective abortion and sex-selective infanticide are functional equivalents, etc.—we may
hope to bring family planning past and present, East and West, into a common
analytical framework. A recent analysis of missing females in China (Coale
and Banister 1994) documents the transition from infanticide to sex-selective
abortion and the changing role of sex-selective adoption (that is, various
mixes of birth control, child control, and child transfer) over the course of half
a century, as Chinese parents have struggled to shape their offspring sets in a
dramatically changing political economy.

Let me now pursue issues of family planning in patrilineal joint family systems, with reference to Korea and India/Bangladesh as well as China. It will
not do simply to say that such family systems imply a strong son preference
and hence daughters are killed or neglected. The ideally configured offspring
set is not all male by any means. One or more daughters provide crucial help
to mothers in keeping family members adequately clothed and fed and in caring for younger children. More critically, a daughter is of potential structural
importance to her family—and in two distinct ways. In the unfortunate case
when no son lives to procreate grandsons, a favored solution to the cultural
dilemma is to bring in a son-in-law on condition that at least some of the
offspring take the surname of the family in which they are born (rather than
that of their father) and function sociologically as patrilineally descended
heirs of the sonless couple. This solution is possible only when at least one
daughter survives. Daughters are also crucial to "network expansion" strate-

Table 3.1
Stopping Ratios at Parity 4 by Sex of
Existing Offspring, Taiwan, 1973

Sex Balance of Existing Offspring		Percent Stopping at Four
Male	Female	
4	0	55
3	1	66
2	2	64
1	3	42
0	4	31

NOTE: These data are for a subsample exhibiting traditional family values.

gies (Greenhalgh 1988); marrying a daughter into a high-status family[20] forged a link of potential instrumental value even as it enhanced the family's social status within the community. Where customary brideprice obtains, yet another structural need for daughters comes into play: The net income from marrying daughters can help parents in mustering brideprices for their sons. Data for a Taiwan sample in 1973, shown in table 3.1, is typical (Coombs and Sun 1978, table 12). These are parity-stopping ratios by sex of living children at parity 4; the figures shown are the percentage of couples who stopped at four, that is, who did not continue on to a fifth birth. Thus, a higher percentage indicates greater satisfaction with the gender configuration of the offspring set. Despite the clear male bias (e.g., 66 percent stop after three sons and one daughter, while only 42 percent stop after three daughters and one son), it is notable that couples with one or two daughters are more satisfied than those with all sons, 45 percent of whom went on to another child, presumably in hopes of a daughter.

Data on stopping ratios from the 1974 World Fertility Survey for Korea are presented by Park (1983) according to the precise configuration of existing offspring. Fourth-parity patterns are particularly revealing (see table 3.2). As expected, all female sets are the least desirable, but it is notable that all male sets are no more acceptable than some of the configurations containing three daughters. The most acceptable configurations are gender balanced with the youngest a boy, and in general, holding gender composition constant, sets are more desirable the earlier-born the daughters. (This last finding, which emerges from comparable data for offspring sets in a variety of family systems, appears to be related to the valued role of older sisters as caretakers of their younger siblings.)

A reworking of data from the 1961–62 National Sample Survey of India (Pakrasi and Halder 1971[21]) indicates extensive child control in pursuit of acceptable offspring sets. These data show the gender configuration of the first

Table 3.2
Stopping Ratios at Parity 4
by Configuration of Existing Offspring,
Korea, 1971

Sex Sequence of Existing Offspring	Percent Stopping at Four
MMMM	29
3M 1F	34
2M 2F ending M	42
2M 2F ending F	35
FFFM	34
FFMF	30
FMFF	28
MFFF	27
FFFF	19

NOTE: The sex sequence is shown beginning with the firstborn at left.

N children in completed offspring sets of N or more children. These, then, are sequenced configurations of surviving children. It is generally the case in human populations that, in the absence of differential treatment of boys and girls, the high secondary sex ratio is balanced out by the higher mortality risks of boys, so that by late childhood sex ratios are roughly balanced. On that assumption, and in the absence of sex discrimination in child control, one would expect equal frequencies of same-size offspring sets regardless of their gender configuration. However, the frequencies for each value of N that occur in this Indian sample are far from equal. Table 3.3, for instance, shows the figures for N = 3 in the rural portion of the sample. The most frequent (i.e., the preferred) configuration is that of two boys and a girl with the sexes alternating, while the least frequent (most strongly disfavored) is, as expected, that of three girls.

What can be inferred about the sequential decisions that lie behind such frequency differentials? Consider the 6054 (3206 + 2848) couples whose first two surviving offspring are both girls. In theory, half of them (3027) would have ended up with a surviving son in third position and half with a surviving daughter. It is highly likely that virtually all of the couples granted a son were pleased, whereas the equal number of couples who had a daughter included many who were disappointed. The figures imply that of the 3027 couples who would otherwise have had the FFF configuration, 358 annulled or otherwise disposed of the third girl and tried again for a son. Assuming that half of the survivors of these second-try offspring were male and half female, we end up with the frequencies given: 3027 + 179 = 3206 FFM and 3027 − 358 + 179 = 2848 FFF. On this logic, approximately 12 percent (358/3027) of girls born

Table 3.3
Frequencies of Offspring Sets by
Configuration of the First Three
Surviving Children, Rural India,
1961–62

Configuration of the First Three Surviving Children	Frequency of Offspring Sets
MM M	3920
MM F	4015
MF M	4239
MF F	4004
FM M	3522
FM F	3183
FF M	3206
FF F	2848

NOTE: The sex of the oldest child is at left.

Table 3.4
Frequencies of Offspring Sets by Configuration of
the First Five Surviving Children, India, 1961–62

FMFFM	827	FMFFF	767	FMMFF	813	FMFMF	818
MFMMF	1044	MFMMM	1091	MFFMM	1033	MFMFM	1078
Ratios	79.2%		70.3%		78.7%		75.0%

NOTE: The number of cases are those in the rural and urban sample combined. The sex of offspring are shown in order of age, beginning with the eldest at the left. The percent shown for each pair is the frequency ratio of the upper configuration to its gender obverse, shown underneath.

to couples with two existing daughters had disappeared. Comparable calculations for other third-position offspring indicate "missing" children as follows: 10 percent of girls born to couples with an existing FM sequence, 6 percent of girls born to couples with an existing MF sequence, and 2 percent of boys born to couples with an existing MM sequence.

The cumulative effect of child control (and, to an unknowable extent, also child transfer) in this Indian sample yields sharp differences in the frequencies at higher Ns. The point may be illustrated by comparing gender-obverse configurations where N = 5 and the first two surviving offspring are of mixed sex (table 3.4). In each case, the less desirable female-heavy set is listed first, with the preferred male-heavy set underneath. The percent is the frequency ratio of the former to the latter. The deficit of undesirable offspring sets is a putative indication of the cumulative effect of child control and child transfer that has removed one or more girls from originally female-heavy sets, converting them to more desirable male-heavy configurations.

Is it possible to model the decision-making that lies behind such findings in

patrilineal joint family systems? Starting with the cultural injunction to continue the patriline, we may deduce that a son is more highly valued by his
parents (1) the fewer his brothers, and (2) the higher up (earlier born) his
position in the brother series. Two or three sons reduce the risk that one may
not survive or be suitably filial, but three or four sons increase the risk that
progeny will suffer downward mobility at the time of family division. Important here is the simple fact that sons mature in order of birth, which means
that parental hopes will rest on the eldest—to be displaced onto the second
only if frustrated. The calculus differs for daughters. Because they are normally lost to their natal family through marriage into another family, daughters are of markedly less value than sons. As we have seen, they take on importance for continuing the patriline only if they have so few brothers that one
may not survive. The daughter whose uxorilocal marriage may save the patriline is normally the eldest. Thus a daughter is more highly valued by her parents (1) the fewer her brothers and (2) the higher up (earlier born) is her position in the sister series (Skinner 1992). These propositions, designed to apply
to completed sibling sets, can readily be respecified with respect to existing
siblings at the time of birth. A newborn son will be more highly valued the
fewer his older surviving brothers, and a newborn daughter will be more
highly valued the fewer her older brothers *and* the fewer her older sisters.

This simple model is supported by recent empirical work on child survival
in South Asia (Das Gupta 1987; Muhuri and Preston 1991). In a beautifully
designed study of child survival in Bangladesh, Muhuri and Menken found
that "boys with two or more older brothers experience about 40 percent
higher risks than those with few brothers. . . . Girls with one or more older
female siblings have 90 percent higher mortality odds than girls with no older
female siblings. When the first-born is a boy and a girl follows, she has about
50 percent higher mortality risks. . . . These findings indicate different valuings
of children on the basis of the composition of the sibling set" (1993:15). Indeed—and those differential evaluations accord with a structural model derived from the family system.[22] A formal model of family planning in patrilineal joint family systems, which would require a function that links the
formulas for evaluating sons and daughters separately (is a first-born girl more
valuable than a third-born or a fourth-born boy?),[23] would make possible
some revealing research comparing birth control and child control in various
populations (e.g., Korea and North China, Northwest and Southeast India,
Egypt and Turkey).

Since societies with matrilineal joint family systems exhibit an analogous
cultural concern for continuity of the matriline, one would expect parents to
strive for female-heavy (though, of course, not exclusively female) offspring
sets. And the propositions enunciated above for patrilineal joint family systems would be turned on their head: a newborn daughter will be more highly
valued the fewer her older surviving sisters, and a newborn son will be more

highly valued the fewer his older sisters *and* the fewer his older brothers. While we have qualitative evidence of daughter preference in several of the Asian matrilineal cases already mentioned,[24] for relevant quantitative data we must look beyond Eurasia to sub-Saharan Africa. In a recent longitudinal analysis of the Gwembe Tonga of southern Zambia, Elizabeth Colson and her colleagues document patterns of child control that accord with the above-mentioned expectations. "Gwembe women must have daughters to perpetuate their *basimukoa,* or matrilineage. When a daughter is born, women customarily give two cries of joy as opposed to one for the birth of a boy. Women who have given birth to a disproportionate number of boys have told Colson that they are criticized by their kin for their failure to provide for the continuity of their matrilineage. Men also prefer daughters whose marriages will bring them wealth in the form of marriage payments. . . . A man with a large number of sons and few or no daughters sees himself as disadvantaged" (Clark et al. 1995:105). Gwembe data for the period 1956–1991 show a reported sex ratio at birth of 92 boys for every 100 girls. "Presumably these missing boys were simply never reported, either because they died very early in childhood and were forgotten, or because they were victims of infanticide or conscious neglect and were deliberately not reported" (1995:107). The data on sex-specific infant mortality are also eloquent: 104 deaths per 1000 for singleton male infants vs. 85 for singleton females, with the sex bias even sharper for twins. Thus, the patterning of sex-selective child control in matrilineal and patrilineal joint family systems appear remarkably similar—apart, that is, from the reversal in sex bias.

The principles followed in shaping offspring sets would, of course, be very different in a stem family system with cognatic kinship, even when the stem is explicitly matrilineal or patrilineal. In an analysis of Tokugawa-era villages in the Nôbi Plain of central Japan, I have shown that families in auspicious circumstances sought to shape offspring sets that were headed by a daughter and gender-balanced, preferably with the sexes alternating (Skinner 1987, 1988, 1993). In this population family planning objectives were pursued largely through infanticide (of both sexes and at all parities, including the first), but also through abortion, natural contraceptive methods to space out births and stop childbearing (early), and adoption. I cannot take the space to expound this case here, but a bit of illustrative data can point up the contrast with offspring-set strategizing in unilineal joint family systems. These data show the sex ratio of fourth registered births to a subset of couples with three surviving offspring.[25]

Two pairs of gender-obverse sequences of existing offspring (table 3.5) exemplify the underlying rationale. Families with one girl and two boys, one of whom is the youngest (i.e., families with the FMM and MFM sequences), are strongly motivated to have a girl, in the interests of both gender balance and gender alternation, and it appears that a high proportion of those whose

Table 3.5
Sex of Fourth Registered Birth
by Configuration of Existing
Offspring, Nishijo and
Asakusanaka Villages, Mino
Province, Japan, 1717–1868

Sex Sequence of Existing Offspring	Percent Male of Fourth Births
FMM	9
MFF	69
MFM	18
FMF	55

NOTE: These data are for a subset (N = 113) that excludes landless tenant households.

fourth birth was male have killed the infant to try again for a daughter. Families with one boy and two girls, one of whom is the youngest (MFF and FMF), are motivated for the same reasons to have a boy, and it appears that many couples whose fourth birth was female have killed the infant to try again for a son. It will be noted that the percentages for the first pair of existing-sibling configurations (FMM/MFF) are more extreme than those for the second. This difference, too, reflects the concern to alternate the sexes. A fourth-born child of the "wrong" sex would yield three in a row of that sex for the first pair but only two in a row for the second.

Findings from the same analysis support an argument about fertility-cum-infant mortality that parallels one already made concerning nuptiality, namely, that the mean number of offspring who survived neonatal risks may be expected to vary systematically by family structure. The critical variation may be characterized as that along the range from a favorable/auspicious structural situation to one that is vulnerable/precarious. At the auspicious extreme are intact stem households in which the senior male is head and at the precarious extreme are conjugal families, with other family types intermediate, namely, those exhibiting more or less auspicious combinations of headship with grandmother-only and grandfather-only stem family structure. In these villages, the mean number of registered births varied from 5.4 for couples who began childbearing in an intact stem family to 4.8, 4.4, and 4.0 for those who began childbearing in family structures lacking one grandparent, to 3.7 for those who began childbearing in the conjugal phase of the cycle. I expect to be able to show that couples in these different structural situations in fact followed somewhat distinctive strategies in building their offspring sets.

This example suggests that phase in the domestic cycle may be an important control in analyzing fertility in other societies with corporate family systems.

Adult Mortality

Family systems affect adult mortality in many ways. I illustrate here with four examples concerning, in order, the mortality of young married women, the longevity of mothers, differential longevity by family status, and the mortality of the widowed elderly.

The first argument is obvious. Whereas in conjugal family systems and in uxorilocal stem family systems, the status of the "young married woman" is very often a happy one, in the patrilineal joint family systems of East and South Asia it is the status of highest stress. The bride enters her husband's home as a stranger. It is in the nature of the go-between system of spouse selection that she will turn out to be a disappointment to virtually all members of the groom's family. "Perhaps most painful of all to the young woman," Margery Wolf recounts with respect to Taiwan, "is her sense of isolation, of emotional aloneness. It is considered bad form for her to visit her natal family often, and even her mother discourages frequent trips home. If she is seriously maltreated by her husband or his family, her father and brothers might intervene, but occasional slaps and frequent harsh words are too unexceptional to rate more than commiseration by her mother" (1975:124). In a word, her life is usually (and normatively) miserable, and until she has a child (preferably of course a male child) her life is unlikely to improve. If she should bear a string of daughters, it will get much worse. In the first months and years of marriage in such a system, some women crack, some develop psychosomatic ailments, some go mad, and not a few hang themselves or jump down a well. In societies with patrilineal joint family systems, then, we might expect a rise in female mortality in accordance with nuptiality patterns that is not replicated for men in the same societies or for women in other societies where marriage involves less traumatic discontinuities in women's lives.[26] In fact, the suicide rates for women aged 20 to 24 in the first decade of this century were ten times higher in Taiwan than in Spain and Sweden, and two times higher than in Japan, where virilocal residence obtained in a less patriarchal stem family system (Wolf 1975).[27] Thus, we may expect the elevated age-specific female mortality rates often associated with the childbearing years to have a characteristic trajectory in populations with patrilineal joint family systems.

My second example relates more specifically to the burdens of childbearing. Demographers have demonstrated the deleterious effects of close spacing on infant and early child survival. Careful studies suggest that the most plausible mechanism for the baneful effect of short previous intervals is maternal depletion. As stated by Hobcraft, McDonald, and Rutstein, "The mother has one child and the pregnancy and birth deplete her resources. Further, she commonly breastfeeds, another resource drain. She may well continue breast-feeding until she is already clearly pregnant again, especially when intervals are short and the earlier of the pair survives. Thus she has little or no time for proper recovery following the previous birth. Because her bodily resources are depleted, the next pregnancy results in a small baby, perhaps with increased risk of prematurity. Low birth weight is associated with very poor survival chances . . ." (1985:376–77). This scenario is focused on early child survival (and thus might have been integrated into arguments in the preceding section), but what about the mother depleted by a lifetime of closely spaced pregnancies? It seems quite likely that her subsequent health and longevity would suffer in comparison with mothers whose offspring were well spaced out.

Another factor affecting maternal health is the extent to which a mother can enlist help with child care from other family members. When, as is so often the case with gender divisions of labor, child care is the responsibility of females, not only mothers-in-law but also early-born daughters can relieve the mother's burden. In particular, when the first surviving child is a girl the mother can count on help in rearing the second and subsequent children. Older daughters are also positioned to relieve harried mothers by taking on other household chores.

As it happens, the family system of the Japanese villagers whose household registers I have been analyzing involves a normative preference that children be spaced out *and* a clear preference for offspring sets headed by a girl. This latter norm is sanctioned by a saying that had widespread currency in Japanese society: *ichihime nitarô* (first a girl, then a boy). Three considerations appear to lie behind this well-known bit of folk wisdom. For one, given a norm of male primogeniture, a daughter-first strategy had instrumental value for fathers who married young. In the ideal domestic cycle, the son and heir should be ready to take over management of the farm at about the time the father is ready to cease heavy farm labor and acquiesce in the transfer of authority. In a system with a normative retirement age of 60, a son born when his father was still in his twenties might be expected to challenge his father's authority prematurely (cf. Cornell 1983). If the female-male sequence were pursued via infanticide, the age of the father at the heir's birth would be increased on average not only by the spacing between two normal births, but also by the time lost through killing unwanted male firstborns and unwanted female second-borns. Fathers who married young would thus favor girls as firstborns in the interests of unchallenged authority in middle age. A second rationale concerns child care. As one villager explained to an early ethnographer, the preferred gender sequence means that "the girl can care for the boy." The third consideration is that with their first child mothers lack experience and assurance; if the chances of botching the job are greater with the firstborn, better it should be a girl than a boy. Since we are dealing with a system in

Table 3.6

Mean Age at Death, Ever-Married Women, by Average Intervals
between Registered Births, and by Sex of First Registered Birth,
Nishijo and Asakusanaka Villages, Mino Province, Japan, 1717–1868

Mean Birth Interval in Years*	Woman's Mean Age at Death by Sex of First Registered Birth		Number of Cases		
	Male	Female	Male	Female	Total
–2.3	48.8	52.2	16	12	28
2.4–3.7	57.4	60.8	53	42	95
3.8–4.1	61.3	62.7	28	28	56
4.2–	67.9	73.4	14	22	36
Total	58.4	63.0	111	104	215

* This is the mean of all intervals between births registered to women who have completed child-bearing; the interval from marriage to the first birth is not included.

which the putative single heir is the eldest son, providing him with an older sister may be seen as improving his "quality" on two counts: not only a less harried mother, assured of help in child care, but also a more experienced mother. In table 3.6 we see that mothers who followed the conventional wisdom lived longer. Both spacing and the sex of the first registered child are shown to have independent effects on the mother's longevity.

The next example is also drawn from my study of Japanese villages (Skinner 1987). Investigating the differential mortality risks associated with distinctive family roles, I found evidence that the proverbial oppression of brides by their mothers-in-law appears to have had lasting effects. In the case of virilocally married women, the early death of the mother-in-law increased the woman's longevity. Furthermore, when present, the mother-in-law's negative effect on a woman's longevity was reduced when the father-in-law was also present and when the husband was head, suggesting that a woman fared better when the mother-in-law was held in check by the father-in-law and better still when her husband was positioned to protect her. This finding led me to check out the mortality of *mukoyoshi*, married-in sons-in-law, who suffered stresses analogous to those of incoming daughters-in-law as well as a degree of social stigma on account of their anomalous status. It turns out that a man in that status suffered no mortality disadvantages provided he had assumed the headship of the family at the time of his marriage. However, when the wife's father retained the headship, the usual case when he was alive and well at the time, the son-in-law tended to die young. Propositions of this kind are, of course, geared to the domestic cycle of patrilineal corporate family systems. They might well hold in China and India, say, but presumably not in matrilineal corporate family systems—and certainly not in conjugal systems where these family statuses are not generated by the domestic cycle.

The specific examples just cited suggest a more general argument, namely, that unrelieved powerlessness and structural vulnerability to oppression are in the long run life-negating. Following an inductive strategy, then, one could classify the various family statuses in any family system according to the implicit life-course experience with power and then test hypotheses concerning differential mortality. It is possible that the experience of wielding power within the household enhances longevity everywhere, but to find out one must analyze the workings of particular family systems separately.

My final example concerns the mortality of the widowed elderly. Here, at long last, we have a topic about which tenable generalizations can be made in terms of the three broad classes of family systems. I propose that, other things being equal, the mortality of the elderly widowed will be highest in conjugal family systems and lowest in joint family systems, with stem family systems generally intermediate and highly variable. The logic is straightforward. In joint family systems, a couple grows old in the family they had controlled as adults and, in the typical case, the family is divided only after both have died; even in the unusual case where division occurs earlier, the junior couple remaining in the original household has clear responsibility for their care in old age. In conjugal families, by contrast, couples grow old in their independent households, by then in the empty-nest phase. Even when one of them dies, the widowed parent is not automatically taken into the household of one of the married children, and norms are lacking as to which child ought to take on that responsibility, which is typically viewed as a burden. The intermediate status of the widowed elderly in stem family systems—and, I suspect, a good part of the variability—hinges on arrangements for formal retirement of the elderly couple. In some systems, the senior couple is no less secure in old age than in the usual joint system, whereas in others the retired couple may be shunted off to a separate hut and treated as a fifth wheel by the new family head (cf. Rebel 1978; Nakane 1967). The historical demographic literature for Western Europe and Japan provides such a wide array of relevant cases that it should be possible to design a study to account for observed variation in the mortality of the widowed elderly in different stem family systems.

Migration

How family systems may affect migration is nicely illustrated by the generic problem of nonheirs in any stem family system. Consider male primogeniture, which was a common variant of such systems in both Western Europe and Japan. In an era of high mortality, younger sons served as backup to the putative heir, but once the heir's conjugal unit was safely launched, those younger sons became something of a burden to their natal family. The pros-

pects were little better for younger daughters. Families typically strategized by focusing their resources on only one daughter, usually the eldest, who was given a dowry suited to her natal family's station and married to another family's heir. The variations on this theme are many, but in general it can be said that nonheirs who remained in their native community suffered severe downward mobility. Those from respectable landowning families became cottagers at best. If they married at all, it was usually beneath their station. Some remained as celibate servants in their married sibling's home, while others took positions as live-in servants elsewhere in the village. Nonheirs with any gumption cleared out, whence their prominence in migration streams. It was nonheirs from stem families who supplied most of the Crusaders in the Middle Ages, who manned the armies that expanded European empires, and who filled the monasteries and served as priests. As the stem family system expanded its geographic scope in Europe, nunneries became a primary repository for female nonheirs (Hager 1992).

As a general proposition, then, we may assert that by their nature stem family systems promote out-migration. In a rich study of eighteenth-century Zürich, for instance, Rudolf Braun (1978) shows that emigrants from the rural areas of the canton to the New World as well as to the city of Zürich hailed largely from the farming regions of the canton, where owner-cultivators followed a stem family system, rather than from the "industrialized" areas, where a conjugal family system obtained.

Which offspring count as heirs and which do not in any given stem family system will, of course, strongly shape the composition of migrant streams. A comparison of internal migration in Japan and Thailand is instructive in this regard. The Tokugawa era in Japan, especially the seventeenth and early eighteenth centuries, was characterized by rapid urbanization; by 1800 the population of Edo, the shogun's capital, had grown to a million and Japan was the most urbanized society in the world. The rural to urban migrants who effected that change were largely later-born offspring, an outcome that follows directly from the fact that primogeniture was the norm in most villages. (Even when the customary rule was male primogeniture, it was usually the eldest daughter who married in the village.) Thus, early-borns of both sexes were greatly underrepresented among migrants to the city. A similar if less dramatic urbanization of Thailand occurred during the present century, with Bangkok's population reaching a million around 1950. But in this case there was no overrepresentation of youngest and other late-born siblings. Birth order rank was more or less random for male migrants, but the female migrant stream was dominated by eldests and other early-borns; their younger sisters disproportionately remained in their natal villages. The explanation, of course, is grounded in the version of female ultimogeniture that is a feature of the Thai matrilineal stem family system. By mid-century, as pressure on agricultural land increased, the prospects for older daughters in large offspring sets at home diminished even as employment opportunities in Bangkok expanded, and a large proportion took off for the big city, taking their boyfriends and husbands with them.

In some European stem family systems, heirship was by custom discretionary (Park 1962). That is, while the heir was preferentially male, he was not preordained by birth order but rather selected by the father after he saw how his sons turned out. Fathers were often motivated to delay that selection as long as possible to take advantage of the labor of all sons and maintain effective authority into their old age. Thus, sons were in more or less open competition for the heirship, and a first-born son might be forty before it became clear that he was not to be the heir. The net effect was to inhibit out-migration and keep proportionately more sons unmarried in their natal households. Where the heir is determined by and at birth, not only can the chosen lad be socialized into the role of heir from an early age, but his siblings will be socialized into the role of nonheir. It is the nonheirs who *know* they are nonheirs who are prime candidates for out-migration.

William Douglass (1971) plays on this distinction in a neat comparison of two Spanish Basque villages during the twentieth century. The number of *baserriak* (the house-cum-estate that was passed down intact) was stable in both villages on into the second decade of this century, and the paradox to be explained is why, during the next forty years, estates were abandoned at a far higher rate in one village (Echalar), despite its richer resource base, than in the other (Murelaga). During these decades the economic desirability of the agricultural way of life, which was centered on the landed estates, diminished to the vanishing point. The roles of master and mistress of a *baserria* had been the most prestigious in the local system, clearly superior to townspeople and others in nonfarm occupations (perceived, of course, as nonheirs and their descendants), but by the 1960s peasant agriculturalists retained little of their former prestige or economic advantage. The key to the different experiences of the two villages lies in their distinctive heirship customs. In Murelaga the heir was preordained as the eldest son, whereas in Echalar the heir or heiress was selected by the father. Given the reversal in the economic worth and prestige of the baserria way of life, the thrust of sibling competition in Echalar was reversed. By the 1960s siblings were competing to *escape* the heirship and parents were forced to name as heir the least qualified of their offspring. By contrast, in Murelaga, parents, howsoever demoralized by overall trends, continued to socialize one of their offspring into the role of heir. Thus, the system of male primogeniture that had facilitated out-migration in premodern times now served to brake the prevailing rural exodus.

Family systems also influence the gender composition of migration streams. In both China and Japan in the eighteenth century, net migration for employment was primarily from the peripheries of regional systems in the direction of their more urbanized cores. In Japan, as we have seen, migrants included both men and women, and if anything the cityward thrust was stronger for women than for men. But in China, the net in-migration that characterized cities and regional cores consisted primarily of men. As a result, sex ratios varied through regional space from high in the urbanized cores of regions to low in their peripheries. Japan exhibited just the reverse pattern of gender-in-space, though less pronounced.

The explanation is by now transparent. In societies with patrilineal joint family systems such as that of traditional China, young women were kept close to home (if not at home) under the watchful eyes of parents before marriage[28] and of parents-in-law after marriage. Only men were sufficiently mobile to take advantage of economic opportunities away from home. Those opportunities were concentrated in cities, and the sojourning strategies that were a characteristic feature of the premodern Chinese economy were largely limited to men—whence the male-heavy populations at the core of regional economies. By contrast, in preindustrial societies with cognatic stem family systems, females were not secluded, and there was institutional scope for economic opportunities to develop for women as well as men and for female migration to take on significant proportions. If the opportunity structures of men and women differed in their spatial distribution, sex-selective migration alone could yield significant patterns of gender differentiation. In the Nôbi regional economy of central Japan, which I have studied in some detail, men were drawn to the mountainous periphery to work in lumbering, mining, and quarrying, whereas young women found their employment in the paddy fields, fisheries, and cities of the coastal plains, working as rice transplanters, pearl divers, fishnet makers, domestic servants, textile workers, waitresses, and courtesans. Thus, populations in the fertile lowlands and the cities that dominated them were disproportionately female.

Relocation to take advantage of economic opportunity is, of course, but one form of migration. Another, migration for marriage, should be seen as an integral component of many family systems. In the patrilineal joint family systems of East and South Asia, where marriage is customarily virilocal and village and lineage exogamy obtain, women perforce migrate on marriage. Indeed, migration for marriage may well exceed migration for employment. The 1981 population census of India, for instance, enumerated 196 million persons (some 30 percent of the population) whose locality of residence differed from their place of birth, and of these nearly 80 percent were women who gave marriage as the reason for their move (Stark 1991, ch. 6; cf. Skelton 1986). In an original analysis of these and comparable data from other Asian countries, Oded Stark argues that marital migration across villages serves "to mitigate income risk and facilitate consumption smoothing under conditions in which there are informational costs and spatially covariant risks" (1991:63).

In societies with matrilineal joint family systems, of course, it is men rather than women who migrate on marriage. Among the Minangkabau and several other Sumatran populations (cf. Jayawardena 1977), sons-in-law are brought in for daughters, who normally remain in their natal households. But in Sumatra as in India, migration for employment and sojourning, including rural-to-urban migration, is overwhelmingly male (Kato 1982). Thus, whereas in India one gender dominates short-distance migration for marriage and the other dominates long-distance migration for employment, in Sumatra males dominate both migration streams and females are remarkably sedentary throughout their lives.

A final example will serve to remind us that the differentiating effect of distinctive family systems is also apparent in international migrations. In her recent book (1993), Cynthia Enloe analyzes the significance of the Gulf War for women. There had been a vast influx of laborers to the oil-rich countries of the Middle East from all around the rim of the Indian Ocean. Although South Asians (i.e., Indians, Bangladeshis, and Pakistanis) among the stranded migrants outnumbered Southeast Asians, Enloe focused her discussion on the plight of women from the Philippines and Thailand. In fact, there weren't any stranded South Asian women to speak of. Migration streams from Pakistan, Bangladesh and northern India to the Middle East were almost exclusively male, whereas women and men came in roughly equal numbers from Southeast Asia, delimited for present purposes to exclude Vietnam and include Sri Lanka. Family systems provide the critically relevant contrast between the two groups of societies. Even within the class of countries with patrilineal joint family systems, mainland South Asian societies stand out for their strict seclusion of women.[29] Traditionally South Asian women did not go out to work, and even today most would not consider or would not be allowed to consider traveling across the ocean unchaperoned to take up employment. In Southeast Asia, by contrast, the sex egalitarianism that informs the prevailing cognatic family systems had long since drawn women into full participation in the pre-industrial extradomestic economy. The senior woman in the family usually controlled the purse strings, and women vendors predominated in local markets (Infante 1975). As local economies were integrated into national and international economic systems, the horizons of Southeast Asian women kept pace.[30] Today, women from the Philippines are employed as domestics, as workers in light industry, and as sex workers throughout Asia and the Middle East. Thus does the international labor market reflect cross-cultural variation in family systems.

Demographic Fate

In northern India a third-born daughter with older brothers is at risk for her life; in Thailand, a third-born daughter with older brothers is cherished above any of her older siblings. I have belabored the point that offspring position entails differential mortality risks for infants and children in a given population and that the calculus of differentiation is rooted in family system norms. I want to draw attention in this final section to the fact that the same family system calculus often shapes the demographic fate of those who survive to adulthood.

When pursuing my dissertation fieldwork in what was still a very traditional local system in the far west of China Proper (Skinner 1951), I was struck by the sizable number of middle-aged bachelors. They were a pitiful lot, disparaged for failing to continue their patrilines and socially marginalized within the community. Whenever I interviewed one of these "bare sticks," as they were called, I would get an earful of their bad fate: why his parents could not muster a brideprice, how he was victimized by scheming older brothers, how he allowed himself to be tricked by a dissembling go-between, how his fiancée died of consumption just weeks before the wedding day. These men were almost all from desperately poor families, to be sure, but most were also younger sons. They and millions like them were disadvantaged not only by their poverty but also by the workings of the family system. From historical data that have since been compiled and analyzed, we can now estimate that in late imperial China the percent of men (i.e., males who survived to age eighteen) who never married ranged from 10 to 20 percent and that another 10 to 15 percent married late, at age twenty-five or over (Telford 1992, 1995; Liu 1995). A man was less likely to marry the more brothers he had and the lower his place in the brother series. The same calculus that governed child control, birth control, and child transfer in Chinese society marked out certain persons for a foul social and demographic fate: late marriage or celibacy, low fertility, and an early death.

But in China, unlike Western Europe, the late age at marriage and high celibacy rate for men were themselves demographic phenomena produced by the family system: there were simply not enough women to go around. The discriminatory child-control strategies fostered by a patrilineal joint family system produced the deficit of marriageable females that in turn ensured high celibacy for men. In the last analysis, a fifth son in one family was consigned to bachelorhood because in another family a second daughter with three brothers was culled. The links between family system and population growth are thus multiple and contingent.

As we might expect, life-course prospects were even more sharply differentiated in stem family systems than in joint family systems. In his analysis of the Portuguese nobility in the fifteenth and sixteenth centuries, a population favoring male primogeniture, Boone (1986) documents how men's demographic fate varied with birth order. The proportion who married declines monotonically from over 80 percent of first-born males to less than 45 percent of the fourth-born; fertility net infant mortality declines from 3.1 to 1.7 surviving children; and death in war increases down the brother series from 18 to

26 percent. Those marked out by the logic of their family systems for discrimination were less likely to marry, less likely to reproduce themselves, and less likely to live long.

Conclusion

In company with sociology and economics, with which it has long-standing ties, demography developed not only *in* the Western world but as the study *of* Western societies. Despite increased attention to the Third World and considerable transnationalization, a good deal of family system parochialism remains. In particular, many demographic conventions reflect the particulars of Western conjugal family systems. To this day, demographers use the term "family size" to refer to the size of the offspring set. Why? Because in Western family systems there is normally only one offspring set per family. And they commonly use the term "family formation" as jargon for marriage. The reason once again is that where marriage is neolocal, as in the conjugal family systems of the West, it is indeed equivalent to family formation. But these ethnocentric usages make no sense in the stem and joint family systems that obtain elsewhere in the world and thus have no place in the technical terminology of a "universal" or transnational discipline. This chapter has invited demographers not simply to recognize the parochial biases in their conceptualization of family but also to consider how family systems might provide an analytical framework for certain demographic analyses and afford analytical controls for cross-societal comparisons.

A central argument here is that a given family system virtually specifies the relative desirability of differently configured offspring sets, thereby setting effective goals for family planning within the society. When family planning is conceived broadly to include child control (direct and indirect infanticide) and child transfer (adoption in and out, fostering, abandonment and retrieval, and buying and selling of children) as well as birth control (contraception, the various "natural" methods of averting pregnancy, and induced abortion), then we must recognize that it is no Western or modern innovation. In many if not most societies, families did what they could and continue today to do what they can to shape the size and configuration of their offspring sets. In this manner, family systems affect not only fertility but also infant and child mortality and adoption.

The same family system calculus that regulates infant and child survival may also affect the demographic prospects of those who survive to adulthood. Offspring devalued by a given family system are often less likely to marry early or to marry well or to marry at all. The composition of migrant streams is shaped by family system norms: male-heavy in one society, gender-balanced in another, disproportionately male early-borns here but female early-borns there. And, finally, particular family systems imply distinctive mortality schedules. So, for instance, in societies with patrilineal joint family systems, females exhibit relatively high mortality in childhood and again during the five years following the customary marriage age, but relatively low mortality in the decades following the end of childbearing—reflecting the usual progression from daughter to daughter-in-law to mother-in-law. Family system norms, then, impinge directly on every term of the population equation.

While I have written this chapter as an anthropologist addressing demographers, I do so from a glass house that invites a full complement of reciprocal stones. Reading between the lines of this paper, the anthropologist can hardly miss the point that an adequate analysis of any family system must rest on and, indeed, incorporate demographic processes. As an interdisciplinary field, comparative family demography is no less critical for anthropology than for demography.

NOTES

I have benefited from the critical comments of Monique Borgerhoff Mulder, Bill Chu, James Cramer, Jack Goldstone, Susan Greenhalgh, Eugene Hammel, Stevan Harrell, Sarah Hrdy, Suad Joseph, David Kertzer, Susan Mann, Emily Martin, and John Shepherd. The deficiencies that remain despite their best efforts are mine alone.

1. See Goody 1990 for a very rich, discursive treatment of Eurasian family systems that touches repeatedly on many of the strategic issues treated here.

2. Meyer Fortes (1949, 1958) provided the initial conceptualization of the domestic cycle. He insisted that the family be analyzed as a process, and observed that the various family types found in a population at any point in time are normally phases in a normative developmental cycle.

3. Coresidence is to be understood rather loosely, as when subunits of the family (despite their participation in a single domestic economy) reside in adjacent but separate dwellings. Servants and lodgers are excluded.

Anthropologist readers will doubtless be chagrined to see that I fudge the distinction between family (qua kin group) and household (qua residential unit). For many conceptual and analytical purposes, the distinction is critical, and tomes have been devoted to the ethnographic niceties (e.g., Netting, Wilk, and Arnould 1984). It is indeed the case that some families have overlapping economies, that not all subsystems of a family (with a single economy) necessarily coreside, that some households comprise disjoint family sets, etc., but in the societies treated here such arrangements are exceptional. The simplifying assumptions implicit in my definition of family are designed to facilitate cross-disciplinary communication without introducing systematic bias.

4. In the terminology used here "multi-family household" would mean two or more families (each with a separate domestic economy) residing under one roof, plus any servants or boarders integrated into any one of the families.

5. This approach is not designed to work, and does not work, for family systems in which marital residence is duolocal, that is, where husband and wife remain in their natal households. Duolocal residence characterizes the family systems of the Tory Islanders (Fox 1978) and the Nayars of Kerala (Gough 1959) and figures prominently in the complex family systems of Nambudiri Brahmins in southern India (Yalman 1963) and Shirakawa villagers in the Japanese Alps (Befu 1968). In the matrilineal joint family system of the Moso of Yunnan (Shih 1993), both men and women remain in their natal families; marriage is absent, and men are responsible not for their biological children

but for those of their sisters. While duolocality is an ethnographic rarity, its occurrence demolishes the notion that coresident conjugal units are a human universal, not to mention the widely repeated claim that "nuclear families," "embedded" when not independent, are universal (cf. Murdock 1949).

6. Also known as nuclear family, elementary family, and simple family.

7. It goes without saying that in all family types that include CUs in adjacent generations, one of the spouses in each junior CU will also be a member of the senior CU (or one of the senior CUs). This linking or overlapping member is, of course, normally a son or daughter of the senior couple.

8. Of the many subtypes of joint families that might be distinguished, the two simplest and most commonly occurring forms are the *lineal joint family,* consisting of one and only one CU in the senior generation and two or more CUs in the junior generation, and the *sibling joint family,* consisting of two or more CUs headed by siblings (the term *frérèche* is used when all the siblings are brothers). When doing a count or census of family types within the households of a population, one needs to enumerate units that include no CU. *Subconjugal family* refers to two or more coresiding kin that together do not add up to a minimal CU, e.g., two or more siblings, two or more first cousins, a woman and her unmarried niece. *Singleton* refers to a person coresiding with no other kin.

9. Hammel (pers. communication, 1995) observes that his objective at the time was to develop a consistent notational system designed to look at cross-sections without knowledge of the underlying dynamics of family process. Nonetheless, it is the inherent classification system rather than the notational system that has been widely adopted by historical demographers, leading (in my view) to systematic bias in interpretations.

10. It doesn't just happen, of course, but that is another story, outside the scope of this chapter, as explained at the outset.

11. In the Philippines, where family systems are cognatic conjugal or stem, often with little gender bias, the median observed spousal age difference is 2.5 years and the wife is older in 16 percent of marriages. By contrast, in Bangladesh, where family systems are patrilineal joint, the median age difference is 9.1 years and the wife is older in less than 1 percent of marriages. These findings are based on survey data collected from once-married women within ten years of their marriage. These cases are the two extremes among the 29 countries whose World Fertility Survey data are analyzed comparatively by Casterline, Williams, and McDonald (1986).

12. Hiving-off patrilineal stem family systems and hiving-off patrilineal joint family systems are similar in that daughters-in-law are brought in for all sons. They differ in that junior CUs never coreside in the stem system whereas they always do for a spell in the joint system. Thus, the domestic cycle of the hiving-off joint system involves an alternation between lineal-joint and stem phases, in contrast with the hiving-off stem system, which has no joint family phase.

13. A notable omission is the fraternal polyandrous family system, found among many Tibetan groups in the Himalayan highlands. (General polygyny, the term used by anthropologists for marriage systems in which polygyny is the general norm, is not found among Eurasian societies.) Polygamous present no particular problem to family systems analysis, but space does not permit elaboration or illustration here.

14. Nonetheless, the prevailing shortage of females of marriageable age (roughly 14 to 20 in these populations) meant that those men disadvantaged by the class system (i.e., poor peasants) and by the family system (i.e., boys with several older brothers) had to postpone marriage or miss out altogether. Table 3.7 provides data for 766

couples (in 515 families), the total population in 1931 of one rural district in Ding xian, a county in Hebei province. Whereas only one-third of the husbands in smallholder families had married before age fifteen, the proportion was over 80 percent among landlord and other largeholder families. Within the entire population of 766 couples, the husband was older in 24.6 percent, husband and wife were the same age in 8.5 percent, and the wife was older in 69.6 percent. The distribution was less extreme in a comparable survey of 1,540 couples in three market towns in the same county. Of those town couples, the husband was older in 46.3 percent, husband and wife were the same age in 5.7 percent, and the wife was older in 48.0 percent (Gamble 1954:58–59).

Table 3.7
Age at Marriage by Sex and by Family Landholdings in *mu* (.0667 ha.),
Ding xian, North China, 1931

Age at Marriage	(N = 490) Under 50 *mu*		(N = 219) 50–99 *mu*		(N = 57) 100 *mu* and over	
	Male	Female	Male	Female	Male	Female
	(percentage)		(percentage)		(percentage)	
–11.9	8.2	0	9.2	0	17.5	0
12–14.9	25.2	8.6	39.7	4.5	63.0	12.4
15–17.9	27.6	36.3	31.8	40.6	14.1	45.4
18–20.9	11.9	40.5	9.1	43.9	3.6	38.7
21–	27.1	14.6	10.2	11.0	1.8	3.5
Total	100	100	100	100	100	100

15. These two examples from China point up the fact that much of the demographic variation stemming from family system differentiation is muted or obscured by the usual demographic practice of working with data aggregated to the national level. The various populations in South China where delayed-transfer marriage was the norm probably total over ten million. The portion of North China where wife-older marriages were preferred has a population of several tens of millions. A region of China larger than most of the twenty-nine countries covered in Casterline, Williams, and McDonald's study of spousal age differences shows a distribution totally outside the range of that worldwide sample of developing countries. But even if China were included in that country study, the North China pattern would be overwhelmed by the characteristic spousal-age norms (that is, those typical of patrilineal joint family systems) obtaining in other regions of the country, thus placing China well within the "established" range.

16. The disruption of marriage through death or divorce and the remarriage of widowed and divorced persons are all family events closely intertwined with demographic processes. What should happen when an in-marrying spouse is divorced or widowed is a normative matter that varies from one corporate family system to another. Norms on widow remarriage range from outright proscription ("celibate widowhood") to enjoined marriage to a brother of the widow's late husband (the levirate). In populations where husbands are normatively much older than their wives and life expectancy is short, the proportion of women widowed during their childbearing years can be quite high, so that remarriage norms may have great significance for total fertility. For reasons of space, however, I must eschew here any systematic comparative treatment of marriage termination and remarriage. See Goody 1976 and 1990 for insightful comparative analyses.

17. Hu and Goldman 1990. Of course, marriage is also selective such that never-married adults include a higher proportion of those with serious health problems. Indeed, Hu and Goldman find in their cross-societal comparison that the smaller the proportion of persons who never marry, the more likely are those persons to have high risks of mortality. Still, selectivity on health cannot have been determinative where 15 percent or more of male or female adults never married.

18. Of course, the bride's parents were also eager to place their daughter in an auspiciously configured family. It would be a distortion to interpret the situation as either "female choice" (in which families with marriageable daughters dominated the marriage market) or "male choice."

19. The much smaller traffic in boys was largely limited to those with two or more older brothers sold by their parents to brokers, who transported them to distant areas for sale as adopted heirs (cf. Wolf and Huang 1980; Watson 1980).

20. Hypergamy for women is more or less normative in virtually all patrilineal joint family systems. The range of variation in this regard may be suggested by the following comparison. In most subcastes of northern India, some degree of hypergamy is considered essential, and even isogamous unions are mildly stigmatized. By contrast, in China, isogamy per se is the cultural ideal; still, if there is to be any departure from "matched doors," it must be in the direction of hypergamy for the bride.

21. I wish to dissociate myself from the authors' interpretation of the data they present.

22. As the size of the desired offspring set declines in societies with patrilineal joint family systems, a single daughter may be considered optimal. And with the spread of sex-determination technology, parents are positioned to abort all female fetuses after they have their one daughter. Thus, while sex ratios may fall in the normal range for parity 1, the ratios tend to rise at later parities. The nationwide data for China, Taiwan, and Korea shown in table 3.8, illustrate the typical pattern (Park and Cho 1995).

Table 3.8
Sex Ratio at Birth by Birth Order (Parity), China, 1989; Taiwan, 1990; Korea, 1989

	Parity			
	1	2	3	4
China	105	120	125	133
Taiwan	108	110	134	159
Korea	104	113	185	209

23. Such a model would have to take into account the dynamics of customary marriage payments. True dowry, groomprice, brideprice, and indirect dowry are all implicated in one or another of the Eurasian patrilineal joint family systems. In very general terms, when customary payments go both ways (i.e., brideprice *and* dowry, or indirect dowry) there is a slight push in the direction of gender balance within offspring sets. Brideprice to the exclusion of dowry countervails the general family system pressures for male-heavy sets, while dowry (and a fortiori groomprice) to the exclusion of brideprice reinforces those pressures. The punishing groomprice system obtaining in many subcastes of northern India today can, quite literally, be ruinous to families with more daughters than sons (Sharma 1984; Billig 1991; Rao 1993; Jain 1992).

24. For cross-societal treatments of daughter preference, see Williamson 1976, ch. 4, and Cronk 1991.

25. This analysis has not yet been pursued with the entire eight-village sample, so these results are provisional.

26. A more analytical formulation of this point is suggested by the work of Karasek and Theorell (1990). With respect to work environments, they show that it is precisely when the psychological demands of a job are high, the worker's decision latitude in the task is low, and helpful social interaction is unavailable from co-workers and supervisors, that one finds the most adverse reactions of strain: fatigue, anxiety, depression, and physical illness. In patrilineal joint family systems, the status of young daughters-in-law is closely analogous to this worst-case work environment. The combination of high psychological demands with low decision latitude yields a high-strain situation that is exacerbated by the lack of social support.

27. Qualitative evidence suggests that the situation for young daughters-in-law today is far more difficult in northwest India than in any Chinese society (e.g., Calman 1992). However, I have not been able to find age- and sex-specific suicide data for India.

28. A Chinese woman at the turn of the century made a telling point in her oral history: "When a family wanted to know more about a girl who had been suggested for a daughter-in-law and asked what kind of a girl she was, the neighbors would answer 'We do not know. We have never seen her.' And that was praise" (Pruitt 1945:29).

29. In his classic analysis, Mandelbaum (1988) refers to the northern purdah zone, which includes northern India along with Pakistan and Bangladesh. Seclusion practices in the Dravidian areas of southern India were far less strict (Dyson and Moore 1983).

30. In general, Filipino families more often choose to send a daughter rather than a son to work in the city or abroad. Lauby and Stark argue that this manifests "a strategy for advancing familial well-being" and that an out-migrant daughter "can be relied upon to help support her parents and the education of brothers and sisters" (1988:475, 485). It may be that parental, and especially maternal, efforts to socialize offspring to family loyalty, filiality, and altruism are (across societies) more successful with daughters than with sons, so that other things being equal daughters would be more responsive than their brothers to the needs of parents and siblings. But if so, it would be only in societies where male bias is muted or absent in both the family system and the opportunity structure that family migration strategies could take advantage of this gender difference.

REFERENCES

Arrizabalaga, Marie-Pierre. 1994. "Family Structures, Inheritance Practices and Migration Networks in the Basses-Pyrénées in the Nineteenth Century: Sare." Ph.D. diss., University of California, Davis.

Barbagli, Marzio. 1991. "Three Household Formation Systems in Eighteenth- and Nineteenth-Century Italy." In *The Family in Italy from Antiquity to the Present*, ed. David I. Kertzer and Richard P. Saller, 286–303. New Haven, Conn.: Yale University Press.

Befu, Harumi. 1968. "Origins of Large Households and Duolocal Residence in Central Japan." *American Anthropologist* 70:309–19.

Berkner, Lutz K. 1972. "The Stem Family and the Developmental Cycle of the Peasant Household: An Eighteenth-Century Example." *American Historical Review* 77: 398–418.

Billig, Michael S. 1991. "The Marriage Squeeze on High-Caste Rajasthani Women."
    Journal of Asian Studies 50:341–60.
Boone, James L. 1986. "Parental Investment and Elite Family Structure in Preindustrial
    States: A Case Study of Late Medieval–Early Modern Portuguese Genealogies."
    American Anthropologist 88:859–78.
Braun, Rudolf. 1978. "Protoindustrialization and Demographic Changes in the Can-
    ton of Zurich." In *Historical Studies of Changing Fertility,* ed. Charles Tilly, 289–
    334. Princeton: Princeton University Press.
Caldwell, John C., P. H. Reddy, and Pat Caldwell. 1984. "The Determinants of Family
    Structure in Rural South India." *Journal of Marriage and the Family* 46:215–29.
Calman, Leslie J. 1992. *Toward Empowerment: Women and Movement Politics in In-
    dia.* Boulder, Colo.: Westview Press.
Casterline, John B., Lindy Williams, and Peter McDonald. 1986. "The Age Difference
    between Spouses: Variations among Developing Countries." *Population Studies* 40:
    353–74.
Chan, Anita, Richard Madsen, and Jonathan Unger. 1984. *Chen Village: The Recent
    History of a Peasant Community in Mao's China.* Berkeley: University of California
    Press.
Clark, Sam, Elizabeth Colson, James Lee, and Thayer Scudder. 1995. "Ten Thousand
    Tonga: A Longitudinal Anthropological Study from Southern Zambia, 1956–
    1991." *Population Studies* 49:91–109.
Coale, Ansley J., and Judith Banister. 1994. "Five Decades of Missing Females in
    China." *Demography* 31:459–79.
Coale, Ansley J., and Susan Cotts Watkins. 1986. *The Decline of Fertility in Europe.*
    Princeton: Princeton University Press.
Coombs, Lolagene C., and Te-hsiung Sun. 1978. "Family Composition Preferences in
    a Developing Culture: The Case of Taiwan 1973." *Population Studies* 32:43–64.
Cornell, Laurel L. 1983. "Retirement, Inheritance, and Intergenerational Conflict in
    Preindustrial Japan." *Journal of Family History* 8:55–69.
Crafts, Nicholas F. R. 1989. "Duration of Marriage, Fertility and Women's Employ-
    ment Opportunities in England and Wales in 1911." *Population Studies* 43:
    325–35.
Cronk, Lee. 1991. "Preferential Parental Investment in Daughters over Sons." *Human
    Nature* 2:387–417.
Das Gupta, Monica. 1987. "Selective Discrimination against Female Children in Rural
    Punjab, India." *Population and Development Review* 13:77–100.
Davis, Kingsley. 1955. "Institutional Patterns Favoring High Fertility in Underdevel-
    oped Areas." *Eugenics Quarterly* 2.
Douglass, William A. 1971. "Rural Exodus in Two Spanish Basque Villages: A Cul-
    tural Explanation." *American Anthropologist* 73:1100–14.
Dyson, Tim, and Mick Moore. 1983. "On Kinship Structure, Female Autonomy, and
    Demographic Behavior in India." *Population and Development Review* 9:35–60.
Enloe, Cynthia H. 1993. *The Morning After: Sexual Politics at the End of the Cold
    War.* Berkeley: University of California Press.
Errington, Frederick. 1984. *Manners and Meaning in West Sumatra.* New Haven,
    Conn.: Yale University Press.
Errington, Shelly. 1990. "Recasting Sex, Gender, and Power." In *Power and Difference:
    Gender in Island Southeast Asia,* ed. Jane M. Atkinson and Shelly Errington, 1–58.
    Stanford: Stanford University Press.

Fortes, Meyer. 1949. "Time and Social Structure." In *Social Structure: Studies Presented to A. R. Radcliffe-Brown.* Oxford: Oxford University Press.

———. 1958. Introduction. to *The Developmental Cycle in Domestic Groups,* ed. Jack Goody, 1–14. Cambridge: Cambridge University Department of Archaeology and Anthropology.

Fox, Robin. 1978. *The Tory Islanders: A People of the Celtic Fringe.* Cambridge: Cambridge University Press.

Freeman, J. Derek. 1958. "The Family System of the Iban of Borneo." In *The Developmental Cycle in Domestic Groups,* ed. Jack Goody, 15–52. Cambridge: Cambridge University Press.

Friedlander, Dov, Jona Schellekens, and Eliahu Ben-Moshe. 1991. "The Transition from High to Low Marital Fertility: Cultural or Socioeconomic Determinants?" *Economic Development and Cultural Change* 39:331–51.

Fuchs, Rachel. 1984. *Abandoned Children: Foundlings and Child Welfare in Nineteenth-Century France.* Albany: State University of New York Press.

Gamble, Sidney D. 1954. *Ting Hsien: A North China Rural Community.* New York: Institute of Pacific Relations, International Secretariat.

Goody, Jack. 1976. *Production and Reproduction: A Comparative Study of the Domestic Domain.* Cambridge: Cambridge University Press.

———. 1990. *The Oriental, the Ancient, and the Primitive: Systems of Marriage and the Family in the Pre-industrial Societies of Eurasia.* Cambridge: Cambridge University Press.

Gough, E. Kathleen. 1961. "Mappilla: North Kerala." In *Matrilineal Kinship,* ed. David M. Schneider and Kathleen Gough, 415–22. Berkeley: University of California Press.

———. 1959. "The Nayars and the Definition of Marriage." *Journal of the Royal Anthropological Institute* 89:23–34.

Greenhalgh, Susan. 1988. "Fertility as Mobility: Sinic Transitions." *Population and Development Review* 14:629–74.

Hager, Barbara J. 1992. "Get Thee to a Nunnery: Female Religious Claustration in Medieval Europe." *Ethology and Sociobiology* 13:385–407.

Hajnal, John. 1982. "Two Kinds of Preindustrial Household Formation System." *Population and Development Review* 8:449–94.

Hammel, Eugene A., and Peter Laslett. 1974. "Comparing Household Structure over Time and between Cultures." *Comparative Studies in Society and History* 16:73–109.

Harrell, Stevan, and Thomas W. Pullum. 1995. "Marriage, Mortality, and the Developmental Cycle in Three Xiaoshan Lineages." In *Chinese Historical Microdemography,* ed. Stevan Harrell, 141–62. Berkeley: University of California Press.

Hobcraft, John N., John W. McDonald, and Shea O. Rutstein. 1985. "Demographic Determinants of Infant and Early Childhood Mortality: A Comparative Analysis." *Population Studies* 39:363–85.

Hu, Yuanreng, and Noreen Goldman. 1990. "Mortality Differentials by Marital Status: An International Comparison." *Demography* 27:233–50.

Infante, Teresita R. 1975. *The Women in Early Philippines and among the Cultural Minorities.* Manila: Unitas Publications.

Jain, Ranjana S. 1992. *Family Violence in India.* New Delhi: Radiant.

Jayawardena, Chandra. 1977. "Women and Kinship in Acheh Besar, Northern Sumatra." *Ethnology* 16:21–38.

Kahn, Joel S. 1980. *Minangkabau Social Formation: Indonesian Peasants and the World Economy*. Cambridge: Cambridge University Press.

Karasek, Robert, and Töres Theorell. 1990. *Healthy Work: Stress, Productivity, and the Reconstruction of Working Life*. New York: Basic Books.

Kato, Tsuyoshi. 1982. *Matriliny and Migration: Evolving Minangkabau Traditions in Indonesia*. Ithaca: Cornell University Press.

Kertzer, David I. 1984. *Family Life in Central Italy, 1880–1910: Sharecropping, Wage Labor, and Coresidence*. New Brunswick, N.J.: Rutgers University Press.

———. 1989. "The Joint Family Household Revisited: Demographic Constraints and Household Complexity in the European Past." *Journal of Family History* 14:1–15.

———. 1991. "Household History and Sociological Theory." *Annual Review of Sociology* 17:155–79.

———. 1993. *Sacrificed for Honor: Italian Infant Abandonment and the Politics of Reproductive Control*. Boston: Beacon Press.

Kertzer, David I., and Dennis P. Hogan. 1989. *Family, Political Economy, and Demographic Change: The Transformation of Life in Casalecchio, Italy, 1861–1921*. Madison: University of Wisconsin Press.

———. 1991. "Reflections on the European Marriage Pattern: Sharecropping and Proletarianization in Casalecchio, Italy, 1861–1921." *Journal of Family History* 16: 31–45.

Keyes, Charles F. 1975. "Kin Groups in a Thai-Lao Community." In *Change and Persistence in Thai Society*, ed. G. William Skinner and A. Thomas Kirsch, 274–97. Ithaca, N.Y.: Cornell University Press.

Knodel, John E. 1987. "Starting, Stopping, and Spacing during the Early Stages of Fertility Transition: The Experience of German Village Populations in the Eighteenth and Nineteenth Centuries." *Demography* 24:143–62.

Landers, John. 1990. "Fertility Decline and Birth Spacing among London Quakers." In *Family and Resources*, ed. John Landers and Vernon Reynolds, 92–117. Cambridge: Cambridge University Press.

Laslett, Peter. 1972. Introduction to *Household and Family in Past Time*, ed. Peter Laslett and Richard Wall, 1–89. Cambridge: Cambridge University Press.

———. 1983. "Family and Household as Work Group and Kin Group: Areas of Traditional Europe Compared." In *Family Forms in Historic Europe*, ed. Richard Wall, 513–87. Cambridge: Cambridge University Press.

Lauby, Jennifer, and Oded Stark. 1988. "Individual Migration and Family Strategy: Young Women in the Philippines." *Population Studies* 42:473–86.

Liu, Ts'ui-jung. 1995. "A Comparison of Lineage Populations in South China, ca. 1300–1900." In *Chinese Historical Microdemography*, ed. Stevan Harrell, 94–120. Berkeley: University of California Press.

Mandelbaum, David G. 1988. *Women's Seclusion and Men's Honor: Sex Roles in North India, Bangladesh, and Pakistan*. Tucson: University of Arizona Press.

Miller, Barbara D. 1981. *The Endangered Sex: Neglect of Female Children in Rural North India*. Ithaca, N.Y.: Cornell University Press.

Muhuri, Pradip K., and Jane E. Menken. 1993. "Child Survival in Rural Bangladesh: The Circumstances of Greatest Jeopardy." Paper prepared for the Stanford-Berkeley Colloquium in Demography, Berkeley, June 10.

Muhuri, Pradip K., and Samuel H. Preston. 1991. "Effects of Family Composition on Mortality Differentials by Sex among Children in Matlab, Bangladesh." *Population and Development Review* 17:415–34.

Murdock, George Peter. 1949. *Social Structure.* New York: Macmillan.

Nakane, Chie. 1967. *Kinship and Economic Organization in Rural Japan.* London: Athlone.

Netting, Robert McC., Richard R. Wilk, and Eric J. Arnould, eds. 1984. *Households: Comparative and Historical Studies of the Domestic Group.* Berkeley: University of California Press.

Pakrasi, Kanti, and Ajit Halder. 1971. "Sex Ratios and Sex Sequences of Births in India." *Journal of Biosocial Science* 3:377–87.

Park, Chai Bin. 1983. "Preference for Sons, Family Size, and Sex Ratio: An Empirical Study in Korea." *Demography* 20:333–52.

Park, Chai Bin, and Nam-Hoon Cho. 1995. "Consequences of Son Preference in a Low-Fertility Society: Imbalance of the Sex Ratio at Birth in Korea." *Population and Development Review* 21:59–84.

Park, George K. 1962. "Sons and Lovers: Characterological Requisites of the Roles in a Peasant Society." *Ethnology* 1:412–24.

Peletz, Michael G. 1988. *A Share of the Harvest: Kinship, Property, and Social History Among the Malays of Rembau.* Berkeley: University of California Press.

Potter, Sulamith Heins, and Jack M. Potter. 1990. *China's Peasants: The Anthropology of a Revolution.* Cambridge: Cambridge University Press.

Pruitt, Ida. 1945. *A Daughter of Han: The Autobiography of a Chinese Working Woman.* New Haven, Conn.: Yale University Press.

Rao, Vijayendra. 1993. "Dowry 'Inflation' in Rural India: A Statistical Investigation." *Population Studies* 47:283–93.

Rebel, Hermann. 1978. "Peasant Stem Families in Early Modern Austria: Life Plans, Status Tactics, and the Grid of Inheritance." *Social Science History* 2:255–91.

Reher, David Sven. 1990. *Town and Country in Pre-Industrial Spain: Cuenca, 1550–1870.* New York: Cambridge University Press.

Rich, George W. 1978. "The Domestic Cycle in Modern Iceland." *Journal of Marriage and the Family* 40:173–83.

Rogers, Susan Carol. 1975. "Female Forms of Power and the Myth of Male Dominance: A Model of Female/Male Interaction in Peasant Society." *American Ethnologist* 2:727–56.

———. 1991. *Shaping Modern Times in Rural France: The Transformation and Reproduction of an Aveyronnais Community.* Princeton: Princeton University Press.

Scheper-Hughes, Nancy, ed. 1987. *Child Survival: Anthropological Perspectives on the Treatment and Maltreatment of Children.* Boston: Reidel.

Scrimshaw, Susan C. M. 1983. "Infanticide as Deliberate Fertility Regulation." In *Determinants of Fertility in Developing Countries; Vol. 2: Fertility Regulation and Institutional Influences,* ed. Rodolf A. Bulatao and Ronald D. Lee, 245–66. New York: Academic Press.

Segalen, Martine. 1983. *Love and Power in the Peasant Family: Rural France in the Nineteenth Century,* trans. Sarah Matthews. Chicago: University of Chicago Press.

———. 1992. "Exploring a Case of Late French Fertility Decline: Two Contrasted Breton Examples." In *The European Experience of Declining Fertility, 1850–1970: The Quiet Revolution,* ed. John Gillis, Louise A. Tilly, and David Levine. Cambridge, Mass.: Blackwell.

Selden, Mark. 1993. *The Political Economy of Chinese Development.* Armonk, N.Y.: M. E. Sharpe.

Sharma, Ursala. 1984. "Dowry in North India: Its Consequences for Women." In *Women and Property: Women as Property,* ed. Renée Hirschon, 62–74. London: Croom Helm.

Shih, Chuan-kang. 1993. "The Yongning Moso: Sexual Union, Household Organization, Gender, and Ethnicity in a Matrilineal Duolocal Society in Southwest China." Ph.D. diss., Stanford University

Skelton, Ronald. 1986. "On Migration Patterns in India during the 1970s." *Population and Development Review* 12:759–79.

Skinner, G. William. 1951. "A Study in Miniature of Chinese Population." *Population Studies* 5:91–103.

———. 1987. "Infanticide and Reproductive Strategies in Two Nobi Plain Villages, 1717–1869." Paper prepared for the first workshop of the Nôbi Regional Project, Stanford University, March.

———. 1988. "Reproductive Strategies, the Domestic Cycle, and Fertility among Japanese Villagers, 1717–1869." Paper prepared for the Rockefeller Foundation Workshop on Women's Status in Relation to Fertility and Mortality, Bellagio, Italy, June 6–10.

———. 1992. "'Seek a Loyal Subject in a Filial Son': Family Roots of Political Orientation in Chinese Society." In *Family Process and Political Process in Modern Chinese History,* ed. Ch'en Ch'iu-Kun. Taipei: Academia Sinica.

———. 1993. "Conjugal Power in Tokugawa Japanese Families: A Matter of Life or Death." In *Sex and Gender Hierarchies,* ed. Barbara D. Miller, 236–70. New York: Cambridge University Press.

Smout, Christopher. 1980. "Aspects of Sexual Behavior in Nineteenth-Century Scotland." In *Bastardy and Its Comparative History,* ed. Peter Laslett, Karla Oosterveen, and Richard M. Smith, 192–216. Cambridge: Harvard University Press.

Stark, Oded. 1991. *The Migration of Labor.* Cambridge, Mass.: Blackwell.

Stockard, Janice. 1989. *Daughters of the Canton Delta: Marriage Patterns and Economic Strategies in South China, 1860–1930.* Stanford: Stanford University Press.

Suenari, Michio. 1972. "First-Child Inheritance in Japan." *Ethnology* 11:122–26.

Telford, Ted A. 1992. "Covariates of Men's Age at First Marriage: The Historical Demography of Chinese Lineages." *Population Studies* 46:19–35.

———. 1995. "Fertility and Population Growth in the Lineages of Tongcheng County, 1520–1661." In *Chinese Historical Microdemography,* ed. Stevan Harrell, 48–93. Berkeley: University of California Press.

Tilly, Louise A., Rachel G. Fuchs, David I. Kertzer, and David L. Ransel. 1992. "Child Abandonment in European History: A Symposium." *Journal of Family History* 17: 1–23.

Tomasson, Richard F. 1976. "Premarital Sexual Permissiveness and Illegitimacy in the Nordic Countries." *Comparative Studies in Society and History* 18:252–70.

Watson, James L. 1980. "Transactions in People: The Chinese Market in Slaves, Servants, and Heirs." In *Asian and African Systems of Slavery,* ed. James L. Watson, 223–50. Berkeley: University of California Press.

Williamson, Nancy E. 1976. *Sons or Daughters: A Cross-Cultural Survey of Parental Preferences.* Beverly Hills: Sage.

Wolf, Arthur P., and Chieh-shan Huang. 1980. *Marriage and Adoption in China, 1845–1945.* Stanford: Stanford University Press.

Wolf, Margery. 1972. *Women and the Family in Rural Taiwan.* Stanford: Stanford University Press.

————. 1975. "Women and Suicide in China." In *Women in Chinese Society,* ed. Margery Wolf and Roxane Witke, 111–41. Stanford: Stanford University Press.

Yalman, Nur. 1963. "Female Purity in Ceylon and Southern India." *Journal of the Royal Anthropological Institute* 93.

————. 1967. *Under the Bo Tree: Studies in Caste, Kinship, and Marriage in the Interior of Ceylon.* Berkeley: University of California Press.

Zink, Anne. 1993. *L'Héritier de la maison: Géographie coutumière du sud-ouest de la France sous l'ancien régime.* Paris: E.H.E.S.S.

Chapter Four

Reproduction in Anthropology and Demography

Nicholas Townsend

Both anthropology and demography are concerned with the relationship between elements and structures and with the coordinated reproduction of both individuals and the structured relationships within which they exist. The picture of reproduction in demography, represented by the concept of fertility, is essentially a biological one in which children are attributed unproblematically to the women who gave birth to them. Anthropological theory, on the other hand, has emphasized social reproduction: the recreation over time of structures of relationships and the reproduction of social positions rather than of physical individuals (Fortes 1958; Goody 1976; Goody 1982; Bourdieu 1977; Bourdieu and Passeron 1990). In both biological and social theories of reproduction, the relationship described as parenthood is pivotal, though the concept is differently defined. This chapter examines the features of social parenthood, and applies a social analysis to the concept of fertility. It contributes to the socialization of demography by making fertility itself a subject for theorizing rather than an unproblematic biological event. Anthropology not only contributes to the study of the determinants of fertility, it also contributes a revised vision of what fertility is.

In formal demography, the relationships involved in the reproduction of individuals and populations are described and analyzed in the coordination of individual life courses into demographic rates and population structures. Once born, the demographic individual ages but does not develop; the life course is defined by a handful of events (notably marriage, childbearing, and death) and states (single, married, divorced, widowed). Individual events and transitions are simply aggregated to produce population rates, and the sex and age of individuals are summed to describe population structure.

In social anthropology, on the other hand, issues are discussed in terms of the perpetuation and transformation of social structure, the socialization of individuals, and human agency. Individuals are neither unchanging nor interchangeable, but grow and differentiate through processes of development and socialization; time is not homogeneous but rather a matrix of history and experience; structures are not merely aggregations, but exist *sui generis* and play a determinative role in people's lives.

The differences and similarities of the two approaches to reproduction could be profitably developed at length to examine the multiple meanings that lie concealed beneath a shared vocabulary of "life course," "aging," "transition," and "generation." Both disciplines, however, share the critical

importance they place on the specific moment of reproduction[1]—the creation, production, or recruitment of a new element to the structure through a
relationship with specific existing elements of the structure. For both anthropology and demography, reproduction is a process whereby structures are
maintained, even though the individual elements pass through them, because
those individual elements, in the course of their passage, combine to create
new elements. In both approaches, reproduction is endogenous: an integral
aspect of the structure and sharply distinct from replacement as we would see
it, for instance, in the population of automobiles.

Demography analyzes reproduction through the concept of fertility. Fertility as a category is formalized as one of the crucial elements of the mathematical theory of population statics and dynamics which Schofield and Coleman
describe as "the specific technical property of demography" (1986:5). The
mathematical connection of vital rates and age structure is a thing of beauty
in its own right as well as bringing into order an array of otherwise bewil-
dering phenomena. The very success of the model, however, obscures its
limitations.

Schofield and Coleman propose that "the subject matter of demography
may be imagined as being arranged within a sphere with a hard mathematical core and a softer socio-economic and biological rind" (1986:5). This image, in which "rind" suggests the unappealing outer skin of a fruit while
"sphere" and "core" recall the almost celestial mechanics of mathematical
order, expresses the authors' argument that demographic theory is incom-
pletely integrated. On the one hand, they clearly approve of the mathematical
core ("demography without numbers is waffle," they remark) and value the
"hard" facts of biology. On the other hand, they recognize that the "hard core
of demography does not touch the surface of the real world directly" but must
be connected to phenomena by a structure of facts and theories about biology,
society, and economy (Schofield and Coleman 1986:5).

For Schofield and Coleman, the numerical techniques of the core act as a
"common currency" allowing the coordination of other disciplines in the explanation of demographic processes. The definite categories and precise relationships of the core are privileged over the imprecision of sociological terms
and the specificity of particular populations. A concept of fertility based on an
assumption of unproblematized biological reproduction is adequate to the
modeling of population structure and dynamics and to demographic theory at
the level of, for instance, stable population theory.

However, demography as a social science has ambitions that reach beyond
the formal modeling of population processes. While much demographic work
is content to be usefully descriptive, and some is restricted to development
of the mathematics of population, the project underlying the bulk of demographic publications is to connect demographic events, rates, and structures
to other social and economic events and structures. This project is frequently

implicit or completely taken for granted—for instance, in most work concerned with policy. At other times the task of connecting demographic structures to other processes is made more explicit, as in discussions of the determinants or causes of fertility, mortality, marriage, and migration. Sometimes the nature of the connections has been made the focus of influential works of theory. The social sciences have been recruited into demographic theories to provide causal explanations and to suggest, define, and justify the use of a variety of independent variables in demographic models. Relatively recently, demographers have displayed interest in the contribution of anthropological theory and the concept of culture, to the reduction of the distressingly large amount of residual variation remaining after traditional economic variables have been employed (Watkins 1986; and references in Hammel 1990:455).

In this chapter, rather than mining anthropology for contributory independent variables, I apply anthropological theory to the concept of fertility itself in the expectation that a sociologically informed concept of fertility is more suitable for our purposes. I illustrate what it means to understand fertility as a social phenomenon through a parallel treatment of parenthood in anthropology and demography.

The Specificity of Fertility

The basic project of linking purely demographic rates and structures to "social institutions, cultural norms, economic and environmental conditions" is most clearly illustrated in the analytic frameworks proposed for the analysis of fertility (Freedman et al. 1983:10; see also Easterlin and Crimmins 1985). These frameworks form the conceptual basis for the statistical study of fertility, where some particular measurement of fertility is the dependent variable, and a variety of independent variables are deployed in attempts to reduce the unexplained variance in that measurement. Sometimes fertility is used as an independent variable to help explain some intractable aspect of social life, for instance in Easterlin's treatment of birth cohort size and life chances (1980). In both cases, whether fertility is seen as cause or consequence, an unproblematized biological concept of fertility provides order in the analysis and structure to the analytic framework.

Within this framework, the influence of institutions and individual socioeconomic characteristics operates on fertility through variables organized within the tripartite division of demand for children, supply of children, and costs of fertility regulation (Easterlin 1978). These variables have their direct effects on motivation to control fertility, on fertility regulation, and ultimately on achieved fertility.

Two features of this framework are particularly significant for my argument. The first feature is that "fertility" is taken as unproblematic, while the effort of theory building, variable definition, and elaboration of the models is directed at the left hand, independent variable, or causal side of the model.

Demographers measure or quantify fertility in many ways, and the utility of cohort, period, age, and parity-specific measurements is not at issue (Lutz 1989; Ryder 1980; Van de Walle and Foster 1990), but the underlying definition of fertility as biological event is not questioned by these measures. The second noteworthy feature of these frameworks is the feedback from fertility as the dependent variable to fertility as an independent variable. The feedback loop may be explicitly illustrated with a causal arrow from "cumulated family size" to "reproductive history" (Freedman et al. 1983:10) or from "fertility" to "institutions; social and economic structure; norms; external conditions, etc." (Birdsall et al. 1985:13). Or the feedback may be incorporated by including "current number of children" as an independent variable in a model predicting "period births" (Cochrane 1979:60) or "reproductive history" as a predictor of "fertility" (Rofman 1992:5).

In combination, these two features severely undermine the apparent clarity of the analytic frameworks. The concept of fertility as biological reproduction is being conflated with the goal of human motivation and with the reproductive history and current reproductive situation of the people involved. However, neither reproductive goals nor reproductive statuses can be assumed to be equated with giving birth: goals and statuses to do with family size can be, and are, achieved by social mechanisms as well as by biological events.

The demographic picture of fertility is not only biological as opposed to social, it is also historically and culturally specific, structured by a particular set of social assumptions. The model of fertility in demography assumes a particular family structure and a particular economic context. For instance, the entire discussion of opportunity costs and fertility not only assumes that mothers take the burden of the time costs of children, it also assumes that the productive labor of women takes place only in a wage-labor market economy. In many societies, however, the distribution of childcare among women, and among women of different generations, as well as the structure of productive labor for women, make the concept of opportunity costs applicable only with great modification. The theory is not, however, modified accordingly. Similarly, concentration on marital fertility has sprung from two assumptions— that marriage is a single event, a transition at one point in time, and that a woman's marriage precedes her fertility. Premarital fertility has been a problem for demographic analysis just as it has been constructed as a social problem. In general, severe problems in the collection and analysis of fertility data—notably the emphasis on marital fertility and the almost total neglect of men in any approach to fertility—can be attributed to concentration on a limited concept of fertility. While this concept of fertility appears to be based satisfactorily on the hard facts of biology, it is inadequate to the connections to human activity that are essential for the level of explanation to which we aspire.

One approach to the problem of defining a biological outcome in terms of social, economic, or cultural causes has been to concentrate on the strictly biological antecedents of that outcome through the analysis of proximate determinants (Bongaarts 1978). Changes in the proximate determinants may be understood more easily as the result of deliberate action or as the consequences of social changes than would changes in fertility levels themselves. This chapter takes an alternative, but not necessarily opposed, approach by treating fertility itself as a social institution embedded in social processes. In the process of reproducing itself, a social structure recruits individuals and groups for particular positions and functions. By looking at this social recruitment, and the changes in it, as the object to be explained or understood, we can avoid many problems in contemporary explanations of fertility.

Parenthood as a Social Phenomenon

To speak of "parenthood" as opposed, for instance, to "parenting" is to underscore the point that the sociological discussion of reproduction is about statuses and roles and not only about physical individuals. "It is extremely hard for us to maintain a distinction in our thinking between statuses and the people who hold them" warned Linton sixty years ago (1936:113), and it has remained hard through all the subsequent evolutions and reformulations of status and role. The distinction is crucial to sociological analysis, however, and underlies the disjuncture between sociology and the individualism of microeconomic analysis. The concerns of many anthropologists have shifted since Linton wrote, focusing more attention on human subjectivity and human action (Ortner 1984), but the distinction between an individual person and a social status, and between individual attributes and aspects of social structure, has remained vital to the discipline. Where "fertility" is an attribute, "parenthood" is a status, "a collection of rights and duties" (Linton 1936: 113). Because it is a collection, it may be analyzed into constituent elements combined in a variety of ways.

There are three overlapping but analytically distinct senses in which parenthood can be seen as a social phenomenon. First, the *ascription* of parent and child is a social process, not a biological given—the selection of persons involved in the relationship of parenthood is social. Second, the *content* of the role of parent varies historically, cross-culturally, and within societies. Third, the *distribution* of the various rights and responsibilities that might be, or have been in different contexts, attributed to parents are, in any particular setting, distributed among a number of social actors and institutions.

Ascription of Parenthood as a Social Process

The first sense in which parenthood must be considered social—that the people occupying the relevant statuses are socially selected—is both obvious from the standpoint of role theory and subversive of a biological paradigm.

The concept of fertility depends for its analytic power on the unambiguous connection of each child to its biological mother. The distinction between the socially contingent relationship of fatherhood and the more essential, biological, and natural relationship of motherhood has been widely accepted within the anthropological study of kinship, which has made motherhood the core element of kinship (Fortes 1949; Fox 1967; Goodenough 1970). This theoretical conclusion has been readily accepted because in the United States hegemonic theories of relationship in general (Schneider 1968), and of parenthood in particular (Modell 1986), are founded on an ideology of blood. It is commonly assumed that the genetic connection between parents and children brings about the social relationship between them, and occasions the transition to the status of parenthood.

The congruence of a theory with taken-for-granted models may explain, but does not excuse, the easy acceptance of that theory. Particular categories of comparative analysis should not be privileged simply because they happen to be the folk categories of the analyst. Collier and Yanagisako (1987) extend Schneider's (1984) critique of kinship studies by separating all categories of kinship and gender from folk theories of biology. Recent theoretical approaches in anthropology question many traditional analytic categories in the light of ethnographies concerned with the processes and practices of people's everyday life. The phenomena of kinship and parenthood are discussed as constructions arising out of activity rather than as structures imposed on life. Trobriand accounts of parenthood, which deny the biological contribution of fathers (Malinowski 1929), and Arunta beliefs, which attribute the social position of children exclusively to the social relations between their parents (Montagu 1937), demonstrate the possibility of theories of kinship divorced from biological descent.

In my research on family connections among the Tswana, I was investigating a situation in which social paternity may be ascribed to a man who is not the biological father—for instance, when payment of bridewealth gives a man paternal rights over his wife's previous children; to a dead man under the rules of the levirate (Schapera 1971); or to the mother's father when the mother does not marry (Townsend and Garey 1994). The biological relationship is recognized by the Tswana, but in every socially important interaction of authority, responsibility, succession, and inheritance the social father has the status of parent, whether or not he is the biological father.

In many (if not all) societies, clandestine sexual relations between men and women not married to each other produce offspring who are raised as the children of men who are not their biological fathers. Sexual relations outside marriage may not be clandestine, they may even be the norm, and the strongest contender for a universal characteristic of marriage is not the exclusivity of a bond between a man and a woman but the establishment of a relationship which provides a culturally accepted and legitimated social position for children (Gough 1959). Mathieu (1979) has used the evidence of abortion and infanticide among the Rukuba of Nigeria, of infanticide and adoption among the Mundugumor of New Guinea (Mead 1935), and of adoption among the Mossi of Burkina Faso to argue that maternity is also a social relationship. Becoming pregnant and bearing a child do not make a woman a mother because biological destiny can be socially averted both pre- and post-natally. Newman (1985) points out that cultural ideas about menstrual regularity, combined with the use of emmenagogues, allow women to regulate their fertility as an aspect of regulating menstruation. Use of any form of birth control brings out the social and cultural aspects of maternity because it makes clear that there are social situations in which births are seen as desirable and appropriate and others in which they are not. Birth control makes visible the distinction between biological procreation and social reproduction.

The clearest evidence for the social nature of the attribution of parenthood to particular people is in adoption, when the full rights and responsibilities of parenthood are transferred and the child's social and kinship position is transformed. Adoption in the contemporary United States is sometimes simply a reintegration of a child from an anomalous position into one in which the adoptive parents are complete substitutes for the "natural" parents, for instance after the death or desertion of the biological parents. Adoption also functions, however, as a way for people without children to become parents. The motivating force for this form of adoption is more the desire of the adults than the anomalous situation of the child. Motives of social reproduction are explicit in the Chinese practice of adopting a son to marry one's daughter and be both son and son-in-law in order to perpetuate the family name and lineage (Wolf and Huang 1980). In all these cases of adoption, a social person is created by appropriation, and people become parents in every sense other than the genetic.

Fosterage, which is employed as a blanket term for a variety of social arrangements (Goody 1978, 1982), is much more widespread than total adoption, particularly in Africa where it is an important feature of social structure (Page 1989). As Bledsoe argues from West African evidence, fosterage is bound up with people's life strategies and manipulation of political and economic claims on others (Bledsoe and Isiugo-Abanihe 1989; Bledsoe 1990). In some cases fosterage may be a substitute for biological fertility, but is usually deployed alongside it as part of a more general strategy. While fosterage provides further evidence for the social attribution of parenthood, at least in those variants where significant elements of the bundle of parental rights and responsibilities are transferred, its primary importance in my argument is as an example of social parenthood in the third sense—that is, the distribution of parenthood among several people or groups.

Social Determination of the Content and Distribution of Parenthood

The second and third senses in which parenthood is social are that the content of parenthood (the rights and responsibilities associated with the status) is socially determined, and that those rights and responsibilities are socially distributed. Content and distribution overlap in their application, and their relative significance will depend on the definition that is given to parenthood and on the perspective of a specific investigation.

Esther Goody, in her discussion of parenthood in West Africa, includes under "parenthood" all the things that have to be done "in producing a society's new recruits, and rearing them so that they can effectively assume adult roles in society" (1978:230). With this definition, the question of the distribution of rights and responsibilities between statuses and institutions becomes most salient, but variation in content remains both between and within societies. In any comparative analysis we must consider variation in parenthood along the two dimensions of content and distribution. We ask, that is, how the content of parenthood varies between societies and within them, and how the distribution of that content also varies.

For example, formal education is a necessary element of parenthood in literate, industrial societies, and must be provided if children are to "effectively assume adult roles." Formal education has not always existed, however, and there remain some societies in which it is not necessary. It is therefore an element that may or may not be part of the content of parenthood in Goody's broad definition. In terms of distribution, different societies may distribute responsibility for formal education differentially between individual parents, other people, churches, and the state. Distribution will vary also within societies. In the United States, the general remark that formal education is an element of parenthood that is the responsibility of the state would need to be modified to take account of class-specific notions of "responsible parenthood" which make the provision of private education a part of individual parental status.

Goody's approach of defining parenthood broadly and functionally is eminently suitable for cross-cultural comparison since it allows aspects of parenthood to be analyzed within a framework or list of categories not embedded in any particular cultural context. It has the added advantage of bringing to our attention functions and elements of social organizations that we might not think of as parental. For instance, protection of the child's physical person from external violence, and exacting retribution for violence that did occur, would be an element of parenthood distributed variously to kin groups, feudal patrons, or the state.

The disadvantages to so broad a definition of parenthood, and to the accompanying salience of the distribution of functions throughout the social

structure, are: (1) that all elements of society may be included within parenthood, (2) that clear-cut analytic categories may be blurred in actual societies,
and (3) that the categories used in analysis may be meaningless to the people
being analyzed. When our interest is in motivation, or in the direct provision
of goods and services to children, we will want to deploy a more restricted and
perhaps culturally specific definition of parenthood. In her own investigation
of parenthood, Goody concentrates on those elements of the broader definition that are linked to the physical presence of the child. That is, her discussion
of the distribution of parental activities follows children as they move for
schooling, apprenticeship, and to create and reinforce the social position of
adults (1978).

There is a danger that any restricted approach to parenthood will col-
lapse into the tautology that parenthood is what parents do. As we approach
that restricted definition, the variation of the content of parenthood assumes
greater significance, and the distribution of that content becomes less apparent
and may become invisible. Attention to parenthood as a socially constructed
status rather than a biologically given attribute, however, allows an examination of parenthood from within a cultural context as well as from an external
analytic position. Keesing (1970) describes how he used the "natural experiments" provided by atypical instances of foster, step, and adoptive fatherhood
to separate "the role of the Kwaio father" into constituent identities. Keesing
found that what was usually included in the single category "father" could be
separated both analytically by him, and in practice by the Kwaio themselves,
into the elements of head of household, jural guardian, jural father (transmit-
ter of kinship position, rights, and property), and nonjural father (provider of
support and subsistence). Keesing argues that it was through the study of the
distribution of these identities among different men in atypical cases that he
was able to understand the much more common case in which the identities
were merged in a single man. "By focusing on the typical, we sacrifice the
power to understand the atypical. The 'building blocks' approach reveals how
and why the typical occurs, while rendering intelligible the full range of possibility" (1970:440).

Both the focus of our investigation and our definition of parenthood determine the relative salience of content variation and distribution. In comparative
or analytic investigations we will define parenthood broadly and focus on
variation in the distribution of rights and responsibilities towards children; in
investigations of local meanings and motivations we will define parenthood
more narrowly and will notice variations in the content of the status of parent.
In any thoroughgoing analysis we must proceed from both directions, asking
not only what parents are expected to do for and claim from children, but also
how all the other needs of children are to be provided, and how the benefits to
be derived from them are to be distributed.

Cross-cultural and historical comparisons provide evidence on the variability of parenthood along all three dimensions. The six-culture study of child-rearing directed by Beatrice and John Whiting (Whiting 1963) revealed not only the diversity of patterns of parental responsibility, but also the peculiar focus of parenthood in the United States on an isolated and unsupported mother. Of the six cultures, parenthood in the white middle class of the United States (which provides the implicit cultural context for demographic theorizing about fertility) was the most firmly attributed to biological parents, and the least distributed. Demos (1986) and Pleck and Pleck (1980) describe the history of fatherhood in the United States in terms of the changing content in the role of the father, with the central aspect being variously moral guide, pedagogue, benefactor, controller, companion, moral support to the mother, child-rearer, provider, and friend. Changing cultural norms for the division of moral labor between fathers and mothers have accompanied changes in legal and social relations, with a shift in the natural or custodial parent from father to mother.

These examples illustrate the social nature of parenthood and emphasize that what is frequently labeled "fertility" in demographic models is in fact not a biological event but a socially constructed relationship of parenthood. Parenthood as a status and relationship does not require, nor is it necessitated by, a biological connection. On the other hand, social reproduction, as brought about through parenthood, does require that new individuals be created. Since demographic theories of fertility are concerned with the link between new biological individuals and social institutions, it follows that fertility must be considered a social relationship with strong similarities to parenthood. In the next section I describe the similarities and connections between fertility and parenthood through the sustained examination of a single example from the contemporary United States.

A Contemporary Example of Social Parenthood and Fertility

The complexities of social parenthood, and some of the consequences for analysis of fertility, are illustrated concretely in the following exchange between advice columnist Ann Landers and one of her correspondents. Examination of this story reveals how the rights and responsibilities associated with parenthood are distributed among a variety of people, and also how the claims of these people are in conflict and competition. As this example makes clear, parenthood is contested terrain in which the unambiguous ascription of biological fertility is only one element.

> Dear Ann,
>   My husband of two years and I get along great except for one problem that is driving me nuts.
>   "Kevin" was married before we met. He had no children with "Belle," but she has two daughters from her previous marriage. Kevin helped raise these girls since they were toddlers.

These ex-stepdaughters are now 12 and 14. They look to Kevin for everything. Their father doesn't pay child support regularly, so they ask Kevin for money for bikes, clothes, CDs, and even school lunches. The girls call Kevin "Dad." He helps them with their homework, runs errands and takes them and their friends to the mall.

They refuse to have any kind of relationship with their real father or their mother's current husband, although both men have tried.

Kevin and I want to have a family of our own. I'm afraid his relationship with his ex-stepdaughters will diminish his interest in OUR children.

I feel strongly that parents should be responsible for the financial, emotional and other needs of their children. I don't understand why Kevin's ex-wife and her husband are unable to provide these things for them. On the other hand, Kevin doesn't seem to mind that the girls pretend he's their father. I think they are working him for all they can get.

Which of us is right? Should Kevin give up being a pretend-dad to his ex-stepdaughters, or is it perfectly okay to continue this relationship? How can we work this out?

—Frustrated in Utah

[Ann Landers replied:] Since Kevin helped raise these girls, they consider him their father, and apparently, he feels very close to them. If you attempt to interfere with this relationship, you will find yourself on the outside looking in.

Kevin, however, should not be supporting the girls. This is the responsibility of Belle and the children's father. And it is perfectly okay for you to tell him so. In fact, I recommend it.[2]

We should first of all note that the two children have remained, through divorces and remarriages, with their biological mother. Legal decisions about custody and the default parent have reinforced the optional status of fatherhood in the United States and the cultural emphasis on the basic biological bond between women and children. Recently, well-publicized custody decisions have undermined the mother's position as natural custodial parent in cases where the father contests custody, but they have not affected the position of women as the default parent, the optional status of paternal custody (men have the option of seeking custody), or the legal centrality of biological relationships. As I have argued, however, neither the biological relationship nor our own cultural emphasis on it should conceal the social nature of parenthood.

While this little story features two women, three men, and two children, and is perhaps already complex enough, the facts we have are only part of a larger network of relationships. In particular, we may imagine that Belle's first and current husbands have, over the last fourteen years, had relationships with women and children who are not included in this account. As it is, both men appear only briefly in the narrative, but their lives may well have been as eventful as those of Kevin and Belle. For instance, Belle's first husband may have remarried and may have had more biological children, or may have adopted or become stepparent to a new wife's children. We may then wonder about the relationship he has with these new children, and may temper our first impression that he is a neglectful father with the consideration that he has different classes of children to whom he may stand as father in different ways. We might also wonder if his (hypothetical) current wife has concerns about the effects his relationship with his biological children may have on the quality of his relationship with his new family. From this perspective, "Frustrated" and the second wife, not to mention Belle and two sets of siblings, all have interests in the man's family activities.

Fatherhood in this account is socially determined in all three of the dimensions I have considered. The biological father has apparently played very little part in the physical or emotional sides of rearing his daughters. "Frustrated" combines the "financial, emotional, and other needs" of children as the responsibility of the "parents" and goes on to say that they should be met by "Kevin's ex-wife and her husband"—that is, by the biological mother and her current mate. "Frustrated" also refers to the biological father as the "real father" but is not clear about what role she thinks he should play. Ann Landers acknowledges the division of fathering into two aspects: one of closeness, which she sees as the result of Kevin's association with and parenting of the girls, and one of support, which she attributes to the biological mother and father. (The biological father, however, seems to have done little to support his children financially, and that burden is more likely, as "Frustrated" assumes, to be borne by the biological mother and her current husband.)

In the attribution of fatherhood, there are three possible claimants: (1) the biological father, who has contributed relatively little, (2) Kevin, who, by virtue of the labor of fathering, has established an emotional relationship and who, for a number of years, presumably shared the financial costs, and (3) the biological mother's current husband, who has taken on the "package deal" of wife and children.[3] For different people, and in different contexts, each of these men may be considered the father.

The content of fatherhood is distributed between these three men and is differentially distributed by the different parties concerned. For "Frustrated," none of the content should be with her husband; for her own reasons she wants to make a clear claim that children and parents should be exclusively related—a married couple and their coresident children. This clear-cut definition flies in the face of the facts of the relationships. This story is a single example selected for its clarity. It is, however, illustrative of very widespread social patterns. Divorce and remarriage are common features of family life in the United States (Cherlin 1981), affecting the lives of millions of parents and children (Furstenberg and Cherlin 1991). The complicated patterns of relationship that result from stories just like Kevin and Belle's are described by Stacey (1990).

The distribution of parenthood is not only the result of impersonal rules and social processes, but also of previous actions. Notably, in this situation, the children themselves are active participants in the creation of parenthood. This is something frequently ignored in analyses of parenthood that treat it as an attribute of a parent rather than, in an elementary application of role theory, as (at least) a dyadic relationship.

The fertility implications of the distribution of fatherhood, which are what will be of interest to demographers, follow the distribution of the content of the relationship. It is because of this that demographers cannot afford to ignore the complexities of social relationships. The current costs of the children in this story, and the current and future benefits to be derived from them, have been variously apportioned over their lives. So also has their presence in an accounting of fertility.

Belle's fertility has been perhaps least problematic, having moved simply from zero, to one, and then to two, where it has stayed. Her first husband's fertility, however, is more open to question: has his reproductive behavior since his divorce from Belle been conditioned by the existence of two biological children? The fertility status of Belle's subsequent relationships has also been determined by her own fertility in combination with that of her husbands. Among the questions to be asked are whether the absence of biological children in her marriage with Kevin was in any way caused by the existence of children from a previous marriage. That is, in looking at marital fertility, should we consider Belle's fertility (two previous births), Kevin's (no biological births), or that of the couple (two custodial children)? We may then ask the same question of Kevin's second marriage. His current wife states the situation very clearly: "[we] want to have a family of our own. I'm afraid his relationship with his ex-stepdaughters will diminish his interest in OUR children." That is, "Frustrated" is concerned with the fertility status of her own union. Biologically both husband and wife have zero fertility, but Kevin's social paternity, even at one remove, is influencing the context in which the future fertility of this couple is being considered.

Conclusion—The Implications for Fertility Studies

Fertility and parenthood are in analogous positions in their respective disciplines, for they function similarly as key elements in those small local groups variously seen as families, households, and domestic units. It is within these small groups that the creation of new people is centered, and these groups are the focus of much attention in attempts to link social phenomena at the micro and macro levels. For demography and social science, an adequate definition must make central the fact that fertility describes a relationship and is not simply an attribute of an individual. A person does not "have" some particular fertility all on his or her own; fertility is a description of relationships with offspring. Indeed, a person's fertility is a description of a place in a web of relationships with offspring, with other kin, and with a range of social groups and institutions. The analogy between parenthood and fertility may be extended. The three dimensions along which parenthood is socially constructed may also be applied to a socialized concept of fertility.

To consider first the attribution of fertility, births can not be unproblematically attributed to the women who bore them if we are interested in either the causes or consequences of these births. Evidence of this may be found particularly in adoption, but also in fosterage and stepparenthood. It has been an accepted fact in anthropology that fatherhood is social, and much of culture and social organization is explained by men's attempts to guarantee their rights to children. But maternity is also social, as abortion, infanticide, adoption, and stepparenthood have demonstrated for a long time and as new reproductive technologies forcibly make clear.[4] Histories of illegitimacy emphasize the social determination of the transition to parenthood within the context of a system of marriage and inheritance (Laslett, Oosterveen, and Smith 1980; Kertzer 1993). Demographic theory has made fertility both a cause and an effect—for instance, in the way achieved fertility feeds back upon contraception to produce parity-specific control as the major feature of declines in fertility. For this feedback loop to operate as proposed, fertility must be attributable to a couple unambiguously, but socializing fertility reveals that this attribution must be examined rather than taken for granted.

Variability in the content of fertility is also socially determined. This is recognized in some demographic treatments of the costs and values of children, which find differences between populations and between men and women.[5] But psychological or cultural values of children have taken a back seat in demographic analysis, and the culturally variable economic returns of child labor or old age support (Cain 1981; Nag, White, and Peet 1978) have had to compete for theoretical recognition with an assumption of unchanging tastes (Becker 1976). Seeing fertility as social allows us to include a range of values and costs. Though not all values and costs operate in all contexts, all must be considered. Of the three dimensions of variability in social fertility, demographic studies have been most successful in acknowledging the variable content of the relationship, and in using variation in content to explain variation in fertility levels. However, lack of attention to variability in the attribution and distribution of fertility has limited the effectiveness of these analyses.

The distribution of fertility, the third dimension of variability, is the most subversive of the biologically-based definition of fertility. Attribution of fertility to a single individual is compatible with the accounting procedures of mathematical demography, and variation in the costs and benefits of fertility can frequently be handled within an economic framework (Easterlin 1978). Demographic techniques have been much less successful in attributing fertility to two people, one male and one female, simultaneously. One implication of seeing fertility as a social relationship is that the inclusion of men in fertility studies is made easier as well as more necessary. Demographic models of fertility function adequately as accounting procedures while considering only women, but analysis of social relationships with a one-sex model is doomed to distortion.

To see fertility as a social relationship, and as distributed between people, is to see fertility not as fixed and unproblematic but as subject to negotiation and renegotiation between people: to see it inevitably as a social relationship. Bledsoe (1990) cites Berry's observations on competing claims to tree crops in Nigeria as an example of the way in which certain social relationships are better understood in terms of claims than of rights. Negotiated and renegotiated ambivalence in ownership is a source of social cohesion as well as conflict (Mauss 1967). I observed a similar process in Botswana, where discussion of cattle ownership is a major occupation, and the definition of claims on particular animals is an idiom for talking about relationships between people (cf. Comaroff and Roberts 1981:175–215). Bledsoe, like Esther Goody, emphasizes how distributed parenthood strengthens and transforms social relationships.

Sexual relationships are subject to cultural norms and rules, creating new social units and linking existing ones. Children are born into a nexus of social links, and the way they are socially positioned transforms the network. One specific anthropological contribution in this area has been to emphasize the importance of other people, particularly senior kin, in decisions about sexual relations, use of birth control, and resource allocation to children, which demographic theories have assumed to be the province of couples alone. Another contribution has been to demonstrate that the costs and benefits of children accrue to others besides the biological parents. A broad approach to the distribution of fertility in all its aspects will allow, among other benefits, a more realistic treatment of the externalities of childbearing, of intergenerational relations and equity, and of the relationship between the family and the state. To understand fertility motivation and fertility levels, we must investigate the claims made on children, the negotiation of these competing claims, and the alternative strategies for achieving the values that are claimed from children. To do so involves us immediately in analyses of relations of power, and gives a redefined notion of fertility a central place in political economy.

I have argued that, for anthropology, parenthood is a social relationship embedded in a matrix of other relationships. Who is defined as a parent, the rights and responsibilities associated with that status, and the ways in which those rights and responsibilities are shared or competed for, are all social phenomena. If fertility is to be a theoretically useful category for linking biological reproduction to social forces, human action, and motivation, it must also be reconstructed as a social category.

NOTES

1. By "moment" I mean to acknowledge, but not to accentuate, the way that reproduction occurs at a point in time. My emphasis is rather on the meaning of reproduction as an element of a whole, an aspect of a process, and a turning point in a qualitative transformation.

2. Ann Landers, "Children Still Lean on Ex-Stepdad," *Providence Journal*, 16 August 1994, E6.

3. I have discussed the idea of the "package deal" as a description of fatherhood and as an element in the male life course in an account of family formation in a California community (Townsend 1992). Constituent elements of the package are that men discuss their relationships with their children as operating through their wives, and that marriage, children, employment, and home ownership are linked in their picture of a successful life.

4. *In vitro* fertilization of an embryo which is then implanted in the uterus of a woman who is not the source of the egg, but who carries the fetus to term, separates a genetic mother from a birth mother in the same way that adoption separates a biological mother from a social mother. In both cases the identity so often assumed to be necessary is revealed as contingent.

5. Values of children have usually been described in terms of psychological states and social identities (e.g., Arnold et al. 1975), while variable costs and benefits have generally been economic (e.g., Cain 1981; and the industry inspired by Caldwell 1982).

REFERENCES

Arnold, Fred, Rodolfo Bulatao, Chalio Buripakdi, Betty Jamie Chung, James T. Fawcett, Toshio Iritani, Sung Jin Lee, and Tsong-Shien Wu. 1975. *The Value of Children: A Cross-national Study*. Honolulu: East-West Center.

Becker, Gary. 1976. *The Economic Approach to Human Behavior*. Chicago: University of Chicago Press.

Birdsall, Nancy, Bryan Boulier, W. Parker Mauldin, Robert J. Lapham, and David Wheeler. 1985. *The Effects of Family Planning Programs on Fertility in the Developing World*. World Bank Staff Working Paper No. 677. Washington, D.C.: World Bank.

Bledsoe, Caroline. 1990. "The Politics of Children: Fosterage and the Social Management of Fertility among the Mende of Sierra Leone." In *Births and Power: Social Change and the Politics of Reproduction*, ed. Penn Handwerker, 81–100. Boulder, Colo.: Westview Press.

Bledsoe, Caroline, and Uche Isiugo-Abanihe. 1989. "Strategies of Child-fosterage among Mende Grannies in Sierra Leone." In *Reproduction and Social Organization in Sub-Saharan Africa*, ed. Ron J. Lesthaeghe, 442–74. Berkeley: University of California Press.

Bongaarts, John. 1978. "A Framework for Analyzing the Proximate Determinants of Fertility." *Population and Development Review* 4:105–32.

Bourdieu, Pierre. 1977. *Outline of a Theory of Practice*. Cambridge: Cambridge University Press.

Bourdieu, Pierre, and Jean-Claude Passeron. 1990. *Reproduction in Education, Society, and Culture*. 2d ed. Newbury Park: Sage.

Cain, Mead. 1981. "Risk and Insurance: Perspectives on Fertility and Agrarian Change in India and Bangladesh." *Population and Development Review* 7:435–74.

Caldwell, John C. 1982. *Theory of Fertility Decline.* New York: Academic Press.

Cherlin, Andrew. 1981. *Marriage, Divorce, Remarriage.* Cambridge: Harvard University Press.

Cochrane, Susan H. 1979. *Fertility and Education: What Do We Really Know?* World Bank Staff Occasional Papers No. 26. Washington D.C.: World Bank.

Collier, Jane F., and Sylvia J. Yanagisako. 1987. "Toward a Unified Theory of Gender and Kinship." In *Gender and Kinship: Essays Towards a Unified Theory,* ed. Jane F. Collier and Sylvia J. Yanagisako, 14–50. Stanford: Stanford University Press.

Comaroff, John L., and Simon Roberts. 1981. *Rules and Processes: The Cultural Logic of Dispute in an African Context.* Chicago: University of Chicago Press.

Demos, John. 1986. "The Changing Faces of Fatherhood." In *Past, Present, and Personal: The Family and the Life Course in American History,* John Demos, 46–67. New York: Oxford University Press.

Easterlin, Richard. 1978. "The Economics and Sociology of Fertility: A Synthesis." In *Historical Studies in Changing Fertility,* ed. Charles Tilly. Princeton: Princeton University Press.

———. 1980. *Birth and Fortune.* New York: Basic Books.

Easterlin, Richard A., and Eileen M. Crimmins. 1985. *The Fertility Revolution: A Supply-Demand Analysis.* Chicago: University of Chicago Press.

Fortes, Meyer. 1949. "Time and Social Structure: An Ashanti Case Study." In *Social Structure: Essays Presented to Radcliffe-Brown,* ed. Meyer Fortes. Oxford: Oxford University Press.

———. 1958. Introduction to *The Developmental Cycle in Domestic Groups,* ed. Jack Goody. Cambridge: Cambridge University Press.

Fox, Robin. 1967. *Kinship and Marriage: An Anthropological Perspective.* Harmondsworth: Penguin.

Freedman, Ronald, Richard Easterlin, Jane Menken, Robert Willis, Robert Lapham, and Rudolfo Bulatao. 1983. "A Framework for the Study of Fertility Determinants." In *Determinants of Fertility in Developing Countries. Volume 1. Supply and Demand for Children,* ed. Rudolfo Bulatao and Ronald D. Lee. New York: Academic Press.

Furstenberg, Frank F., and Andrew Cherlin. 1991. *Divided Families: What Happens to Children When Parents Part.* Cambridge: Harvard University Press.

Goodenough, Ward. 1970. "Epilogue: Transactions in Parenthood." In *Adoption in Eastern Oceania,* ed. Vern Carroll. Honolulu: University of Hawaii Press.

Goody, Esther. 1978. "Some Theoretical and Empirical Aspects of Parenthood in West Africa. In *Marriage, Fertility, and Parenthood in West Africa,* ed. Christine Oppong, Gemma Adaba, Manga Bekembo-Priso, and John Mogey, 227–72. Canberra: Australian National University.

———. 1982. *Parenthood and Social Reproduction: Fostering and Occupational Roles in West Africa.* Cambridge: Cambridge University Press.

Goody, Jack. 1976. *Production and Reproduction: A Comparative Study of the Domestic Domain.* Cambridge: Cambridge University Press.

Gough, Kathleen. 1959. "The Nayars and the Definition of Marriage." *Journal of the Royal Anthropological Institute* 89:23–34.

Hammel, Eugene A. 1990. "A Theory of Culture for Demography." *Population and Development Review* 16:455–85.

Keesing, Roger M. 1970. "Toward a Model of Role Analysis." In *A Handbook of Method in Cultural Anthropology,* ed. Raoul Naroll and Ronald Cohen, 423–53. Garden City, New York: Natural History Press.

Kertzer, David I. 1993. *Sacrificed for Honor: Italian Infant Abandonment and the Politics of Reproductive Control.* Boston: Beacon Press.

Laslett, Peter, Karla Oosterveen, and Richard M. Smith, eds. 1980. *Bastardy and Its Comparative History.* Cambridge: Harvard University Press.

Linton, Ralph. 1936. *The Study of Man.* New York: Appleton-Century.

Lutz, Wolfgang. 1989. *Distributional Aspects of Human Fertility: A Global Comparative Study.* New York: Academic Press.

Malinowski, Bronislaw. 1929. *The Sexual Life of Savages.* New York: Harcourt, Brace, and World.

Mathieu, Nicole-Claude. 1979. "Biological Paternity, Social Maternity: On Abortion and Infanticide as Unrecognized Indicators of the Cultural Character of Maternity." *Sociological Review Monograph* 28:232–40.

Mauss, Marcel. 1967 [1925]. *The Gift: Forms and Functions of Exchange in Archaic Societies.* New York: Norton.

Mead, Margaret. 1935. *Sex and Temperament in Three Primitive Societies.* New York: William Morrow.

Modell, Judith. 1986. "In Search: The Purported Biological Basis of Parenthood." *American Ethnologist* 13:646–61.

Montagu, Ashley. 1937. *Coming into Being among the Australian Aborigines.* London: Routledge.

Nag, Moni, Benjamin. N. F. White, and Richard C. Peet. 1978. "An Anthropological Approach to the Study of the Economic Value of Children in Java and Nepal." *Current Anthropology* 19:293–306.

Newman, Lucile F. 1985. "Context Variables in Fertility Regulation." In *Women's Medicine: A Cross-Cultural Study of Indigenous Fertility Regulation,* ed. Lucile F. Newman and James M. Nyce, 179–91. New Brunswick, N.J.: Rutgers University Press.

Ortner, Sherry. 1984. "Theory in Anthropology Since the Sixties." *Comparative Studies in Society and History* 26:126–66.

Page, Hilary. 1989. "Childrearing Versus Childbearing: Coresidence of Mother and Child in Sub-Saharan Africa." In *Reproduction and Social Organization in Sub-Saharan Africa,* ed. Ron J. Lesthaeghe, 401–41. Berkeley: University of California Press.

Pleck, Elizabeth H., and Joseph H. Pleck. 1980. Introduction to *The American Man,* ed. Elizabeth H. Pleck and Joseph H. Pleck, 1–49. Englewood Cliffs: Prentice-Hall.

Rofman, Rafael. 1992. "How Reduced Demand for Children and Access to Family Planning Accelerated the Fertility Decline in Colombia." Working Paper 924. Washington, D.C.: World Bank.

Ryder, Norman B. 1980. "Components of Temporal Variations in American Fertility." In *Demographic Patterns in Developed Societies,* ed. Robert W. Hiorns, 15–54. London: Taylor and Francis.

Schapera, Isaac. 1971 [1940]. *Married Life in an African Tribe.* Harmondsworth: Penguin Books.

Schneider, David M. 1968. *American Kinship: A Cultural Account.* Englewood Cliffs, N.J.: Prentice Hall.

———. 1984. *A Critique of the Concept of Kinship.* Ann Arbor: University of Michigan Press.

Schofield, Roger, and David Coleman. 1986. Introduction to *The State of Population Theory: Forward from Malthus,* ed. David Coleman and Roger Schofield, 1–13. Oxford: Blackwell.

Stacey, Judith. 1990. *Brave New Families: Stories of Domestic Upheaval in Late Twentieth Century America.* New York: Basic Books.

Townsend, Nicholas. 1992. "Paternity Attitudes of a Cohort of Men in the United States: Cultural Values and Demographic Implications." Ph.D. diss., University of California, Berkeley.

Townsend, Nicholas, and Anita Ilta Garey. 1994. "Men, Households, and Children in Botswana: An Exploration of Connections over Time and Space." Paper presented at the annual meeting of the Population Association of America, Miami, May 1994.

van de Walle, Etienne, and Andrew Foster. 1990. *Fertility Decline in Africa: Assessment and Prospects.* Washington, D.C.: World Bank.

Watkins, Susan Cotts. 1986. "Conclusion." In *The Decline of Fertility in Europe,* ed. Ansley J. Coale and Susan Cotts Watkins, 420–49. Princeton: Princeton University Press.

Whiting, Beatrice B., ed. 1963. *Six Cultures: Studies of Child Rearing.* New York: Wiley.

Wolf, Arthur P., and Chieh-Shan Huang. 1980. *Marriage and Adoption in China, 1854–1945.* Stanford: Stanford University Press.

Chapter Five

Similarities and Differences: Anthropological and Demographic Perspectives on Gender

Nancy E. Riley

In anthropology, the study of gender has received sustained attention for over two decades. Jane Guyer (1991) has described the work on gender in anthropology as consisting of at least three phases. First, she argues, "the intellectual space to cultivate gender studies within anthropology was created by a series of bold and sweeping attacks on the undergrowth of naturalistic assumptions, reporting biases, and sheer neglect of the topic" (1991:257). From there, feminist anthropology moved to develop theories, drawing on work outside the field and experimenting with new concepts and empirical approaches. Feminist anthropologists are now working to "explore the space created and decide how to use it" (1991:257).

In demography, we are still at the early stage of trying to create intellectual space for gender studies. Demographers working on data from a wide variety of societies and historical periods have begun to express interest in understanding the role of gender in demographic processes. However, demography has barely begun to address the neglect of attention to gender within the field, there have been few bold and sweeping attacks, and very little borrowing from work on gender in other fields. But is developing a gendered demography—a feminist demography—a necessary endeavor? Is it in the interest of demographers in general? Answers to these questions come from examination of the development of gender studies in anthropology and the potential parallels in demography.

As fields, demography and anthropology share some similarities, but there are also significant differences between them, differences that may partly account for the lag in demography. In this chapter I will explore some of those differences. I will highlight one issue that is key to both anthropology and demography, given the cross-cultural focus of both, an issue that is central to discussions within feminist theory as well,[1] namely, how each understands the differences and similarities among women.

The focus of this chapter is how work in anthropology can enrich demography's research on gender. I begin by looking at the status of gender studies in demography. I then explore developments of gender research in anthropology, their relationships with feminist theory generally, and the implications of this history and development for demography. I end by examining how the structures, philosophies, and methodologies of the two fields have contributed to the current situation of gender studies in each.

Gender in Demographic Research

Although research on women is certainly plentiful in demography, there is much less attention to gender. In fact, evidence from the demographic literature makes a strong case for distinguishing these two concepts, gender and women, and the contributions of each to our understanding of social processes.

Fertility studies are at the heart of demography, and, especially there, demography has amassed vast amounts of information on women's lives in the past few decades. But it is perhaps because of that focus on fertility and the rather narrow approach demographic studies have generally used to examine it that we have available information on only a few (albeit important) aspects of women's lives.

The World Fertility Survey (WFS) probably best represents the kinds of information on women's childbearing patterns available from demographic research (Cleland and Hobcraft 1985). From that survey alone, we have information from sixty-one countries on such variables as age at first marriage, contraceptive use, breastfeeding patterns, and number of children born and surviving. Numerous studies using these data have compared the family-building patterns and fertility preferences of women (and men) around the world.

Much less central to demographic research is attention to gender. The distinction between women and gender is important; gender is more than an individual attribute, more than a question of whether a person is male or female. Its more pervasive and important effect is at the societal level. Gender influences the way societies are organized, and it is part of all social institutions in any society—part of the economy, part of the institution of the family, part of the state. "The gender perspective simultaneously emphasizes the symbolic and the structural, the ideological and the material, the interactional and the institutional levels of analysis" (Ferree 1990:868). Gender in this sense is rarely a part of research in demography, even when that research is focused on women.

Attention to gender requires attention to the social and cultural context of fertility and other demographic behaviors. This context is not easily captured in large-scale surveys like the World Fertility Survey (WFS), the Demographic Health Surveys (DHS) or even many national surveys (Caldwell 1985); without that context, the meaning of fertility or the reasons for fertility change are difficult to discern.

Especially in recent years, demographers have tried to capture the effect of what is often termed "women's status" on demographic outcomes. Caldwell (1986), for example, has argued that women's status is one of the primary "routes to low mortality" in Third World countries. In much of such work, the effect of gender is measured at an individual level, by adding to the equation a variable or two purported to be an indicator of women's status.[2] These measures are rarely culturally specific, and because they are merely added to models (rather than using them to re-evaluate the model itself), rarely can account for or reflect the complexities of gender in any society.[3]

To develop a demography that attends to gender, there are several issues that need to be raised, discussed, and examined. I now turn to the development of gender in anthropology to highlight the importance of these issues.

The Development of Gender Theory in Anthropology

Studying the history of gender theory in anthropology is useful to demography for several reasons. First, the theoretical discussions in anthropology have both influenced and been influenced by empirical approaches and methodology in ways which might be paralleled in demography. Second, tracing the history of feminist anthropology makes it clear how transformative these debates and projects have been to anthropology as a field. Third, and perhaps most importantly, the development of gender theory and feminist anthropology has produced issues, arguments, and perspectives which are useful in the study of demographic processes as well. Particularly important have been discussions about understanding gender as a social construction and the conversations about universals and differences among women.

In keeping with the general approach of anthropology (Rosaldo 1989), early feminist anthropologists began their focus on gender with an attempt to find similarity within cultural difference.[4] A number of anthropologists developed theories in an effort to understand the seemingly universal subordination of women. Rosaldo focused on the division of the public and private spheres in most societies, and argued that the subordination of women cross-culturally can be attributed to women's confinement to the private (Rosaldo 1974). Ortner (1974) connected women's reproductive functions with women's universal association with nature; she argued that women are subordinate to men in most cultures because culture, with which men are associated, is valued more highly. These early attempts to develop a subfield held to the rules and philosophy of anthropology and could be seen as an attempt to combat a male-dominated field and to garner evidence for a new field of gender studies within anthropology (Lamphere 1987:14; Quinn 1977).

Almost immediately, anthropologists began to question those unifying theories; within anthropology, evidence of differences among cultures was relatively easy to gather. Disagreements and critiques came from many directions. Some argued against the notion of universal female subordination (Schlegel 1977; Leacock 1981), while others argued that the theories developed to explain women's subordination were flawed (Rosaldo 1980) or were not supported when tested cross-culturally (MacCormack and Strathern 1980). Critiques of early theories and the development and testing of new perspectives relied on both broad-based studies of gender (e.g., Sanday 1981) and small-scale studies focused on single societies (e.g., Wolf 1972; Bledsoe 1980; Weiner 1976; Collier 1988; Shostak 1981). The interconnectedness of empirical, local studies on the one hand and theoretical pieces on the other helped to underscore the need to develop gender theory based on cultural specificities of gender and to understand the diversity of gender constructions among and even within different cultural settings.

Work at this stage of gender research and theory also relied on mainstays of anthropological theory and approaches (di Leonardo 1991), in particular the importance of seeing a society as a whole and seeing a behavior or action as part of that whole (Lutz 1988). For example, Rosaldo argued for attention to potentially different meanings of what might seem similar behavior: "women's place in human social life is not in any direct sense a product of the things she does, but of the meaning her activities acquire through concrete social action" (Rosaldo 1980:400). Such perspectives have led to further recognition of the difficulty and problematics of theories that tried to account for universal notions of gender (Mohanty 1991; MacCormack 1980).

The results of these endeavors in feminist anthropology also began to call into question basic assumptions in anthropology and contributed to new directions in the field as a whole (Shapiro 1983). Early discussions of the relationship between kinship and gender (Schneider 1984; Rubin 1975) led to Yanagisako and Collier's argument that anthropological studies of both kinship and gender are flawed by assumptions that "biological facts of sexual reproduction" underlie gender or kinship systems in any society (1987:15). Abu-Lughod (1991) has used the perspectives of feminists and "halfies" (people of mixed national or cultural identity) to redefine culture; she argues that anthropological perspectives of culture have served to underscore and create differences and hierarchies between "self" and "other."

In addition, in several self-reflective pieces, scholars have attempted to understand how some of the theories developed to explain the universal subordination of women were built on philosophy and values located in Western history and perspectives (Rosaldo 1980, 1989). Thus Collier and her colleagues addressed the connections between our current thinking and research on family and kinship and its origins in early Victorian notions of evolution, the role of women as nurturers, and ideas about the separate spheres of public and private (Collier, Rosaldo, and Yanagisako 1992; see Lamphere 1993; Tsing and Yanagisako 1983).

In many of these critiques, scholars have underscored the way that Western sciences (like anthropology) frame thinking and research through the use of dichotomies that are often unquestioned and yet are problematic in their ability to understand the complexities and differences of gender across cultures (Jay 1981; Yanagisako and Collier 1987; Rosaldo 1980). Errington, for example, has argued that Western observers often presume that other societies base their notions of gender on biological differences between male and female in a way that mirrors Western societies, rather than understanding that other societies may organize gender much differently, and may see gender differences as less important or based on other characteristics, such as work preferences (Whitehead 1981; Errington 1990).

As in many other disciplines (Harding 1991:51ff.; Stacey and Thorne 1985; Scott 1987–1988; Lutz 1990), feminist anthropologists have struggled with the reaction of their field to new feminist scholarship and have discussed how it is often ignored or criticized (Mascia-Lees, Sharpe, and Cohen 1989; Howell and Melhuus 1993; del Valle 1993; Strathern 1987). But however contested feminist work in anthropology might be, the study of gender within the field nevertheless has made progress and has seen success completely foreign to the field of demography. Feminist demographers are still trying to find intellectual space for their ideas within demography; one of the most common complaints from feminist anthropologists seems to be that feminist anthropology or the study of gender is accepted only as one of many anthropological perspectives and has not been as transformative of the field as a whole as they had hoped (Shapiro 1983; Strathern 1987).

Discussions within anthropology have paralleled and interacted with those in the more broadly defined field of feminist studies, and both anthropology and feminist studies have gained from these interactions. As feminist scholars within anthropology were working through the meaning and implications of difference, a similar discussion was at the center of many debates in feminist theory. Discussions about how to see both commonalities among women, which might allow political action, while at the same time recognizing differences among women because of their class, nationality, race, religion, or sexuality have been sources of tension, lively debate, and important scholarly works (Alcoff 1988; Haraway 1985; Spelman 1988).[5] Within feminist scholarship there is now a much stronger and more visible acknowledgment that there are as many differences among women as there are between women and men.

Work examining the implications of gender's socially constructed nature has been the site of one of the most fruitful interactions between feminist anthropology and feminist studies. From anthropology came solid support for differences in the meaning and shape of gender across cultures (Whitehead 1981; Rubin 1975; Martin 1987; MacCormack and Strathern 1980; Moore 1988; Ortner and Whitehead 1981)—evidence that has further underscored the importance of seeing beyond and through the biological differences of women and men as well as beyond any framework that reduces women's position to biological reproduction (Rosaldo 1980; Errington 1990; Yanagisako and Collier 1987).

In many respects, findings from feminist anthropology have strengthened the position of feminist poststructuralists—that is, those who emphasize the lack of unity within the concept of woman (Haraway 1985; Fraser and Nicholson 1990; Flax 1987; Seidman 1994). Feminist anthropology also has been an important contributor to poststructuralist perspectives on the role of experience in understanding women's situations; it has helped to shape discussions about the advantages and problems of using experience as evidence and the need to theorize beyond individual experience in order to understand the larger processes and influences of gender (Scott 1992; Ong 1987; Callaway 1992; Bell 1993).

Along with these substantive contributions, feminist anthropology has also contributed to the process of feminist theorizing. Feminist anthropology generally builds theory based on evidence collected from small areas, with appropriate attention to the context of gender relations in a society. The contributions from this work have been twofold: scholars began to understand the detailed context of gender organization better, and to see the importance and use of connections between theory and data—the process of combining culturally specific examples with theory that extends beyond a specific cultural example. Thus Errington's study of power and prestige in Southeast Asian cultures (1990) helps us to understand the difficulties of measuring women's status cross-culturally; whereas power in the West is related to economic control, activity, and coercive force, in many Southeast Asian societies those same characteristics suggest a lack of power and prestige. That comparative perspective, she argues, suggests that it would be misguided to measure women's power as a function of their economic or instrumental roles in all societies, for this would ignore the very important cultural differences that determine power in different societies.

Feminist anthropology has benefited from feminist theory as well. The development of feminist poststructuralist theory (Hartsock 1987) and the usefulness of that perspective in understanding connections and differences among women have shaped the ways that feminist anthropologists address issues within their field (Bell 1993; Gordon 1991; Kirby 1993; Mascia-Lees, Sharpe, and Cohen 1989; Strathern 1987). Discussions about what the role of the "postmodern turn" in anthropology might mean for the field and for the study of gender and women within it have been informed by work of feminist theories. Mascia-Lees and her colleagues, for example, argued that "what appear to be new and exciting insights to these new postmodernist anthropologists—that culture is composed of seriously contested codes of meaning, that language and politics are inseparable, and that constructing the 'other' entails relations of domination—are insights that have received repeated and rich exploration in feminist theory for the past forty years" (Mascia-Lees, Sharpe, and Cohen 1989:11).

Scholars in both feminist theory and feminist anthropology continue to struggle with what differences mean for the concept "woman" and for the fields of inquiry within which difference has been acknowledged. Questions about the political implications of an emphasis on difference rather than unity have been at the center of many writings (DiStefano 1991; Downs 1993; Scott 1993). If women are so different from one another, is there a way to rally around an issue that is common to women across cultures or groups? If not, how do feminists interested in political action effect change (Haraway 1988)? If and when we find differences among women, what do we do with those differences, how do we use them to understand a society more fully or to understand how gender is constructed? How do we understand and acknowledge the importance of individual experience without decontextualizing it from the social arena in which it occurs (Scott 1992; Callaway 1992)? As we have seen, in anthropology these kinds of questions have led on the one hand to rethinking notions of dichotomy, and on the other to understanding how we might better analyze relationships, similarities, and differences among women—differences based on a variety of social attributes such as race, nationality, class, and age (Moore 1993; Mohanty 1991; Lamphere 1993; Mukhopadhyay and Higgins 1988). The results of these examinations and debates have underscored both the ways and the difficulties of combining empirical evidence from individual societies or groups and the importance of broad-based theories.

Implications for Demography

What lessons do the findings and debates from feminist anthropology have for demography? Some of the potential implications for demography are more obvious than others. I want to discuss four aspects of the development of feminist anthropology that might have lessons for demography: methodological issues, the idea that the cultural/social context is necessary to understand human behavior, the particular argument that gender is a social construction, and feminist anthropology's productive relations with feminist studies. Each of these issues has important implications for demography.

One of the easiest cross-fertilizations between anthropology—feminist and other—and demography has been the use of anthropological data within demography. The cultural details surrounding birth, death, migration, or contraceptive use which have been provided by anthropologists have contributed to demography's understanding of these processes (Scheper-Hughes 1992; Massey et al. 1987; Ginsburg and Rapp 1991; Greenhalgh 1994; Browner 1986), and account for the increasing acceptance of some of the methodologies used by demography (Caldwell 1985; Knodel, Chamratrithirong, and Debavalya 1987:13ff.).

However, although there is some recognition within demography of the importance and contribution of anthropological method, the role of methodology in understanding gender and developing new perspectives on gender has not been the subject of much discussion in demography to date; such discussions would be helpful as part of a debate about how demography could refocus its study of gender. Barrett and Phillips argued that (in social sciences generally) attention to differences among women has led to an interest in micro-level analyses, an approach, they claim, that lends "itself better to complex interplay of different aspects of inequality" (1992:4). Others have also argued that the ethnographic approach allows attention to the processes and complexities involved in gender constructions, ideologies, and resistance (Wolf 1993:17, 173ff.). Although large-scale survey data collection is useful for certain aspects of any study of gender, we must consider whether demography's near-total allegiance to large-scale quantitative survey methods has contributed to its difficulty in tackling issues of gender in any depth. Susan Greenhalgh characterized such surveys as having a "lack of flexibility, inability to probe sensitive matters, [and neglecting] . . . social, cultural and economic context" (1990:92); she argued that anthropologists, on the other hand, employ methods that are more likely to bring "the full range of social, cultural, economic, and political processes into the picture" (1990:91; see also Greenhalgh 1995; Stacey and Thorne 1985).

Other social scientists have discussed the difficulties of using the types of methods and data most common in demography to understand human behavior. In the process of analyzing data and in the development of models to explain behavior, characteristics and behavior are often removed from their social, economic, and cultural context. In discussing the problems inherent in this approach, one scholar argues that "it is not possible to decontextualize a phenomenon without changing its significance. Thus research should be conducted insofar as possible without violating the social embeddedness of the subject" (Gergen 1988:89).

Data gathered through large-scale surveys obviously have much to add to our understanding of gender. But we need to recognize the contribution that intense ethnographic work has made to the development of thoughtful and far-reaching theories on gender in anthropology. Sandra Harding (1987) has argued that methods and theory are linked, and that the ways gender is conceptualized have, in fact, led different fields to different methods of collecting data and evidence. "For example, discussions of how sociobiology, or psychoanalytic theory, or Marxist political economy, or phenomenology should be used to understand various aspects of women and gender addressed by different disciplines are methodology discussions that lead to distinctive research agendas—including ways of gathering evidence" (1987:22).

That demographers have begun to see the value of anthropological method is important. It is possible that new methodologies in demographic research might open a door to other changes in the way that demography conceptualizes gender. However, working in both directions—developing theories on gender that suggest new methods of collecting data even as data collection informs our changing perspectives on gender—would produce an even richer understanding of the impact of gender on demographic outcomes.

Furthermore, demography adds important perspectives to current methodological debates. There would be benefits to all concerned if demographers were to be part of both discussions about the advantages and disadvantages of qualitative methods, and discussions that focus on the linkages and similarities between qualitative and quantitative methods (Jayaratne and Stewart 1991; Cook and Fonow 1990). We also need to begin discussions about how to use the large-scale surveys so common in demography in new ways that could be especially illuminating to issues of gender (Entwisle and Coles 1990). These surveys offer a breadth and statistical depth unavailable from most anthropological data collection. Such discussions, which are likely to be very different than those taking place within anthropology, could add valuable input to the exchanges between feminists working in anthropology and demography.

One of the central contributions that anthropology can make to demography is its emphasis on studying behavior within its cultural and social context—the idea that understanding the society as a whole is key to understanding any part of it. That approach is often missing from demography (Greenhalgh 1990; Riley 1994). For the study of gender, such an approach is a fundamental necessity; Evelyn Fox Keller has argued that the recognition of gender as a cultural construction is contemporary feminist theory's most important contribution (Keller 1989; Connell 1985).

Findings from feminist anthropology and feminist theory contain some useful warnings to demographers about how women and gender should be brought into models of demographic change. Especially important are arguments about why additive models are not widely accepted in either feminist anthropology or feminist theory (Shapiro 1983). Gender takes on different meanings in different contexts and among different groups; thus, for example, in the United States an African American woman is not like a white woman in everything except her race (Spelman 1988), but rather her race and gender interact in significant ways. Seeing gender as more than the property of individuals—seeing it as a principle of social organization—allows such a perspective (Stacey and Thorne 1985).

Those interested in gender in demography can learn from the struggles that have taken place within anthropology and feminist studies. These debates have been important to our understanding of gender. Theories develop, are challenged, and are redeveloped based on new evidence or different interpretations of earlier evidence. I have outlined those debates not because scholars have been able to define gender or its influence succinctly or to find universal traits which define, influence, or underlie gender inequality or ideology; rather, their significance lies in how the discussions and disagreements themselves have served to deepen our understanding of gender and its complexities.

The substance of the debates, however, is also important. In their efforts to find cross-cultural similarities and patterns, feminist anthropologists (and others) have come to emphasize the difficulty of doing so. This process and its outcome are a powerful suggestion to demography about the problems of trying to find universal meaning in "women's status," let alone a measure of status that can be used cross-culturally. If, as Lamphere argues, debate over the universal subordination of women has reached a dead end within feminist studies (1987:23), what does this imply for demographers who continue to focus on finding cross-cultural patterns and similarities? We have to consider whether demographers are doing just what anthropologists have warned against, "speak[ing] of the statuses of 'men' and 'women' as though they could be discerned globally, not only assum[ing] that 'status' is measurable cross-culturally but also presuppos[ing] that the species falls into two natural categories, 'men' and 'women' without any cultural 'work' or interpretation to construct these categories" (Errington 1990:9).

It is also necessary for demographers to understand how vital anthropology's connections to other fields have been in its development of gender studies, and how these interdisciplinary discussions have enriched the fields of both anthropology and feminist studies. Demography has played a much smaller role in the development of gender theory, and demographers have been less willing to borrow from and use feminist studies. Demography has much to gain by doing so, and can also make vital contributions to the debates within feminist theory. The lack of contact with current debates in feminist theory or cultural studies is particularly notable because of demography's claim as a field with cross-disciplinary influences and cross-cultural focal points. Unfortunately, its lack of participation in these debates to date may make it more difficult to enter them at this point.

A demography informed and influenced by developments in feminist anthropology would have several features currently absent or underrepresented in demography. Instead of emphasizing a search for a universal definition of women's status (Mason 1987) or examining similarities across societies (Caldwell 1986), demography might borrow anthropology's insight that "gender systems are embedded in and generated by local contexts. This recognition shifts attention from women only to gender relations, from immutable roles to intercultural and intracultural variability, and from the universal features of gender to the implications of different contexts for the sociocultural construction of 'natural' biological facts" (Mukhopadhyay and Higgins 1988: 484). The centrality and enormous contribution of this perspective—that is, the cultural and social construction of gender—suggests that demography would do well to acknowledge this powerful perspective, even as demography's own huge data collection efforts might contribute important comparative insights. It is clear to many of us that methodological diversity is key to bridging gaps between demography and disciplines such as anthropology.

Gender theory and theory development within anthropology suggests that demography would benefit from using new methodology and perspectives from other social science fields (including anthropology and feminist studies) to develop new models and ways to examine the effects of gender on demographic processes. Particularly key will be attempts to capture the effect of gender above the level of individuals; we need to find ways to measure gender by doing more than adding variables to equations meant to predict demographic behavior or intentions. Projects—many of them done at the local level—which examine how gender is constructed, including the ways that gender shapes and is shaped by other social institutions, and the complex ways those institutions are implicated in demographic change, should be a key area of concern.

Some work already done in demography suggests the value of these kinds of insights. Obermeyer (1992) reviews demographic change in Islamic countries and raises issues about the "fateful triangle" of Islam, women's status, and demographic outcomes and research that attempts to make global assessments of the impact of Islam on women's status and mortality. She argues that the effects of Islamic traditions are culturally specific and cannot be adequately explored through aggregate-level analysis. Although she focuses on women rather than gender per se, she calls for in-depth investigations that allow us to "develop more complex models that contribute to an explanation of how changes in broad structures and ideas are correlated with individual decisions" (1992:50). Her findings of enormous variability within an area of the world often considered monolithic point to how the problems of the search for commonalities and universals—in this case a transnational and transcultural effect of Islam on women's position—has ignored the many variations and the great complexities of gender in Islamic societies.

Two other pieces of research illustrate the value of projects focused on understanding how cultural constructions of gender influence demographic outcomes. Mead Cain's work (1988; 1991) examines reproductive failure (that is, the failure to bear a son who survives and is able to care for his elderly parents) in Bangladesh. His findings illustrate that women are especially vulnerable in this setting because of the gendered structure of the society and its institutions. These institutions include the different roles of women and men, with men providing the most economic support; family organization and norms, which include patrilocal and patrilineal living arrangements; and marriage norms resulting in women marrying much older men. Because women are more likely than men to be widowed, and because of their economic and social dependence on men (husbands and sons), reproductive failure has particularly dire consequences for them, including a decline in economic well-being and early death. Cain's research suggests underlying motivations for high fertility, reasons that are not fully captured by individual levels of analysis but require broader and deeper understandings of the society and its institutions to fully appreciate the importance of sons.

Susan Greenhalgh's study of a village in central China (1994) also illustrates the value of an in-depth analysis of the tensions produced by different institutions in Chinese society. Whereas family norms and organization continue to encourage the birth of at least one son, the state's family planning program has considerably tightened the constraints around fertility for these villagers. Because of the way that males are privileged in all social institutions in China—from the family to the economy and from schools to the state (including the population control program)—females are severely disadvantaged, and women are subject to enormous and conflicting pressures from their families and the state-run population program.

These pieces of research illustrate the value of perspectives that are not now widespread within demography. Obermeyer argues persuasively for the need to examine Islam's influence on fertility and women's lives within a cultural context, and points out the dangers of global survey and measurement. Cain's and Greenhalgh's work, focused on local areas, attends to the cultural specificities of gender and connects individual behavior with social institutions and structures. Cain's work suggests motivations for fertility that lie outside those captured by international surveys, although similar pathways are likely to be found in other societies (Cain 1988; Nugent 1985; Wolf 1972). Greenhalgh's work suggests how locally specific tensions, resistance, and disagreements among different members of households, communities, and societies might underlie reproductive behavior. Again, we can expect that such tensions might exist in other societies (e.g., see Browner 1986) but they would be society-specific as well. A demography informed by anthropology would include more research that is better able to capture these important complexities and specificities.

Comparing Demography and Anthropology

One of the questions that arises when we compare the fields of anthropology and demography is why anthropology has been so far ahead of demography in work on gender. Whereas theories about gender and the role of gender in demographic change are scarce, at best, in demography (Greenhalgh 1995; Riley 1994; Watkins 1993), many have cited anthropology as leading other fields in its approach to gender (Stacey and Thorne 1985; Shapiro 1983; Rapp 1992). Indeed, Rayna Rapp describes anthropology as "one of the most audacious sites of feminist thinking in the social sciences" (1992:79). An important clue to its relative success is provided by Rapp's observation that those working in anthropology have had available to them the "minimal scaffolding" of "classical anthropology discourse," scaffolding on which feminist anthropologists have been able to depend and which they have used to develop gender theory and understanding (1992:80). Looking at the scaffolding available to anthropologists and comparing it to what is available in demography allows us to understand the different directions and outcomes of work in gender in the two fields, and has implications for future directions as well.

I will briefly discuss four issues that can be considered basic "scaffolding" for the development of any research or theoretical agenda: underlying philosophy, methods, substantive focus, and politics.

As we have seen, recognition of the cultural construction of any human action has always been at the heart of anthropological endeavor and is a focus of feminist anthropology as well (Stacey and Thorne 1985). Data collected with such an understanding of both society and gender have also played a key role in discussions within feminist studies about the tensions between acknowledging differences among women (or between women and men) and recognizing universal patterns and characteristics.

In contrast, demography's interest in finding universal influences on demographic change may be one of the reasons that gender (and other behavior and structures) is more often decontextualized in demographic research. Rather than emphasizing the diversity among different cultures, demography is often focused on finding common patterns and, through that kind of analysis, understanding past and especially future population changes. As Gergen has argued, "attempts to establish general laws of human functioning . . . mean that any given phenomenon is viewed as an expression of universal law. The major problem for the scientist is to determine these laws by testing the relationship among isolated entities" (1988:89). In this kind of approach, the complexities of gender are often lost.

Methodology plays a role in the ways that research and thinking about gender have developed differently in anthropology and demography. But although methodology follows and brings with it certain assumptions and perspectives, it is not at all certain that methods like those of demography prevent the development of sophisticated theories of gender. Such theories might be very different from those that have arisen from other fields. Thus, although demographic methods might hamper demographic scholars from agreeing part and parcel with other feminist scholars, such theoretical diversity could well be beneficial to our overall understanding of gender.

Many of these issues of philosophy and method are connected to epistemology. Anthropology is more interpretive than the highly positivistic field of demography. Stacey and Thorne (1985) have argued that fields with interpretive frameworks are more accepting of feminist approaches because feminist concerns fit with the overall efforts of these fields to understand how knowledge is created or accepted. Positivist fields, on the other hand, are less tolerant of openly political standpoints or perspectives.

Fuchs and Ward (1994a; 1994b) argue that (radical) deconstruction is unlikely to take place in fields in which the production of facts and objective knowledge is of central importance. I would argue that demography is one of those fields, where practitioners are focused on "pragmatic realism," believing in "facts, method, representation and progress." Demographers would thus "have little time or reason to undermine the epistemic and social authority of their own practices as merely contingent or culturally relative. . . . [F]actual fields do not view their basic constructions *as* constructions, but as the way reality is, or at least, as approaching Truth" (Fuchs and Ward 1994b). Given feminist scholarship's focus on the social construction of knowledge, its questioning of facts, methods, and representation, feminist scholars can be expected to make greater inroads in interpretive fields such as anthropology than in demography, with its strong positivist inclinations.

Differences in the substantive focus of anthropology and demography also affect the ways that gender studies has developed in each. At first glance, it might seem that demography's focus on fertility would encourage sophisticated analyses of both women's lives and gender. However, demography's focus on fertility may have had just the opposite effect. For one thing, such a focus may make it more likely that gender is seen as simply a function of biology (e.g., reproduction) rather than as an organizing principle of society (Yanagisako and Collier 1987; Errington 1990). But the substantive focuses alone certainly cannot account for the differences between the two fields.

In addition, demography's focus on fertility often contains an explicit or implicit interest in the policy implications of fertility change, which may make it easier to decontextualize this aspect of women's lives, rather than seeing fertility as only one aspect which shapes and is shaped by other social relationships and behaviors. Hodgson (1983) has argued that there are times when demography and its practitioners are focused less on understanding human behavior than on changing it. A strong interest in policy changes the focus of demographic research and the way it is conducted. In policy-oriented research, Hodgson argues, there is less attention to the influences of social structures on individual behavior and a more mechanistic attitude, an attempt to find the necessary behavior or action needed to effect a particular change.

Both demography and anthropology are fields in which Western researchers are involved in the lives of people in poorer countries; thus, international politics have played a role in both fields. But in recent decades, scrutiny and analysis of the role of politics have been a very important part of anthropology (Trouillot 1991; Marcus and Fischer 1986) in a way that has not been true in most demographic research. It is true that those working in areas of family planning and other programmatic concerns have, in fact, been discussing the roles—past, current, and preferred—of Western governments, international agencies, and local political or women's groups and their impact on the outcome of the programs (Dixon-Mueller 1993; Pritchett 1994a, 1994b; Knowles, Akin, and Guilkey 1994; Bongaarts 1994). The turmoil before and during the 1994 International Conference on Population and Development in Cairo attests to the significant role that international politics play in population policies. But discussions of how politics underlie the focus, methods, and findings of demographic research more generally is noticeably lacking (but see Hodgson 1983, 1991; Szretzer 1993; Greenhalgh 1996; Reidmann

1993). I argue that feminist anthropology has benefited from (or at least has been less easily dismissed by) being in a field where scrutiny of political origins and connections has been, at least recently, common practice. The reflexive theoretical pieces important in feminist anthropology (Rosaldo 1980; Abu-Lughod 1991) mirror what has been occurring in anthropology more generally.

Implications and Conclusions

My goal in this chapter has been to explore the ways that anthropological work on gender might inform and enrich demography. I have found myself comparing the two fields and in that comparison, demography seems to come up short; scholarship on gender in anthropology and demography is at such different stages that it is sometimes very difficult and not always fruitful to compare the fields. In this chapter I have looked at the lessons that anthropologists, and in particular feminist anthropologists, have learned from the last twenty years of their research, exploration, discussions, debates, and arguments about gender, and I have asked: is there something here that demography can learn or borrow? is it possible to apply the lessons learned through feminist anthropology to demographic research?

I have discussed a number of anthropological issues and perspectives which might be informative and useful in demography. Primary among them is the importance of acknowledging the cultural and social construction of gender and its implications for research. That idea, of course, is one that demography could borrow from anthropology generally, applying it not only to the study of gender but using it to understand many human behaviors, including fertility (see ch. 4), education, motherhood, or marriage, to name just a few. Making more effort to understand context, which is at the root of such a perspective, would be likely to influence the way that demographers conceptualize their ideas, conduct their research, and draw conclusions.

From feminist anthropologists, demographers might not only draw insights but develop heightened sensitivity to a debate of extreme importance to gender studies in a variety of fields. The difficulties and importance of balancing a view of women as being similar at the same time that differences among them are recognized has been the subject of intense and illuminating discussions among feminist scholars. Both the substantive developments arising from those discussions and the engagement with scholars from other fields have been important in the development of feminist anthropology and could have similar positive benefits for demographers.

Gender studies in demography are fledgling at best but relatively advanced in anthropology, and that difference makes it difficult to view the two fields and the way they handle gender within the same framework. But it is also true that these two fields overlap in their focus of study. What might happen if feminist scholars in these two fields began to work together? I believe that this would be a useful collaboration and would inform a variety of debates and fields. Demography may provide particular insights into the universal/ difference debate. Many feminist scholars have argued for the importance of recognizing the historical, economic, social, cultural and religious differences among women, and hence the difficulty (some have argued the impossibility) of thinking of women as a unified group (Mohanty 1992). Others, however, have argued that this dispersal of the concept of woman has gone too far and has paralyzed both feminist thought and especially political action (Walby 1992). What these different perspectives suggest is the need to have *both* comparative global perspectives and localized accounts that allow us to understand the meaning and complexities of the ways gender is constructed, maintained, challenged, and dismantled.

It is in this tension that demography might have an important role and that feminist anthropology and feminist demography might find a common meeting place. Demography is much more closely tied to policy than is anthropology, although anthropological findings have clear implications for policy decisions (see Gordon 1991; Scheper-Hughes 1991 and chapter 8 in this volume; Ginsburg 1991). Bringing together anthropological perspectives and demographic concerns and issues may allow a productive tension between understanding the complexities of gender and the need for policy that often deals with the concrete immediate concerns of many women's lives. At the same time that we need to be able to "catch complexity" (Walby 1992:39), we need the tools for developing social policy.

Demographic research provides important data that can be used for political action. Those data are not uncontested, nor should they be. But demography might act as a political action arm of feminist studies. I would argue that demography needs to be involved in many of the debates occurring in feminist studies, including those in feminist anthropology. Demographic perspectives enrich our understanding of the situation and needs of women across the globe and could form an important part of feminist scholars' discussions about the need to keep feminist studies tied to political action and the ways that might occur (hooks 1989; Lees 1991).

A recent publication by the United Nations illustrates the potential uses of demographic data for political action and policy development. In 1991 (and again in 1995) the United Nations published *The World's Women 1970–1990, Trends and Statistics*. It contains information on many aspects of women's lives from many societies, presenting "telling and often shocking statistics on the conditions under which women and girls live, conditions not shared by their male counterparts" (Mason 1992:184). This book, which depends heavily on demographic data, is valuable for the broad overview of the situation of women in different parts of the world and is a useful tool for advocacy for change. By itself it is thus a useful volume. It is not, however, unproblematic. As a volume that uses "standard" definitions for hundreds of different cultures, it cannot attend to the cultural contexts and the variations in meaning of many of the concepts that are used within it. That contradiction between the use of broad overviews and the need for cultural specificity represents the tension between demographic and anthropological perspectives. Rather than ignore it, demography as a field would benefit from exploring that tension in writing and research. Using the combined strengths of anthropology and demography would allow us fuller understanding of both women's and men's lives and the role that gender plays in our societies, and provide us with the tools to change the inequities.

Juxtaposing the perspectives of anthropology and demography again reminds us that we cannot transcend the tensions between sameness and difference, and we should not attempt to. "However frustrating the lesson, feminism must learn to 'embrace the paradox' for 'there is no transcendence, no third cause'" (Vogel 1993:5, quoting Snitow 1990). Feminist anthropology and feminist demography could be fruitful partners in exploring that tension.

But the lack of methodological and theoretical scaffolding available in demography remains an important issue. I have noted the significance of this scaffolding for feminist anthropology. Feminists working in demography do not enjoy the advantage of such supporting frameworks. I believe that this is and will be for some time the major impediment to the development of work on gender within demography.

This suggests that to study gender within demography, we will need to build new scaffolding. But the history of feminist scholarship within anthropology also leaves me with some optimism. Feminist anthropologists have struggled with the lack of impact their work has had on the field in general. That might be at least partially a function of how a field like anthropology has space for many perspectives; thus feminist perspectives can be absorbed into it without changing the fundamental nature of the field (Fuchs and Ward 1994a; Strathern 1987). In contrast, building the groundwork necessary for the development of a feminist demography might be the beginning (or part) of major changes and transformations in the field of demography—transformations which would allow for better understanding of demographic processes.

NOTES

I would like to thank the following for their comments and suggestions: Sara Dickey, Tom Fricke, Anastasia Gage, Robert Gardner, Susan Greenhalgh, David Kertzer, and Susan Watkins.

1. In this chapter I will be making a distinction between feminist anthropology and feminist theory and scholarship, although these two areas of scholarship are often intertwined. I do so to allow a focus on current feminist thinking in anthropology. Further, I am focusing on feminist anthropological work in cultural anthropology.

2. Some demographic research does acknowledge that gender is more complex than a single variable might indicate. But because this recognition most often occurs at

the stage of interpreting the results of the equations and models, what is being interpreted is still an overly simple measure of women's status.

3. An exception to this type of approach is Desai and Jain (1994). In a study of a poor rural area in South India, the authors argue that employment status and child health are not automatically linked; "nonworking" mothers must perform domestic activities that make them as likely as women working in waged work to be away from their children for long periods of time. The authors also examine the links between discrimination in the labor market and women's household drudgery. This research, which attends to the cultural context of women's lives and child health, results in a deeper understanding of the mechanisms through which women's position and work influence demographic outcomes.

4. In this description of the history of feminist anthropology, I draw heavily from Lamphere 1987; see also Sanday 1990 on anthropologists' search for gender universals before the 1970s.

5. Questions about the similarities and differences among women and the importance of those differences arose from the development of feminist studies in the West in the last three decades. In the 1970s feminist academic writing was often tied to political action. Because of the need for political cohesiveness and expediency and the relative homogeneity of class, race, and nationality of those involved, differences among women were minimized. In recent years, such feminist writings have been strongly criticized for their exclusion of issues related to race, ethnicity, class, nationality, and sexuality (Mohanty 1992); these critiques have become central to feminist studies today and address such issues as the importance of national, racial, class, and sexual context of any gender construction (Spelman 1988; Dill 1983; Mohanty, Russo, and Torres 1991). Mohanty argued persuasively that differences among women in different cultural and national settings are ignored in much research on Third World women, and that much of this research assumes—without question or documentation—similarities across great geographic and cultural spans.

REFERENCES

Abu-Lughod, Lila. 1991. "Writing Against Culture." In *Recapturing Anthropology: Working in the Present,* ed. Richard Fox, 137–62. Sante Fe: School of American Research Press.

Alcoff, Linda. 1988. "Cultural Feminism Versus Post-Structuralism: The Identity Crisis in Feminist Theory." *Signs* 13(3):405–36.

Barrett, Michele, and Anne Phillips. 1992. Introduction to *Destabilizing Theory: Contemporary Feminist Debates,* ed. Michele Barrett and Anne Phillips, 1–9. Stanford: Stanford University Press.

Bell, Diane. 1993. "Yes, Virginia, There Is a Feminist Ethnography: Reflections from Three Australian Fields." In *Gendered Fields: Women, Men and Ethnography,* ed. Diane Bell, Pat Caplan and Wazir Karim, 28–43. London: Routledge.

Bledsoe, Caroline. 1980. *Women and Marriage in Kpelle Society.* Stanford: Stanford University Press.

Bongaarts, John. 1994. "The Impact of Population Policies: Comment." *Population and Development Review* 20(3):616–20.

Browner, Carole. 1986. "The Politics of Reproduction in a Mexican Village." *Signs* 11(4):710–24.

Cain, Mead. 1988. "The Material Consequences of Reproductive Failure in Rural South Asia." In *A Home Divided: Women and Income in the Third World,* ed. Daisy Dwyer and Judith Bruce, 20–38. Stanford: Stanford University Press.

———. 1991. "Widows, Sons, and Old-Age Security in Rural Maharashtra." *Population Studies* 45:519–28.

Caldwell, John. 1985. "Strengths and Limitations of the Survey Approach for Measuring and Understanding Fertility Change: Alternative Possibilities." In *Reproductive Change in Developing Countries: Insights from the World Fertility Study,* ed. John Cleland and John Hobcraft, 45–63. Oxford: Oxford University Press.

———. 1986. "Routes to Low Mortality in Poor Countries." *Population and Development Review* 12(2):171–220.

Callaway, Helen. 1992. "Ethnography and Experience: Gender Implications in Fieldwork and Texts." In *Anthropology and Autobiography,* ed. Judith Oakley and Helen Callaway, 29–49. London: Routledge.

Cleland, John, and John Hobcraft, eds. 1985. *Reproductive Change in Developing Countries: Insights from the World Fertility Survey.* Oxford: Oxford University Press.

Collier, Jane. 1988. *Marriage and Inequality in Classless Societies.* Stanford: Stanford University Press.

Collier, Jane, Michelle Rosaldo, and Sylvia Yanagisako. 1992. "Is There a Family? New Anthropological Views." In *Rethinking the Family,* ed. Barrie Thorne and Marilyn Yalom, 31–48. Boston: Northeastern University Press.

Connell, Robert W. 1985. "Theorizing Gender." *Sociology* 19(2):260–72.

Cook, Judith, and Mary Fonow. 1990. "Knowledge and Women's Interests: Issues of Epistemology and Methodology in Feminist Social Science Research." In *Feminist Research Methods: Exemplary Readings in the Social Sciences,* ed. Joyce Nielsen, 69–93. Boulder, Colo.: Westview Press.

del Valle, Teresa. 1993. Introduction to *Gendered Anthropology,* ed. Teresa del Valle, 1–16. London: Routledge.

Desai, Sonalde, and Devaki Jain. 1994. "Maternal Employment and Changes in Family Dynamics: The Social Context of Women's Work in Rural South India." *Population and Development Review* 20(1):115–36.

di Leonardo, Micaela. 1991. "Gender, Culture, and Political Economy: Feminist Anthropology in Historical Perspective." In *Gender at the Crossroads of Knowledge,* ed. Micaela di Leonardo, 1–48. Berkeley: University of California Press.

Dill, Bonnie Thorton. 1983. "Race, Class, and Gender: Prospects for an All-Inclusive Sisterhood." *Feminist Studies* 9(1):131–50.

DiStefano, Christine. 1991. "Who the Heck Are We: Theoretical Turns Against Gender." *Frontiers* 12(2):86–108.

Dixon-Mueller, Ruth. 1993. *Population Policy and Women's Rights: Transforming Reproductive Choice.* Westport, Conn.: Praeger.

Downs, Laura Lee. 1993. "If 'Woman' Is Just an Empty Category, Then Why Am I Afraid to Walk Alone at Night? Identity Politics Meets the Postmodern Subject." *Comparative Studies in Society and History* 35(2):414–37.

Entwisle, Barbara, and Catherine Coles. 1990. "Demographic Surveys and Nigerian Women." *Signs* 15(2):259–84.

Errington, Shelly. 1990. "Recasting Sex, Gender, and Power: A Theoretical and Regional Overview." In *Power and Difference: Gender in Island Southeast Asia,* ed.

Jane Atkinson and Shelly Errington, 1–58. Stanford: Stanford University Press.

Ferree, Myra Marx. 1990. "Beyond Separate Spheres: Feminism and Family History." *Journal of Marriage and the Family* 52:866–84.

Flax, Jane. 1987. "Postmodernism and Gender Relations in Feminist History." *Signs* 12(4):621–43.

Fraser, Nancy, and Linda Nicholson. 1990. "Social Criticism without Philosophy: An Encounter between Feminism and Postmodernism." In *Feminism/Postmodernism,* ed. Linda Nicholson, 19–38. New York: Routledge.

Fuchs, Stephan, and Steven Ward. 1994a. "Deconstruction: Making Facts in Science, Building Cases in Law." *American Sociological Review* 59(4):481–500.

———. 1994b. "The Sociology and Paradoxes of Deconstruction: Reply to Agger." *American Sociological Review* 59(4):506–10.

Gergen, Mary. 1988. "Toward a Feminist Metatheory and Methodology in the Social Sciences." In *Feminist Thought and the Structure of Knowledge,* ed. Mary Gergen, 87–104. New York: New York University Press.

Ginsburg, Faye. 1991. "What Do Women Want?: Feminist Anthropology Confronts Clitoridectomy." *Medical Anthropology* 5 (March): 17–19.

Ginsburg, Faye, and Rayna Rapp. 1991. "The Politics of Reproduction." *Annual Review of Anthropology* 20:311–43.

Gordon, Daniel. 1991. "Female Circumcision and Genital Operations in Egypt and the Sudan: A Dilemma for Medical Anthropology." *Medical Anthropology* 5 (March): 3–14.

Greenhalgh, Susan. 1990. "Toward a Political Economy of Fertility: Anthropological Contributions." *Population and Development Review* 16(1):85–106.

———. 1994. "Controlling Births and Bodies in Village China." *American Ethnologist* 21(1):3–30.

———. 1995. "Anthropology Theorizes Reproduction: Integrating Practice, Political Economic, and Feminist Perspectives." In *Situating Fertility: Anthropology and Demographic Inquiry.* ed. Susan Greenhalgh, 3–28. Cambridge: Cambridge University Press.

———. 1996. "The Social Construction of Population Science: An Intellectual, Institutional, and Political History of Twentieth Century Demography." *Comparative Studies in Society and History* 38(1):26–66.

Guyer, Jane. 1991. "Female Farming in Anthropology and African History." In *Gender at the Crossroads of Knowledge,* ed. Micaela di Leonardo, 257–77. Berkeley: University of California Press.

Haraway, Donna. 1985. "A Manifesto for Cyborgs: Science, Technology, and Socialist Feminism in the 1980s." *Socialist Review* 80 (March/April): 65–108.

———. 1988. "Situated Knowledges: The Science Question in Feminism and the Privilege of Partial Perspective." *Feminist Studies* 14(3):575–99.

Harding, Sandra. 1987. "The Method Question." *Hypatia* 2(3):19–35.

———. 1991. *Whose Science? Whose Knowledge? Thinking from Women's Lives.* Ithaca, N.Y.: Cornell University Press.

Hartsock, Nancy. 1987. "Rethinking Modernism." *Cultural Critique* 7 (fall): 187–206.

Hodgson, Dennis. 1983. "Demography as Social Science and Policy Science." *Population and Development Review* 9(1):1–34.

———. 1991. "The Ideological Origins of the PAA." *Population and Development Review* 17(1):1–34.

hooks, bell. 1989. *Talking Back: Thinking Feminist, Thinking Black*. Boston: South End Press.

Howell, Signe, and Marit Melhuus. 1993. "The Study of Kinship; The Study of Person; A Study of Gender?" In *Gendered Anthropology*, ed. Teresa del Valle, 38–53. London: Routledge.

Jay, Nancy. 1981. "Gender and Dichotomy." *Feminist Studies* 7(1):38–56.

Jayaratne, Toby, and Abigail Stewart. 1991. "Quantitative and Qualitative Methods in the Social Sciences: Current Feminist Issues and Practical Strategies." In *Beyond Methodology: Feminist Scholarship as Lived Research*, ed. Mary Fonow and Judith Cook, 85–106. Bloomington: Indiana University Press.

Keller, Evelyn Fox. 1989. "Just What IS So Difficult About the Concept of Gender as a Social Category? (Response to Richards and Schuster)." *Social Studies of Science* 19:721–24.

Kirby, Vicki. 1993. "Feminisms and Postmodernisms: Anthropology and the Management of Difference." *Anthropological Quarterly* 66(3):127–33.

Knodel, John, Apichat Chamratrithirong, and Nibhon Debavalya. 1987. *Thailand's Reproductive Revolution: Rapid Fertility Decline in a Third World Setting*. Madison: University of Wisconsin Press.

Knowles, James, John Akin, and David Guilkey. 1994. "The Impact of Population Policies: Comment." *Population and Development Review* 20(3): 611–15.

Lamphere, Louise. 1987. "Feminism and Anthropology: The Struggle to Reshape Our Thinking About Gender." In *The Impact of Feminist Research in the Academy*, ed. Christine Farnham, 11–33. Bloomington: Indiana University Press.

———. 1993. "The Domestic Sphere of Women and the Public World of Men: The Strengths and Limitations of an Anthropological Dichotomy." In *Gender in Cross-Cultural Perspective*, ed. Caroline Brettell and Carolyn Sargent, 67–77. Englewood Cliff, N.J.: Prentice Hall.

Leacock, Eleanor. 1981. *Myths of Male Dominance*. New York: Monthly Review Press.

Lees, Sue. 1991. "Feminist Politics and Women's Studies: Struggle, Not Incorporation." In *Out of the Margins: Women's Studies in the Nineties*, ed. Jane Aaron and Sylvia Walby, 90–104. London: Falmer Press.

Lutz, Catherine. 1988. *Unnatural Emotions: Everyday Sentiments in a Micronesian Atoll and Their Challenge to Western Theory*. Chicago: University of Chicago Press.

———. 1990. "The Erasure of Women's Writing in Sociocultural Anthropology." *American Ethnologist* 17(4):611–27.

MacCormack, Carol. 1980. "Nature, Culture, and Gender: A Critique." In *Nature, Culture, and Gender*, ed. Carol MacCormack and Marilyn Strathern, 1–24. Cambridge: Cambridge University Press.

MacCormack, Carol, and Marilyn Strathern, eds. 1980. *Nature, Culture, and Gender*. Cambridge: Cambridge University Press.

Marcus, George, and Michael Fischer. 1986. *Anthropology as Cultural Critique: An Experimental Moment in the Human Sciences*. Chicago: University of Chicago Press.

Martin, Emily. 1987. *The Woman in the Body: A Cultural Analysis of Reproduction*. Boston: Beacon Press.

Mascia-Lees, Frances, Patricia Sharpe, and Colleen Cohen. 1989. "The Postmodernist Turn in Anthropology: Cautions from a Feminist Perspective." *Signs* 15(1):7–33.

Mason, Karen Oppenheim. 1987. "The Impact of Women's Social Position on Fertility in Developing Countries." *Sociological Forum* 2(4):718–45.

———. 1992. Review of *The World's Women 1970–1990* (United Nations). *Population and Development Review* 18(1):184–85.

Massey, Douglas, Rafael Alarcon, Jorge Durand, and Humberto Gonzalez. 1987. *Return to Aztlan: The Social Processes of International Migration from Western Mexico.* Berkeley: University of California Press.

Mohanty, Chandra. 1991. "Under Western Eyes." In *Third World Women and the Politics of Feminism,* ed. Chandra Mohanty, Ann Russo, and Lourdes Torres, 51–80. Bloomington: Indiana University Press.

———. 1992. "Feminist Encounters: Locating the Politics of Experience." In *Destabilizing Theory: Contemporary Feminist Debates,* ed. Michelle Barrett and Anne Phillips, 74–92. Stanford: Stanford University Press.

Mohanty, Chandra, Ann Russo, and Lourdes Torres, eds. 1991. *Third World Women and the Politics of Feminism.* Bloomington: Indiana University Press.

Moore, Henrietta. 1988. *Feminism and Anthropology.* Minneapolis: University of Minnesota.

———. 1993. "The Differences Within and the Differences Between." In *Gendered Anthropology,* ed. Teresa del Valle, 193–204. London: Routledge.

Mukhopadhyay, Carol, and Patricia Higgins. 1988. "Anthropological Studies of Women's Status Revisited; 1977–1987." *Annual Review of Anthropology* 17:461–95.

Nicholson, Linda, ed. 1990. *Feminism/Postmodernism.* New York: Routledge.

Nugent, Jeffrey. 1985. "The Old-Age Security Motive for Fertility." *Population and Development Review* 8(3):449–94.

Obermeyer, Carla M. 1992. "Islam, Women, and Politics: The Demography of Arab Countries." *Population and Development Review* 18:33–60.

Ong, Aihwa. 1987. *Spirits of Resistance and Capitalist Decline.* Albany: State University of New York Press.

Ortner, Sherry. 1974. "Is Female to Male as Nature Is to Culture?" In *Woman, Culture, and Society,* ed. Michelle Rosaldo and Louise Lamphere, 67–88. Stanford: Stanford University Press.

Ortner, Sherry, and Harriet Whitehead, eds. 1981. *Sexual Meanings: The Cultural Construction of Gender and Sexuality.* Cambridge: Cambridge University Press.

Pritchett, Lant. 1994a. "Desired Fertility and the Impact of Population Policies." *Population and Development Review* 20(1):1–55.

———. 1994b. "The Impact of Population Policies: Reply." *Population and Development Review* 20(3):621–30.

Quinn, Naomi. 1977. "Anthropological Studies on Women's Status." *Current Review of Anthropology* 6:181–225.

Rapp, Rayna. 1992. "Anthropology: Feminist Methodologies for the Science of Man?" In *Revolutions in Knowledge: Feminism in the Social Sciences,* ed. S. Zalk and J. Gordon-Kelter. Boulder, Colo.: Westview Press.

Reidmann, Agnes. 1993. *Science That Colonizes: A Critique of Fertility Studies in Africa.* Philadelphia: Temple University Press.

Riley, Nancy E. 1994. "Challenging Demography: Contributions from Feminist Theory." Unpublished manuscript.

Rosaldo, Michelle. 1974. "Woman, Culture, and Society: A Theoretical Overview." In *Woman, Culture, and Society,* ed. M. Rosaldo and L. Lamphere, 17–42. Stanford: Stanford University Press.

————. 1980. "The Use and Abuse of Anthropology: Reflections on Feminism and Cross-Cultural Understanding." *Signs* 5(3):389–417.

————. 1989. "Moral/Analytic Dilemmas Posed by the Intersection of Feminism and Social Science." In *Interpretive Social Science: A Second Look,* ed. Paul Rabinow and William Sullivan, 280–301. Berkeley: University of California Press.

Rubin, Gayle. 1975. "The Traffic in Women: Notes on the 'Political Economy' of Sex." In *Toward an Anthropology of Women,* ed. Rayna Reiter, 157–210. New York: Monthly Review Press.

Sanday, Peggy. 1981. *Female Power and Male Dominance.* Cambridge: Cambridge University Press.

————. 1990. Introduction to *Beyond the Second Sex: New Directions in the Anthropology of Gender,* ed. Peggy Sanday and Ruth Goodenough, 1–19. Philadelphia: University of Pennsylvania Press.

Scheper-Hughes, Nancy. 1991. "Virgin Territory: The Male Discovery of the Clitoris." *Medical Anthropology* 5 (March): 25–28.

————. 1992. *Death without Weeping: The Violence of Everyday Life in Brazil.* Berkeley: University of California Press.

Schlegel, Alice. 1977. *Sexual Stratification.* New York: Columbia University Press.

Schneider, David. 1984. *A Critique of the Study of Kinship.* Ann Arbor: University of Michigan Press.

Scott, Joan. 1987. "Women's History and the Rewriting of History." In *The Impact of Feminist Research in the Academy,* ed. Christie Farnham, 34–50. Bloomington: Indiana University Press.

————. 1988. *Gender and the Politics of History.* New York: Columbia University Press.

————. 1992. " 'Experience.' " In *Feminists Theorize the Political,* ed. Judith Butler and Joan Scott, 22–39. New York: Routledge.

————. 1993. " 'The Tip of the Volcano.' " *Comparative Studies in Society and History* 35(2):438–43.

Seidman, Steven. 1994. *Contested Knowledge: Social Theory in the Postmodern Era.* Oxford: Blackwell.

Shapiro, Judith. 1983. "Anthropology and the Study of Gender." In *A Feminist Perspective in the Academy,* ed. Elizabeth Langland and Walter Gove. Chicago: University of Chicago Press.

Shostak, Marjorie. 1981. *Nisa: The Life and Words of a !Kung Woman.* Cambridge: Harvard University Press.

Snitow, Ann. 1990. "A Gender Diary." In *Conflicts in Feminism,* ed. Marianne Hirsch and Evelyn Fox Keller, 9–43. New York: Routledge.

Spelman, Elizabeth. 1988. *Inessential Woman: Problems of Exclusion in Feminist Thought.* Boston: Beacon Press.

Stacey, Judith, and Barrie Thorne. 1985. "The Missing Feminist Revolution in Sociology." *Social Problems* 32(4):301–16.

Strathern, Marilyn. 1987. "An Awkward Relationship: The Case of Feminism and Anthropology." *Signs* 12(2):276–82.

Szreter, Simon. 1993. "The Idea of Demographic Transition and the Study of Fertility: A Critical Intellectual History." *Population and Development Review* 19(4):659–701.

Trouillot, Michel-Rolph. 1991. "Anthropology and the Savage Slot: The Poetics and Politics of Otherness." In *Recapturing Anthropology: Working in the Present,* ed. Richard Fox, 17–44. Sante Fe: School of American Research Press.

Tsing, Anna, and Sylvia Yanagisako. 1983. "Feminism and Kinship Theory." *Current Anthropology* 24(4):511–16.

United Nations. 1991. *The World's Women 1970–1990, Trends and Statistics.* New York: United Nations.

Vogel, Lise. 1993. *Mothers on the Job: Maternity Policy in the US Workplace.* New Brunswick, N.J.: Rutgers University Press.

Walby, Sylvia. 1992. "Post-Post-Modernism? Theorizing Social Complexity." In *Destabilizing Theory: Contemporary Feminist Debates,* ed. Michelle Barrett and Anne Phillips, 31–52. Stanford: Stanford University Press.

Watkins, Susan. 1993. "If All We Knew About Women Were What We Read in *Demography,* What Would We Know?" *Demography* 30(4):551–78.

Weiner, Annette. 1976. *Women of Value, Men of Renown.* Austin: University of Texas Press.

Whitehead, Harriet. 1981. "The Bow and the Burden Strap." In *Sexual Meanings: The Cultural Construction of Gender and Sexuality,* ed. Sherry Ortner and Harriet Whitehead, 80–115. Cambridge: Cambridge University Press.

Wolf, Diane. 1993. *Factory Daughters: Gender, Household Dynamics, and Rural Industrialization in Java.* Berkeley: University of California Press.

Wolf, Margery. 1972. *Women and the Family in Rural Taiwan.* Stanford: Stanford University Press.

Yanagisako, Sylvia, and Jane Collier. 1987. "Toward a Unified Analysis of Gender and Kinship." In *Gender and Kinship: Essays Toward a Unified Analysis,* ed. Jane Collier and Sylvia Yanagisako, 14–50. Stanford: Stanford University Press.

Chapter Six

Population and Identity

Philip Kreager

OVERLAP w/ N S-H

A quarter of a century has passed since Ansley Coale, drawing on the work of Lesthaeghe and Leasure, remarked that attempts to correlate socioeconomic variables with fertility declines might stand a better chance of succeeding if data were grouped into regions defined by common language and culture (Coale 1969). Since then the complexity of this seemingly straightforward piece of advice has come to be more widely appreciated. Data collected according to standard administrative units, like provinces, generally give an incomplete and approximate picture of the distribution of constituent national, ethnic, and linguistic groups. Even where official sources report people's stated affiliations with some regularity, these markers are by nature neither discrete nor immutable. Groups frequently share familial, labor, consumption, and popular cultural values with neighboring populations. Individuals may answer to one collective identity in some circumstances but not in others. There are inevitable internal differentials since populations apparently homogeneous with respect to religion or ethnicity nonetheless recognize class, caste, and genealogical distinctions among their members. These differences, together with collective memory of past events and relations between certain sub-groups, may shape behavior more significantly than wider affiliations. Put another way, several collective identities may be at issue in a given context, and they are unlikely all to have the same status. In light of all of these and other circumstances, it is hardly surprising that attempts to correlate fertility declines with stated ethnicity, religion, or other blanket cultural markers have tended to give mixed results (see Berelson 1977; Anderson 1986; Hammel 1995).

Macrosociological approaches attempting to develop Coale's proposition have, in consequence, faced a doubly daunting task. On one side, the uneven and often scanty data available on collective identities at levels other than the nation-state have meant that complex sandwiches of proxy variables (party political voting behavior, persistence of traditional modes of production, observance of traditional marriage ceremonies, etc.) have been needed to try to capture distinctive cultures or regions (Leasure 1963; Livi-Bacci 1971; Lesthaeghe 1982, 1983, 1992; Lesthaeghe and Wilson 1986; Le Bras and Todd 1981). The resulting picture is nonetheless very interesting, but it is something of an unfinished jigsaw puzzle, with some parts of the map of Europe (like Flemish and Walloon areas of Belgium) coming to be well-delineated, whilst large expanses elsewhere have some pieces suggestively fitted in (e.g., Germany, Spain), or have given rise to competing hypotheses

139

difficult to resolve with the data available (France). One of the foremost proponents of macro-level culture approaches, Ron Lesthaeghe, soon expressed skepticism of this exercise. His remarks remain worth citing: "the lessons to be drawn from Western European fertility transition lie not so much in the fact that geographical dispersion patterns are detectable or that fertility transition followed linguistic and cultural boundaries, but rather in the fact that . . . diversifications emerged in the timing and format of the marital fertility decline that were closely associated with the development of differential and sometimes compartmentalized ideological codes" (1982:539).

What we are to understand by such codes, and how they may best be characterized, has become the second daunting task. Coale's influential argument, it will be remembered, was linked to diffusionism. Not only did it require that some way be found to distinguish cultures and regions as "natural units" of demographic change, within which contraceptive and related information flowed readily through customary networks; it implied that, whilst particular cultures have the capacity to give their own twists and turns to the spread of modern methods of birth control, gender relations, modes of production, and so forth, there nonetheless remains a fundamental commonality underlying different people's experience of emergent modernity. According to this view, different cultures may assign their own meanings and adaptations to ideas, practices, and technologies in the course of diffusion, but the several adjustments they make are effectively similar, or at least analogous, and therefore can be treated as systematic and directly comparable. Attempts to typify these analogous changes and to relate them to concurrent patterns of institutional development have relied on a wider and perennially controversial set of terms drawn from political and philosophical discourse, of which individualism, secularism, capitalism, and socialism are probably the most familiar. Data now available from multinational attitude surveys have added a number of further "isms" (postmaterialism, fundamentalism, consumerism, etc.; see Lesthaeghe 1983; Lesthaeghe and Surkyn 1988; Simons 1986, 1994), and doubtless there are more to come. Talk of ideology and "isms" in population studies is, of course, rather like waving red conceptual flags in the face of one's colleagues; researchers will generally accept a discourse couched in "ismatic" terms up to a point, especially if it allows them to pay lip service to the need for a comparative historical and analytical framework. Sooner or later, however, they will look to the empirical evidence which their own work may or may not provide for such generalizations, and then they are likely to be much more critical.

How and whether cross-cutting ideological codes like secularization and fundamentalism can be related to the regional and cultural demography to which Coale pointed also remains a subject of uncertainty. To the extent that national value surveys and census data at a provincial level remain the primary sources, then Coale's proposition is bound to remain an incomplete patchwork confined to those areas that happen to provide relevant data. At worst, as Hammel notes, the careful assembling of proxy variables and analogous secularizing adjustments that different peoples are supposed to make may add up to little more than a labeling exercise (1990:439) Anthropological area studies, for example in Brittany (Segalen 1992), Sicily (Schneider and Schneider 1992) and Alpine communities (Viazzo 1989), would appear in many respects to fit Coale's bill rather better. The focus of these studies, however, is emphatically on internal differences and the plurality of demographies to be found within these areas.

Thus, Segalen's study differentiates the timing of fertility declines in two Breton communes in terms of contrasting institutions and values (family organization, agricultural types, labor arrangements, church influence, social class, and political activity), which are the same criteria Lesthaeghe (1983) has used to differentiate traditional and secularized regions in select parts of Europe at an earlier period. Though not citing Lesthaeghe, Segalen is conscious that her study is "a local version of a general tune," and her two communes conform reasonably well to the opposed traditional and secularized ends of the spectrum of modernization that Lesthaeghe outlines. There are some interesting twists, such as the major role of the church in actively promoting rationalizations for the spread of modern contraception or the continuity of marriage exchange (e.g., two sisters in one family marrying two brothers in another). The overall interpretation she gives to her materials, however, runs sharply counter to Lesthaeghe's thesis on the pervasive influence of secular individualism. The fact that the demographic behavior of Breton communes may be observed sooner or later to reflect wider aggregate trends and the general secular drift of European values is, from her point of view, little more than trivially true, a labeling exercise in which academic categories are read in a predetermined way over local experience. For Segalen, the fundamental mechanisms of adjustment and change lie not in the pervasive diffusion of secularism, but in what I have called the "twists and turns": the capacity of human collectivities to generate or improvise their own solutions. It may be noted that a number of recent syntheses, drawing variously on survey and ethnographic sources, have come to view the continuing pluralization of household and community demographies as a more significant feature of modern demographic change than the convergence of fertility and mortality trends at higher levels of aggregation and the processes hypothesized to lie behind them (Berrington et al. 1993; Kuijsten 1994; Kreager 1986; Greenhalgh 1995; Viazzo, n.d.).

Culture or Identity?

There is a danger that differing interpretations, such as those of Segalen and Lesthaeghe, may appear to be little more than business as usual in the social sciences. A stereotypical quest of the social demographer, after all, is for generalizations which hold true at higher levels of aggregation, whilst anthropologists sing a no less perennial song about the peoples they study being really very diverse in a way that escapes deterministic models. This impression of *status quo revivus* is unfortunate, since it misses the substantial (if unfinished) rethinking of Coale's initial proposition, to which both interpretative tendencies have made major contributions.

As Coale described it, the Princeton group's interest in cultural and regional demographies began in a kind of paint-by-numbers exercise, reminiscent of a child's coloring book. William Leasure drew a map of Spain in which different levels of marital fertility were colored-in and—lo and behold!—the units of color resembled the distribution of languages and dialects. The several spaces on the map Coale took to be "natural units," the populations of shared culture and historical experience in which people had lived since before the modern era. Language boundaries and cultural identities were assumed to be effectively synonymous and were viewed as fixed social phenomena. Coale's next methodological step was to compose a kind of checklist of cultural attributes relevant to fertility decline (especially supposed barriers to diffusion, like linguistic boundaries and religious dogmas) which modernizing trends in variables (like education and improved living standards) might be expected to influence.

The notion of culture as a checklist of traits by which peoples can be identified is one that has for some time ceased to appear adequate in anthropology. As Hammel bluntly puts it in a recent review, "no theory of social action is embedded in this [conception of] culture" (1990:459).[1] As the difficulties with this conception (such as those noted at the beginning of this chapter) have become apparent in population studies, demographic thinking has likewise moved on to consider ways to extend and redevelop the concept of "culture-as-identifier" so that social action (in this case, behavior relating to demographic outcomes) may be tied more closely to the reference groups or collective identities which people recognize and within which they live. As the work of Coale and his successors makes clear, it is not a theory of culture *tout court* that population studies is seeking, but a more limited comparative framework that would enable specific demographic changes to be understood as a dimension of specific cultural differentials and changing relationships between groups. More particularly, the hope has remained that such an approach would allow formalization, in which identity could serve as a proxy for complex patterns of cultural change.

This general approach is one, I shall argue, that anthropologists interested in population can and should accept, albeit not in the form Coale originally proposed. The range of anthropological theory and ethnography addressed to culture is vast and contains subjects, from paleobotany to semiotics, entailing issues and imposing conceptual requirements that extend very far beyond demographic interests. It is really an encumbrance to expect population studies to begin from an elaborate theory of culture. A cultural approach that would satisfy anthropologists is unlikely in any case since they themselves are not in agreement about cultural theory, as Hammel in his review has taken some pains to demonstrate.

More important is that a concept of culture be developed that builds on the several advances from Coale's proposition just outlined. To begin with, it is possible and desirable to formulate culture in a more dynamic way. If identity is to provide a directed focus on the cultural dimension of demographic change, the first question that must concern us is the account of human agency which arises from this approach. Discussion of agency leads us, in turn, to the question of evidence, a problem to which Hill, Hammel and other authors in this volume make pointed reference. As an active ingredient of demographic change, collective and personal identities, or people's attempts to manage and develop them, have the capacity to shape not only population trends, but the accuracy and bias of the demographic record. With the concept of identity, culture ceases to be important only as a factor amongst the so-called "independent" variables. As we shall see in the next two sections of this chapter, identity figures amongst the materials and methods of demography in the strict sense, entering not only into the interpretation but the selection of "dependent" variables and of the basic parameters used to define population structures and compositions.

The section entitled "Identity and History" then puts this perspective in historical context by reviewing briefly the role of collective identity in the development of population inquiry in the nineteenth century, the period to which we owe the establishment and spread of the principal sources and methods of demographic data collection. The problem of culture, as it re-emerged in the work of Coale and his successors in the postwar era, turns out to be a recapitulation of nineteenth-century models and problems. These historical sections are not just background. They provide us with criteria for a concept of identity construction that escape the charge of reducing the role of culture-as-identifier in population studies to a mere labeling or proxy exercise. The concluding section of the chapter then takes up these criteria by considering briefly an example drawn from the Census and Ethnographic Survey of India in the early years of this century. Limitations of space inevitably mean that discussion here is confined to collective aspects of identity construction, leaving aside personal aspects.

A major advantage of taking identity as a central concept in population research, rather than the broad domain of culture, may be noted at the outset. In seeking to explain the diversity of modern demographic transitions, we do not have to make a radical choice between the agency of broad historical shifts in ideology or economy on the one hand, and the strength of local and regional traditions on the other. As the vast body of writings on demographic transition testifies, such distinctions generally result in culture being cast in a passive role. Coale is but one of many who have seen culture as a localized repository of tradition, a barrier or blockage to change having supposedly latent susceptibilities which might be conducive to change if exogenous forces handle them in the "right" way. Bound up with this picture are the usual stereotypes of Western versus non-Western cultures, macro- versus microlevels of phenomena, and infra- versus superstructural changes. As the work of Segalen, Lesthaeghe, and others shows, however, demographers and anthropologists have for some time recognized the dangers of these sweeping and reductive oppositions, and have recognized that the crucial data lie in processes of selective adjustment occurring at several levels of social and cultural organization which are at once symbolic and material. The point is obvious enough: wider social, economic, and cultural factors do not act on localities in a simple stimulus-response fashion, but are translated by people according to their historical experience. In the process, the nature and significance of supposedly exogenous factors are likely to be quite transformed. In this way people manage to incorporate major historical shifts (identifying themselves with modern values and practices to a greater or lesser degree) whilst at the same time reaffirming what they consider to be their own traditions.[2]

The challenge for anthropological demography, then, is clear. An account of how demographic behavior constitutes and maintains a particular population composition and structure should be integral to our understanding of how and whether that population constitutes and maintains a given identity or identities. Likewise, the way in which a population constitutes and maintains its identity should be integral to understanding the demographic composition and structure of that population.

Identity and Agency

A few elementary definitions may serve as our starting point. Culture, as commonly defined, refers to sets of symbols, linguistic and otherwise, that are used by people to construct their collective life. Identity refers to a series of subsets of culture by which people represent, both to themselves and to others, the many different sorts of associations and groups to which they belong and in terms of which they recognize other collectivities and their members. Demography, as a system for classifying, measuring, and modeling people(s) as "populations" is one such subset. As demographers are sometimes made painfully aware, they do not exercise sole prerogative over how the populations they measure are defined, nor over how their data and analyses are interpreted. There are always several voices to be considered. In the example considered at the end of this chapter, at least six perspectives are recognizable, each of which, on closer examination, reflects a number of differing parties. There are the priorities of national and colonial administrations; the logistical concerns of registrars and census-takers; the involvement of scientific experts (demographers, linguists, ethnologists); the several ethnic, religious, and other identities seeking representation; the differing scholarly, religious, and political authorities belonging to these collectivities; and the local press and other media of communication. Clearly these perspectives are not discrete points of view, especially as administrative and scientific bodies are likely to contain members of one or more relevant collective identities.

The demographic record as it eventually emerges in census and survey documents, and in analyses thereof, is a kind of composite, reflecting the relative influence which these several voices have succeeded in exercising over its contents. A central issue in all of this is bound to be identity: who and what should be counted and the manner of classification and measurement appropriate to them. In formulating identity as an agency of historical change, we may note that the making and contesting of the demographic record is generative in several readily recognizable senses.

The first sense is simply that demography, like any science, produces new knowledge: emerging trends and unexpected patterns in events commonly point to the need for collecting new data series; newly available series in turn pose problems which stimulate more refined statistical methods; and successive refinements feed back into the selection of variables and the phrasing of questions in further data collection. The process as a whole generates not only new facts but parameters used to identify societies, their members, and their problems.

Merely making demographic information available is thus not a static phenomenon. By changing the state of knowledge, demographic research effects displacements across a range of existing social, political, and economic values. These changes constitute a second generative function, since they permit interventions into ever wider debates, and thence become bound up in recurring disputes of various kinds. Take, for instance, the rise of cohort analysis in the 1940s and 1950s. Cohort methods arose in part as a response to a long debate over the significance of declining fertility in Europe. The measures that had been employed before World War II showed a precipitous drop in reproductive levels, encouraging extreme hypotheses: European civilization was said to be dying out; reproductive differentials between upper and lower class groups—and eugenic arguments pertaining to them—were used to suggest that declining fertility was both a cause and consequence of moral and racial deterioration (Pearson 1909). Cohort techniques subsequently showed, however, that such hypotheses were unnecessary. The apparent inability of European populations to replace themselves disappeared once it was recognized that previous measures had failed to distinguish changes in the quantum and tempo of fertility between successive age groups.

Better data and analysis, however, are rarely able in themselves to put an end to supposed crises and the kinds of argument they engender. The French demographic establishment was recently rocked by a renewal of the old debate over the significance of declining fertility (Keyfitz 1993). Its national demographic institute was accused by one of its own senior fellows of a cynical neglect of cohort measures, an effective plot to exaggerate the low level of French fertility. On the one hand, by consistently presenting selective evidence of fertility below replacement level, the institute created a continuing "crisis" in French fertility, thereby strengthening and legitimizing its own importance. On the other hand, its obsession with deficient reproduction was linked to right-wing political interests, racism, and to policies of the Vichy government (Le Bras 1992). Not surprisingly, the national press had a field day, and eventually both the director of the institute and its accuser left the organization. Such examples are a reminder that the methodological validity of categories and measures is not all that determines what population trends "really are." Measurement and analysis are repositories of people's values; they are icons of wider significance and possess varying and renewable symbolic power.

The number of voices that participate in making the demographic record grows, of course, when the people(s) being counted are allowed or encouraged to voice their own points of view. The third generative aspect of identity follows from the interaction between these voices and the administrative and scientific voices just noted. Every demographer probably has his or her own favorite (or not-so-favorite) examples. I shall list here three main aspects: (1) changes of self-identification; (2) identity changes which reflect popular responses to scientific, political, and administrative priorities; and (3) the impact that both of these aspects have on the classification and trend of core demographic variables.

(1) To begin with, ostensibly secondary changes of identity may produce radical changes in the stock and flow of a population which dwarf changes in fertility, mortality, and migration. The rate of growth and distribution of American Indian populations in the United States has of late become a well-known case in point. More than half of the Indians born in California, for example, who were between ages ten and nineteen in 1980, had been reported as belonging to some other identity in the previous census (Eschbach 1993). Such changes appear due not only to popular fashion and changing attitudes to relations between social groups, but to the role which recorded ethnic numbers play in entitlements to federal funds. The former Soviet sphere of influence is now a source of many further instances, in which reasserted Greek, Jewish, German, and other identities appear to have elastic properties in response to changing opportunities. As one Polish colleague put it, the more members of these groups are "repatriated" (i.e., to Greece, Israel, and Germany, where they have never lived), the more members there appear still to be living in the former Soviet bloc.

(2) Obviously, such shifts are not simply due to redefinitions internal to the ethnicities or minorities in question. They arise as part of long-standing relations between collectivities, and may be imposed wittingly or unwittingly by some collectivities on others. As Dobroszycki (1981) notes, a variation

in the phrasing of nationality and language questions in the Polish census of 1930 resulted in a 15 percent increase in the Jewish population over the preceding ten year period. Such a change is not merely an artifact; it is potentially important evidence of a state of relations within and between collective identities and the groups to which they refer. Lengthening our historical perspective and taking related cases into account proves instructive. Many Jews of the period 1870–1930 saw themselves as Germans and Poles as well as Jews, and often preferred these identities to their Jewish identity. Some Jews became ardent German nationalists. However, the inter-war period witnessed a rise of anti-Semitism and the spread of the idea of a Jewish state. The marked increase in Jewish numbers noted by Dobroszycki reflects these conflicting influences (cf. Bartosz 1992). Later in the 1930s, Jews were to discover that apparently they had never been Germans at all, and that the one identity left to them was an immense fatality.

(3) Thus far we have considered the mutability of collective identities as a factor in population measurement as if it were simply a matter of questions addressed to englobing ethnic, national, or religious affiliations. The fate of European Jewry is a forcible reminder, however, that shifting identities in turn affect determinants of mortality, fertility, and migration. Put more precisely, patterns of mortality, fertility, and migration are manifestations and expressions of shifting identities. Fortunately, in most cases a given identity is not synonymous with brute demographic outcomes, as in the wartime German Jewish case. Nonetheless, sociodemographic research on ethnic and religious identity has long been characterized by an attempt to move directly from broad ideological aspects of collective identities to changes in dependent variables, as if the relation was, in effect, causal. In reviewing this literature, Anderson (1986) remarks that particularized ideology hypotheses tend to tautologies in which, for example, Catholicism is posited as an explanation of higher fertility in Catholic parts of a population.

As noted some years ago (Kreager 1982, 1986), demographic systems in their cultural dimension exercise their effects not directly on numerical outcomes, but on the structure of personal and social categories which constitute collective identities, and the strategies that are recognized as acceptable in them. I illustrated this point using some well-known case studies from rural Africa and historical Europe, but a large amount of bread-and-butter analysis of population statistics can be used to make the same point. Sam Preston and his colleagues (1992), for example, recently remarked that the significant overcounting of black widows at younger and older ages in the U.S. census of 1910 appears to have been due to attempts by these women to disguise births out of wedlock. Adult black mortality and the corresponding propensity to widowhood were at the time quite high, so these women were availing themselves of a plausible alias. The matter does not stop there, however, as if reported widowhood was merely an alias, a bias in the data to be corrected.

These women's claims to widowhood were also statements about the acceptable identity of marriages and families at the time, and about negotiating black identities in a dominant white society. Preston et al. rightly remark that a longitudinal perspective on identity manipulations of this kind is important for gauging the significance of current numbers of single-parent households and births outside of marriage. They are part and parcel of a long-term relationship between black and white (and Indian, and other) identities in American society, in which black widows and demographers have occupied a number of different identities and used strategies that go with them.

In sum, the processes by which people identify themselves and others and how they come to be classified in and out of groups are, and have ever been, integral to population dynamics and their analysis. Processes of identity construction and reconstruction are primary demographic phenomena, since they shape the size, composition, and structure of recognized and contested populations. Analytical experience, after all, makes this something of a truism: how we define a population for demographic purposes predetermines much of the subsequent findings. The accuracy and usefulness of demographic information depends on how certain identities rather than others are or have been affixed to persons and groups. It is inevitable in this at once classificatory and mensurational exercise that the identities of groups existing in particular localities and regions should often come to be central issues in critical debates across the whole range of applied demography, from discussions of the adequacy of coresidence as an identifier of domestic and kin groups in historical sources to the logistics of counting refugees. The tendency to treat the multiplicity and mutability of identities only to the extent that they pose technical problems of bias and misreporting in effect throws out a major dimension of population dynamics.

In this critical activity our concerns bear an important similarity to those of the peoples we study. For members of a given collectivity, from the family to the state, deciding who is and who is not included in the group generally determines its capacities. The estimated capacities of one group in comparison with others have a direct bearing on courses of action for all the collectivities that may be implicated. The fact that people may report their ethnic, religious, and other identities differently from one census to the next and may tailor birth, marital, occupational, and migration histories to suit currently preferred statuses, is significant not only as a potential source of bias affecting the analysis of trends but as evidence of the active adjustment of population composition and structure to changing circumstances.

Identity and Evidence

The old trinity of birth, death, and migration thus turns out to be not all there is to the most elementary constituents of a population. At least, the matter of who and what to count as belonging in one population as opposed to some other can no longer be taken as given by the conventions that happen to have been employed in extant censuses and surveys. The familiar balancing equation, in which total population at a given time (t + 1) is the additive outcome of an initial population (t) plus natural increase and net migration, needs to be rewritten to include a denominator:

$$\frac{\text{population}(t) + \text{births} - \text{deaths} + \text{net migration}}{\text{identity}} = \text{population}(t + 1).$$

In other words, the membership of population (t+1) depends on the extent to which its members can be considered continuous with population (t); the births, deaths, and migrations of the intervening period must likewise conform to criteria of membership.

From one point of view, this restatement contains no surprises. Demography, as ever, faces the difficulty of classifying and recording events in a way which both captures local entities and realities whilst retaining general comparative value. From another perspective, however, potential mutability and multiplicity in the identity of a population's members may appear to raise troubling questions about the nature of demographic evidence. In short, it appears to open the door to a class of evidence that can not be falsified by usual quantitative procedures. As a collective phenomenon, identity appears to be of a different order than the vital events themselves. This difference is in fact a misimpression.

The births, deaths, and migrations that make up the demographic record are generally taken to refer to physical events. Their attributes (age, sex, parity, and so forth) are assumed likewise to describe physical states and properties. Demographic data, in this respect, are as "hard" as any one could hope to find in social inquiry. Moreover, as a record of material aggregates, demographic data are subject to statistical regularities as are any data on physical processes. Thus, in some of the early and seminal statements of advanced mathematical demography, parallel instances from vital statistics and chemistry could be treated together in a single article (Lotka 1907).

From a physical datum point of view, shifts of identity, whilst they may arise from material circumstances and have some decidedly material consequences (as in the Jewish, black and Indian examples, above), appear to consist essentially in changes of classification. The black American women described by Preston et al. would seem at first glance to illustrate this very well. At the level of physical events, a demographer wishing to check the identity "widows" claimed by these women may discover that their claims are falsified by reference to other vital series, namely, the absence of sufficient adult male mortality over the relevant period to account for the increase in widowhood. Subsequent correction of this misreporting will require adjustment of other data series. A certain number of legitimate births, for example, may need to be corrected to illegitimate ones. However, as we have seen, the authors raise a question of identity which unsettles this tidy picture. Is reported widowhood merely a statement about the timing of physical events (marriage and death)? Might the response of these black women be more closely related to the moral judgment implicit in a classification scheme that recognizes only certain partnerships and their offspring as legitimate? If so, can this definition of marriage be expected to yield accurate data on this population? And if it does not reflect the pattern of unions relevant to fertility, will it provide suitable demographic correlates for studying the causes behind changes in family and group composition?

These questions subtly shift the ground of discussion. The nature of demographic evidence is no longer decided, as common sense might suppose, at the level of recorded physical events. What counts as an event is decided, rather, at the level of the population: ostensibly discrete physical events are of course interdependent; they obtain their significance according to relationships in a number of interdependent series which together compose the units of family and wider collective membership. The usual methods of falsification and correction remain informative, since they are consistent with the census definitions employed at the time. However, such falsification and correction are no longer definitive, because more than one identity of the population and its constituent units is at issue.

The physical datum view of demographic evidence thus turns out to be a convenient myth. Demographic textbooks do not, in any case, claim that established methods produce data that are a pure and absolutely literal recording of vital events as a physical stratum. Rather, the demographic record is what can be achieved using systematic census, registration, and survey procedures backed up by mathematical models and statistical checks. Falsification is relative not to brute reality, but to the conventions used to define it. Recognizing identity as the denominator of population processes requires us to take the conventional nature of the demographic record seriously.

In this respect, the fundamental contribution of the Princeton group's findings lies not just in the prominent role they came to assign to cultural factors, but in the major turning toward the problem of collective identities which their methodology (with its attempt to specify demographic changes for cultural entities at sub-national and regional levels) set in motion. The shift is from what Anderson describes as the earlier attitude, in which "cultural factors were often treated as contaminating influences to be controlled away" (1986:299–300), to one in which the units used in the study of a population are supposed to reflect people's experience of demographic change over time. The "contaminating influences" are, of course, the several voices that have contributed to making the institutions, categories, and measures that compose the demographic record. To the extent that methods of reducing bias succeed in clarifying and substantiating the record of events, they remain essential tools. But insofar as in these methods what counts as bias (or, indeed, what counts as an event) is decided solely from the perspective of certain voices and not others, such methods can only be a part of the scholarly and technical apparatus by which data and trends are evaluated.

Analyzing the role of culture in demographic change in terms of its identity functions therefore leads us to four fundamentally historical questions: How have certain collective identities come to be the conventional aggregate units employed in demographic and related record systems? What historical relations exist between these identities and others? Has exclusion or inclusion in the official record subsequently influenced the several identities at issue? What bearing does this feedback have on the demographic record over time? This last question, as we have seen, is likely to be particularly important for understanding variations of quantum and trend in vital and familial events where self-identification and official classification are at odds. If the four questions have not been asked and reasonable working answers provided there is good reason to regard data and analyses as subject to doubt.

We have entered here on the critical problem with which Allan Hill concludes his contribution (chapter 9 in this volume). He remarks on the plethora of contemporary census and survey data that provide the standard, ready-made units of population on which most research and policy studies rely, and he goes on to note how forces at work within the scientific and policy community push research and analysis into accepting these units at face value. The complex relation of demographic patterns to their context is in consequence reduced to cross-tabulation. This "easy definition of a population," Hill argues, "has blinded us to more complex thoughts about what holds people together and what divides them."

As the above illustrations indicate, understanding people's memberships and their oppositions to other collective identities means asking how the demographic record enfranchises certain voices, and whether these voices are representative. Some, like those of Preston's black "widows," are present in the record, but speak to us obliquely through the categories and measures employed at the time. Still other voices—and potentially no less significant ones— are often effectively silenced. Hill's provocative remarks, like the example from Preston et al., refer not only to populations of the kind specified by englobing classifications like nationality, religion, and ethnicity, but to sub-populations within and amongst these identities, as defined by variables like age, marital status, and fertility.[3]

One implication of Hill's argument, with its emphasis on the capacity of professional realities to shape the research agenda, is that the tendency to accept easy definitions of population comes not just from the misimpression that reported identities are of a different order of events than births, deaths and migrations. The problem also lies in the nature of "normal science" (cf.

Kuhn 1962). In general, when presented with searching questions that point beyond customary research paradigms, scientific communities will carry on very largely as before; the normal response is to make relatively modest adjustments using available data sets and procedures on the assumption that the field must get on with its usual tasks and that troubling questions may be accommodated by an accumulation of relatively modest adjustments. In the case of population studies, this tendency means that the inaccuracy and incompleteness of easy definitions continue to affect the formulation of hypotheses about the peoples in question.

Coale's suggestion that research on the influence of culture in demographic change can be reduced to the study of diffusion may be seen in this light. As I have described elsewhere, the concept of diffusion has a checkered history in the social sciences, closely associated with the very theories of economic development and modernization that the findings of Coale's Princeton researchers called into question. Talk about diffusion as a possible cultural framework for explaining major social trends has been fashionable at roughly thirty-year intervals since the 1890s, but none of the formulations has provided conceptual and methodological tools suitable to understanding the mutability and multiplicity of values and practices that the heterogeneity of demographic behavior presents (Kreager 1993, in press). Diffusion research of course requires that identifiable subpopulations exist; examples are media audiences sharing a common culture and local networks of interpersonal exchange. However, when it comes to specifying these units of population, research has followed the easy option Hill has criticized: the presence and historical reality of populations is simply taken as given and attention is focused on tracing a limited number of diffusion pathways presupposed by such a definition of a population. Criticism of diffusionism is now becoming more widespread (see, e.g., Mason 1992; McNicoll 1992; Greenhalgh 1996).

Identity and History

The main outcomes of the preceding sections of this chapter may be summarized in three points. The first and most basic is that the mutability and multiplicity of collective and personal identities is a normal feature of the way populations adjust to changing circumstances. The structure, quantum, and tempo of population trends are bound to be influenced by shifting identities since changes in people's reproductive and other vital values and practices are fundamental means by which they express and represent themselves. In important instances changing demographic patterns may be constituted largely by changes people make in their own or others' collective representation. Observing and monitoring the dynamics of identity should be regarded as a central task of population research.

Second, in facing up to the importance of identity, we are confronted by an ambiguity underlying demography's central concept, the idea of a population. Whenever we try to understand the role of population in history, we enter that history. The formal study of populations and their constituents then becomes subject to the voices of some or all of the parties having an interest in the demographic record and its analysis. The ingenuity of formal procedures, the simplicity of common-sense reference to the population record as a physical stratum, and the logic of cross-tabulation, were never intended to provide a framework that would reconcile these voices and their histories. The much more limited and critical function of these devices is supposed to be confined to evaluating and making allowance for the effects of the voices as they distort the accuracy of established record-keeping procedures. We are thus presented with two rather different notions of population. One reflects a model of professional inquiry that allows the scientist or registrar to stand somehow outside of history, as if his or her identity, and the history of methods and concepts, are of no consequence. The second concept of population would put the demographic record and its keeping back into history in order to understand how the interplay of voices has shaped the nature and pattern of vital events and the role of the inevitably selective quantitative record we have of them.

Recognizing that there is more than one idea of population at issue in any given setting should not, as some anthropologists appear to suggest, lead us to try to subvert or abandon demography's formal methodology.[4] The formal record and the methods used to develop and maintain it remain a major voice (or voices) with a capacity to shape policy and opinion; the ability of science and administration to construct people(s) as populations needs to be understood in its own terms and placed amongst the other voices. Viewed historically, this methodology is closely bound up with the making of many modern collective identities; its generative capacity is part of the agency of cultures as they interact with others.

The third outcome, therefore, is that the problem of identity requires a systematic approach to understanding the production of demographic knowledge in history. To this end, I outlined a framework of four questions in the preceding section. Here, however, we again encounter the forces of normal science that have tended to push identity to the margins of population research. It is one thing to examine historical sources, including censuses and registrar's reports, as part of ethnographic (or, indeed, of any careful) inquiry into the peoples of some part of the world. It is another to embark upon a general history of the relationship between quantitative and other definitions of population. The latter task appears all the more daunting since the development of demography is integral to the immense subject of the rise of modern government and scientific institutions over the last two centuries.

Fortunately, the story of the statistical movement in the nineteenth century has recently become the object of much historical attention, embracing technical aspects of the development of probability (see, e.g., Institut National de la Statistique et des Etudes Economiques 1976; Porter 1986; Stigler 1986; Hacking 1990) and the central place that descriptive statistics came to play in political, economic, and social reforms of the period (Desrosières 1993; Bourguet 1989; Perrot 1984; Alonso and Starr 1987). Taken as a straight subject in the history of science, these developments stand outside the usual interests of anthropologists and demographers. There is more, however, than the technical complexity of this subject that is likely to make it appear an unpromising avenue to understanding problems in population research. For much of the nineteenth century, quantitative approaches were bound up with a scientific attitude now regarded as a naive empiricism. On the one hand, extensive numerical compilations were supposed to provide the quantitative basis from which universal laws of human society would be derived; on the other, the application of laws of probability to this corpus supposed that the human element could be eliminated from the exercise. As one of the statistical enthusiasts put it, "introduce a numerical theory into the most confused assemblage of facts, and they start at once into a science" (Guy 1839:45).

There is no need to relive these old debates. They are being dealt with already in the above-mentioned literatures, and neither demographers nor anthropologists show much inclination to return to the project of a "social physics." There is, however, another side of this history which has received remarkably little attention, and which has direct bearing on the cultural dimension of population change as a current problem of substance and method. The rise of statistics as a scientific, social, and governmental reform movement belongs to the same era as the spread of nationalism. The intimate relation between the two was essential not only to the logic that established demography's role in government but to the central place that fertility, more than any other demographic variable, has come to play in the preoccupations of modern states. From this point of view, the production of demographic knowledge in history ceases to be a technical and academic specialty of historians of science. It was integral to the making of many populations and identities both in the demographic record and as now popularly recognized.

My argument can now move on a further step. Having outlined the implications of identity as a conceptual framework for studying the agency of culture in demographic behavior and its implications for demographic evidence, we can now begin to look at the impact of competing collective identities as they have shaped the population record and attempts by demographers and others to interpret it. I shall begin by tracing briefly the problem of collective identity as a factor in the development of population inquiry in the nineteenth century. This history turns out to have an immediate interest since it enables us to see that the approach to culture put forward by Coale, far from being a new direction in population studies, returns us to a nineteenth-century conundrum. I conclude with an example of how the multiplicity of voices underlying the demographic record can be disentangled.

Nationalism and the Rise of Demography

The integral role of population and population statistics in the logic of nationalism and the emergence of fertility as a central concern of modern nation-states, may be summarized as follows.[5] Nationalism as a political philosophy arose in the attempt to resolve the authoritarianism of the ancien régime. One of its principal innovations was to give a new and apparently definitive meaning to the concept of population. The old empires and states of Europe had been cobbled together by princely fiat, marriage, and war. Their populations included peoples of diverse ethnicities, religions, and so forth. From the standpoint of princes and rulers, the diverse character of the nationalities of which a state was composed was a secondary matter. The boundaries convenient to princes might divide peoples amongst several states and lump them together with other nationalities. What was important about a population was its loyalty and productivity; the arrangement of boundaries and units of state should ensure this by assembling zones of production and ports of trade together within a single defensible condominium. The concerns of seventeenth- and eighteenth-century political arithmetic were a direct reflection of this attitude to the state and its members.

In contrast, early and influential writers on nationalism like Herder and Fichte, along with spokesmen of the French and American revolutions, began from the view that sovereignty rests not in the manipulations of an aristocratic elite, but in national populations as a whole. What defines such populations? According to these writers of the late eighteenth and early nineteenth centuries, a nation is a people who have a common linguistic, cultural, and historical experience, together with associated material conditions such as residence in a common territory and shared descent. Of these characteristics, common language and culture were considered most important and were often traced to ancient periods and sources. In addition, nations were characterized not only as historical and cultural but natural phenomena in several senses. Their habitation of particular geographical regions, entailing characteristic modes of livelihood, material culture, and natural symbols were considered to give them organic ties to their territory and environment. Residence in one's homeland from time immemorial gave peoples natural rights to such places in addition to the right of self-determination to which, as original peoples, they were entitled under prevailing ideas of natural law. Such natural associations were often further legitimized by reference to God's laws of nature.

As a wider movement of political, social and economic reform, nationalism came to entail more than a doctrine involving certain ideas about the identity and destiny of supposedly autochthonous national cultures. As Seton-Watson

(1977), Anderson (1983), Gellner (1983), Hobsbawm (1983), and other writers on the history of nationalism and ethnicity have described, the identification of the state with a nation or national culture availed the state of all the legitimizing symbolism of that culture, whilst making available, in turn, the rituals of state and its bureaucratic apparatus to articulate and further develop identity. Such "official nationalisms" came to characterize not only states formed in the nineteenth century, like Germany, Italy, Japan, and Thailand, but established states and multinational empires, like Britain, Austria-Hungary, and Russia. A burgeoning anthropological and historical literature now exists on "imagined communities," "invented traditions," and the like. Amongst the themes of this literature is an emphasis on the modular character which the state, with its ability to influence popular opinion via education, economic policies, and the media, could give to national culture. Especially important was the presiding influence of professional groups such as doctors, teachers, clergymen, scientists, businessmen, and lawyers. In this respect, a brief glance across the list of famous nineteenth-century vital statisticians, who were generally drawn from such groups—Farr, Quetelet, Engel, Southwood-Smith, Guy, Schwartner, Villermé, and so on—or at the fervent prose style in which they often wrote, is a reminder that scientific, sanitary, and social reform movements of the mid-century were seen at the time as elements in the realization of inherent national capabilities and propensities for greatness.

Logically, the need for public statistical institutions follows merely from an equation of popular and national sovereignty: if the state is based on all the people, then their number, condition, and distribution must be known so that policies can be designed appropriate to their needs, and so that the people will themselves be informed of their rights and responsibilities. In this way the identification of the state with a nation or people extends directly to the concept of a population. Ancien régime ideas about population thence began to give way: once the legitimacy of states ceases to be based on dynastic legacies, conquests, and factional allegiances and comes instead to depend on what are felt to be natural and primordial national communities, then it becomes necessary to take a different approach to the way populations are created and maintained. Henceforth the population on which each state depends must, so to speak, be home-produced.

Populations come to be viewed as closed in three important senses. First, and obviously, they are cut off from other peoples by the boundaries of states. Second, this administrative and political closure introduces an important epistemological closure as a precondition of demographic ideals of complete enumeration and registration. This proved highly convenient for the application and further development of population models like the life table. Third, it was noted that national populations are economically and environmentally constrained since their growth is ultimately limited by the territory and nature of the ancestral domain. National populations therefore have to guard themselves especially against overpopulation. This argument appears independently, but at the same time, in the works of the two modern authors whose formative theories remain most famous and perennially controversial in the domains of population (Malthus 1890 [1798]) and nationalism (Fichte 1988 [1801]). Their works were taken up, popularized, and applied by the professional cadres already remarked. An interesting corollary to the study of official nationalism is that it requires us to revise the stereotype of nationalist attitudes to population as more or less automatically pronatalist. Prominent continental political economists whose writings have a strongly nationalist tenor, like List, were solidly Malthusian, whilst Malthusian vital statisticians, like Farr, were fervent nationalists.

The realignment of ideas of nation, state, and population in the first half of the nineteenth century also helps us to understand the abrupt emergence of public statistical bodies on a large scale in this period. Demographers have often been puzzled by this (see Glass 1973). General resistance to census taking in the ancien régime is well known. As Hecht (1976) notes, only Sweden and Prussia managed to establish regular enumerations in the eighteenth century, but the circulation of such information was generally restricted. The appearance of national statistical offices is thus a kind of litmus test for the diffusion of ideas of nation-building amongst the challenged aristocratic elites as well as the emerging intelligentsia and middle classes of the period. Following France (1800), Prussia (1805), and Bavaria (1808), national statistical offices appeared in the Grand Duchy of Tuscany (1818), in the dozen or so German-speaking principalities (beginning with Wurtemburg in 1820 and ending in Saxony in 1831), and in Holland (1828), Austria (1829), Belgium (1831), Sicily (1832), Denmark (1833), Norway (1837), and England (1837). Census and registration functions were the primary responsibility of these offices; the term demography had entered European vocabularies by the 1850s. Government statisticians and reformers recognized their role as an international movement by convening a series of eight international statistical congresses between 1854 and 1878. The ostensible purpose of these meetings was to exchange information on technical matters, standardize measures, and promote application of statistics to a wider field of what they considered essential problems.

It was at this point, at the very inception of demography as a national and international institution, that the problem of collective identities manifested itself in a big way. The sequence of summaries of Congress proceedings reports successive attempts to formulate methods of registration for constituent national populations, defined in various ways (Congrèss Général de Statistique 1872). Although considerable progress was made, the recommendations put forward by the congressistes were never widely adopted by member states. The first Congress (in 1854) asserted as a fundamental principle the importance of studying actual populations ("population de fait") rather than merely collecting data according to the administrative boundaries of states and provinces ("population de droit"). The distinction aroused some debate: it was clear that the latter phrase referred to legacies of the ad hoc arrangements of the ancien régime; the former, however, implied some unspecified amalgam of quantitative and cultural criteria.

The difficulty of carrying out this proposition was acknowledged four years later at the meeting in Vienna, which proposed that all states compile a "statistique ethnographique," in which the territory, customs, language, physical characteristics, and several relations between national populations constituent of states would be compiled (see also Heuschling 1847). At this stage, it was hoped that this task could be carried out using the apparatus provided by existing administrative units. At London in 1860 it was decided that information on central nationalist questions, notably language, whilst perhaps not indispensable in all states, should nonetheless be required wherever practicable. Seven years later the issue was still on the agenda in Florence, where a more elaborate demographic system, or "community statistics," was proposed. At this meeting it was agreed that inquiry could not be confined to administrative data collected according to the boundaries of provinces and standard registration districts but should record characteristics according to the boundaries of "influential local populations." The proposal is impressive by current standards no less than those of the time. It acknowledges a need to understand hierarchical relationships between groups in a community and acknowledges that such groups have a capacity to stimulate action and to adopt varying forms of solidarity, making them a real complement to public institutions. The need for community or ethnographic statistics was extended to colonial areas at the meeting in The Hague in 1869, coupled with the suggestion that local elites would need to be developed for this purpose. At Budapest in 1876, a Russian delegate again put the subject on the agenda, this time calling it "local statistics" and noting that units of population "not defined by arbitrary administrative boundaries" are as relevant to the states of Western Europe as in the East (Neuvième Session 1876: 185–7).

As Kedourie observed, a characteristic feature of the idea of national self-determination is its inherent instability (1961). Translating this observation into demographic terms, we can say that the mere collection of data on a constituent national population is effectively to enfranchise it, enabling members of that population and others to point to its relative advantage or disadvantage according to several indices of national development, from birth and death rates to social and economic indicators. Such enfranchisement carries obvious dangers from the standpoint of the state. If, as early writers on nationalism argued, each "original people" is entitled to its own statehood, then evidence of relative disadvantage may legitimize not only claims to rectify disadvantages but possibly claims for secession. These ideas remain very active in the world today. A *New York Times* article published February 7, 1993, cited forty-eight states in which ethnic conflicts were currently in process; at the time the Soviet Union had yet to break up. According to the *United Nations Statistical Yearbook*, however, only a handful of states are as yet willing to make a sustained effort to collect data relative to membership of constituent nationalities.

Had the Congress proposals for a statistical ethnography been widely adopted by nineteenth-century states, an immense body of data would have been generated on precisely the questions of cultural specification that have become topical since the Princeton European Fertility Project. The work of the Princeton group has returned us to the problem that our statistical forebears recognized a century ago: the question of whether, and to what extent, it is possible to define units of population that reflect the social aggregates in which demographic change is actually experienced and arbitrated.

The Postwar Reprise

It is in some ways an awkward fact for demography that the statistical movement was bound up in the problematic thesis that "state equals national culture equals people equals population." Demography gained a professional identity from the nation-state, and certain undoubted methodological and analytical advantages associated with the fiction that national populations are closed.[6] But the price of this fiction has been a dialectic in which entry into the demographic record is perennially contestable. On the one hand, once a state begins to collect data which can be used to attribute identity and assess the relative advantages and disadvantages of different subpopulations, it is inevitable that some constituent groups will find it politic to capitalize on this data. Claims and counter-claims by other groups may ensue. On the other hand, as Grebenik notes, modern states and party interests within them have often used quantification not just to specify but to demonize particular groups (1989). He cites race and overpopulation as the main forms of this dire tendency.

A classic case is British eugenics, from Galton's early article on the differential fertility of social classes (1873) to Pearson's measurement of "reproductive selection" (1909). These eugenic pioneers set out to establish that a growing percentage of the native British population was composed of inferior genetic stock. Writing before the rediscovery of Mendel and the rise of genetics, they relied on simple population measures to construct the collective identities that they believed were a threat to national development. At the time the decline of British fertility, as in all of Western Europe, was lamented. But Galton and Pearson pointed to what they considered an even more serious threat: an increasing proportion of British fertility was contributed by the working classes. Equating class differences directly with differences of genetic quality, they predicted the rapid deterioration of the genetic stock of Britain and a radical decline of national strength.

Such arguments, with their supposed demographic supports, became common in the inter-war period. In Italy in the 1930s, the Consiglio superiore di statistica, directed by the distinguished demographer Corrado Gini, used a battery of simple measures like the ratio of births to marriages to establish the identity of subfertile groups within the population and to legitimize Mussolini's pronatalist legislation (Ipsen 1993). Family histories provided Nazi Germany with documentation of supposedly pure Aryan stock, underwriting eugenic policies applied to Jewish and Gypsy populations. Following the war, of course, emphasis shifted to economic rather than hereditary sources of national strength. A global rather than merely European perspective was seen as appropriate. The major threat nonetheless continued to be seen as the excessive reproductive performance of relatively poor and disadvantaged populations. Following Notestein, these populations were identified as national and ethnic groups living in, or immigrating from, the Third World.[7]

The continuity that Grebenik suggests between the overpopulation family of demon identities and the eugenic family is neatly illustrated by a publishing detail which complements the important commentaries recently published on this period (in addition to Grebenik 1989, see Hodgson 1983 and Szreter 1993). Just prior to the war, Professor Gini was invited to give a lecture in Chicago, in which he eloquently and passionately presented the rationale for nationalist population policies such as Italy's. His lecture was published in the prestigious series of Harris Foundation Lectures (Gini 1930). The next volume to appear in the series, immediately after the war, is well-known to demographers because it contains Notestein's first and seminal formulation of demographic transition theory (Notestein 1945). What has rarely, if ever, been remarked is the other demographic contribution to this volume, clearly intended as a complement to Notestein's and a riposte to demographers like Gini. Written by the distinguished American demographer Frank Lorimer and entitled "Population as a Problem of Quality," this paper highlights the shift in the choice of identities believed to pose a threat to national and international development.

Lorimer's essay explicitly refutes nationalist population policies, especially eugenic ones. "Qualitative differences among nations and races," Lorimer wrote, "have commonly been ascribed to differences in biological heredity . . . but the whole weight of scientific evidence today indicates that most interpretations of this sort are fallacious." "The popularity of such doctrines," he continued, "rests in part on the psychological tendency for every person to identify himself with a particular group and to overevaluate both himself and the group." Lorimer then develops a contrast between "rational" societies, associated with adaptability to modern economic forces, and societies characterized by adherence to tradition. The latter he characterizes in terms of "types of religion which emphasize compensation . . . rather than ways of controlling nature or ways of living . . . [and] . . . accentuated personal conflict or excessive use of stimulants and narcotics." Such cultural traits, he concludes, "reflect relations between conquerors and subject peoples, or between masters and slaves" (1945:59–61).

In the same vein, Notestein makes his famous remark that traditional cultures are regulated by "older taboos" which lead people to accept high fertility passively (1945:39–40). Construction of demographic categories and measures with which to establish this identity, from the Khanna Study to the KAP surveys, followed in due course. As Hodgson and Szreter have noted, this emphasis on traditional culture nonetheless allowed these cultures to be seen as manipulable: family planning programs would target selected cultural obstacles at a local level. Put another way, as the war experience receded, the powerful and potentially threatening association of nationalism and traditional culture became less of an issue. Refutations and condemnations like Lorimer's no longer seemed necessary.

Nonetheless, a major shift was effected by these classic formulations of demographic transition in two closely related respects. First, the significance of culture in population change was displaced from the macro- to the micro-level. Second, and more particularly, this shift changed culture from a primary characteristic of nations to one significant only in respect to local (and, indeed, chiefly domestic) groups. At the time this probably appeared to be good sense. National culture as an important influence on population (and particularly on fertility) was tainted by its association with the eugenic policies of national socialism. Demographic transition theory, whilst dissociating itself from these approaches, nonetheless retained a major tenet of demography's involvement in nineteenth-century ideas of nationalism and state intervention: the idea that fertility measurement and control are essential to national development. In effect, postwar demography sought to distance itself from qualitative approaches, as defined in Lorimer's essay, whilst keeping the old equation that treated national populations as homogeneous or (in the new dispensation provided by ideas of economic development) as tending more or less inevitably to homogeneity. Rationalist assumptions about the nature of modern culture, with its progressive individualism, were substituted for the old discussion of the rootedness of national cultures. Certain traditional identifiers like religious affiliation of course remained, but the negative significance of such factors was made clear by their function as lag effects on fertility transition. They were not expected to play a positive role, or to stand as explanations on their own.

What remained of culture, then, as a potentially significant demographic factor was its role in microlevel phenomena. Lorimer's subsequent and more thoughtful work (1954) set out to show that the demographic transition as a paradigm for research did include an important niche for culture, and one which called especially for anthropological expertise. This expertise, however, was viewed as definitive primarily in the context of societies perceived as backward or exotic; more generally, anthropological data might complement quantitative approaches. The fact that the intellectual and scientific contributions of anthropology were seen to lie in its field methods reinforced culture's exile as a major problem at higher levels of aggregation. As anthropology was also perceived at the time to be a subject that did not study European populations, the politically loaded relation between national and other cultures in this area was likewise avoided.

In sum, whilst the marginalization of culture in postwar demography gave a decidedly secondary place to anthropology in the emerging field of population and development research, the sources of this relegation derived less from any specific attitude to anthropology than from a wider consensus against taking culture as a major force in modern history. As we have seen, banishing identities and the problems of recording them was not a new solution. The failed program of "statistique ethnographique," however, was by this time forgotten.[8] As the results of the Princeton European Fertility Project (not to mention the resurgence of contested identities worldwide) have shown, past attempts to banish the problem of collective identity have not suppressed ethnic, national, and other differences. Such attempts have, however, created ambiguities and gaps in the historical record on which competing interpretations continue to feed.

The attempt in postwar population studies to put aside the problem of culture as a major factor at the macrolevel undoubtedly encouraged the easy definitions of population that Hill criticizes. Marginalization made possible a style of interpretation, from Notestein's first essay in transition theory up to Coale's reconsideration, in which national data derived from standard survey and governmental sources could be taken without qualm as untainted by problematic cultural differences, nationalist, ethnic, or otherwise. The consequences, however, have turned out to be quite the opposite of what Lorimer and Notestein expected. Ironically, the easy definition of population as standardized by the modern state enabled the old nineteenth-century nationalist equation to triumph at precisely the point at which nationalism was thought to be in eclipse. The idea of "nation" or "people" once again attained an equivalent value to that of the state and could be identified unequivocally with its population. This was not the only irony. By excluding the problem of national culture and its relation to other collective identities, classic demographic transition theory also set the stage for the manner in which the problem was rediscovered by Coale. As noted above, when Coale came to report the findings of Leasure and Lesthaeghe, he returned, quite unself-consciously, to a language and form characteristic of nineteenth-century discourse, in which cultures located traditionally in certain European regions were taken to be effectively timeless natural units of population.[9]

Parameters

The short history of modern population and identity outlined above helps to put in perspective the almost syndrome-like character of collective identities. History may well repeat itself in the oppositions and enmities of national, ethnic, and other collective identities. But this process is no less evident in the repeated tendency of scientific and administrative communities to marginalize the problem.[10] We thus return to the agency or generative capacity of the symbolic systems by which collective and personal identities are constructed, and the power of this agency to shape the demographic record.

As I noted above, the fundamental balancing equation on which all demography rests would be expressed more accurately if identity were introduced as its denominator. The equation then provides us with a simple way of summarizing changes that have been a major factor in shaping population theory and measurement during the last two hundred years. With the rise of nationalism in the nineteenth century, the denominator came to equate the state with the idea of a dominant and homogeneous national culture, thus setting in motion a dialectic of alternative identities (nationalities, peoples, ethnicities, minorities, etc.). As nationalism came to be interpreted in this century in terms of national socialism, the denominator of "national culture" narrowed to a racial and eugenic definition. Demographic transition theory, with its socioeconomic conception of national development, proposed a radical correction: the denominator would be removed altogether from the equation . . . only to be reintroduced by Coale and his followers.

Events in Central and Eastern Europe since perestroika have without doubt brought about a much wider awareness that the cultural integration of nation-states is a far from settled matter. At least one demographer, Geoffrey McNicoll (1992), has suggested that assertion of "primordial loyalties to tribe and ethnos" may actually increase the potential of income differentials and environmental deterioration to exacerbate perceived group differences. From this viewpoint, modernization and differential demographic transition, far from expunging nationalism and ethnic diversity, become mechanisms for their perpetuation.

It is hardly in the interests of a scientific community like population studies to treat phenomena widely observed to have a major demographic dimension as peripheral to its primary subject matter. The continuity and change of national, ethnic, and minority groups are surely a case in point. Population research might do well to take advantage of prevailing concerns about world turbulence (and the funding which tends to be associated with such concerns) in order to make the demography of collective identities one of its principal interests. As I have suggested, the implications of identity are not confined to englobing ethnic, religious, and national labels, but act through the ramifications of shifting and competing identities on principal demographic variables. The payoff of such a research strategy is likely, therefore, to include significant improvements in the range and quality of data.

That said, what are the parameters of identity construction, maintenance, and change that need careful observation and analytical definition? Four general descriptive properties are apparent from the preceding discussion:

(1) *Openness.* In most cases there is no one-to-one correspondence between a recognized collective identity and the human aggregate which demographic records of its membership are supposed detail. Memberships are neither closed nor mutually exclusive. People commonly belong to several reputed groups: family, religion, occupation, firm, class, tribe, party, lineage, ethnicity, nation, state. People vary their affiliations and allegiances according to context, abandoning old identities and embracing new ones. Such changes may be imposed on them. The shifting composition and structure of collectivities is an important part of how these entities, severally and together, respond to changing economic, political, environmental, and other circumstances. This elasticity of response does not mean that the established fiction of a complete enumeration, or the analytical devices built upon it, must be discarded. Demographic methods remain a central and useful way of freezing identities in a given duration for purposes of analysis and discussion. Clearly, the effects of the particular characteristics chosen as collective identifiers requires critical scrutiny. But this is no less the case for ethnography which, as a cultural refrigerator, merely works more slowly and unevenly.

(2) *Simultaneity or multi-dimensionality.* As people hold multiple identities which are not mutually exclusive, and may vary some or all of them over time, the model of social action adopted in the study of collective identities must be able to handle shifts in several dimensions of identity simultaneously. We need to be able to examine the effects that a change in one dimension may have on others.

(3) *Reflexivity.* As population studies is itself an important player in the process of identity construction, any model of this process should be applicable to collective identities as created via demographic and related methods.

(4) *Selective amnesia.* Adopting or changing a given identity often activates past identities, for example, of other groups to which a person may be considered to have belonged or to which his or her ancestors were reputedly members. Sudden rememberings of this sort are often not acknowledged. Registration and survey procedures likewise establish patterns of exclusion and inclusion in which past classifications are retained as a scattered part. The attempts to correct and adjust series and relations between them may become as much a part of selective amnesia as the irregularities they seek to remove. The "accountancy core" of demography, as it is sometimes called, appears to contain a great deal of evidence, direct and indirect, on the properties and trends of collective mutability and multiplicity.

Evidently these parameters are not mutually exclusive, items (2) through (4) being corollaries of (1). All four items, whilst general in nature, derive from observation of historical and contemporary societies, and are therefore descriptive rather than prescriptive in character. It is appropriate to proceed by examining particular instances.

The Census and the Colonial State: An Indian Example

The nineteenth-century statistical congresses, as we have seen, were quick to recognize that the study of demographic diversity requires a correspondingly major and long-term commitment to the study of cultural diversity. Their recommendation at The Hague congress in 1869 that colonial administrations have particular responsibilities of this kind follows logically from the observation, made at the Florence meeting two years before, that statistical data reveal hierarchical relations between constituent populations. In India these issues had already entered administrative thinking by the 1850s. As part of the consolidation of colonial rule over an agrarian society, one of the first tasks embarked upon by British administrators was a comprehensive land register which would establish people's rights and tax liabilities on a village-by-village basis. As Smith (1984) notes, these "settlement reports" from the 1850s onwards relied on a method that was at base a household census supplemented by commentaries on marriage, religion, caste, and other factors necessary to understand the transmission of property. During the next twenty years, the need to synthesize and compare experience led to ever wider compilations at district and provincial levels. These compilations, styled variously as statistical reports, gazetteers, medical and topological surveys, and provincial censuses, contained a mixture of quantitative and qualitative observation of the kind advocated by the statistical congresses. They reflected a serious and sustained attempt to accommodate shifting native classifications to the rigor of a standardized census inquiry.

In consequence, when the first all-India census was taken in 1871–72, it could begin from procedures pioneered in these compilations, defining constituent "nationalities" in terms of an elaborate classification of peoples based on racial, religious, and caste criteria, and tabulating differences of age and sex structure accordingly. The twenty-odd identities recognized in the first census grew to several hundred by the fourth census of 1901, in which caste came to be cross-tabulated with education, occupation, and marriage.

The admixture of ethnography and demography contained in these publications, although flawed from the standpoint of present-day methodology, was nonetheless far in advance of anything European censuses attained in the same period, with the possible exception of Austria-Hungary. In them the unity of ethnographic and demographic perspectives is as much a commonplace as the separation of these subjects came to be in population studies after 1950. An early notice of the Ethnographic Survey of India, for instance, took for granted that the census is "an ethnographic document of great value"; the Survey itself was presided over by a census commissioner (H. H. Risley) who was an "accomplished ethnographist" (Foster 1901:139). Likewise the Linguistic Survey of India, which began to appear in 1903, was described by its compiler G. A. Grierson, himself the author of several early ethnographic accounts, as "for the most part based on figures from the Census of 1891" (Grierson 1919:1).

Given the close association of demographic, linguistic, and ethnographic record systems and their continuing importance as the largest body of data on nineteenth- and early twentieth-century Indian populations, there can be little surprise that a critical literature has gradually come to surround them. In evaluating the concepts and methods employed in these sources, a fairly consistent line of argument has been shared by historians and anthropologists from Cohn (1987 [1970]) and Jones (1976; 1981) to the recent Foucault-inspired syntheses of Smith (1984) and Appadurai (1993). This perspective may be summarized in two broad theses.

The first is that the census, although advocated at the time as a neutral, scientific procedure for collecting data, served to fix explicit identities onto shifting collective representations, thereby creating new relationships amongst constituent groups. Although the ostensible rationale for the census, like the statistical reports that preceded it, was purely administrative, its main contribution was in fact conceptual. The decades preceding the census had witnessed a kind of bureaucratic voyage of discovery: the institutions and groups most appropriate for observation and administrative control were not obvious; their identity and nature as units of landholding, household membership, village organization, and so forth, had to be worked out. Caste and communal identities emerged as a central organizing principle of statistical reports gradually from 1850, in response to the need for a social morphology which assimilated data on tens of thousands of villages into a coherent discourse about the state and its problems. From 1870, the Indian census became the modus operandi of this morphology. "It would not be an exaggeration" Cohn remarks, "to say that until 1950 scholars' and scientists' views of the Indian caste system were shaped mainly by data and conceptions growing out of the census operations" (1987:242).

Although the census did fix collective identities to a considerable degree, it paid the inevitable price of setting in motion the dialectic of nationalist, ethnic, communal, and other identities I have described. The second thesis of recent critical writings on the Indian census, however, points provocatively beyond this dialectic, arguing that the census effectively established the ground of present-day communal and ethnic conflict in South Asia. Thus Appadurai, remarking on recent cases of self-immolation and other violent and symbolically charged expressions of caste and communal consciousness, concludes that "this cultural and historical tinder would not burn with the intensity we now see, but for contact with the techniques of the modern nation-state, especially those having to do with number" (1993:335–6).

There can be little question that census data and operations gave rise to new strategies of social mobility and status, and of political and electoral competition. Census classifications were directly relevant to educational and military preferments. They provoked competition between Muslims, Hindus, and Christians by publishing tables which showed the growth and decline of caste groups as a function of religious conversion. The state epitomized the power of its schema by granting separate electorates to major communal identities. It also developed certain classifications for the express purpose of stigmatizing particular groups, notably with respect to female infanticide (Pant 1987). Caste groups responded by petitioning Record Offices to have their registered identity changed, or their place in caste ranking improved (Cohn 1987:248–50). Emerging religious movements likewise sought entries that would distinguish them from more general classifications like "Hindu"; census counts of sects and castes were reported in the popular press and actively debated as indices of relative strength and legitimacy (Jones 1981:87). Many of these issues, from political representation to sex ratios remain controversial today (see Frykenberg 1987; Das Gupta 1987).

Whilst the quantitative devices of the census are indeed crucial to understanding the mutability and contestability of collective identities, it is difficult to isolate the seeds of contemporary violence as flowing from its specifically numerical methodology. Of course, the image of enumeration as a potentially sinister ploy of the state is as old as taxation and conscription; remarks like Appadurai's are very possibly intended as polemical, and to that extent belong to a long-established tradition. That the image on which they rely is a considerable oversimplification is evident from the many historical cases in which registrars and vital statisticians opposed and even subverted the designs of states that employed them.[11]

A less polarized approach is shown in Burghart's account of how the interplay of indigenous, scientific, and administrative interests shaped the record of collective identities in Bihar (1993). In Bihar a subtle indigenous demarcation of caste and occupational statuses on linguistic grounds preceded and survived the standardizing functions of the census. Local scholars, politicians, and journalists were able to maintain different interpretations of this "folk classification" according to circumstance. Colonial authorities, for their part, proposed not one but a sequence of standardizations. Bihar included language groups in which Grierson specialized, and he not only revised his classification of languages and dialects in light of subsequent experience, but invented categories where his schema appeared to require them. Although Grierson worked very closely with the census, his schema were only partly accepted as the basis of its classification of indigenous groups. The meaning and composition of supposedly primordial identities ("Mithala," "Bihari," "Jangali," "Hindi") thus remained fluid. Burghart's article is a good example of why none of the communities that try to shape the demographic record may be assumed to act in a single-minded or monolithic way.

Concluding Note

The history of the Indian census and its related surveys is a further reminder that the project of an anthropological demography is not new. Since the early nineteenth century, the agency of collective identities and of culture more generally have been integral to the idea of the modern nation-state and to many of the groups that comprise its populations. Anthropological demography cannot, therefore, be understood as simply another academic specialty within population studies or anthropology. Nor can it be understood as a subject concerned chiefly with microlevel social phenomena, or with non-Western, less developed peoples. The mutability and multiplicity of collective identities, and their witting and unwitting deployment by states and constituent populations, have been important in shaping population theory and measurement, and hence in shaping population history as we know it. They remain important to the repertoire of adjustments people employ in the face of changing circumstances. Clarification of the agency of collective identities in history has an important bearing on how we collect data and interpret trends in contemporary populations, and could give population studies a significant role in attempts to come to grips with the current round of national, ethnic, and religious conflicts in the world today.

NOTES

This essay is much improved in consequence of comments and questions raised by Jane Schneider, Daniele Bélanger, Tom Fricke, and David Kertzer. The advice of Elizabeth Krishna on Indian sources was particularly helpful. To all of them my sincere thanks.

1. Hammel notes further that the concept of culture-as-identifier has two important implications: "The first is that the individuals who produce the demographic pattern are members of a communicative system, sharing the pattern and transmitting it, one to another in some degree. . . . The second implication is that demographic behavior is part of a larger, more complex whole of behavior patterns, learned as part of the general repertoire of behavior in a social group. In some unspecified way, these elements are thought to cohere in space and time, although not perfectly" (1990:459). As we shall see, the "unspecified way" has nonetheless been the object of very particular and enduring specifications, which continue to shape our whole view of the problem of regional cultures.

2. The continuity-in-change of values and practices as they pertain to population are discussed more fully in Kreager 1986.

3. The problem of "misplaced concreteness" remarked by Hammel and Friou (chapter 7 in this volume), provides many further instances of the need for attention to collective identity in the choice and interpretation of specific demographic variables. Amongst the examples they give are collective representations of marriage and pater-

nity that run counter to the family models of Western demographers and the possible use of formal classifications to stigmatize and demonize certain individuals and groups. We shall return to the latter problem below.

4. Some of the arguments put forward by Riley and Scheper-Hughes (chapters 5 and 8 of this volume, respectively) may lend themselves to this interpretation.

5. This section draws on Kreager 1988, 1991, and 1992.

6. The usefulness of assuming for purposes of calculation that a given population is closed to the new entry or departure of members, and to other impinging events as well, is implicit in Graunt's *Observations*, the earliest population arithmetic (1662). Analytical development of the idea was also possible in the early modern period, as is shown by the long line of probabilists, from Halley to LaPlace, who turned their hands to life-table calculation. Around 1800 there was also beginning to be a sufficient body of empirical data available from life-assurance offices to test and modify the mathematical developments suggested by early modern mathematicians. The important step, which was not possible without the intervention of the state into data collection, was to extend the practice of exhaustive enumeration of a population by age (which the life offices could do on the basis of detailed records of members) to the population of a nation-state as a whole. Immediately after such data became available, Farr used it to calculate the first national life table. The development of descriptive and analytical concepts of population were at this stage very closely linked.

7. The postwar literature on overpopulation, like Galton's eugenic ideas, were commonly traced by their authors to the inspiration of Malthus. There is not sufficient space to pursue their similarities in this respect, nor the reductive view of Malthus's *Essay* which they shared.

8. The "statistique ethnographique" was also forgotten by anthropologists who, following the qualitative ethnographic tradition pioneered by Malinowski and others working early in this century, reacted against comparative frameworks in which culture was treated in national, statistical, and racial terms. As this reaction coincided with a general retreat from the ethnography of European populations in favor of colonized ones, anthropologists may be said to have actively participated in marginalizing the study of culture as a dynamic force shaping modern society. In recent years Stocking (1982) has noted how the Boasian school of anthropology nonetheless incorporated basic ideas of collective identity deriving from Herder and nineteenth-century writings on national culture. Dumont (1983) provides a parallel example from Durkheimian anthropology, and the involvement of British anthropology in perpetuating the construction of nationalities is implicit in my discussion of British India.

9. Coale was not alone in this choice of phrasing. Sauvy, for example, employed a concept of population that reads like a nineteenth-century dictionary entry for "nation" (1954: vol. 2, 304). Henry's (1961) development of natural fertility may also be seen in this light.

10. The conceptual and methodological limitations of diffusionism, noted in passing at the end of the section on "Identity and Evidence," would appear to renew the possibility of a cultural approach to population which once again side-steps the problem of identity.

11. This is a theme that also begins at the same time as the attempt to equate nation, state, people, and population. Thus, the regional compilers of the Statistique Générale in France succeeded entirely in frustrating Napoleon's attempt to use it for purposes of surveillance. Engel likewise opposed Bismarck's centralization. British vital

statisticians, from Farr to Stevenson, made admirable use of the Registrar General's reports to demonstrate the need for health and economic reforms often not popular with the governments of the time, and to try (not always successfully) to limit the influence of eugenics.

REFERENCES

Alonso, William, and Paul Starr, eds. 1987. *The Politics of Numbers.* New York: Russell Sage Foundation.

Anderson, Barbara A. 1986. "Regional and Cultural Factors in the Decline of Marital Fertility in Western Europe." In *The Decline of Fertility in Europe.* ed. Ansley J. Coale and Susan C. Watkins, 293–313. Princeton: Princeton University Press.

Anderson, Benedict. 1983. *Imagined Communities.* London: Verso.

Appadurai, Arjun. 1993. "Number in the Colonial Imagination." In *Orientalism and the Postcolonial Predicament,* ed. Carol A. Breckinridge and Peter van der Veer, 314–39. Philadelphia: University of Pennsylvania Press.

Bartosz, Adam. 1992. *Tarnowskie Judaica.* Warsaw: Wydawnictwo PTTK Kraj.

Berelson, Bernard. 1977. "Ethnicity and Fertility: What and So What?" Center for Policy Studies, Working Papers. New York: The Population Council.

Berrington, Anne, Eva Lelièvre, Kathrine Kiernan, and Michael Murphy. 1993. "Changes in Living Arrangements in Great Britain Over the 1980s: A Review." Paper for the IUSSP General Conference, Montreal, August 24–September 1, 1993.

Bourguet, Marie-Noel. 1989. *Déchiffrer la France.* Paris: Editions des archives contemporaines.

Burghart, Richard. 1993. "A Quarrel in the Language Family: Agency and Representations of Speech in Mithila." *Modern Asian Studies* 22(4):761–804.

Coale, Ansley J. 1969. "The Decline of Fertility in Europe from the French Revolution to World War II." In *Fertility and Family Planning,* ed. Samuel J. Behrman, Leslie Corsa, and Ronald Freedman. Ann Arbor: University of Michigan Press.

Cohn, Bernard. 1987 [1970]. "The Census, Social Structure and Objectification in South Asia." In *An Anthropologist amongst the Historians and Other Essays,* 224–54. Delhi: Oxford University Press.

Congrèss Général de Statistique. 1872. *Compte Rendu Général.* St. Petersbourg: Impr. Trenké et Fusnot.

Das Gupta, Monica. 1987. "Selective Discrimination against Female Children in Rural Punjab." *Population and Development Review* 13(1):77–100.

Desrosières, Alain. 1993. *La Politique des Grands Nombres.* Paris: Editions la Découverte.

Dobroszycki, Lucjan. 1981. "The Fertility of Polish Jewry." In *Modern Jewish Fertility,* ed. P. Ritterband, 64–77. Leiden: Brill.

Dumont, Louis. 1983. "Interaction between Cultures: Herder's Volk and Fichte's Nation." In *Ethnicity, Identity, and History,* ed. J. B. Maier and C. I. Waxman, 13–26. London: Macmillan.

Durkheim, Emile. 1982. *The Rules of Sociological Method,* ed. S. Lukes, trans. W. D. Halls. London: Macmillan.

Eschbach, Karl. 1993. "Changing Identification among American Indians and Alaska Natives." *Demography* 30(4):635–52.

Fichte, Johannes. 1988 [1801]. *Der Geschlossne Handelsstaat.* Vol. 87, *Werke 1800–*

1801, ed. R. and H. Gliwitzky. Stuttgart-Gad Cannstatt: Friedrichfrommann Verlag.

Foster, M. 1901. "Letter [on behalf of the British Association for the Advancement of Science] to the Secretary of State for India." In "Ethnographic Survey of India in Connection with the Census of 1901." *Man* 1(13):137–41.

Frykenberg, Ronald E. 1987. "The Concept of a 'Majority' as a Devilish Force in the Politics of Modern India." *Journal of Commonwealth History and Comparative Politics* 25(3):267–74.

Galton, Francis. 1873. "The Relative Supplies from Town and Country Families to the Populations of Future Generations." *Journal of the Statistical Society* 36:19–26.

Gellner, Ernest. 1983. *Nations and Nationalism*. Oxford: Blackwell.

Gini, Corrado, Shiroshi Nasu, Robert Kuczynske, and Oliver Baker. 1930. *Population*. Chicago: University of Chicago Press.

Glass, David. 1973. *Numbering the People*. Farnborough, U.K.: D. C. Heath.

Graunt, John. 1662. *Natural and Political Observations on the London Bills of Mortality*. London. Printed by Tho. Roycroft, for John Martin, James Allestry, and Tho. Dicas, at the Sin of the Bell, in St. Paul's Churchyard.

Grebenik, Eugene. 1989. "Demography, Democracy, and Demonology." *Population and Development Review* 15(1):1–22.

Greenhalgh, Susan. 1995. "Anthropology Theorizes Reproduction: Integrating Practice, Political Economic, and Feminist Perspectives." In *Situating Fertility: Anthropology and Demographic Inquiry*, ed. S. Greenhalgh. Cambridge: Cambridge University Press.

———. In press. "The Social Construction of Population Science: An Intellectual, Institutional, and Political History of Twentieth-Century Demography." *Comparative Studies in Society and History* 38(1):26–66.

Grierson, George A. 1919. *The Linguistic Survey of India and the Census of 1911*. Calcutta: HMSO.

Guy, William A. 1839. "On the Value of the Numerical Method as Applied to Science, But Especially to Physiology and Medicine." *Journal of the Statistical Society* 2: 25–47.

Hacking, Ian. 1990. *The Taming of Chance*. Cambridge: Cambridge University Press.

Hammel, Eugene A. 1990. "A Theory of Culture for Demography." *Population and Development Review* 16(3):455–86.

———. 1995. "Economics 1, Culture 0, Fertility Change and Differences in the Northwest Balkans, 1700–1900." In *Situating Fertility: Anthropology and Demographic Inquiry*, ed. Susan Greenhalgh. Cambridge: Cambridge University Press.

Hecht, Jaqueline. 1976. "Idée de dénombrement jusqu'a la révolution." In *Pour une Histoire de la Statistique*. Vol. I., 21–82. Paris: Institut National de la Statistique et des Etudes Economiques.

Henry, Louis. 1961. "Some Data on Natural Fertility." *Eugenics Quarterly* 8:81–91.

Heuschling, Xavier. 1847. *Manuel de Statistique Ethnographique*. Bruxelles: A. Wahlen.

Hobsbawm, Eric. 1983. "Mass-Producing Traditions: Europe, 1870–1914." In *The Invention of Tradition*, ed. E. Hobsbawm and T. Ranger. Cambridge: Cambridge University Press.

Hodgson, Dennis. 1983. "Demography as Social Science and as Policy Science." *Population and Development Review* 9(1):1–34.

Institut National de la Statistique et des Etudes Economiques. 1976. *Pour une Histoire de la Statistique*. Paris: Institut National de la Statistique et des Etudes Economiques.

Ipsen, Carl. 1993. "The Organization of Demographic Totalitarianism: Early Population Policy in fascist Italy." *Social Science History* 17(1):71–108.

Jones, Kenneth W. 1976. *Arya Dharm: Hindu Consciousness in Nineteenth-Century Punjab*. New Delhi: Manohar.

———. 1981. "Religious Identity in the Indian Census." In *The Census in British India*, ed. N. G. Barrier. New Delhi: Manohar.

Kedourie, Elie. 1961. *Nationalism*. London: Hutchinson.

Keyfitz, Nathan. 1993. Review of *Marianne et les lapins: l'obsession démographique*, by Hervé Le Bras. *Population and Development Review* 19(2):365–74.

Kreager, Philip. 1982. "Demography in Situ." *Population and Development Review* 8(2):237–66.

———. 1986. "Demographic Regimes as Cultural Systems." In *The State of Population Theory*, ed. D. Coleman and R. Schofield, 131–55. Oxford: Blackwell.

———. 1988. "Machiavelli, Burckhardt, and the Making of Florentine Historical Identity." *Journal of the Anthropological Society of Oxford* 19(1):1–24.

———. 1991. "Early Modern Population Theory: A Reassessment." *Population and Development Review* 17(2):207–27.

———. 1992. "Quand une Population et-elle une Nation? Quand une Nation est-elle un état? La Démographie et l'émergence d'un Dilemme Moderne, 1770–1870." *Population* 6:1639–56.

———. 1993. "Anthropological Demography and the Limits of Diffusionism." In *International Population Conference, Montréal, 1993*, 313–26. Liège: International Union for the Scientific Study of Population.

———. In press. "The Limits of Diffusionism." In *New Approaches to Anthropological Demography*, ed. Alaka M. Basu. Oxford: Oxford University Press.

Kuhn, Thomas. 1962. *The Structure of Scientific Revolutions*. Chicago: University of Chicago Press.

Kuijsten, A. 1994. "Changing Family Patterns in Europe: A Case of Divergence?" Paper presented at the BSPS Annual Conference, Durham, Aug. 31–Sept. 2, 1994.

Leasure, J. William. 1963. "Factors Involved in the Decline of Fertility in Spain, 1900–1950." *Population Studies* 16(3):271–85.

Le Bras, Hervé. 1992. *Marianne et les lapins: l'obsession démographique*. Paris: Olivier Orban.

Le Bras, Hervé, and Emmanuel Todd. 1981. *L'Invention de la France*. Paris: Editions de Minuit.

Lesthaeghe, Ron. 1982. "On the Social Control of Reproduction." *Population and Development Review* 6(4):527–48.

———. 1983. "A Century of Demographic and Cultural Change in Western Europe: An Exploration of Underlying Dimensions." *Population and Development Review* 9(3):411–35.

———. 1992. "Beyond Economic Reductionism: The Transformation of the Reproductive Regimes in France and Belgium in the Eighteenth and Nineteenth Centuries." In *Fertility Transitions, Family Structure, and Population Policy*, ed. Calvin Goldscheider, 1–44. Boulder, Colo.: Westview Press.

Lesthaeghe, Ron, and Johan Surkyn. 1988. "Cultural Dynamics and Economic Theories of Fertility Change." *Population and Development Review* 14(1):1–46.

Lesthaeghe, Ron, and Chris Wilson. 1986. "Modes of Production, Secularization, and the Pace of Fertility Decline in Western Europe, 1870–1930." In *The Decline of Fertility in Europe,* ed. Ansley J. Coale and Susan C. Watkins, 261–92. Princeton: Princeton University Press.

Livi-Bacci, Massimo. 1971. *A Century of Portuguese Fertility.* Princeton: Princeton University Press.

Lorimer, Frank. 1945. "Population as a Problem in Quality." In *Food for the World,* ed. T. W. Schulz, 58–65. Chicago: University of Chicago Press.

———. 1954. *Culture and Human Fertility.* Paris: UNESCO.

Lotka, Alfred J. 1907. "Studies on the Mode of Growth of Material Aggregates." *American Journal of Science* 24(141):199–216.

Malthus, Thomas Robert. 1890 [1798]. *An Essay on the Principle of Population,* London: Ward Lock.

Mason, Karen O. 1992. "Culture and the Fertility Transition: Thoughts on Theories of Fertility Decline." *Genus* 48(3,4):1–14.

McNicoll, Geoffrey. 1992. "The Agenda of Population Studies: A Commentary and Complaint." *Population and Development Review* 18(1):399–420.

Neuvième Session du Congrèss International de Statistique à Budapest. 1876. *Rapports et Résolutions,* 185–7. Budapest: Athenaeum.

Notestein, Frank. 1945. "Population—The Long View." In *Food for the World,* ed. T. W. Schulz, 36–57. Chicago: University of Chicago Press.

Pant, Rashmi. 1987. "The Cognitive Status of Caste in Colonial Ethnography: A Review of Some Literature on the Northwest Provinces and Oudh." *Indian Economic and Social History Review* 24(2):145–62.

Pearson, Karl. 1909. *The Groundwork of Eugenics.* London: Dulau and Co.

Perrot, Jean-Claude. 1984. "The Golden Age of Regional Statistics." In *State and Statistics in France, 1789–1815,* ed. J.-C. Perrot and S. Woolf. London: Harwood Academic.

Porter, Theodore M. 1986. *The Rise of Statistical Thinking.* Princeton: Princeton University Press.

Preston, Samuel H., Suet Lim, and S. Philip Morgan. 1992. "African-American Marriage in 1910: Beneath the Surface of Census Data." *Demography.* 29(1):1–15.

Sauvy, Alfred. 1952, 1956. *Théory Générale de la Population.* 2 vols. Paris: Presses Universitaires de France.

Schneider, Jane, and Peter Schneider. 1992. "Going Forward in Reverse Gear: Culture, Economy, and Political Economy in a Rural Sicilian Town." *The European Experience of Fertility Decline,* ed. John R. Gillis, Louise A. Tilly, and David Levine, 146–74. Oxford: Blackwell.

Segalen, Martine. 1992. "Exploring a Case of Late French Fertility Decline: Two Contrasted Breton Examples." In *The European Experience of Fertility Decline,* ed. John R. Gillis, Louise A. Tilly, and David Levine, 227–50. Oxford: Blackwell.

Seton-Watson, Hugh. 1977. *Nations and States.* London: Methuen.

Simons, John. 1986. "Culture, Economy, and Reproduction in Contemporary Europe." In *The State of Population Theory,* ed. D. Coleman and R. Schofield, 256–78. Oxford: Blackwell.

———. 1994. "The Cultural Significance of Western Fertility Trends in the 1980s." Paper presented to the IUSSP Seminar on Values and Fertility Change. Sion, Switzerland, February 16–19.

Smith, Richard S. 1984. "Rule-by-Records and Rule-by-Reports: Complementary Aspects of the British Imperial Rule of Law." *Contributions to Indian Sociology*, n. s. 19(1):153–76.

Stigler, Stephen M. 1986. *The History of Statistics*. Cambridge, Mass.: Belknap Press.

Stocking, George W., Jr. 1982. *Race, Culture, and Evolution*. Chicago: University of Chicago Press.

Szreter, Simon. 1993. "The Idea of Demographic Transition and the Study of Fertility Change: A Critical Intellectual History." *Population and Development Review* 19(4):659–702.

Viazzo, Pier Paulo. In press. "Anthropology, Family History, and the Concept of 'Strategy.'" In *Economic and Social Aspects of the Family Life Cycle*, ed. R. Wall and O. Sato. Cambridge: Cambridge University Press. In press.

———. 1989. Upland Communities: Environment, Population, and Social Structure in the Alps since the Sixteenth Century. Cambridge: Cambridge University Press.

Chapter Seven

Anthropology and Demography: Marriage, Liaison, or Encounter?

Eugene A. Hammel and Diana S. Friou

After two centuries of uncertain success in explaining demographic behavior through the use of economic and sociological variables, some demographers have turned to Culture as a source of understanding social action, or at least to ethnographic methods of data collection as a means to improve their data. Some anthropologists, weary of the undefinable variables of traditional interest in their own discipline, have seized on demographic events as certain and measurable. The two disciplines have begun to eye each other with interest. In this chapter we explore some of the opportunities and problems inherent in that mutual interest.[1]

It is important in the construction of any relationship between disciplines, as between persons, to think about how that relationship might ultimately be structured. Is this courtship between anthropology and demography to result in a marriage, in an enduring liaison, or in a series of brief encounters? Will a substantial field of anthropologically informed demography, or of demographically informed anthropology, arise with its own bilaterally competent members? Will there be a few devoted but monospecialized collaborators across the disciplinary boundary, or will we see only occasional and transient connections, more the result of chance than of plan?

Similarly, in constructing a disciplinary relationship, it is important to be honest about the past. Without that understanding any encounter, however durable, may turn out like that between the lovers in Gover's *One Hundred Dollar Misunderstanding* (1961). Each, although experiencing events that were objectively identical, would interpret them differently. This point emerges strongly from any discourse between anthropologists and demographers, especially between more recently trained social/cultural anthropologists and technical demographers who, after all, on account of their age, might be expected to meet, connect, and perhaps prove intellectually fertile. We begin with a review of some of the problems offered by the respective histories of the two disciplines.

Differences between the Disciplines

From the outset, demography has had a strong positivist, quantitative, and policy-oriented tradition. It emerged from two roots, one in the political arithmetic of William Perry and the theoretical concerns of the Scottish moral philosophers, the other in the increasingly sophisticated mathematics of Gaunt, Halley, Lotka, and others.[2] It was driven on the one hand, as in the work of

Malthus, by a concern with the relationships between socioeconomic conditions and other measurable aspects of the populations displaying those conditions, and on the other by a fascination with formal modeling. In these characteristics and history it is much like modern statistics, and its relation to anthropology is much like that between statistics and sociology.

Moreover, demography has always been close to the seat of power, employed in the study and execution of policy. Kreager's essay (chapter 6 in this volume) shows how the development of census taking is closely tied to the emergence of powerful, centralized states. The rare politically sensitive and reflective reviews of demographic theory (Hodgson 1983, 1988; Donaldson 1990), like those of statistics (Hacking 1990), show how close and problematic the relationship with power has been. The view of demography as an instrument of the state can cause trouble in a relationship. Scholars who go into demography are relatively untroubled by any guilt that may arise from association with power, and are most comfortable with well-ordered and preferably elegant constructions of the social world. Disorder spurs them to make such constructions.

Demographers have another interesting characteristic. In the purest form of their work they concentrate on the statistical mechanics of populations rather than on the actions of individuals. Their proper calling is the analysis of aggregates even if they often justify aggregate analysis by reference to individual behavior and thereby move into the domains of other social sciences, whether economics, sociology, or anthropology. Townsend (chapter 4 in this volume) refers to the "hard core–soft rind" simile employed by Schofield and Coleman, a figure that seems quite natural to demographers but evokes astonished deconstruction from anthropologists. The compulsion of demographers to consider individual behavior rather than only aggregate results is strongest when they are asked to advise how the behavior of aggregates might be changed, since changes in the aggregates are best approached by asking how the behavior of the constituents of those aggregates might be changed.[3] Sometimes demographers reaching for causality focus on institutions, sometimes on values, and sometimes on markets. Demographers who trespass on the fields of concern of sister social sciences are prompted by that same connection with policy mentioned above. Are demographers simply servants of the state? Yet the trespass of other social sciences on demography's turf is also manifest (for example in this volume), as the disciplines of the soft rind encroach and the hard core shrinks into ever more cabalistic manipulations of data (see, for example, the critique by McNicoll 1992).

Anthropology by contrast has a weak quantitative tradition although it originally had a strong positivist natural science, observational tradition. Further, since the fifteenth century anthropologists or their precursors have been those members of the Western philosophical tradition who have confronted the exotic and the extinct in the struggle to understand the world beyond

Europe and the discovery of their own antiquity. While demographers have dealt with counting the familiar, anthropologists have dealt with understanding the strange. Latterly, the positivist natural science tradition of anthropology has weakened under a critical onslaught, fueled first by left-wing condemnation of its associations with governance in European colonies or the pursuit of American military or diplomatic adventures in less-developed countries, or LDCs (most notably in Southeast Asia), then by a corrosive postmodernist wave of doubt about anyone's ability to be sure of any observation. Some of these characteristics and events have had a strong selection effect on recruitment into anthropology. The field tends to attract those alienated from their own culture to begin with, and especially from its positivist components, the most objectionable of which to them is what they call linear thinking, or what others would call science. They celebrate their innumeracy.

Anthropologists, at least the postmodern variety, are uncomfortable with order and happiest when the world lies deconstructed around their feet. They are also hypersensitive to any association with the interests of states or elites; indeed their code of ethics proclaims a first responsibility to the communities they study.

Anthropologists, or at least ethnographers, frequently have another interesting characteristic. They do not care much for aggregates. Even when they generalize about "cultures," their picture of a culture is individuated and humanistic rather than summary and statistical. Their focus is most often on the individual actor in a broadly defined social and cultural milieu. They specialize in the classical mechanics of populations, focusing on individual motivation, action, and response. Thus they stand to demography as Galileo or Newton did to Einstein, more comfortable with the click of ivory on some institutionally and natively defined table of individual interactions than with a broad and abstract geometry of social space.

To be fair about it, there are demographers who are more concerned with individual behavior than they are with the behavior of aggregates, even though their data may represent aggregates while only their theory involves individuals. Some demographers seek to situate individual demographic behavior in a broader context by using sample survey techniques. Similarly, there are anthropologists whose concern is with ecological and other structural constraints on aggregate behavior, even though much of their field experience lies in extended conversations with individual informants. There are still other anthropologists whose methods are exquisitely quantitative, whether applied to groups or to individuals. There are anthropologists who work as field explorers in human physiology, especially in reproduction. Finally, there are anthropologists who work rather like historians, especially in demographic history, dredging like archaeologists for the detritus of behavior, combining individual with aggregate sources, trying always to relate their findings to broad issues of culture and institutional context (see, for example, the contributions in Greenhalgh 1995). Nevertheless, the picture we have drawn of the demographer as a generalizing number-cruncher and of the anthropologist as a sensitive interpreter of native poetics has some truth in it, as do most caricatures. Further, as McNicoll pointed out in conference discussion, both anthropologists and demographers have particular professional publics to which they must respond and particular traditional constraints within which they must operate. The assaults of the postmodernists on more traditional forms of anthropological investigation and indeed on any objective enterprise are a case in point, and the obstacles they raise to the interdisciplinary cooperation we here discuss are formidable.[4] If one had to put the differences between the disciplines in a nutshell, one would remark that while demographers and old-time anthropologists regarded sex as an independent variable, the new anthropology regards gender as a dependent one (or in their terms, a phenomenon to be deconstructed—see Riley, chapter 5 in this volume).

On account of these differences, complete incomprehension is often the most welcome outcome of interdisciplinary encounter, outright hostility the worst (see Scheper-Hughes, chapter 8 in this volume). Part of anthropologists' struggle to understand the exotic had an intellectual outcome—the realization that familiar Western categories, from language grammar to family classification, could not easily be applied to non-Western phenomena or even some Western phenomena.[5] The struggle had a moral outcome: the conviction that no variant of human culture could be privileged over another—that is, consideration of cultures had to be relativistic. Each culture, the anthropologists held, had to be considered and understood on its own terms, had its own logic, and had its own worth.[6]

Anthropologists are therefore likely not to be able to understand or agree with many demographic analyses. Such analyses often use Western-based cultural categories and ignore the internal logic of local societies. They use quantitative techniques that depend on the willing suspension of disbelief, a quality not well developed in anthropologists. Further, they are often applied in the furtherance of Western political aims such as economic development, modernization, and population stabilization.[7]

Demographers, on the other hand, don't comprehend that their categories and quantitative models can be seen as unnatural and inapplicable. After all, they do occasionally achieve statistically significant results in their regression equations. When demographers protest that they go to uncommon lengths to correct errors in their data, they do not understand that anthropologists may be questioning not only their accuracy but also the very systems of classification they employ. Demographers are also profoundly disturbed by the idea that because they work on policy-relevant endeavors they are the lackeys and running dogs of a hegemonic system. Few of them can spell hegemonic. They are less troubled, for example, by the exportation of white, upper-middle-class, emergent norms of gender relations and the status of women to LDCs than are otherwise socially identical anthropologists who have watched the destruction of whole cultures through the importation of a few important Western ideas like monotheism and T-shirts.

No one easily accepts the questioning of their accustomed cultural categories and deepest values. Anthropologists are likely to be profoundly upset by an enterprise that questions the intrinsic validity of social concepts in a society under study, by any tendency to export to it the categories of others, and especially by the use of approaches or data that ignore the hegemonic influence of the West. They will display little respect for mathematical reasoning because to them it is gibberish. Demographers are likely to be relatively insensitive to the political implications of their work, not to mention the inapplicability of their analytic categories, and unquestioning of the reality of their schema to the social actors they purport to describe.

Using the Idea of Culture

We define culture for the purposes of this exposition as a set of norms or values that influence behavior.[8] By behavior we mean observable human action, including the formulation or enunciation of and response to culture. Defining culture as a set of norms is important to the demographic enterprise since it gives meaning to the causal models employed, generally in economic analyses of demographic behavior. It permits a more flexible and sensitive definition of maximization than that afforded by the anthropologically repugnant notion of the universal economically rational actor. It allows, for example, a social-category definition of taste and the idea of optimization on several dimensions of value, including social value.

The employment of culture in this way is important because it explicates human agency. Human agency is important to realistic modeling of causation in economics and sociology, but it is particularly important to anthropologists, among many of whom the recognition of human agency is a symbolic protest against analyses of social action that depict actors as automatons. The effect of agency to the economist or sociologist is some measurable amount of residual variance in outcome; to the anthropologist it is a beam from the human soul, which will only be extinguished if its source is found.

If demographers and anthropologists could be persuaded to abandon the search for understanding motivation among rational actors, much dispute could be avoided. Anthropologists would be much more likely to accept results that showed that some kinds of people acted one way, while others acted another, if the stories did not contain some subtext about what motivated them to do it. Such descriptive accounts would be in accord with that ethnological tradition that has sometimes been called "butterfly collecting" (Leach 1961), and the thicker the description the better.

Thick descriptions allow the reader to move in clouds of vicarious intuition and symbolic connection in which much can be appreciated even if it is not understood. Is a less mystical approach possible? Completely formalistic depictions might be less likely than causal ones to arouse dispute. Much might be salvaged by abandoning the Aristotelian efficient cause and resting only with formal causality. But there is probably no hope for that since anthropologists do not like formalisms and demographers usually are not bothered by the absence of agency unless they are economists and simply assume it. If we are to pursue the idea of culture as a source of motivation, we are obliged to examine it further.[9]

Although culture has observable manifestations in enunciated texts and bodies of symbols, in its operational sense it must exist in people's heads. Just as you cannot make an omelette without breaking eggs, you cannot see what is in people's heads without destroying or at least altering the evidence. In the absence of some magical scanner, people have to tell you what is in their heads. It is difficult to know whether statements of behavioral norms are descriptions of such norms as they may apply to future behavior, or rationalizations of past behavior, or rationalizations of anticipated future behavior. To be sure, the investigator can try to achieve some control by asking about specific behaviors that occurred in the past (in which instance rationalization might be more likely) versus those that might occur in the future (in which instance rationalization might be less likely), but the ability of persons to imagine what might have been before it even happens makes the task difficult.[10] One can of course try very cleverly to contextualize and contrast behaviors, controlling as much as possible for factors thought to be constraining or causal, but that exercise often involves the investigator's mind more than the informant's. One can elicit the commentary of some actors on the behavior of others, but it is then difficult to understand just why they made the evaluations they did. The problems inherent in this enterprise can be seen by inquiring into behavioral motivation within one's own family or circle of colleagues and friends.

In our view, the use of culture as a causal force in explanations that depend on motivation can have, operationally, only a heuristic value. In their ongoing critique of local social action, the statements of informants about their own culture provide us with plausible motives for that social action. We can construct models using those motives and some will show better correspondence with observation than others. We can continue to accept the motivational principles of those models as analytically useful, but we had better not believe them in any absolute sense. This kind of approach may be congenial to the economists, who can thereby thicken their rational actors. The alternative—to consider institutions and symbols as constraints on otherwise randomly and inscrutably motivated behavior—may be more congenial to sociologists, whose classic style involves the intelligent cross-classification of social action. It is not clear whether the approach would be congenial to many ethnographers, who seem divided into those who desperately want to believe something and those who insist on believing nothing. They would be relieved of this epistemological burden if they could simply work as interpretive opportunists, using whatever natively enunciated commentary or theory of behavior made the most sense when compared to ethnographic observation of that behavior. Only if they moved to intergroup comparison would they be obliged to fit these locally derived models into larger theoretical frameworks. At that point their dilemma would match that of the demographers, whose explanations of demographic behavior are often locally accurate but globally insufficient. It is comparison and broader generalization that forces science to invent truths that may have a hollow ring in their narrowest span.

Using Ethnographic Data

The utility of anthropology to the demographic enterprise may also lie in anthropologists' ability to work at close range and for long durations in the field. The unique contribution of ethnographers in the social sciences (and their epistemological curse, as well) is to be the very instrument of data recording. They often are obliged to observe by participating, by joining the stream of social action, and inevitably affecting it as they record it. Nevertheless, the disadvantages of being the very thermometer in recording social temperature are more often outweighed by the ability to get next to the source of the heat. Many ethnographers are profoundly transformed by this experience, especially if they have done their job right.

In this data-gathering enterprise we seek to record behavior directly pertinent to the most fundamental enterprise of descriptive demography. Our restricted intent is not to explain that behavior but only to observe it and perhaps associated behaviors like resource use that might assist in explanation. Some care needs to be exercised in cooperative enterprises in which the ethnographer provides the facts, while the demographer uses them in explanation. Anthropologists are unlikely to accept the role of gopher quietly, and those who would are probably not the best anthropologists. Indeed, the time for initial cooperation is in the planning stages of the research, and cooperation works best if it is continuous and cyclical. For example, ethnographic information is essential in framing survey questions, but some survey work is essential in selecting the location of ethnographic work and selecting representative informants. Thus waves of ethnographic and survey-analytic work should alternate in an ideal research enterprise.

There are two parts to providing good data. The first is to discover those behaviors in a population that might alter demographic results in unexpected ways. For example, we might discover that some members of a population were addicted to inhalation of the smoke of a noxious weed that seriously increased their mortality. Or we might discover that some females married a mythical being, living in spiritual but not corporeal union with Him, so that their observed fertility was lower than that of women otherwise married in the population. The ordinary observer, unaccustomed to the collection of exotic minutiae, might not observe these phenomena and would thus be less able to explain the demographic heterogeneity resulting therefrom.

The second part is to ask whether we can believe what we observe—whether there are behaviors in the population that affect not the pattern of demographic events but affect our knowledge of those events. For example, we might not realize that in some populations and under some circumstances there was a distinct tendency for people to report a much lower income than they actually enjoyed, while in others the reverse might be true. The reporting behavior does not affect the income, but only our knowledge of it. We might also ask whether the familiar furniture of our own minds prevents us from seeing relationships in the data that would be clear to the actors or to a different investigator who was cursed with a different set of furniture. For example, in some census we might count only people who spent the previous night at a particular address, since normal people who live in normal households come home at night. The U.S. Census Bureau is still struggling with that problem.

What we present is a series of hopefully thought-provoking examples. They are anything but exhaustive, only exemplary. They should serve as a source of humility for the ethnographers and as a clear statement to the demographers of *caveat emptor*. Some of what we offer is based in personal observation; the rest is drawn from published ethnographic sources, among which is that classic of armchair ethnography, *The Golden Bough* (Frazer 1922).

Behaviors That Change Demography

The list of behaviors that introduce demographic heterogeneity into a population is of course almost limitless. In what might be called ethnoepidemiology there are innumerable risk factors that may affect morbidity and mortality, and many of these may be gender-based, rooted in the sexual division of labor and in the treatment accorded to individuals of different sex.

In the study of AIDS in urban America, a good deal of emphasis was placed originally on male homosexuals, resulting in more than the ordinary stigmatization of an STD. If AIDS had been transmitted only through homosexual contact the epidemic would have been self-limiting and resolutely ignored by policy makers. It broke out of the homosexual population through bisexual behavior and needle-sharing among drug users. Heterosexual transmission was acknowledged, and emphasis placed on female (and sometimes male) prostitutes as the primary vectors spreading the disease to male clients. The prevalence of AIDS as a heterosexually transmitted disease within the sanctity of marriage was first noted in Africa, where prostitutes probably served as the primary vectors in infecting the male heterosexual population, but where AIDS may have been long endemic at low levels. In LDCs where needle use is low but prostitution often rampant, this transmission route is very important.

In more-developed countries (MDCs) where needle use is high, it may not be as important as needle sharing. But wherever prostitution is a factor, it is interesting that the behavior of men outside the brothel is largely ignored in policy action.[11] Emphasis is on getting men to use condoms when having sex with prostitutes, not on using condoms when having sex with their wives, nor on avoiding sex with prostitutes. Thus, there is a large segment of the adult population (approximately half in most LDCs), namely married women, whose own behavior does not place them at risk but whose husbands' behavior places them at risk. To fail to understand this is to fail to understand the epidemiology of AIDS and its demographic consequences. Not to develop a john-based strategy to limit AIDS leads to misguided policy and ineffective intervention. The mistake is doubtless related to the cultural perceptions of the men who control such policy. After all, boys will be boys.[12]

Similar examples could be adduced in the important area of infant and child mortality, where heterogeneity of maternal competence within or between societies can lead to major differences. We can point to the sometimes contradictory effects of maternal education often observed in survey results—the ethnographic work of Scrimshaw (1978) and Das Gupta (1990), which concentrates on instrumental competence, or that of Nancy Scheper-Hughes (1985, 1992), which finds a phenomenon of hopelessness she sees rooted in larger political and economic structures.

In the area of fertility, Nag (1962) has claimed that very early marriage may reduce total fecundity, rather than increasing it, through longer exposure to risk of pregnancy. He argues that stillbirths and miscarriages are more common in the pregnancies of very young women, and that damage to the reproductive organs may result from such events, depressing fecundability and fertility. He has also noted that a number of factors involved in "modernization," such as the introduction of bottle-feeding, may increase fecundability (1980). Gordon (1991) observes that female genital mutilation in Egypt, being illegal, is widespread but concealed, leading to genital infection, infertility, and death in childbirth (see also James 1994; Kopelman 1994). Female genital mutilation is widespread in Africa; its abandonment with modernization may increase fertility by decreasing female morbidity. It has also been surmised that female infibulation, which can make vaginal intercourse painful, may encourage anal intercourse, which involves more frequent rupture of tissue, and thus encourages the spread of AIDS. The effects of botched clandestine abortions on subsequent fertility are well known and are an unintended consequence of social policies that must be considered in comparative analysis. Similarly, the effects of endemic STD on fertility must also be taken into account (Caldwell and Caldwell 1983; Howell 1979; Whiting, Burbank, and Ratner 1986).

Male genital mutilation, ranging from circumcision to subincision, or the use of penis rings or inserts, may also have an effect on fertility. It has been claimed that circumcision is associated with lower rates of penile infection and vaginal cancer. Himes (1970 [1936]) comments that Australian subincision was not intended as a form of fertility control and probably had no effect (see also Segal 1972; Basedow 1927). Brown, Edwards, and Moore (1988) survey the incidence of penis inserts and rings in Southeast Asia with comparative data from southern India, classical antiquity, and European history. These authors claim that male infibulation was used as a form of birth control by inhibiting coitus, to prevent sexual access by slaves to females of their owners, or to prevent masturbation. The explanation for their use in Southeast Asia is the enhancement of female sexual pleasure, but no female witnesses are known to have pronounced on this interpretation. We would imagine Chinese influence, citing the Golden Lotus as an authority (Hsiao-hsiao-sheng 1939; but cf. Brown, Edwards, and Moore 1988 for suggestions of reverse diffusion). Dalton (1837) claims that almost all the Dyak men of Borneo were infibulated and that a third suffered serious consequences, including death from tetanus. Bock (1887) confirms some of Dalton's observations but disputes his data on resulting mortality. Gaffron (1859) suggests that the use of penis inserts in western Borneo may render women infertile. Grubauer (1913) supports Dalton with his observations in Sulawesi. Hovorka (1894) provides an elaborate, illustrated compendium covering classical antiquity and ethnography. Kobak (1970) comments on Alzina's observations in the Philippines in 1668, noting that men might use a penis insert with sharpened points to punish a woman. Kuhlewein (1930) reports an intensive medical survey in Borneo, in which up to 95 percent of men in various tribes were infibulated, leading to inflammation of the urethra, but no apparent consequences for fertility. Morga (1906 [1609]) observes that penis inserts worn by the Pinados of the Philippines cause much bleeding, but does not say to whom. To allay any notion that such practices are restricted to so-called primitive peoples, we refer the reader to Buhrich (1983) who documents infibulation and other forms of piercing in modern Los Angeles.

Apart from Mayer's assertion (1877) that southern Bornean penis pins cause sterility by inducing insensitivity, the literature is almost silent on what any demographer would wonder about, namely, the probable laceration of the vagina by penis pins, the consequent inflammation and infection, and especially the enhanced spread of STDs and resulting secondary sterility.

With regard to nuptiality, many authors have noted important variations in age at marriage of men and women according to wealth, social standing, and the kinds of prestations that accompany marriage (see, for example, Dumont 1970 on India and Trumbach 1978 on preindustrial Europe, among others). Analyses of nuptiality that ignore such heterogeneity and its sources yield only meaningless averages and do not reveal the underlying behaviors, or to coin a phrase, m&m's that melt in your analysis.[13]

Variations in adult management of and adolescent conduct of sexual behavior may induce differences in the likelihood of or the age at marriage within and between societies. Gordon (1991) notes that in Egypt unmarried pregnant women often commit suicide or are murdered by family members, and we would expect such phenomena, or commitment to a life of prostitution, in societies in which female chastity at marriage was a paramount concern. The most fecundable women may thereby be removed from the legitimate marriage market. Most Near-Eastern societies and segments of European society exhibit such anxiety, as do rural Haitians, who couple their disapproval of pregnancy with a tolerant attitude toward adolescent sexuality (Herskovits 1971). By contrast, the Hopi of Arizona supervise their adolescent daughters closely but have a casual attitude toward any pregnancies (Schlegel 1975), as do the Papago toward a class of "playful" women (Underhill 1936). Among the Ijo of Nigeria some men prefer to marry women already proven to be fertile (Hollos and Leis 1986). Similar instances are known from some peasant cultures of Europe, in which cohabitation was initiated but not formalized until pregnancy. Such practices could easily lead to earlier marriage for more fecundable women, increasing their exposure and thus their total fertility and introducing a particular heterogeneity in the data. This effect is the reverse of what one might expect in the Egyptian example just noted.

Sexual abuse may also play a role in nuptial mechanics. Women abused in youth by family members but living in a society that demands virginity at marriage and especially proof thereof on the wedding night may be unmarriageable by anticipation or may be rejected by their husbands. Women who have been raped by anyone may not be able to marry or may be cast out if already married. Even without these extreme effects, conjugal behavior may be affected either because of psychological trauma to the woman which leads her to avoid sexual relations, or because of culturally induced psychological trauma to the husband, who may be unwilling or unable to engage further or often in such relations with that woman (the spoiled-goods syndrome). Korbin (1987), deMause (1961), and Schlegel and Barry (1991) review some of the cross-cultural evidence on incest and child sexual abuse.

Apart from the most extreme examples, we know rather little of the demographic effects of extra-institutional or even of institutionalized punitive sexuality. Institutionalized punitive sexuality should not be ignored. War rape and its effects are not, to our knowledge, treated anywhere in the historical demographic literature, yet if rape is a restraint on conjugal relations, war must induce temporal fluctuations in fertility in at least some societies beyond those attributable to spousal separation. Punitive rape is not unknown, but its demographic effects are. Gregor (1985) reports institutionalized punitive rape for the Mehinaku of central Brazil, as do Murphy and Murphy for the Mundurucu (1974). The phenomenon of men raping their female companions as an alternative or in addition to beating them up in the United States is not unknown, either, and the psychological effects of such behavior are beginning to be known. Ritual rape of a nonpunitive kind is also known. Serpenti (1977) observes that in some New Guinea groups, women or girls are seized and gang-raped by ten to fifteen men solely to serve as vessels for semen, which is then re-collected from the woman's vagina and used medicinally, but Serpenti does not report what the consequences are for nuptiality. The classic American fraternity gang-bang is another kind of institutionalized rape with important psychological and behavioral consequences.

Psychological and physiological inhibitors to fertility are too numerous to highlight here, but one should expect nonrandom distributions across populations. To hint at the complexities we note Wulfften's analysis of the distribution of penis pins in Southeast Asia (1936), in which he proposes that these objects originated as an antidote to *koro*, the psychiatric disease in which a man fears his penis will withdraw inside the body and cause death. If there are social heterogeneities in such behaviors, within or across societies, we are obliged to take them into account in demographic analysis. For example, computing a total fertility rate for a population in which a substantial proportion of women have been forced into or who have fled into prostitution, or who are otherwise excluded from or who participate minimally in conjugal relations, simply distorts the evidence. Demographers who have long depended on the universality of marriage are beginning to understand that institution is a swamp.

Factors That Affect Our Knowledge of Demographic Events

None of the points made thus far would surprise most observers, who would agree that the ferreting out of important covariates, whether obtained through ethnography or blind luck in casting the survey net, was an important part of the research enterprise. More intriguing, however, are factors that affect our knowledge of events rather than the patterns of the events themselves. Demographers are of course very familiar with this problem under the rubric of bias or misreporting. Much attention has been devoted to the phenomenon of age misreporting and its sources in illiteracy, innumeracy, and so on. Yet there are more obscure sources of bias.

In a number of societies it is tabu to mention the dead, or through various social and ceremonial mechanisms their memory has been obliterated. It would be remarkably difficult to collect mortality data under such circumstances. Frazer (1922) provides an extensive catalog of this practice from classical antiquity to the ethnographic present. Opler (1936) reports that among the Apache the memory of the deceased is banished after ritual public expression of grief. The literature suggests that naming the dead may be tabu especially among a number of North American Indian groups.

In some societies a newborn child is named after a person recently deceased (Bloch and Perry 1982). Data collection through genealogical methods would present the same problems encountered in historical demography, in which such practices may also affect the quality of data and the ability to link records. Mandelbaum (1965) describes Kota dual funeral ceremonies. There are two such funerals for any male death, separated by whatever span elapses between the actual date of death and the end-of-year burial ceremony for all persons who died that year. A widow's pregnancy occurring between the death of her husband and her first menstruation after the end-of-year ceremony is attributed to the dead husband. Similar problems arise through name changes, familiar to us in European society when women change names on marriage. Not so well known are name changes in other societies contingent on supernatural experiences, or through the custom of teknonymy, in which a parent is named after one or another of his or her children.

Since so-called primitive sexuality has always been a focus of anthropological inquiry, especially of Victorian anthropologists, the literature is replete with discussion of premarital and extramarital sexual activity. Interesting problems arise in the attribution of paternity, as in the Kota example just given. Gaulin and Schlegel (1980) report that there was high confidence in paternity in only half of the societies surveyed in a sample from the Human Relations Area Files. While the African literature is generally unanimous that the social father of a child is the woman's husband, no matter who the genitor, Gough (1961) reports that among the Nayar of central Kerala it is the woman's current lover rather than her official husband who is regarded as the social father (again, no matter who the genitor); the Nayar are of course unique in their matrilineality and extreme duolocal residence, with household management in the hands of the senior brother of a group of coresiding married sisters who consort with their lovers rather than with their husbands.

In aboriginal Australia, kinship connections establish marriageability in quite strict regimes of marital exchange and alliance. Yet they are often coupled with extreme age differences between spouses that lead to frequent adulterous relations between young wives and bachelor males (Hart and Pilling 1960). While the Tiwi husbands in this example are jealous to the point of homicide, among the pastoral Hima of Africa, a wife who does not give sexual favors to her husband's friends is regarded as churlish and is reprimanded by her husband (Elam 1973). Similar examples exist for the Eskimo (Freuchen 1961, Friedl 1983). A classic case in the literature is from polyandrous Tibet, where Prince Peter (1963) reports that paternity is attributed to the elder brother of a group of men jointly married to one woman. Calculating male fertility rates in such groups is thus a tricky enterprise.

Among some African societies, such as the Nuer (Evans-Pritchard 1951), women may be married to ghosts who are the recognized jural fathers of their children, or women may be married to other women who produce children of their lovers, and such children have the female husband of their mother as their father. Among the Serbs, women with impotent or serologically incompatible husbands could legitimately demand sexual services of the local Orthodox priest, and their children would be filiated to the mother's husband (Filipovic 1982).

We may also note in this connection the reported influence of the Hadith (the reported sayings of the Prophet), which governs strict Muslim behavior, including sexual relations. According to the Hadith, intercourse is to be carried out fully clothed and in the dark (the Orthodox Jewish rules are the same). Some ethnographic and medical evidence suggests that under these conditions penetration can be either uncertain or erroneous, with consequent declines in what might be expected from the Bongaarts model.

Even in the absence of uncertain paternity, the answer to the question "whose child is this?" is not always obvious. Child abandonment is an ubiquitous phenomenon, clearly known in MDCs today, historically known at high levels in countries such as the United States, England, Italy, and France during the eighteenth and nineteenth centuries, and rampant in some LDCs both historically and now, especially in the selling of daughters (Scheper-Hughes 1987; Boswell 1989; Kertzer 1993). Such children are unlikely to be reported in fertility surveys and they may be hard to find in censuses, so that even crude measures of fertility that depend on ratios of age groups will be biased.[14]

Absent these extreme effects, adoption or fosterage can make attribution of parentage uncertain. Highly developed systems of fosterage are well known from Africa (Bledsoe 1990; Caldwell 1977; Etienne 1983; Goody 1982), where they serve not only to confuse the field demographer but also to average the costs and benefits of childbearing across households and to permit competition for the control of children and their contributions. Silk (1987) documents fosterage more broadly. Townsend (chapter 4 of this volume) usefully deconstructs the idea of parentage in a manner analogous to the way British social anthropologists separated the functions of marriage into different kinds of rights and duties (see below). In Townsend's decomposition, not only is an individual foster child the locus of different rights and duties, and not only can that foster child be located in different households at different times, but the different rights and duties can be located in different households at the same time and over time.

Marriage is a particularly difficult process to analyze, both in itself and for its role in the analysis of fertility. Anthropologists generally agree that marriage is an institution or process that legitimizes rights of mutual sexual access, rights of access to spousal labor and other forms of support, and rights of paternity. Of course, most of the literature focuses on the rights of men *in uxorem* and *in genetricem,* but women have corresponding rights in the prevailing institution of marriage as to whom to expect in their bed and who will put food on the table.

Granting even this insight, analyses involving marriage are problematic because, although usually regarded as an institution or a relationship, marriage is a process. Marriage is, as Clemenceau said of war with respect to diplomacy, a continuation of courtship. The various rights that it entails are invoked at different points in the process in different societies and indeed within societies. For example, access to a spouse's labor and material resources begins in some societies with engagement, since at that point those resources are committed. Thus, dowry accumulation is committed, as are the future husband's savings. In days more prudish than the present in our own society, intercourse was sometimes thought permissible if a couple were engaged to be married—at least that is what the boys said—while the girl and most likely the parents of both might have insisted on marriage first, unless the strategy were to use a pregnancy to ensure a marriage.

Marriage in absentia is likely to upset calculation of marital fertility rates if the official date of marriage is taken literally. This is not a problem only of obscure and exotic societies. In today's world, with millions of refugees, one often finds marriages contracted across thousands of miles of separation, in anticipation of ultimate coresidence which may not be realized for years.

Sexual access can occur between menarche and subsequent marriage, between marriage and subsequent menarche, or before menarche. For example, in some societies girls marry extremely early, perhaps in order to guard against premarital pregnancy. Among the Chatino of Oaxaca, girls marry at about age eleven, but sexual relations do not begin until they reach menarche (James Greenberg, personal communicaton, cited in Schlegel and Barry 1991: 98). Similar reports are given in the literature for India. Among the Kikuyu, the young sleep in mixed-sex dormitories, where the practice of sex without penetration is permitted—a custom not so different from our own traditions (Worthman 1986). Among the Ifugao and Bontoc there are similar unsupervised mixed-sex dormitories (Barton 1969). The adolescent Muria of central India may choose husbands and wives peculiar to their ghotul (dormitory) lives who are different from their betrothed. Interestingly, they claim to avoid pregnancy by changing partners frequently, but should it occur the betrothed male marries the pregnant girl and accepts paternity (Elwin 1968). Among some southern Orthodox Slavs the first part of the marriage ceremony may be separated by some months from the second, and coresidence and conjugal relations may be legitimized by the first part alone. In a number of African societies, a husband acquires the various rights to his wife as he pays installments on the bride price. The range of behavior cross-culturally in these respects is very wide (Whiting, Burbank, and Ratner 1986).

What, then, does "marriage" mean to a demographer? Certainly one should not begin to calculate the risk period for fertility calculations with marriage when marriage begins before menarche. Conversely, one ought not to start that risk period with marriage when legitimate sexual access begins before some ceremonial recognition of the union. Demographers have also had difficulty in dealing with various forms of marriage, as for example in much of Latin America and the Caribbean, where formal and recognized unions are often not celebrated either by civil registry or religious proceedings but simply acknowledged by the community (Blake 1961; Handwerker 1986, 1988). When such unions are begun and ended by consent but not marked by datable ceremonies, the demographer is cast adrift; measurement of fertility rates may only be possible from the date of first or subsequent birth, with consequent left-censoring and selection bias. It is not just the differing implementations of some institution of marriage that make analysis difficult; it is the very idea of marriage as an institution and the imposition of such an institution in a foreign context.

Similarly problematic is the notion of household (see Netting, Wilk, and Arnould 1984 for a broad review). Understanding the difference between households as contemporary residence units and households as units developing over time within their own cycle has been a classic problem in social anthropology (see, among others, Fischer 1958; Goody 1958; Goodenough 1956; Hammel 1961, 1972, 1980), but only lately has it been recognized by historians and demographers. Married children sometimes live with the parents of one or the other spouse, sometimes with neither, sometimes alternately with both, and sometimes spouses do not coreside at all. The analytic complexity of systems of household formation has seldom been adequately treated (Geoghegan 1969). The concentration of particular functions of production and consumption and of social control within households and exchanges between households can only be understood through detailed ethnographic investigation. The domestic politics of such arrangements are seldom investigated. Zimmerman (1990), for example, shows how interhousehold support for the education of a nephew is a function of traditional South Indian kinship and marriage expectations in which the nephew ultimately becomes the son-in-law. Demographers, and particularly New Household Economists, err seriously if they impose Western definitions of household in other milieux, notably in polygynous societies. The subject of temporal, cross-sectional, and functional variation in household structure is so vast that we shrink from describing it.

Conclusion

In this chapter we have explored the chances for interdisciplinary bliss that may lie in some union or at least rapprochement between anthropology and demography. We have overlooked larger theoretical issues such as evolutionary theory, ecological adaptation, and the like that might inform the interpretation of demographic analyses, and we have also overlooked potential contributions from biological anthropology that might be of assistance.[15] We have concentrated instead on social analysis and ethnography.

The first part of our effort was to examine the historical differences between the two disciplines. Demography is the statistical mechanics of populations and moves from that position only to explain the behavior of social actors; anthropology is more individualistic. Demography is close to policy, while anthropology is consciously distant from it and is especially antithetical to elite and state positions. Demography is generalizing; much of anthropology (especially in its current state) is particularizing.

The second part of our effort was to consider how concepts of culture fit into the demographic enterprise. We found the elucidation of motivation problematic, so that even when cultural symbols are used to construct such motivations, such motivations might still act only as a proxy for the true underlying causes of behavior. We suggest that an alternative is to consider institutions and cultural values as constraints on otherwise inscrutable behavior, or alternatively that completely formalistic descriptions of institutions and behavior might serve prediction as well, although at the expense of intuitive understanding, since prediction may reduce uncertainty to some extent even if we cannot achieve *Verstehen*.

Finally, we examined how working ethnographers could help demography. The flying armchair survey of the ethnographic literature is a cautionary tale. There are many things that ethnographers can tell demographers about important heterogeneities in behavior that may induce important heterogeneities in demographic phenomena. Demographers need to be alert to unexpected sources of such differences; all too frequently the typical surveys impose Western cultural definitions of marriage, the household, and gender roles on non-Western behavior. Equally importantly, ethnographers must be alert to the potential demographic results of behaviors that interest ethnographers for entirely different reasons, whether these are the fixation of marxists or postmodernists on hierarchy and exploitation or the prurience of Victorian comparativists. Most importantly, ethnographers and demographers need to be aware that there are some kinds of facts they cannot discover or that are likely to be biased by the nature of recall or the social conventions governing demographically relevant behavior. The world, as Alice said, is not what it seems.

The intrinsic difficulties of the social sciences are daunting. There can be no pure social science, so that its practitioners cannot escape moral questions. There can be no purely objective research in it, since its practitioners are also members of social systems in which standard answers to many analytic questions are already formed. There can be no simple models of social behavior, since social action is pervaded by emergent properties, and social actors are themselves evaluators and analysts of their own systems. In observing and recording data, the effect of the observer on the phenomena observed is likely to be very strong. Conversely, in the intense and long-lasting observation that constitute ethnographic fieldwork, the effect of the host society on the observer is likely to be profound. The collection of ethnographic data is difficult, expensive, and time-consuming, and because few societies are ever studied twice by ethnographers, replication of observation is rare; thus tests of validity are restricted to internal consistency, correspondence with theoretical expectation, and the always risky comparison with results from other times and places.

Nevertheless, the joint enterprise is worth undertaking if the participants have their eyes wide open. Each should recognize the individuality of the other and understand their differences. If we are to progress in the interpretation of population dynamics, we have no choice but to cooperate. To return to the introductory metaphors of this chapter, tolerance can be achieved and love may come later.

NOTES

We are especially obliged to Anthony Carter, Philip Kreager, Robert Netting, and Nicholas Townsend for their comments on the original and revised versions of this chapter. They are not responsible for any residual errors of fact or interpretation. Our chapter's title bears an uncanny resemblance to that by Pollak and Watkins (1993), testimony to the power of independent but shared metaphor in social life.

1. See also the treatment of the subject by V. Rao at the conference and Caldwell, Caldwell, and Caldwell 1987.

2. McNicoll (1992) divides the history a bit differently, but the general argument is the same.

3. Of course, in the Notesteinian tradition, one might only have to achieve "modernization" (whatever that is) and let social actors mysteriously adapt, without our understanding just what they are adapting to.

4. This is not to say that the postmodernists have raised no issues of importance. The difficulties of achieving objective observation, if objective observation can be reached other than in the limit, are serious. The question is whether to move doggedly and critically ahead in the face of such obstacles or to succumb to the paralysis of self-analysis. Similarly, feminist theory has made extraordinary contributions to our view of demographic behavior and of social history, but that contribution does not imply that gender is the only worthwhile subject. For discussion of the scientific and humanistic aspects of anthropology see, for example, Hammel 1995b, D'Andrade 1995a, and other comments in the 1995–1996 *Anthropology Newsletter*.

5. Perhaps the first discovery of this problem lay in the inability of Latin grammar to account for the structure of indigenous languages outside Europe. Indeed, it has taken quite some time to appreciate that Latin grammar cannot account for the structure of modern European languages, although most such languages continue to be taught as though the grammatical categories of Latin still had explanatory force.

6. In the strict sense, cultural relativism means that cultural phenomena foreign to the observer should be analyzed in their own terms without the imposition of Western categories and evaluations. In a looser and infinitely more problematic sense, cultural relativism means that one culture is morally as acceptable as any other. See, for example, Edgerton 1992; Gellner 1985; Hammel 1994; Herskovits 1972; James 1994; Kopelman 1994; Schweder 1990; Shore 1990a, 1990b; Spiro 1992.

7. The export of "development" by institutions such as the World Bank and the eager acceptance of such concepts by elites in LDCs are particularly troubling to many ethnographers who have seen the effects of development programs at the bottom of the social structures, where ethnographers customarily do their work. Anthropologists are

often not just the students of such societies but their vehement defenders. For contrasting views, see D'Andrade 1995b and Scheper-Hughes 1995.

8. For a discussion of the potential meanings of culture see Carter 1988, 1995a, 1995b; Fricke, chapter 10 in this volume; Hammel 1990; Keesing 1974, 1990; Kertzer and Fricke, chapter 1 in this volume; Kreager 1982, 1986.

9. We might note in passing that the dispute about agency is just a warmed-up version of the debate about determinism and free will, and we cannot resist quoting the sarcastic observation that economics is about how people make choices, while sociology is about how they have no choices to make (Duesenberry 1960:233).

10. There is a history of discussion on these issues in formal semantic analysis in anthropology. See, for example, Burling 1964a; 1964b; Frake 1964; Hymes 1964; Hammel 1964. For discussions of similar issues in demography and especially attempts to use cultural concepts, see Blake 1961; Caldwell 1977; Caldwell and Hull 1988; Caldwell, Reddy, and Caldwell 1982; Carter 1988, 1995a, 1995b; Cicourel 1974; Clark 1988; Cleland and Wilson 1987; Coale and Watkins 1986; Dyson and Moore 1983; Beckman 1983; Galloway, Hammel, and Lee 1994; Greenhalgh 1988; Hammel 1981, 1985, 1995a; Handwerker 1988; Hull 1983; Knodel, Chamratrithirong, and Debavalya 1987; Kreager 1982, 1986; Lee, Galloway, and Hammel 1994; Lesthaeghe 1977, 1983; Lesthaeghe and Surkyn 1988; Levine and Scrimshaw 1983; McNicoll 1980; Nag 1962, 1980, 1983; Pollak and Watkins 1983; Watkins 1986, 1987, 1991.

11. We are indebted to Sudha Shreeniwas for her comments on this situation in India.

12. American males with military service may recall a series of graphic films sometimes called derisively the "venereal serial." These were shown to military personnel to caution them to avoid contact with prostitutes and to use condoms or other postcoital prophylactic means to avoid infection. The American male co-author of this chapter can recall no instructions about subsequent behaviors with wives or even "nice girls," although in the prevailing culture of the time, one need not have worried at all about nice girls.

13. Deep cultural knowledge, only some of which is shared by American readers, is required to understand this remark. M and m are the coefficients of a well-known analytic method that estimates the level of fertility and the degree to which parity-specific control is being practiced. Readers who have not been exposed to American advertising might just as well forget this phrase.

14. See especially Townsend's treatment of parenthood (chapter 4 in this volume), a concept superior to that of fertility for analysis because it allows more rigorous analysis of the costs and benefits of childbearing and reflects the desire to have children when having children is primarily a way to be a parent.

15. There are several reasons for these omissions. The larger issues raised by ecological adaptation and evolutionary theory often focus on the development of social institutions rather than the behavior of individuals in the presence of those institutions. We are not here concerned with the development of institutions. Where evolutionary theory and particularly sociobiology use concepts of selection and adaptation to explain individual behavior, they often seem thoroughly teleological and not mindful of the fundamental contributions of Darwin and Huxley. Finally, while biological anthropology plays an important role in understanding many demographic processes, especially the collection of information such as hormonal assays in anthropological populations, those contributions form a kind of underpinning to the issues we discuss here.

REFERENCES

Barton, Roy F. 1969. *Ifugao Law*. Berkeley and Los Angeles: University of California Press.

Basedow, Herbert. 1927. "Subincision and Kindred Rites of the Australian Aboriginal." *Journal of the Royal Anthropological Institute* 57:123–56.

Beckman, Linda J. 1983. "Communication, Power, and the Influence of Social Networks in Couple Decisions on Fertility." In *Determinants of Fertility in Developing Countries*, ed. Rodolfo A. Bulatao and Ronald D. Lee, vol. 2, 415–43. New York: Academic Press.

Blake, Judith. 1961. *Family Structure in Jamaica: The Social Context of Reproduction*. In collaboration with J. Mayone Stycos and Kingsley Davis. New York: Free Press.

Bledsoe, Caroline. 1990. "The Politics of Children: Fosterage and the Social Management of Fertility among the Mende of Sierra Leone." In *Births and Power: Social Change and the Politics of Reproduction*, ed. W. Penn Handwerker, 81–100. Boulder, Colo.: Westview Press.

Bloch, Maurice, and Jonathan P. Perry, eds. 1982. *Death and the Regeneration of Life*. Cambridge: Cambridge University Press.

Bock, Carl Alfred. 1887. *Reise in Oost-en-Zuid-Borneo van Koetel naar Bandjarmasim in 1879 en 1880*. s'Gravenhage: Martinus Nijhoff.

Boswell, John. 1989. *The Kindness of Strangers: The Abandonment of Children in Western Europe from Late Antiquity to the Renaissance*. New York: Pantheon.

Brown, Donald, James W. Edwards, and Ruth P. Moore. 1988. The Penis Inserts of Southeast Asia: An Annotated Bibliography with an Overview and Comparative Perspective. Occasional Paper No. 15, Center for Southeast Asia Studies, University of California, Berkeley.

Buhrich, Neil. 1983. "The Association of Erotic Piercing with Homosexuality, Sadomasochism, Bondage, Fetishism, and Tattoos." *Archives of Sexual Behavior* 12:167–71.

Burling, Robbins. 1964a. "Cognition and Componential Analysis: God's Truth or Hocus-Pocus?" *American Anthropologist* 66:20–28.

———. 1964b. "Rejoinder" (to Hymes and Frake). *American Anthropologist* 66:120–22.

Caldwell, John C. 1977. "The Economic Rationality of High Fertility: An Investigation Illustrated with Nigerian Survey Data." *Population Studies* 31:5–27.

Caldwell, John C., and Pat Caldwell. 1983. "The Demographic Evidence for the Incidence and Cause of Abnormally Low Fertility in Tropical Africa." *World Health Statistics Quarterly* 36:2–34.

Caldwell, John C., Pat Caldwell, and Bruce Caldwell. 1987. "Anthropology and Demography: The Mutual Reinforcement of Speculation and Research." *Current Anthropology* 28:25–43.

Caldwell, John C., P. H. Reddy, and Pat Caldwell. 1982. "The Causes of Demographic Change in Rural South India: A Micro Approach." *Population and Development Review* 8:689–727.

Caldwell, John C., and Valerie J. Hull, eds. 1988. *Micro-Approaches to Demographic Research*. London: Kegan Paul International.

Carter, Anthony T. 1988. "Does Culture Matter? The Case of the Demographic Transition." *Historical Methods* 21:164–69.

———. 1995a. "Agency and Fertility: For an Ethnography of Practice." In *Situating*

Fertility: Anthropology and Demographic Inquiry, ed. Susan Greenhalgh, 55–85. Cambridge: Cambridge University Press.

———. 1995b. "Cultural Models and Reproductive Behavior." Paper presented at the Workshop on New Approaches to Anthropological Demography, IUSSP, Barcelona, November 10–13.

Cicourel, Aaron. 1974. *Theory and Method in a Study of Argentine Fertility.* New York: John Wiley and Sons.

Clark, Gregory. 1988. "Economists in Search of Culture: The Unspeakable in Pursuit of the Inedible." *Historical Methods* 21:161–64.

Cleland, John, and Christopher Wilson. 1987. "Demand Theories of the Fertility Transition: An Iconoclastic View." *Population Studies* 41:5–30.

Coale, Ansley J., and Susan C. Watkins, eds. 1986. *The Decline of Fertility in Europe.* Princeton: Princeton University Press.

Dalton, John. 1837 [1831]. "Essay on the Diaks of Borneo." In *Notices of the Indian Archipelago and Adjacent Countries,* ed. J. H. Moore, 41–54. Singapore.

D'Andrade, Roy D. 1995a. "What Do You Think You're Doing?" *Anthropology Newsletter* 36(7):1ff. Washington, D.C.: American Anthropological Association.

———. 1995b. "Moral Models in Anthropology." *Current Anthropology* 36:399–408.

Das Gupta, Monica. 1990. "Death Clustering, Mothers' Education, and the Determinants of Child Mortality in Rural Punjab, India." *Population Studies* 44:489–505.

DeMause, Lloyd. 1961. "The Universality of Incest." *Journal of Psychohistory* 19:123–64.

Donaldson, Peter J. 1990. *Nature against Us: The United States and the World Population Crisis, 1965–1980.* Chapel Hill: University of North Carolina Press.

Duesenberry, James S. 1960. "Comment." In *Demographic and Economic Change in Developed Countries: A Conference of the Universities' National Bureau Committee for Economic Research,* 231–34. Princeton: Princeton University Press.

Dumont, Louis. 1970. *Homo Hierarchicus.* Chicago: University of Chicago Press.

Dyson, Tim, and Mick Moore. 1983. "Kinship Structure, Female Autonomy and Demographic Behavior in India." *Population and Development Review* 9:35–60.

Edgerton, Robert. 1992. *Sick Societies.* New York: Free Press.

Elam, Itzhak. 1973. *The Social and Sexual Roles of Hima Women.* Manchester: Manchester University Press.

Elwin, Verrier. 1968. *The Kingdom of the Young.* Bombay: Oxford University Press.

Etienne, Mona. 1983. "Gender Relations and Conjugality among the Baule." In *Male and Female in West Africa,* ed. Christine Oppong, 303–19. London: George Allen and Unwin.

Evans-Pritchard, Edward E. 1951. *Kinship and Marriage among the Nuer.* Oxford: Clarendon Press.

Filipovic, Milenko S. 1982. *Among the People, Native Yugoslav Ethnography: Selected Writing of Milenko S. Filipovic,* ed. Eugene A. Hammel, Joel M. Halpern, and Robert S. Ehrich. Ann Arbor: Michigan Slavic Publications, Dept. of Slavic Languages and Literatures, Papers in Slavic Philology 3.

Fischer, Jack. 1958. "The Classification of Residence in Censuses." *American Anthropologist* 60:508–17.

Frake, Charles. 1964. "Further Discussion of Burling." *American Anthropologist* 66:119.

Frazer, James George. 1922. *The Golden Bough: A Study of Magic and Religion* (abridged). New York: Macmillan.

Freuchen, Peter. 1961. *Books of the Eskimos 1886–1957.* Ed. and pref. Dagmar Freuchen. 1st edition. Cleveland: World Publishing Co.

Friedl, Ernestine. 1983. "Society and Sex Roles." In *The Pleasures of Anthropology,* ed. Morris Freilich, 196–205. New York: New American Library.

Gaffron, von. 1859. "Over Menschen met Staarten op Borneo." *Natuurkundig Tijdschrift voor Nederlandisch-Indie* 20:227–32.

Galloway, Patrick, Eugene A. Hammel, and Ronald D. Lee. 1994. "Fertility Decline in Prussia 1875–1910: A Pooled Cross-Section Time Series Analysis." *Population Studies* 48:135–58.

Gaulin, Steven, and Alice Schlegel. 1980. "Paternal Confidence and Paternal Investment: A Cross-Cultural Test of a Sociobiological Hypothesis." *Ethnology and Sociobiology* 1:301–9.

Gellner, Ernst. 1985. *Relativism and the Social Sciences.* Cambridge: Cambridge University Press.

Geoghegan, William H. 1969. *Decision Making and Residence on Tagtabon Island.* Language Behavior Research Laboratory Working Paper No. 17, University of California, Berkeley.

Goodenough, Ward. 1956. "Residence Rules." *Southwestern Journal of Anthropology* 12:22–37.

Goody, Esther N. 1982. *Parenthood and Social Reproduction: Fostering and Occupational Roles in West Africa.* London: Cambridge University Press.

Goody, Jack, ed. 1958. *The Developmental Cycle in Domestic Groups.* Cambridge Papers in Social Anthropology, no. 1. Cambridge: Cambridge University Press.

Gordon, Daniel. 1991. "Female Circumcision and Genital Operations in Egypt and the Sudan: A Dilemma for Medical Anthropology." *Medical Anthropology Quarterly* 5:3–14.

Gough, Kathleen. 1961. "Nayar: Central Kerala." In *Matrilineal Kinship,* ed. David M. Schneider and Kathleen Gough, 298–384. Berkeley: University of California Press.

Gover, Robert. 1961. *One Hundred Dollar Misunderstanding, a Novel.* New York: Grove Press.

Greenhalgh, Susan. 1988. "Fertility as Mobility: Sinic Transitions." *Population and Development Review* 14:629–74.

———, ed. 1995. *Situating Fertility: Anthropology and Demographic Inquiry.* Cambridge: Cambridge University Press.

Gregor, Thomas. 1985. *Anxious Pleasures: The Sexual Lives of an Amazonian People.* Chicago: University of Chicago Press.

Grubauer, Albert. 1913. *Unter Kopfjägern in Central-Celebes: Ethnologische Streifzüge in Südost-und Central Celebes.* Leipzig: R. Voightländers Verlag.

Hacking, Ian. 1990. *The Taming of Chance.* Cambridge: Cambridge University Press.

Hammel, Eugene A. 1961. "The Family Cycle in a Coastal Peruvian Slum and Village." *American Anthropologist* 63:959–1005.

———. 1964. "Further Comments on Componential Analysis." *American Anthropologist* 66:1167–71.

———. 1972. "The Zadruga as Process." In *Household and Family in Past Time,* ed. Peter Laslett and Richard Wall, 335–73. Cambridge: Cambridge University Press.

———. 1980. "Household Structure in Fourteenth-Century Macedonia." *Journal of Family History* 5:242–73.

————. 1981. "What Can Anthropologists Say about Fertility?" Paper presented at the National Research Council Workshop on the Anthropology of Human Fertility, Washington, D.C., February 20–21.

————. 1985. "Cultural Receptivity to Fertility Control?" Paper presented to the Seminar on Societal Influences on Family Planning Program Performance, IUSSP and the National Family Planning Board of Jamaica, Ocho Rios, Jamaica, April 10–13.

————. 1990. :A Theory of Culture for Demography." *Population and Development Review* 16(3):455–85.

————. 1994. "Meeting the Minotaur." *Anthropology Newsletter* 35(4) 48. Washington, D.C.: American Anthropological Association.

————. 1995a. "Economics 1: Culture 0. Fertility Change and Differences in the Northwest Balkans 1700–1900." In *Situating Fertility: Anthropology and Demographic Inquiry*, ed. Susan Greenhalgh, 225–58. Cambridge: Cambridge University Press.

————. 1995b. "Science and Humanism in Anthropology: A View from the Balkan Pit." *Anthropology Newsletter* 36(8):52ff. Washington, D.C.: American Anthropological Association.

Handwerker, W. Penn. 1986. *Culture and Reproduction*. Boulder, Colo.: Westview Press.

————. 1988. *Women's Power and Social Revolution: Fertility Transition in the West Indies*. Newbury Park, Colo.: Sage Publications.

Hart, Charles W. M., and Arnold R. Pilling. 1960. *The Tiwi of North Australia*. New York: Holt, Reinhart, and Winston.

Herskovits, Melville J. 1971. *Life in a Haitian Village*. Garden City: Doubleday.

————. 1972. *Cultural Relativism*. New York: Random House.

Himes, Norman. 1970 [1936]. *Medical History of Contraception*. New York: Schocken Books.

Hodgson, Dennis. 1983. "Demography as Social Science and Policy Science." *Population and Development Review* 9:1–34.

————. 1988. "Orthodoxy and Revisionism in American Demography." *Population and Development Review* 14:541–69.

Hollos, Marida, and Phillip E. Leis. 1986. "Descent and Permissive Adolescent Sexuality in Two Ijo Communities." *Ethos* 14:395–408.

Hovorka, Oskar. 1894. "Verstummelungen des Männlichen Gliedes bei einigen Völkern des Alterthums und der Jetztzeit, mit besonderer Berücksichtigung der Sogenannten Infibulation und Kynodesme." *Mittheilungen der Anthropologischen Gesellschaft in Wien* 24:131–43.

Howell, Nancy. 1979. *The Demography of the Dobe !Kung*. New York: Academic Press.

Hsiao-hsiao-sheng. 1939. *The Golden Lotus. A Translation from the Chinese Original of the Novel, Chin P'ing Mei*, trans. Clement Egerton. London: G. Routledge.

Hull, Terence H. 1983. "Cultural Influences on Fertility Decision Styles." In *Determinants of Fertility in Developing Countries*, ed. Rodolfo A. Bulatao and Ronald D. Lee, vol. 2, 381–414. New York: Academic Press.

Hymes, Dell. 1964. "Discussion of Burling's Paper." *American Anthropologist* 66:116–19.

James, Stephen A. 1994. "Reconciling International Human Rights and Cultural Relativism: The Case of Female Circumcision." *Bioethics* 8:1–26.

Keesing, Roger. 1974. "Theories of Culture." *Annual Review of Anthropology* 3: 73–97.

———. 1990. "Theories of Culture Revisited." *Canberra Anthropology* 13:46–60.

Kertzer, David. 1993. *Sacrificed for Honor: Italian Infant Abandonment and the Politics of Reproductive Control*. Boston: Beacon Press

Knodel, John, Apichat Chamratrithirong, and Nibhon Debavalya. 1987. *Thailand's Reproductive Revolution: Rapid Fertility Decline in a Third-World Setting*. Madison: University of Wisconsin Press.

Kobak, Cantius J. 1970. "Alzina's Historia de las Islas e Indios de Bisayas . . . 1668: A Translation of the Lenox text (continued)." *Leyte-Samar Studies* 4:17–28.

Kopelman, Lauretta. 1994. "Female Circumcision/Genital Mutilation and Ethical Relativism." *Second Opinion* 20:55.

Korbin, Jill E. 1987. "Child Sexual Abuse: Implications from the Cross-Cultural Record." In *Child Survival: Anthropological Perspectives on the Treatment and Maltreatment of Children*, ed. Nancy Scheper-Hughes, 247–66. Dordrecht: D. Reidel.

Kreager, Philip. 1982. "Demography in Situ." *Population and Development Review* 8:237–66.

———. 1986. "Demographic Regimes as Cultural Systems." In *The State of Population Theory*, ed. David Coleman and Roger Schofield, 131–55. Oxford: Basil Blackwell.

Kuhlewein, M. von. 1930. "Report of a Journey to Upper Mahakam (Borneo), February–May 1929." *Mededeelingen van den Dienst der Vilksgezondheit in Nederlandische-Indie, Foreign Edition* 19:66–152.

Leach, Edmund. 1961. *Rethinking Anthropology*. London: Athlone Press.

Lee, Ronald D., Patrick Galloway, and Eugene A. Hammel. 1994. "Fertility Decline in Prussia: Estimating Influences on Supply, Demand, and Degree of Control." *Demography* 31:347–73.

Lesthaeghe, Ron. 1977. "On the Social Control of Human Reproduction." *Population and Development Review* 6:527–48.

———. 1983. "A Century of Demographic and Cultural Change in Western Europe: An Exploration of Underlying Dimensions." *Population and Development Review* 9:411–36.

Lesthaeghe, Ron, and Johan Surkyn. 1988. "Cultural Dynamics and Economic Theories of Fertility Change." *Population and Development Review* 14:1–46.

Levine, Robert A., and Susan Scrimshaw. 1983. "Effects of Culture on Fertility: Anthropological Contributions." In *Determinants of Fertility in Developing Countries*, ed. Rodolfo A. Bulatao and Ronald D. Lee, vol. 2, 666–95. New York: Academic Press.

Mandelbaum, David. 1965. "Social Uses of Funeral Rites." In *The Meaning of Death*, ed. Herman Feifel, 189–217. New York: McGraw-Hill.

Mayer, A. B. 1877. "Über de Perforation des Penis bei den Malayan." *Mittheilungen der Anthropologischen Gesellschaft in Wien* 7:242–44.

McNicoll, Geoffrey. 1980. "Institutional Determinants of Fertility Change." *Population and Development Review* 6:441–62.

———. 1992. "The Agenda of Population Studies: A Commentary and Complaint." *Population and Development Review* 18:399–420.

Morga, Antonio de. 1906 [1609]. "Sucesos de las Islas Filipinas." In *The Philippine Islands*, ed. Emma Helen Blair and James Alexander Robertson, vol. 16, 25–209. Cleveland: A. H. Clark Col.

Murphy, Yolanda, and Robert F. Murphy. 1974. *Women of the Forest*. New York: Columbia University Press.

Nag, Moni. 1962. *Factors Affecting Human Fertility in Nonindustrial Societies: A Cross-Cultural Study*. Yale University Publications in Anthropology, no. 66. New Haven, Conn.: Yale University Press.

———. 1980. "How Modernization Can Also Increase Fertility." *Current Anthropology* 21:571–87.

———. 1983. "Sociocultural Factors in Breastfeeding and Sexual Behavior." In *Determinants of Fertility in Developing Countries*, ed. Rodolfo A. Bulatao and Ronald D. Lee, 163–98. New York: Academic Press.

Netting, Robert McC., Richard R. Wilk, and Eric J. Arnould, eds. 1984. *Households: Comparative and Historical Studies of the Domestic Group*. Berkeley: University of California Press.

Opler, Morris. 1936. "An Interpretation of Ambivalence of Two American Indian Tribes." *Journal of Social Psychology* 7:82–116.

Peter, H.R.H., Prince of Greece and Denmark. 1963. *A Study of Polyandry*. The Hague: Mouton and Co.

Pollak, Robert A., and Susan C. Watkins. 1993. "Cultural and Economic Approaches to Fertility: Proper Marriage or Mesalliance." *Population and Development Review* 19:467–96.

Scheper-Hughes, Nancy. 1985. "Culture, Scarcity, and Maternal Thinking: Maternal Detachment and Infant Survival in a Brazilian Shantytown." *Ethos* 13:291–317.

———. 1992. *Death without Weeping: The Violence of Everyday Life in Brazil*. Berkeley: University of California Press.

———. 1995. "The Primacy of the Ethical: Propositions for a Militant Anthropology." *Current Anthropology* 3:409–20.

———, ed. 1987. *Child Survival: Anthropological Perspectives on the Treatment and Maltreatment of Children*. Dordrecht: D. Reidel.

Schlegel, Alice. 1975. "The Adolescent Socialization of the Hopi Girl." *Ethnology* 4:449–62.

Schlegel, Alice, and Herbert Barry. 1991. *Adolescence: An Anthropological Inquiry*. New York: Free Press.

Schweder, Richard A. 1990. "Ethical Relativism: Is There a Defensible Version?" *Ethos* 18:205–18.

Scrimshaw, Susan. 1978. "Infant Mortality and Behavior in the Regulation of Family Size." *Population and Development Review* 4:383–404.

Segal, Sheldon J. 1972. "Contraception Research: A Male Chauvinist Plot?" *Daedalus* 97:486–501.

Serpenti, Laurentius M. 1977. *Cultivators in the Swamps: Social Structure and Horticulture in a New Guinea Society*. Assen (Netherlands): Van Gorcum.

Shore, Brad. 1990a. "Human Ambivalence and the Structuring of Moral Values." *Ethos* 18:165–79.

———. 1990b. "Moral Relativism—Afterword." *Ethos* 18:219–23.

Silk, Joan B. 1987. "Adoption and Fosterage in Human Societies: Adaptations or Enigmas?" *Cultural Anthropology* 2:39–49.

Spiro, Melford. 1992. "Cultural Relativism and the Future of Anthropology." In *Rereading Cultural Anthropology*, ed. George E. Marcus, 125–51. Durham: Duke University Press.

Trumbach, Randolph. 1978. *The Rise of the Egalitarian Family*. New York: Academic Press.

Underhill, Ruth. 1936. *Chona Papago Woman: The Autobiography of a Papago Woman*. Memoirs of the American Anthropological Association 46. Menasha: American Anthropological Association.

Watkins, Susan C. 1986. "Conclusion." In *The Decline of Fertility in Europe*, ed. Ansley J. Coale and Susan C. Watkins, 420–49. Princeton: Princeton University Press.

———. 1987. "The Fertility Transition: Europe and the Third World Compared." *Sociological Forum* 2:645–73.

———. 1991. *From Provinces to Nations: Demographic Integration in Western Europe, 1870–1960*. Princeton: Princeton University Press.

Whiting, John W. M., Victoria K. Burbank, and Mitchell S. Ratner. 1986. "The Duration of Maidenhood across Cultures." In *School-Age Pregnancy and Parenthood: Biosocial Dimensions*, ed. Jane B. Lancaster and Beatrix A. Hamburg, 273–302. New York: Aldine de Gruyter.

Worthman, Carol M. 1986. "Development Dysynchrony as Normal Experience: Kikuyu Adolescents." In *School-Age Pregnancy and Parenthood: Biosocial Dimensions*, ed. Jane B. Lancaster and Beatrix A. Hamburg, 95–112. New York: Aldine de Gruyter.

Wulfften Palthe, P. M. van. 1936. "Psychiatry and Neurology in the Tropics." In *A Clinical Textbook of Tropical Medicine*, ed. C. D. de Langen and A. Lichtenstein, 525–74. Batavia: G. Kolff & Co.

Zimmerman, Frank E. 1990. *South Indian Fertility Decline: The Life Cycle and the Kin Group*. Ph.D. diss., University of California, Berkeley.

Chapter Eight

Demography without Numbers

Nancy Scheper-Hughes

I want to argue here for a particular methodology for an anthropologically informed demography, one that Margaret Lock and I have called a "critical interpretive approach" (Lock and Scheper-Hughes 1990). After a few words on the epistemological divide separating objectivist/positivist approaches from critical/interpretive approaches, I will take up an instance from my intermittent, twenty-five-year study of infant mortality in northeast Brazil in order to demonstrate what qualitative, interpretive, and meaning-centered research—demography without or beyond numbers[1]—can reveal about infant mortality that strictly quantitative and positivist research cannot.

Objectivist and interpretive approaches have been described in terms of incommensurate epistemological differences, conforming to what Thomas Kuhn (1970) called "paradigms" and what Michel Foucault called "epistemes," by which he meant different shapes of thought/knowledge/power (1972:191). A paradigm in Kuhn's sense provides a foundation for the organization of reasoning; it is a source of logical constructions devoted to the systematic production of explanations. Another meaning of paradigm is similar to the concept of *weltanschauung* (or worldview): the paradigm is that which is shared by the members of a particular scientific community (see Kuhn 1970). In other words, it organizes and legitimates the shared values of the group; it monitors the standards of what is to be considered acceptable, permitted, adequate, and good (as well as the reverse) in the conduct of research.

Objectivist and interpretive frameworks constitute paradigms insofar as they constitute very different convictions about the nature of reality, about what is considered useful or respectable data, about research and funding priorities, about the forms that data and theories should take, and about the kind of language researchers should use—in all, about the way scientists and social scientists should go about their business and how research findings should be applied to public policy and to everyday life (see, for example, the debate between D'Andrade [1995] and Scheper-Hughes [1995b] on "scientific" versus "moral" models in anthropology).

Drawing on anthropological metaphors, we could say that the worldviews underlying the two approaches represent "foreign cultures," each one self-contained and autonomous, possessing its own inner logic and standards of truth-seeking. Viewed in these uncompromising terms, it would be next to impossible to invalidate the method of one from the perspective of the other. To appropriate Evans-Pritchard's statement on Azande witchcraft, "In this web of belief every strand depends on every other strand, and a Zande [here read an objectivist or an interpretivist] cannot get out of its meshes because it is the only world he knows. The web is not an external structure. . . . It is the [very] texture of his thought and he cannot think that his thought is wrong" (1937:193–94).

The debate turns on the old question of whether "facts" in the world are uncovered or whether they are produced in the context of research. The objectivist position assumes that rigorous empirical research can lead to a truthful and accurate representation of the objects or events under study (see D'Andrade 1995). Empiricism is a philosophical tradition which advocates (and assumes the possibility of) a neutral, value-free science, one able to apprehend reality without mediations. What is needed to settle complex problems and arguments is always more findings, more facts.

Most epidemiologists and demographers simply take for granted the fundamentally empiricist nature of their scientific practices. In his discussion of modern epidemiology, Kenneth Rothman quotes the respected physicist (but indifferent philosopher) Lord Kelvin: "I often say that when you can measure what you are speaking about, and express it in numbers, you know something about it; but when you cannot express it in numbers your knowledge is of a meager and unsatisfactory kind; it may be the beginning of knowledge, but you can have scarcely, in your thoughts, advanced to the stage of Science, whatever the matter may be" (Rothman 1986:23). Gene Hammel (1990, and chapter 7 in this volume) used to say something similar to the many cohorts of graduate students who took his excellent seminars in research methods. "If you can't count it, it probably doesn't exist." Of course, he would modify this dictum for the hopelessly qualitative cultural anthropologists-in-training. I think he was happy if I managed to number the pages of the research proposals I submitted to his seminar.

Curiously, the hard-wired notion of empiricism and the notions of objective reality and causality which derive from it just about disappeared from Western philosophy when modern science appeared on the scene as a social practice. While there are few radically empiricist philosophers left in the Western world, there are countless practicing and practical scientists and (even worse!) social scientists who operate in the laboratory and in the field as if a radical critique and reassessment of empiricism had not taken place over the past 150 years![2] The commitment to positivism and empiricism is so unconsciously defended that when a radical critique of it appears it is often misunderstood, as recent intellectual biographies of the early philosophical writings of Ludwig Wittgenstein demonstrate (see Malcolm 1994).

The critical interpretive approach in anthropology—and specifically in medical anthropology—calls into question the epistemological status of the objects and the realities under study. It conceives of the body, illness, disease, and death as simultaneously biological and social (Scheper-Hughes 1994a), and conceives of the social as historical, complex, fragmented, conflictive, uncertain, and constantly negotiated. Because research takes place within a social field it cannot possibly be neutral or value free. At the very least it partakes of the culture (and hence the morality) of the scientific community where values are no less strong simply because they remain unarticulated (see Rabinow and Sullivan 1979; Rorty 1979).

In critical interpretive anthropology what matters most are the means through which research data are acquired, the various and complex meanings these findings might have, and the relations between the kinds of knowledge generated and the maintenance of powerful ideologies and forms of dominance, both social/political and biomedical/scientific. In all, interpretive research is less concerned with orderly explanations than with achieving a fuller, richer, deeper understanding of social life as the "negotiation of meanings" (Marcus and Fisher 1986:26). It is part of a broader movement in which reductionist science as a whole is reappraised as a product of its specific historical and cultural contexts.

The Radical Challenge

While conventional research in demography and/or epidemiology can strive to be culturally sensitive and can illuminate, for example, the cultural logic and alternative shapes of rationality that may govern the fertility and reproductive decision-making of Third World women, poor people, immigrants, refugees, and other marginalized "others," there is often a striking lack of awareness of the ways in which the culture of their science structures the questions asked and overdetermines the findings. Rather than simply including or factoring in reductionist and unproblematized cultural variables—and thereby "cutting culture down to size" as Kertzer (in press) put it in his contribution to another volume—a critically interpretive demography would have to become a much more radical undertaking, one which calls into question the neutral and objective status of its research categories as well as the adequacy of its interventions.

Almeida Filho has begun this radical process for the science of epidemiology (1989, 1990, 1991). He has examined the question of the object of knowledge in his field so as to interrogate further the dominant statuses of causality and of risk as they operate in conventional epidemiological inquiries. He argues that to date the best that the radical epistemologic critique can offer epidemiology is "the paradigm of what is missing, of what needs to be construed, what is [still in the process of] becoming in order to fill the gaps" (Almeida Filho 1991:6). I hope that the anthropological essays included in this volume can do the same for the science of demography—that is, to point to demography's gaps, to suggest what may be missing, and to indicate what still needs to be construed.

Recently, T. M. S. Evens referred to anthropology as the most "implicitly revolutionary" of the human sciences (1995:12). The as yet unrealized radicalness of anthropology's epistemology derives from its "constituting interest in otherness" which renders it "open" in a definitive way. However, the lure of easy empiricism constantly undermines and subverts anthropology's radical promise. It does so each time anthropology is presented (or presents itself) as a "body of accumulated knowledge, rather than as a discipline obliged by the character of its subject matter to continually round up for interrogating the presuppositions according to which it proceeds" (Evens 1995:12).

Reality is, of course, always more complex, contradictory, and elusive than our limited and partial theoretical models and methods allow. And even those who, like myself, question the truth claims of objectivist science do not deny that there are any meaningful and discoverable facts in the world. Some things are incontestably factual and these need to be studied empirically. In my own research I am deeply committed to finding better ways of getting at crucial but elusive data, whether through better ways of mapping, predicting, and responding to the global HIV/AIDS epidemic (see Scheper-Hughes 1994b) or of unmasking the culture of silence that hides the new practices of "political disappearances" in Brazilian *favelas* (Scheper-Hughes 1992 ch. 6, 1995b).

Moving toward my main illustration, as I noted elsewhere, either 150 or 350 children die of hunger, diarrheal disease, and dehydration in the Brazilian shantytown of Alto do Cruzeiro in a given year, and the researcher who is exploring infant mortality has a strong scientific and moral imperative to get it right (Scheper-Hughes 1992:23). In Third World situations there are a great many lives and deaths to count among populations generally thought of as not worth tracking at all. But necessary empirical research of this kind need not be empiricist—that is, it need not entail a philosophical commitment to Enlightenment notions of reason, objects, and truth. Empirical work can be guided by critical-interpretive concerns about the inevitable partiality of truths and about the various and contradictory meanings that facts and events have in the existential, cultural, and political sense.

Demography without Numbers: Counting Angels

Since 1964–66 (with subsequent field research in 1982, 1986–87, 1989, 1990, and 1992) I have been working in a northeast Brazilian sugar plantation town I call Bom Jesus da Mata in order to document, analyze, and explain the causes, meanings, and the effects of infant and child mortality on a population of impoverished and chronically hungry sugar cane cutters and their families. My work began during the imposition of the military dictatorship and followed through the years of the so-called Economic Miracle up through the period of democratization.

Keeping track of "angel babies" in the plantation zone of northeast Brazil—the poorest and Third World sector in an otherwise First World nation that boasts the world's eighth richest economy—is as daunting as attempts by

U.S. census workers to count the homeless in American cities. Much of the phenomenon is tucked away from public scrutiny. The reference to a demography without numbers is, in the first instance, descriptive. As anyone working in the Third World knows, both official statistics and survey research are unreliable. An estimated one million children younger than five years old die each year in Brazil (and more than half of these die in the large, impoverished northeast region). But the official statistics are at best a rough approximation of a vastly unreported phenomenon. Brazil's national system of vital statistics was only established in 1974, although local statistics for the municipalities of state capitals and large towns are available for earlier dates. These are, naturally, of greatly varying quality.

As demographers are well aware, public records—whether official censuses, birth and baptismal certificates, marriage and divorce records, or death or burial certificates—are not pure, accurate, or objective sources of information. Nor are they politically, let alone scientifically, neutral. The public records and the statistical inferences based on them are less mirrors of realities than filters and collective representations. At best, official records and statistics reveal a society's particular system of classification as well as some of its basic social values, such as what is deemed worth recording and counting at all.

Censuses and other public records count some things better than others. In rural northeast Brazil the death of a marginalized shantytown baby is an event considered hardly worth documenting at all. The moral economy of public health and medical services in rural northeast Brazil is such that two-thirds or more of those infants who die do so without a medical diagnosis, evaluation, or testimony. The space for recording the infant's cause of death on the official death certificate is simply left blank, a conspicuous semiotic zero representing the inconsequentiality of the infant's civil status in Brazil. Even when the cause of death is recorded the information given is often meaningless, careless, or useless.

Of the 881 infant and child deaths recorded in the civil registry office of Bom Jesus da Mata—a medium-sized sugar plantation town in the northeast state of Pernambuco with a population of roughly 30,000 people—over three sample years (1965, 1985, 1987) only 159 carried a cause of death. And 35 percent of these attributed the baby's death to the incontestable but rather useless diagnosis "heart stopped, respiration stopped." The infants died, we might suppose, of having lived. Other commonly listed causes of death included "prematurity," "weakness," "hunger," "dehydration," "accidental death" (including, more specifically at times, "knock on the head," "fall," "drowned," "poisoning") and the mytho-poetic "acute infantile suffering." As there was no follow-up of any kind, "the state" seemed to demonstrate an appalling lack of curiosity about the "natural" or "accidental" causes of deaths of so many "acutely suffering" angel babies.

As many as a third of all infant deaths are unrecorded altogether. Although by constitutional law poor Brazilians are exempted from paying birth and death registration fees, in small rural towns and rural villas in northeast Brazil the civil registry office is often privately owned and the fees charged for birth, death, and marriage certificates are prohibitive for the poorest population. Consequently, many needy parents postpone birth registration for several years and only register the deaths of those babies they intend to bury in the municipal cemetery. The majority of stillborn and a great many premature infants who die at home are simply buried privately in the backyard *quintal* or in the countryside without the benefit of either a birth or a death certificate. In rural areas where older, traditional customs prevail, the deaths of unbaptized infants of any age are unregistered because as "pagan" infants they are stigmatized creatures. They are buried secretly by their parents at a crossroads, the place where Exu, the African-Brazilian deity, and his host of unbaptized spirit infants gather and congregate to serve as messengers for good and ill in the world.

Fifteen percent of births in the shantytown still take place at home, keeping half a dozen elderly midwives regularly employed. These lay midwives (unlike those attached to hospitals and maternity clinics) work in relative isolation from the agents of medicine and the state and, as they fear running afoul of the law, they do not encourage registration of the births, let alone the infant deaths, in which they have been involved. This is not, however, to malign the skills of the rural *parteiras,* for their record of maternal morbidity/infant mortality fares well in comparison to the very high number of perinatal deaths for "charity" patients at the single, privately owned but publicly supported, municipal hospital of Bom Jesus.

In cross-checking the official vital statistics on children's deaths (from birth to five years) reported for 1984–85 in Pacatuba, Ceara (northeast Brazil) against their own door-to-door household survey and interviews with women and their local healers, Nations and Amaral (1991) found that the civil registry office recorded only 44.4 percent of actual child deaths, underreporting the phenomenon by 56 percent. They also found that the official death registry and household survey techniques were less sensitive than the "folk" demographers and death reporters in detecting the deaths of less-valued females and newborns of both sexes.

In order to capture the social reality of infant and child deaths and to uncover the layers of cultural meaning underlying the metaphorical causes of death listed in the death certificates required cross-checking the official data against the oral tradition. This meant relying on the memories and self-reports of poor shantytown women as mothers and as traditional healers, praying women, and midwives. It meant, first of all, leaving the civil registry office in order to walk the length and breadth of the poor *bairros,* shantytowns, and outlying rural hamlets of Brazil in order to follow pregnancies, births, and sicknesses (and their medical treatments and cultural healings) and the premature death of infants and children. It meant attending wakes, trailing after infant and child funeral processions, examining old and new and reused grave-sites, and talking with all those who are involved with the production, death, and burial of "angel babies."

Among the folk demographers of infant death in rural Pernambuco are the Catholic priests and nuns who baptize infants and babies, the pharmacists who prescribe for them, the hospital attendants who just as often reject as attend to them, the local coffin makers who fashion little shoeboxes of cardboard and crepe paper, the local seamstresses who sew the shrouds for infants and the little white albs with the blue sash for older children, and the shopkeepers at the open air market who sell the other ritual materials used at infant wakes: white candles, blue and white cloth, silver gummed stars, white stockings, flowers, etc. What these people don't know the taxi cab drivers, who carry mothers and sick infants to the clinics and hospitals or who may occasionally transport a father and his dead infant to the public cemetery, might know. What they don't know the local gravedigger is sure to know. Their often stigmatized and rejected knowledge can fill out the social context within which infant deaths occur.

When asked "How many poor and how many rich infants did you bury in the past month?" Seu Chico, the club-footed gravedigger of Bom Jesus da Mata, replied without batting an eye, "Thirty-four paupers and one infant of the bourgeoisie." How did he know? "Only one 'angel' arrived," he said, "in a proper, 'bought' coffin and only one was put into a purchased plot." The graves of all the others could be exhumed and reused for another pauperized angel within a scarce three months time. The data on class affiliation is absent on the official death certificates and so the particular social face of infant mortality and the magnitude of human suffering and loss are also erased.

Eliciting the individual reproductive life histories of poor women is a time-consuming method of investigation, but necessary not only to correct the incomplete official public record but in order to gain a deeper understanding of the context and meaning of infant death, which in rural northeast Brazil is viewed alternatively as "angel life." While the causes of infant death are largely unreported in the official vital statistics collected at the registry office in rural northeast Brazil, mothers can almost always say why a particular infant died. But since their etiological explanations bridge biological, social, political, spiritual, and magical realities, their knowledge is generally rejected by the state and by scientific investigators. The assumptions, models, and paradigms of these women do not fit the secular, biomedical, epidemiological, and demographic notions of causality, rationality, and rational choice that govern scientific research.

Nonetheless, shantytown mothers' interpretations of infant and child death can help clarify the pathogens—both microparasites and macroparasites—

which together carry off shantytown infants in veritable "die-outs": contaminated water, socially produced hunger and scarcity, unpredictable resources, exploitative "bosses," unreliable fathers, and chronic feelings of maternal "inner badness," weakness, and powerlessness. The causes of infant mortality in Bom Jesus da Mata, as the mothers readily recognized, are constitutional, economic, political, and moral/theological.

Women's reproductive histories can be supplemented by the normally overlooked knowledge, memories, and experience of children as potential informants. Children are, after all, the siblings, playmates, and not infrequently the primary caretakers of fated angel babies and even very young children can be painfully willing "informants" on the topic of child death. Twelve-year-old "China," a runaway street child in Bom Jesus, defended his knowledge and expertise as follows:

> I'm small, Tia, but I have learned a few things. I was in charge at home. It fell to me to take care of everything—the cooking, the cleaning, the shopping. You could say that I was the *dona da casa* [the madam, the woman of the household]. There were a whole bunch of us born and today there are only three of us left. I only didn't die myself because I was the oldest and I was in charge. They died of hunger and of *gasto* [weakness from explosive diarrhea]. I was expected to go out every day and find milk for the babies. . . . When they got sick it was up to me to wrap them up and carry them to the hospital. And when they died it was me who went to the mayor to ask for a coffin and it was me who arranged them in their box. It was me who got the flowers and who called the other children to make the procession to the cemetery.

In all, what is remarkable about infant mortality in northeast Brazil is its general acceptance as a fact of everyday life, and not only by *favela* women who are so accustomed to giving birth to "angel babies." Infant death has not entered the public consciousness of even rural doctors and political leaders in Bom Jesus da Mata as a serious problem about which something must be done. Shantytown infants in rural Brazil are presumed to die of "natural causes," just as old people in North America did prior to the medicalization of old age. The death of poor infants is the most natural, routine, ordinary, and even expected of events.

Letting Go—The Moral Economy of Mothering

By the time I completed my study in Bom Jesus nearly a hundred shantytown women had told me their reproductive histories, as well as their thoughts and feelings about their lives, their mostly informal marriages, and the births and deaths of their many children. The average woman of the Alto do Cruzeiro is pregnant 9.5 times and gives birth to eight living children. This, I suspect, represents an underreport of those pregnancies resulting in miscarriage or abortion as well as less-than-memorable stillbirths. Such a woman experiences an average of 3.5 infant and child deaths. This profile looks very much like a classic "pre-demographic transition" pattern—a high fertility driven by "untamed" infant and child mortality.

I found that the high expectancy of child death was, indeed, a powerful shaper of reproductive and maternal thinking and practice in the shantytown, as evidenced in a conditional attachment to newborns who were often treated more like household visitors than as permanent family members. A stance of maternal watchful waiting until the baby manifested a real "hold on life" preceded the full expression of maternal love and attachment. Women's over-prediction of infant death, with its accompanying distanced maternal affections, could be mortal at times and contributed to the premature death of infants who were seen as lacking a *gosto* (taste) or *jeito* (knack) for life. Such babies are described by their mothers as "wanting" or even "needing" to die.

Aided by their female relatives, neighbors, *co-madres*, midwives, and local healing women, mothers distinguished between those infants and babies who were safe to adopt into one's care and affections and those who demonstrated the will, destiny, or innate constitution of angel babies. Such babies could be assisted to die through a gradual reduction and then withdrawal of food, liquid, and care. Women sought thereby to avoid the suffering of a prolonged and agonizing death in a "little creature."

The feminist philosopher Sara Ruddick (1989) identifies a womanly attitude of "holding" as an essential feature of maternal thinking. Holding implies a metaphysical attitude of holding on, holding up, holding close, holding dear. It connotes maternal protectiveness and of conserving and valuing what is at hand. But what of mothering in an environment like the Brazilian shantytown, where the risks to child survival are legion? There, mothers must concede to a certain humility, even passivity, toward a world that is, in so many respects, beyond their control.

Consequently, among the mothers of the Brazilian shantytown, maternal thinking and practice were often guided by another, and quite opposite, metaphysical stance, one (to draw on the mothers' own choice of metaphors) of "letting go." Among the mostly Catholic women of the Alto do Cruzeiro, "letting go" implied a fundamentally religious attitude of calm and reasonable resignation to events that cannot easily be changed or overcome. It implied a leap of faith and a trust that was not easy for most poor women to achieve. The women struggled to conform to the demands that their poverty and scarcity had imposed on the practices and experience of sexuality and motherhood. "Holy indifference" in the face of terrible adversity is a cherished, though elusive, religious value. Secular anthropologists do it a disservice by reducing the phenomenon to "peasant fatalism." Meanwhile, demographers (like children) demand too much of mothers, particularly when they attribute maternal thinking and practice to alienated concepts of rational choice and to mathematical calculations concerning the value of children.

While there is something consoling in Donald Winnicott's forgiving notion of the "good enough" mother—his common sense faith in ordinary mothers to perform the requisite tasks necessary to sustain and support new life under ordinary conditions (1987)—surely "good enough" mothering depends on a "good enough" social and economic environment. And though it is rarely thought about in this way, to what extent does "good enough" mothering depend on the presence of a "good enough" baby? But favela women often speak of being "let down" and "disappointed" by their weak and sickly babies—especially those who seem to lack a certain talent for life.

The kind of thinking that evolves from the experience and practice of mothering in a context of hunger, scarcity, and infant death is somewhat analogous to the social and moral ethic of the battlefield, where triage, thinking in sets, and ideas about the magical replaceability of the missing and the dead predominate, as well as the idea of acceptable or meaningful death. In a world of great uncertainty about human life mothers may approach each new pregnancy with sorrow and dread. If an infant dies young, before it has had a chance to be properly named, baptized, or to express its individual nature, its death may be accepted as a misfortune, but not as a great tragedy. (As one shantytown father remarked when he was hesitantly told by a nurse that all had not gone well with his wife's labor and delivery, "Pois, menos um por meu poquinho de angu"—Well, less one for my little bit of gruel.) On the Alto do Cruzeiro mother love grows slowly, gradually, fearfully, increasing in strength and intensity once a mother senses that the child is not just a casual visitor to the household, stopping off on its way to the afterlife, but intends to remain and enter the *luta*, the struggle that is life.

I have encountered situations in which some impoverished shantytown mothers appear to have suspended compassion, empathy, and care toward some of their weak and sickly children, helping them to die easily and well. I spent many years trying to understand, translate, and to defend the ethical position of these folk Catholic women who refused abortion (and in some cases even birth control) on moral grounds but who confidently asserted that some of their supernumerary infants "wanted to die" so that others, including themselves, might be able to live.

I came to think of the babies of the Alto do Cruzeiro who were "given up" (i.e., offered up) and "given up on" in terms of ritual scapegoating and sacrifice as discussed by René Girard (1987). Girard builds his theory of religion around the idea of sacrificial violence and the need for an agreed-upon or surrogate victim—the "generative scapegoat"—whose suffering or death (like Jesus') helps to resolve unbearable social "tensions, conflicts, and material difficulties of all kinds" (1987:74). The given-up, offered-up angel babies of northeast Brazil were likewise sacrificed in the face of terrible conflicts about scarcity and survival. And that is, in fact, just how their mothers spoke of them. The following theological reflection took place at a Christian "base community" meeting in the Alto do Cruzeiro in 1990:

"What does it mean to say that a baby 'has' to die, or that it dies because it 'wants' to die?" I asked.

Terezinha was the first to speak. "It means that God takes them to save *us* from suffering."

"What she means," broke in Zephinha, "is that God knows the future better than you or I. It could be that if the baby were to live he would cause much suffering in the mother. Why, he could turn out to be a thief, or a murderer, or a *cabo safado,* a good for nothing. The baby daughter could shame her family by turning out a prostitute in the *zona.* . . . And so they die instead as babies, to *save* us from great suffering, not to give us pain. Yes, there are many reasons to rejoice for the death of a baby!"

Luiza added, "Well, I only know that I kept giving birth, and mine just kept on dying. But I never gave up hope. Perhaps the first nine had to die to clear the way, to make space, so that the last five could live."

"I myself," said Fatima "don't have too much hope for this one," referring to the fussy, sickly toddler on her lap. "If God wants her, then I would be happy for her and happy for me! I would be pleased to have a little 'sacred heart' in heaven."

"But why," I persisted in asking, "would God want babies to suffer so much in dying?"

"Don't ask me," said Edite Cosmos. "I did *everything* to keep mine healthy and alive, but God just didn't want me to have them. I think that these deaths are sent by Him to punish us for the sins of the world. And yet the babies don't really deserve this. We ourselves are the sinners, *but the punishment falls on them.*"

"Be quiet, Edite," said another. "They die, just like Jesus died, to save us from suffering. Isn't that right, Sister Juliana?"

But Sister Juliana, a native of the dry *sertão* where (she said) babies did not die like flies as they did in the sugar plantation zone, was not so sure that the women were right in their moral thinking. "I don't think Jesus *wants* all your babies," she said. "I think He wants them to live." But, after all, Sister Juliana was a nun and the women of the shantytown didn't pay her too much attention. What could *she* possibly know about babies?

In searching for an appropriate, respectful way to present the existential dilemmas in the lives of these desperately poor women, who could shrug their shoulders when another hungry or dehydrated infant died and comment philosophically, "Melhor morrer menino do que um de nos mourrer" (Better that a baby die than one of us adults), I found myself walking an ethical and representational tightrope—one familiar, I imagine, to a great many anthropologists. The survivor logic that guides shantytown mothers' actions toward some of their weak babies is understandable. But the moral and political issues still give one reason to pause, and to doubt.

In my reluctance to objectify or romanticize the women of the Alto do Cruzeiro, I avoided the easy lure of victimology and refused to see the women as merely passive victims of cruel fate, as cruel and inhuman as their material realties were. And I also refused to see them as mindlessly indoctrinated Catholics mouthing, like so many parrots, Ecclesiastical platitudes coming down to them from Rome or from the Archdiocese of Recife. These women actively made choices, as constrained as those choices were, and likewise they selected aspects of Catholic teachings that they could use or live with, while readily discarding others. Some of their moral choices—if you will excuse the pun—evidenced more than a touch of bad faith.

I think, for example, of Dona Dora's remark after she explained the folk belief in dead infants as winged angels who fly happily around the thrones of Jesus and Mary in heaven: "Well, this is what we say. This is what we tell each other. But to tell you the truth, I don't know if these stories about the afterlife are true or not. We want to believe the best for our children. How else could we stand all the suffering?" Or, I think of thirteen-year-old Xoxa instructing me on how to behave at the wake of an emaciated infant whose mother had refused to breastfeed: "You must not scold the mother. You must say how very sorry you are that Jesus came to take her baby." "Yes, of course," I replied, "but what do you think?" "Oh, Nanci! That baby never got enough to eat—but you can't *ever, ever* say that!"

The solution I eventually found was to practice what I call *antropologia-pe-no-chão*—anthropology with one's feet on the ground. The phrase refers both to an existentially, methodologically, and politically grounded practice of fieldwork, as well as to a "barefoot" anthropology which, in the language of liberation theology, means assuming "a preferential option" for the poor. I interpreted this to mean allowing myself to be drawn from time to time into local political struggles to "accompany" my Brazilian informants and friends in their daily *luta*.

The Death of Mercea: The Single Case Study

In order to secure my interpretation, I will anchor it in the narrative of the short life and death of Mercea, a three-year-old toddler from the shantytown of Alto do Cruzeiro in Bom Jesus da Mata, who died at home alone and un-attended while her mother and her anthropologist were out dancing carnival in the streets. Perhaps I want to illustrate what a single instance, an "n" of 1, can contribute to demographic inquiry.

The case study, pioneered by Max Gluckman (1963) and the Manchester School of British Social Anthropology, is generally seen as a method for ex-tracting the general from the particular (Evens 1995:17–18). Additionally, the "thickly described" case study can disclose the fundamental principles of

the given social order—the ways in which thought, ideas, and practice interact, and can illuminate the deeper meanings of social events and the moral
economy which governs the resolution of a particular incident. The case study
is essential for capturing the social situatedness of cultural knowledge and
practice.

Three-year-old Mercea was severely ill in February 1989 and had been so
since her birth at Ferreira Lima hospital in Bom Jesus. Her mother, Biu, was a
forty-three-year-old cane worker, a tough woman, slight of build but with
strong arms and long, thick brown hair (her one vanity) that she would pull
back in a knot each morning. She rose in the dark to prepare a cup of black
coffee before setting off on foot for a local plantation where she was employed
with her nine-year-old son as an unregistered field worker earning less than
the official minimum wage. Biu took home about $1.25 a day.

Mercea was left in the care of her thirteen-year-old sister, Xoxa, and she
sat in a dark corner endlessly scratching her infected bug bites and sores. Mercea could not walk and she spoke only a few words, among which were inces-
sant demands for fresh, unsalted meat. There had been no "Papa" in the
household since the night of Sao Joao (St. John's day) when Oscar, Biu's second common-law husband, walked out with the couple's gas stove, bed, and
the healthiest two boys among Biu's seven surviving children (of the fifteen
born to her), to live with a younger woman who, Oscar boasted, still had her
teeth.

"Infants are like birds," Biu once said, "here today, gone tomorrow. Alive
or dead, it's really all the same to them. They don't have that certain attachment to life of the older child." Mercea had, however, already survived over a
dozen medical crises of fevers, respiratory ailments, violent diarrhea, and vom-
iting that had wasted her frail little body, retarded her speech, and brought her
close to death. Next to Mercea's hammock was a wooden table with half-used
medicine bottles, some of which, Biu said, had "worked for a while." They
included antibiotics, antiseptic skin creams, cough medicines, analgesics, tran-
quilizers, and sleeping pills. There was even an appetite stimulant, though the
child had often been denied more than a few tablespoons of "mingau" (a thin
rice or manioc gruel) in a twenty-four-hour period. None of these treatments
had resolved the child's main illness, which Biu described as "weakness" and
"nervousness"—a *nervoso infantil*—that left her child unable to withstand
the *luta*. Mercea, said Biu, never showed a real *gosto* or *jeito* for life.

Mercea was reported by her mother to suffer from periodic and violent
episodes of "child attack," as women of the Alto refer to acute convulsions
with head banging, eye rolling, twitching, and body rigidity. Like many women
of the Alto, Biu regarded the convulsions as an early sign of incurable weakness—a precursor of what would later develop into full blown madness, epi-
lepsy, mental retardation, or paralysis. "Such babies are never right in their
head or their body." And so an antipsychotic medication that was meant for

adults and had been illegally purchased lay next to Mercea. Infants are normally allowed to die by gradually reducing food and liquids. Infant euthanasia is closer to the way shantytown women, many of them practicing Catholics, view their actions. But Mercea was too old for that sort of resolution.

Mercea's final crisis took place in the days before the Brazilian carnival when many shops and most public services were closed. Hospital staff were on strike and would not return to work until Ash Wednesday. Biu and I planned to join the revelers on the first night of carnival, but Mercea continued to have a choking cough. She could not get her breath and her little chest shook rapidly with every effort. Her skin was as dry as parchment. Biu arranged for her sixteen-year-old daughter to look after Mercea. Hospital and clinic attendants had refused to attend to the little girl in the days preceding her death; the local pharmacist sold the mother various cough medicines; and when little Mercea was in her final death throes, the municipal ambulance driver arrived too late to be of help.

The next time Biu and I met was the morning after carnival when we gathered at the home of Biu's older sister, Antonieta, to prepare Mercea's wasted little body for burial in a little painted plywood and cardboard coffin. The only official and paradoxically compassionate response to Mercea's sickness and premature death came in the form of a free pauper coffin provided by the mayor from his makeshift municipal coffin factory attached to the back of the town hall, the *prefeitura*. Biu was in shock; we had barely had time to change out of our carnival costumes. Mercea was laid out in a white Holy Communion dress and we covered her bare feet and her body up to her chin with tiny, sweet-smelling white flowers, as befitted an innocent little angel child. Mercea's uncle and her designated godfather sprinkled her still body with holy water in a ritual of conditional, postmortem baptism. No one was certain whether such a baptism would count in the after life.

Mercea's siblings and their playmates carried her light coffin to the municipal graveyard. Children bury children in many parts of Latin America. It serves, among other functions, to remove the onus from parents and to socialize children from a very early age to "death without weeping." No church ceremony marked the death, of course—300 infant and childhood deaths in a town with only 30,000 people—would be an excessive burden on the single Catholic priest. Meanwhile, the Franciscan Sisters scold women who bring them dead babies to bless rather than sick babies to be helped and possibly rescued. Only a small slip of paper from the civil registry office documents the death. The diagnosis in Mercea's case was left blank on the form. There had been no medical examination. The child had died at home, then, of "natural causes." The gravedigger chided the children for leaving Mercea's coffin lid loose. "The ants will get to your little sister," he told Leonardo, Mercea's older brother, who cried on my shoulder despite the strong cultural injunction against shedding tears that could make the angel baby's path to heaven wet and slippery.

When Xoxa returned home from the plantation (where she was briefly employed during the carnival holiday) to learn that her little sister had died, she too grieved deeply. Xoxa was especially angry that her sister had been buried without stockings, and for several weeks she was bothered by visitations of Mercea's spirit hovering over Xoxa's canvas cot and pointing to her bruised bare feet. "She can't speak," said Xoxa, "because like all angel babies she is mute." On returning to Mercea's grave some months later to bring her a pair of stockings, we found that the area had been cleared and Mercea's space given to unfortunate twin infants. Mercea's remains had been tossed into the deep well called the "bone depository" near the west wall of the cemetery.

Vital statistics and survey research techniques conceal the existence of traditional patterns of selective neglect that only qualitative, existentially driven, and critically interpretive methods of anthropological witnessing are capable of doing and doing in such a way, moreover, as to avoid blaming women for their actions. Nonetheless, research findings continue to be fetishized, objectified, compared, and treated as if they were adequate representations of reality. Worse, they are all too readily translated into indifferent or even iatrogenic health programs and policies based on technological fixes. Among these I would cite both the Oral Rehydration Therapy program (ORT) and the decontextualized promotion of breastfeeding, both of which were supported for many years under UNICEF's international "child survival" campaign.

Misapplication One: ORT and Child Survival

Oral Rehydration Therapy, proclaimed by public health physicians as "an oasis of hope in the developing world" and as a "miracle of modern medicine," (Mull 1984) provides a case in point. The distribution of ORT sachets in communities at high risk for infant mortality is promoted on an assumption that parents everywhere share a common set of parenting goals, foremost among which is the equal value given to the survival and health of each and every child born. The child survival program assumes that once a dehydrated infant is snatched from the jaws of immediate death by a simple application of ORT, the "normal" parental nurturing, caring, and preserving instincts will resume. But where infant death is viewed as a highly probable, expected, and even beneficial outcome of birth, as it sometimes is in the shantytowns of rural northeast Brazil, and where a quarter of all babies die before the close of their first year, poor women may be unwilling to take back into the family an infant already perceived as "giving up" and "given up on." Consequently, I have had the bad fortune to see scores of shantytown babies rescued with ORT and antibiotics half a dozen times or more in the first year of their lives, only to die of chronic diarrhea, wasting, and respiratory ailments after the seventh or eighth medical rescue.

The distribution of ORT sachets does not take into account polluted water supplies, nor does it anticipate local perceptions of the salts as a powerful medicinal infant food that requires little supplementation. Babies raised on ORT, like babies raised on watery "pap," will often die on it. ORT is not a substitute for breast milk, clean water, attentive nurturing, appropriate medical care, adequate housing, fair wages, free and universal public education, or sexual equality, all of which are prerequisites for child survival.

In this instance, is ORT a life-affirming or death-prolonging intervention?

Over the years that I observed Biu and her family, Mercea received ORT on several occasions. She was brought to clinics and immunized against most communicable diseases. She was treated for worms. The apparent pneumonia from which she died in acute distress (the "acute infantile suffering" listed in the death certificates of the civil registry office now begin to take on a human face) was perhaps, as Biu eventually came to see it, a blessing in disguise. Mercea's escape from chronic hunger and sickness would require far more than any technological fix could possibly offer. The child's rescue could not be accomplished without the simultaneous rescue of her mother and other siblings. And the rescue of Biu and her other children depended, in part, on the rescue of her alienated husband, Oscar, whose state of permanent economic humiliation kept him running from household to household in shame. Oscar's poverty made him a promiscuous father and a deadbeat husband. The rescue of Oscar and all the other great-great-great grandsons of plantation slaves throughout the world depends on a realignment of North-South relations and of the capitalist global economy, no matter how naive and counter-intuitive this may seem at the close of the twentieth century.

Misapplication Two: Mother's Milk and Infant Death

A fairly direct correlation has been established through conventional empirical research between infant survival and breastfeeding and between infant death and bottle feeding in the Third World. Yet it is also widely documented that each generation of new mothers in the Third World is less likely to nurse their offspring than the previous generation. More than a decade ago UNICEF (1983) reported the percentage of babies breastfed for any length of time in Brazil had fallen from 96 percent in the 1940s to under 40 percent in the 1970s. This phenomenon was especially marked among rural migrants to urban areas, where wage labor displaces home economies and cottage industries more compatible with breastfeeding and puts a plastic wedge between mother and infant and between infant and breast.

The staple food for the infants of women working for wages is reconstituted powdered milk extended with a starch filler and sweetened with sugar. A great many poor women cannot afford sufficient quantities of commercial powdered milk to satisfy the baby's hunger, in which case they increase the starch and sugar or they eliminate the expensive powdered milk entirely and feed their infants a watery gruel called *papa d'agua*. Their babies readily sicken and die on it.

Why is this irrational practice maintained in the face of such graphic failure? Why did poor women so readily give up the breast for the commerciogenic bottle and powdered milk? How were they turned into consumers of a product that they do not need, cannot afford, and that contributes so directly to the death of their infants? Empirical studies and survey research, including a study sponsored by the World Health Organization of infant feeding patterns in nine countries (see Gussler and Briesmeister 1980), indicated that worldwide the most common explanation given by women for discontinuing breastfeeding was "insufficient milk." This finding led to many unfounded arguments about the biological fragility of breastfeeding as a practice (including height-weight-body fat and other nutritional correlates of successful breastfeeding). In fact, breastfeeding is bio-evolutionarily protected, and even very skinny and malnourished women—not to mention famished women—can adequately breastfeed a young infant. Saying this does not, however, suggest a lack of empathy for the individual and often nutritionally battered bodies of women.

One thing is certain. Mother's milk assumes new cultural and symbolic meanings wherever subsistence economies have been replaced by wage labor. The culture of breastfeeding was lost over a very rapid period in modern northeast Brazilian sugar plantation life. What had changed radically was poor women's beliefs in the essential goodness of what comes out of their own bodies, which they now saw as dirty, disorganized and diseased, as compared to what comes out of clean, healthy, modern objects, like cans of Nestle's infant formula, clinic hypodermic needles, and rehydration tubes.

Moreover, in terms of the bricolage that governs family formation in the shantytowns of Brazil, the ritual that creates social fatherhood today relocates baby's milk from mother's breasts—disdained by responsible, loving women—to the pretty cans of powdered milk formula (bearing corporate and state warnings about the dangers of the product that these illiterate women cannot read), which are carried into the shacks and shanties of the Brazilian *favela* by responsible, loving men. Paternity is transacted today through the gift of "male milk"—Nestle's powdered milk. Father's milk, not his semen, is a poor man's means of conferring paternity and of symbolically establishing the legitimacy of the child.

A new mother on the Alto do Cruzeiro will delightedly say when her boyfriend appears on her doorstep carrying the weekly requisite can of powdered milk, "Clap your hands, baby! Clap your hands! Your milk has arrived!" Conversely, the woman whose breasts flow with milk and who sustains her infant from them is, symbolically speaking, the rejected and abandoned woman, the woman whose baby has no father. For a woman to declare that she has no milk, that she has very little milk, or that her milk is weak and watery may be a proud assertion that both she and her baby have been claimed and are being nurtured by a protective male mother, a milk-giving father. All the UNICEF sponsored posters and classes and ads promoting the "obvious" benefits of maternal breastfeeding cannot turn around this new practice which has transformed gender and generativity in such profoundly modern and technological ways.

Toward a Demography beyond Numbers

At the heart of the anthropological method is the practice of witnessing, which requires an engaged immersion, as far as possible, in the lived phenomenological worlds of anthropology's subjects. Looking, touching, seeing, feeling and reflecting with people on the key experiences and moral dilemmas of their lives—and our own lives with them—as these are happening in the field constitutes the method of participant-observation—a method that is hard to categorize and harder still to teach. This always flawed, human encounter demands that the researcher take stands, make mistakes, move in, pull back, and move in again. In northeast Brazil it meant living with and absorbing the protective guise of indifference to hunger and death until I could not stand it any more and allowed the repressed horror to return. Witnessing means taking people at their word sometimes and second guessing them at others. It means keeping an open dialogue with people who are just as morally conflicted and challenged and horrified, by turns. It means, above all, not standing above and outside the fray, coolly observing and recording objective facts and turning these into scientific models which are nothing of the sort, and never were.

Against this "little tradition" and "minor practice" of traditional humanistic and engaged anthropology are arrayed all the mighty forces and guns of high-powered and high-tech scientific research. The basic quantitative methods of demography and epidemiology were introduced to Brazil in the 1960s through large grants from North American foundations, including the Ford Foundation and the MacArthur Foundation. These grants have established academic departments as well as doctoral and postdoctoral training programs which have produced by now an almost unassailable tradition of scientific positivism. Demography in particular has assumed enormous power and influence in the formation of social and government policy and programs in Brazil, Mexico, India, and elsewhere in what used to be called the "developing" world. We might begin by interrogating the particular political and economic history that has lead to the dominance of these approaches and traditions of research and the status of their "objective" measures of health and well-being, as Arjun Appadurai (1991) has done for colonial India and David Armstrong (1986) has done for late-nineteenth-century medicine in Britain.

We are today so accustomed to thinking that official and government policies can only be built around hard data—an accumulation of neutral and objective facts and on statistical figures and flow charts—that we can scarce
imagine serious public policies and programs emerging from in-depth case
studies or from interpretive analyses and moral-philosophical arguments. But
until very recently in the United States and elsewhere, public policies were
argued and decisions were reached by relying on historical, ethical, and philosophical arguments, while facts, figures, statistics, and other quantitative measures were used, if at all, as supporting evidence. Quantitative data were not
expected to argue the final case as they so often do today.

Although its influence has been stunted in the late twentieth century, interpretive research has introduced human rights and ethical concerns into
various scientific research programs and agendas. Culturally sensitive, qualitative, ethnographic research on reproduction and population issues in India,
Africa, and Latin America clarified very early on the crucial difference between family planning and population control and revealed the tensions
between the individual good and the common good as these were socially constructed within different polities (Polgar 1976; Mamdani 1967). Thanks to
qualitative, interpretive research, the ethical considerations and the cultural
appropriateness of various kinds of governmental interventions are now being
explored in philosophical and moral-political language. Calls for research and
new policy initiatives by the World Health Organization, the MacArthur
Foundation, and the Ford Foundation, among other research funding giants,
are beginning to affirm and to promote reproductive rights, women's rights,
and broader issues of social and political equity (Martine 1990; Ford Foundation 1991; Scheper-Hughes et al. 1991). For example, in 1992–94 the Ford
Foundation office in Rio de Janeiro sponsored a critically applied research program on "AIDS, Women, and Reproductive Rights" (Scheper-Hughes et al.
1991) that attempted to discover ways to bring the particular reproductive
issues of women to bear on a grassroots AIDS education and prevention program, which was until then focused almost exclusively on "condom literacy"
(Scheper-Hughes 1994b; Goldstein 1994).[3]

Obviously, what I am calling epidemiology and demography without numbers requires anthropologists who are free agents and who will not work as
handmaidens to medicine, the biomedical sciences, or the statistical demographic sciences in a dependent and/or auxiliary capacity.[4] There is really no
need for more collaborations between qualitatively-trained anthropologists
and epidemiologists or demographers in which the realm of the social is reduced to a set of reified and lifeless variables. The piling up of quantitative
data that relies on biomedical and Western categories will not generate fresh
insights. Instead, a praxis-oriented, critically applied, and politically engaged
anthropology is needed to illuminate the complex and multifaceted existential, cultural, medical, moral, and political dilemmas of vulnerable popula-

tions such as those confronting shantytown women and children in Brazil. Critically interpretive research begins with a series of negative questions: What is being hidden from view in the official statistics? Whose economic or political interests are reflected in the kinds of records kept? How are the records kept? What events are tracked? What is thought hardly worth counting at all? And what can this tell us about the collective invisibility of certain groups and classes of people—women and small children in particular? Only a paradigm shift toward a theoretically-driven and critically interpretive and analytical work can open up new areas of knowledge about the relationship between the way people live and the way they die.

NOTES

1. There is an anecdote that goes with this title which in its self-mocking may undercut whatever expertise I might claim from the outset. In the spring of 1979 a Brazilian psychiatrist studying for his doctorate in social epidemiology at the University of North Carolina, Chapel Hill came to my seminar in research methods in medical anthropology. Dr. Almeida Filho enthusiastically presented me with several dozen fairly complicated quantitative computer printouts related to his study of mental health and migration in Salvador, Bahia. After poring over the printouts with him—and finding much that I could not follow in his statistical formulas—I said (to his shock and embarrassed confusion), "I can't help you; you had better discuss these with a statistician." "Oh, excuse me," he replied, "I thought you were a kind of social epidemiologist." "I am," I replied, "but an epidemiologist . . . without numbers!" As Dr. Almeida Filho himself became more concerned with philosophical, qualitative, and theoretical issues in social epidemiology and medical anthropology, he found time to write an excellent monograph on the central problem of the object in epidemiological studies, arguing that what is constituted as the object of knowledge overdetermines the method of investigation. The title of his book, which I have now adapted for this chapter, is *Epidemiologia sem Numeros*—Epidemiology without Numbers.

2. Excellent reviews of this intellectual history can be found in Habermas 1968; Rabinow and Sullivan 1979; Rorty 1979; see also Megill 1991.

3. Goldstein and I tried to persuade grassroots activists and medical workers that the current AIDS education programs, based as they were on phallocentric assumptions and fairly universal notions of what I call basic sexual citizenship, were incapable of protecting poor women and other sexually vulnerable groups. Poor women and other "classificatory females" (i.e., "sexual passives" within the Brazilian sex/gender domain), such as street children and female transvestites, lacked the phallus and therefore the ability to make rational sexual choices or the power to control the transgressive autonomy of those who possessed the phallus (see Scheper-Hughes 1994b). Goldstein (1994) suggested that the sexual transmission of HIV hinged on this hitherto rejected knowledge in the present climate of male and exclusively "sex positive" AIDS activist discourse.

4. I expand this point elsewhere arguing that critically applied medical anthropologists need to establish greater distance from the centers and sources of biomedicine and bio-power and to assume a role of voluntary marginality—and voluntary poverty shall follow! Medical anthropology can provide "that small, sometimes mocking, often

ironic, but always mischievous voice from the sidelines . . . afflicting the comfortable, and living anthropology as the 'difficult science'" (Scheper-Hughes 1990:195).

REFERENCES

Almeida Filho, Naomar. 1989. *Epidemiologia sem Numeros*. Rio de Janeiro: Campus.
———. 1990. "O Problemo do Objeto de Conhecimento na Epidemiologia." In *Epidemiologia: Teoria e Objeto*, ed. D. Costa, 203–20. Sao Paulo: Hucitec.
———. 1991. "Paradigms in Epidemiology." Paper presented at the roundtable, Theoretical Challenges for Epidemiology, First Brazilian Conference on Epidemiology, Campinas, Brazil, September.
Appadurai, Arjun. 1993. "Number in the Colonial Imagination." In *Orientalism and the Post-Colonial Predicament*, ed. Carol Breckenridge and Peter van der Veer, 314–39. Philadelphia: University of Pennsylvania Press.
Armstrong, David. 1986. *Political Anatomy of the Body*. Cambridge: Cambridge University Press.
D'Andrade, Roy. 1995. "Moral Models in Anthropology." *Current Anthropology* 36(3):399–408.
Evans-Pritchard, Edward E. 1937. *Witchcraft, Oracles, and Magic among the Azande*. Oxford: Oxford University Press.
Evens, Terrence M. S. 1995. *Two Kinds of Rationality*. Minneapolis: University of Minnesota Press.
Ford Foundation. 1991. *Reproductive Health: A Strategy for the 1990s*. A Program Paper of the Ford Foundation (June). New York.
Foucault, Michel. 1972. *The Archeology of Knowledge*. New York: Pantheon.
Girard, Rene. 1987. *Things Hidden Since the Foundation of the World*. Stanford: Stanford University Press.
Gluckman, Max. 1963. *Order and Rebellion in Tribal Africa*. London: Cohen and West.
Goldstein, Donna. 1994. "AIDS and Women in Brazil." *Social Science and Medicine* 39(7):919–30.
Gussler, Judith, and Linda Briesmeister. 1980. "The Insufficient Milk Syndrome." *Medical Anthropology Quarterly* 4(2):146–74.
Habermas, Jürgen. 1968. *Knowledge and Human Interests*. Boston: Beacon Press.
Hammel, Eugene. A. 1990. "A Theory of Culture for Demography." *Population and Development Review* 16:455–86.
Kertzer, David. In press. "The Proper Role of Culture in Demographic Explanation." In *The Continuing Demographic Transition*, ed. Gavin W. Jones, John C. Caldwell, Robert M. Douglas, and Rennie M. D'Souza. Oxford: Oxford University Press. In press.
Kuhn, Thomas S. 1970. *The Structure of Scientific Revolutions*. Chicago: University of Chicago Press
Lock, Margaret, and Nancy M. Scheper-Hughes. 1990. "A Critically Interpretive Approach in Medical Anthropology." In *Medical Anthropology: Contemporary Theory and Method*, ed. Thomas Johnson and Carolyn Sargent, 47–72. New York: Praeger.
Malcolm, Norman. 1994. *Wittgenstein: A Religious Point of View?* Ithaca, N.Y.: Cornell University Press.
Mamdani, Mahmood. 1967. *The Myth of Population Control*. New York: Monthly Review Press.

Marcus, George, and Michael Fisher. 1986. *Anthropology as Cultural Critique.* Chicago: University of Chicago Press.

Martine, George. 1990. *Population in Brazil: Agenda for a Country Strategy.* Report prepared for the John D. and Catherine T. MacArthur Foundation (June). Mimeograph.

Megill, Allen, ed. 1991. "Four Senses of Objectivity." In *Rethinking Obectivity* I (special issue), *Annals of Scholarship* 8(3/4):301–20.

Mull, J. Dennis. 1984. "ORT: An Oasis of Hope in the Developing World." *Journal of Family Practice* 18: 485–87.

Nations, Marilyn, and Mara L. Amaral. 1991. "Flesh, Blood, Souls, and Households: Cultural Validity in Mortality Inquiry." *Medical Anthropology Quarterly* 5(3): 204–20.

Polgar, Steven. 1976. "The Search for Culturally Acceptable Fertility Regulating Methods." In *Culture, Natality, and Family Planning,* ed. J. Marshall and Steven Polgar, 204–18. Chapel Hill: Carolina Population Center.

Rabinow, Paul, and William M. Sullivan, eds. 1979. *Interpretive Social Science.* Berkeley: University of California Press.

Rorty, Richard. 1979. *Philosophy and the Mirror of Nature.* Princeton: Princeton University Press.

Rothman, Kenneth J. 1986. *Modern Epidemiology.* Boston: Little Brown.

Ruddick, Sara. 1986. *Maternal Thinking.* Boston: Beacon Press.

Scheper-Hughes, Nancy. 1990. "Three Propositions for a Critically Applied Medical Anthropology." *Social Science & Medicine* 30(2):189–98.

———. 1992. *Death without Weeping: The Violence of Everyday Life in Brazil.* Berkeley: University of California Press.

———. 1994a. "Embodied Knowledge: Thinking with the Body in Medical Anthropology." In *Assessing Cultural Anthropology,* ed. Robert Borofsky, 229–42. New York: McGraw-Hill.

———. 1994b. "AIDS and the Social Body." *Social Science & Medicine,*39(7): 991–1004.

———. 1995a. "Demilitarization and Death Squads in Post-Democratic Transition Brazil." Paper delivered at the Colloquium on Consolidating Freedom: The Role of Civil Society, San Jose, Costa Rica, February 16ñ21.

———. 1995b. "The Primacy of the Ethical: Propositions for a Militant Anthropology." *Current Anthropology* 36(3) (June): 409–20.

Scheper-Hughes, Nancy, Michael Adams, Sonia Corea, and Richard Parker. 1991. *Reproductive Health and AIDS in Brazil.* A Consultants' Report. Prepared for the Ford Foundation, December, Rio de Janeiro, December.

UNICEF. 1983. *State of the World's Children.* James Grant, ed. Oxford: Oxford University Press.

Winnicott, Donald. 1987. *Babies and Mothers.* Reading, Mass.: Addison-Wesley.

Chapter Nine

"Truth Lies in the Eye of the Beholder": The Nature of Evidence in Demography and Anthropology

Allan G. Hill

At the core of any scientific inquiry is the set of conventions that define what the investigators and their critics will accept as proof that a particular line of argument is either true or false. Even if the investigators are followers of Karl Popper (1961), the issue of what is required to satisfactorily demonstrate that a particular argument is false is still a central consideration. The recent descent of demography to the microlevel and its extended flirtation with anthropology and ethnography has revealed some mutual misunderstandings. Although demography (a largely technical subject) and social anthropology are hardly on the same level in terms of their disciplinary standings,[1] it is fair to compare the approaches of anthropologists and demographers to similar problems. Here we focus on joint attempts to account for variations in the levels and trends of human fertility in different times and social contexts. We have chosen to focus on fertility but in many ways the argument might apply equally to attempts by both demographers and anthropologists to account for variations and trends in the survival of adults and children as well as to other demographic processes.

Rather than conduct this argument on an abstract level, I have chosen to illustrate the main points with reference to a recently concluded research project in rural West Africa (The Gambia) conducted jointly with social anthropologist Caroline Bledsoe. The project was an opportunistic exploitation of several coincidences. One was my long association with the populations of forty villages which since 1982 had been the subject of many epidemiological experiments by the U.K. Medical Research Council on the control of mortality and morbidity from malaria (Greenwood and Baker 1993). Another was the decision by the Gambian Ministry of Health to provide family planning services as part of its Primary Health Care program and through the maternal and child health services. Western family planning methods were being introduced into a rural agricultural population with little formal education and low incomes. The project thus began with more than the usual richness of demographic information. In all forty villages, containing around 17,000 people in 1995, we found a compliant group of men and women ready to discuss many intimate aspects of their fertility behavior with outsiders because of the health benefits they had received in the past.

The basic idea behind the research was first to describe the pattern of fertility and its proximate determinants with a simple cross-sectional survey of all women of reproductive age (about 3,000 in all) and then to follow a subset of these women from one birth to the next pregnancy. Since we had an idea of when women would pass through the different reproductive states (pregnant, infertile after a delivery, fertile a subsequent time and then pregnant again), we hoped to collect statements from couples about their behavior and intentions at every stage of this cycle. Earlier work by Hill in Mali had suggested that the desire to engineer long birth intervals (the intervals turned out to average over thirty months—see below) was widespread in different ethnic groups and that the portrayal of the resulting fertility patterns as "natural" (i.e., subject only to biological, nonvolitional limitations) was misleading (Hill 1985). Along the way, the project spawned many additional subprojects as well as resulting in the collection of a wealth of naturally non-numerical information from conversations and interviews.

This chapter is thus an attempt to identify whether the sources of the differences between demographers and anthropologists are technical or epistemological. I argue here that the two approaches have very different origins and assumptions so that convergence may not be possible. Further, it may be wholly undesirable to combine the two since the two separate perspectives both have their flaws as well as their strong points. Good will and respect for the biases of others should not lead us to disguise the much more fundamental differences between the two sets of practitioners. Here, the aim is not to start a philosophical argument about the nature of scientific inquiry and how it differs from the approaches of the social sciences generally and social anthropology in particular, but to show through some examples how our views about "proof" and what constitutes convincing evidence are at the core of the difference between demography and anthropology. These notions about evidence are more important than we think since they seem to determine our methods and ultimately our theories. Demographic theorizing is driven by data—from sources such as censuses and surveys or from other routine sources of numbers. The numbers demographers work with are generally very concrete—births, deaths, residents in a geographic area—and are thus not very difficult to conceptualize. Although demography is not entirely atheoretical, the collectors and analysts of the primary data are in a dominant position with regard to the rest of the profession. Demographers have so many statistics to work with—what other social science has governments and international aid agencies paying for their primary data collection?—that as a result, theory construction is generally in a subsidiary position compared to the process of seeking patterns in the mountains of statistics demographers have at their disposal.

The Corrosive Effect of Too Many Numbers

The first point about evidence in demography is that the statistics on population size, structure, and dynamics by their very nature refer to large samples or whole national populations. This leads naturally to the calculation of aggregate measures of structure and change since there is little need to work with the data for separate individuals. When comparisons are drawn between fertility or mortality in different populations, we rarely see variances presented except for very small subpopulations. Then we use an epidemiological approach. A typical set of questions is thus: Controlling for the confounding variables (i.e., the variables excluded from the explanatory theory), what significant differences remain, based on a comparison of means and the confidence limits around those means? Thus in demography, many of our ideas about the causes of change are based on very aggregate indices, inevitably masking some of the complexities that emerge at more local scales of analysis. Perhaps the best known illustration of this point is the series of indices Coale and his collaborators developed at Princeton for the study of the European fertility transition (Coale and Watkins 1986).

There is another unfortunate effect of having such ready access to statistics on large numbers of people. It is the debilitating effect on methodology. Until recently, most analysis of census and large-scale household surveys consisted of simple cross-tabulations. Regression analysis of different forms is well-established in the research field but for most administrative and policy purposes, basic two- or three-way tables are the most common form used for presenting the data. A glance at the U.N. Demographic Yearbook, at any national census report, at the series of country monographs produced by the U.S. National Academy of Sciences, at the Taeubers' tome on the U.S. population (Taeuber and Taeuber 1971), or even at one of the national reports from the Demographic and Health Survey project will confirm this. In all such publications, we are rarely shown the diversity which surrounds the published aggregate figures.

A related difficulty created by this glut of raw information is that with such large numbers, disaggregation to quite small geographic areas—census tracts or enumeration districts, for example—does not require much alteration in the basic plan of analysis. The same cross-tabulation, the same rates and proportions can be generated for a few thousand people in a restricted geographical area as for the millions of individuals in a national population. Again, turn to the latest subnational data available for the United States in machine-readable form for confirmation of this point. For local level planning and administration, the U.S. Census Bureau makes available data for census tracts, blocks, counties, and other geographical units on CD-ROMs. The software for making the required tables appears on the same diskette—the user simply picks the unit of analysis and the variables to be cross-tabulated and the numbers appear in neat rows and columns.

Thirdly, there is so much richness in the officially generated data on a population that it may seem churlish to demand more detail or additional variables when the basic information has yet to be fully digested. Adding together the demographic information we have on even data-poor countries—data from censuses, household surveys, routine administrative activities, the health sector, municipal censuses (the list is very long)—we can quickly appreciate that the supply of raw numbers is not a problem. More innovative inquiries which probe the motives and underlying reasons for the population trends are always going to look like the poor relations of the major national censuses and surveys. The professionalism of the national census and survey organizations is everywhere impressive. The shared international goals of counting the people and assessing their rate of growth has led to codification and standardization of the approaches. Terms such as "family," "household," "resident," and "migrant" all have standard definitions. Manuals exist in several languages for performing the calculations required for the national report (see, e.g., United Nations 1983).

The upshot of being awash in this sea of information is that much of the thinking about demographic processes and their underlying social and economic factors has been emasculated by the effects of not having to reflect on which data we might collect or to be forced to interpolate or to extrapolate from the known to the unknown. To answer most ordinary demographic questions—How fast is the population growing? What is replacement level fertility?—there is a data set somewhere that can provide the answer or at least some suggestive information surrounding the answer. As a result, the gurus of the demographic profession have rarely needed to design surveys themselves, to conduct substudies to bridge the gaps in existing data, or to agonize very long on what analysis to do next. The data have been there waiting for a capable analyst with a strongly empirical frame of mind to make use of the raw numbers. To provide some substance to these assertions, let us consider the demographic approach to accounting for variations in fertility in different populations and follow this with an example of how the conventional approach can be very misleading.

Studying Fertility: Some Data from Rural Gambia

In addition to producing standardized measures of reproduction in human populations—basic fertility rates and ratios—demographers have worked out a neat accounting framework for explaining differences in the fertility of different populations based on the list of proximate determinants originally proposed by Davis and Blake (1956). In the format made operational by John Bongaarts, the indices of the fertility-reducing effects of the four or five main determinants can only be calculated for populations; the indices cannot be calculated for individuals (Bongaarts 1982). Admittedly, the approach called "fertility exposure analysis" (Hobcraft and Little 1984) does allow the force of each individual woman in the study to be calculated but the overall aim of the analysis is to account for fertility trends and differentials for groups of people, usually large populations.

In a study in rural Gambia, an initial analysis of fertility and its proximate

Table 9.1
Fertility and Its Proximate Determinants in the MRC Main Study Area Villages,
North Bank Division, The Gambia, 1992

Age of Women	C(m)	C(c)	C(i)	Age-Specific Fertility	Number of Women
15–19	0.56	0.95	0.56	0.076	590
20–24	0.93	0.96	0.60	0.287	450
25–29	0.97	0.95	0.59	0.338	410
30–34	0.99	0.94	0.58	0.286	450
35–39	0.98	0.94	0.55	0.238	422
40–44	0.98	0.94	0.32	0.150	357
45–49	0.97	0.94	0.17	0.070	218
All	0.88	0.96	0.53	7.225	2900

NOTE: Data from the 1992 fertility survey around Farafenni. Each index can theoretically take a value between 0 and 1, with 1 indicating that the variable has no effect on overall fertility. Thus, 1 minus the index is the proportional contribution of the variable to the reduction of fertility from some theoretical level, potential fecundity, usually taken to be between 14.5 and 16 births per woman. The full model is explained in Bongaarts and Potter 1983.

determinants was conducted using data from a baseline survey conducted in 1992. The initial survey included the now standard approach to measuring demographic processes in the field. First, we listed the "production" of births, the phenomenon to be "explained," using a full history of births and other pregnancies. Then, we asked the study women questions about their current reproductive status to measure the force of the proximate determinants of fertility as well as estimating potential fecundity.

The results of this process of data collection followed by a standard analysis of the data have a satisfying coherence. The results show that we can account for the prevailing rate at which couples in the study population are having children with little more information than was collected on a four-page questionnaire (see the rates shown in table 9.1). The analysis indicates that the fertility-reducing effects of Western contraception are modest and that the main reasons for the difference between potential fecundity and the realized level of total fertility is because women prolong the infertile period following a birth by extended breastfeeding (see Wood 1994, ch. 8 for a good summary of the underlying physiological mechanisms). The total fertility rate is 7.2 when estimated through the framework of the proximate determinants using model estimates of age-specific potential fecundity (Bongaarts and Potter 1983:115) and 7.5 when measured directly from the birth histories. There is thus a good correspondence between the measures arrived at by different routes. The conclusion to be drawn is that the model has indeed captured most of the sources of variability in fertility in this population. At this level, there appears to be little left to explain; in the current vocabulary of demographers, we are dealing with a largely "natural" fertility regime in a population relatively unaffected by pathological sterility or exceptionally high miscarriage rates. People are not breeding like beasts, with fertility limited by biological factors alone, but the scope for individual decision-making seems limited. Periods of exposure to the risk of conception constitute a relatively small part of each woman's total reproductive life (large blocks of time are spent either pregnant or temporarily infertile after a birth), which seems to limit the role of intentionality and decision-making with reference to the timing of the next birth or the cessation of childbearing.

Views of the Couples Involved

At another level of analysis, this calm picture of a population in a steady "natural" state breaks apart. As a follow-up to this single-round survey, we have been following a subsample of couples originally interviewed in March–April 1992. Each month over a period of eighteen months, interviewers have been visiting approximately 350 women of reproductive age and inquiring about different aspects of their reproductive lives. At intervals, the interviewers also spoke with the husbands of these women. In addition to the factual questions on pregnancy status, breastfeeding patterns, and contraceptive use, the monthly rounds included many open-ended questions as well as longer, free-ranging discussions on selected topics which changed from month to month. In longer interviews with husbands, we tried to reconstruct the history of marriage and fertility through the husbands' eyes—not, as is usually the case, through the eyes of mothers alone. The result is that we have both the easily quantified information about the reproductive performance and the time spent in each of the reproductive states of our sample men and women as well as an account in their own words of their current circumstances and their thoughts about both the past and the future. The information on husbands is less dense but has the same general format—some fairly numerical information together with accompanying views and opinions. This is the luxury of fieldwork in a living population, one that historical demographers and interpreters of past processes and trends cannot enjoy to the same extent.

What have we learned from this experience? First, it is clear that there is a great deal of planning and discussion around each event, be it an act of coitus or the decision to wean the child from the breast. Although private matters, the circumstances and consequences of such events are of concern to a wide range of individuals and hence are subject to social controls. Refusing coitus may signal the beginning of a marital rift. Refusing to wean an infant may be the way a woman demonstrates control over her husband, since it is unseemly to fall pregnant whilst still breastfeeding a child. There are well-known terms for the abrupt withdrawal of breastfeeding and premature weaning in all three main languages in the area.[2] Thus, refusing sex is not necessarily a sign of reduced libido and continuing to breastfeed is not necessarily a sign of the

Table 9.2
Birth-Interval Length in Months by Age of Women at Interview

Age of Women	Mean Birth Interval	✷ Standard Deviation	Number of Cases
15–19	23.9	9.2	60
20–24	29.5	16.5	494
25–29	30.0	11.8	1084
30–34	32.0	16.2	1772
35–39	32.5	17.0	2148
40–44	32.5	19.0	1997
45–49	34.2	21.1	1241
50–54	33.4	22.1	435

SOURCE: 1992 fertility survey, Farafenni area.

mother's firm commitment to improved child health and nutrition. Behaviors associated with reproduction are not what they seem at face value.

Secondly, even through the survey data we can readily observe huge variations around the mean. There is a great deal of diversity that is not readily explicable by controlling for additional sources of variation—again, the medical / epidemiological solution to this problem. There are strongly held normative views about what the sequence and timing of events should be but we find that the relative variability of the calculated averages is very large. Fertility behavior is quite diverse and this range of experiences may be one of the ways in which some women learn from others. Without the luxury of a survey, the couples in this or any similar study cannot know the mean behavior or duration; this is purely a statistical concept. Indeed, it may be the one or two aberrant cases which provide the model to emulate or to eschew rather than the so-called average cases. Certainly, in another study looking at maternal mortality in the same villages, it was the traumatic experience of a few mothers that conditioned most women's attitude to the risks of childbearing.

Take the example of birth intervals as an illustration of this point. As shown in table 9.2, rural Gambian women are achieving birth intervals of over thirty months with relatively little use of Western contraceptives. Not all women manage to achieve birth intervals of this length, however, as the standard deviations indicate. There is thus a diversity of experience in the population reflecting a combination of biological and behavioral factors. It became clear from the more detailed interviewing that this diversity of individual experiences is widely recognized and forms the basis for comparing the benefits and risks inherent in different approaches to family building. This is probably how contraception gains hold—through one woman's positive experience being duplicated by others. Women in especially favored positions—who have enough education to communicate their wishes to outsiders or who have family links to the medical establishment or to pharmacists, for example—try out the devices and report their experiences to others. Generally, we found a frankness in exchanges on sexuality and reproduction not commonly found in Western society, where written materials from impersonal sources are more important. Thus, Gambian women's knowledge of contraception is richer in personal detail than can be found in the printed instructions provided with the contraceptives or in the official medical literature.

The interviews revealed additional problems with the conventional tabulation of the demographic data. The concept of a birth interval, whilst apparently simple, turns out to be very complex. The clear distinction made in demography between parity (live births) and gravidity (more common in medical circles) is unknown in the study population. In the course of earlier mortality studies and during the collection of the data on the full maternity histories, we had inquired about the ages of children's deaths. Immediately, the new category of unbaptized children emerged—children born alive but dying before the naming ceremony had been conducted. Such children were generally buried in the family compound rather than in the public cemetery. This is one reason why the measured neonatal mortality rates are implausibly low even in the longitudinally collected data in the Medical Research Council's surveillance system.

It is interesting to note that this separate classification of children who die very soon after birth has direct parallels in the statistical systems of France, Belgium, Spain, and Russia. There, live births dying before the legal period allowed for registration (usually three days) require neither a birth nor a death certificate. They are referred to as *faux mort-nés* and are included in a separate statistical category called *morti-naissances* (Vallin 1985:11–12). Further, Western medicine is generally concerned to separate miscarriages from stillbirths. The distinction is drawn at an estimated gestational age of twenty-eight weeks. In The Gambia, we could find little difference between a stillbirth and a miscarriage—in both cases, the fetus was buried without ceremony in the compound.

The purpose of the foregoing discussion is to show that even in Western medical contexts, boundaries between categories are not always as hard and fast as imagined. This awareness is essential when it comes to the much more difficult task of explaining how intervals between births in previous pregnancies are determined. In the 1992 survey, we attempted to collect data on all pregnancies (not just live births as in some surveys) regardless of the outcome of that pregnancy or of the survival of the child. As always in retrospective surveys, miscarriages, stillbirths, and neonatal deaths are underreported. Part of the reason for these omissions is surely a desire to avoid reference to unhappy experiences but another part is the more systematic blurring of the above categories.

If we begin to look at how birth or pregnancy intervals have been examined by Western social scientists, we can see more clearly the stark differences in views and behavior prevailing in rural Gambia. Today, most of the fertility analysis emanating from the Demographic and Health Surveys project and other national fertility surveys emphasizes the period age pattern of fertility, placing particular stress on age-specific fertility rates and the total fertility ratio. Further analysis examines other measures such as parity progression ratios, birth interval length, and of course the "unmet need" for contraception (Westoff and Ochoa 1991). In all, the quantity (quantum) and the timing (tempo) of fertility are the dominant concepts, with relatively few references to the conditions of mothers or their plight during the reproductive process.

We must remind ourselves that this obsession with births, birth intervals, and the total number of children born was not always the dominant paradigm. Well before the advent of modern contraceptives, Europeans and others had adopted numerous strategies to postpone pregnancy (see van de Walle and Muhsam 1995 for some recent evidence from eighteenth-century France). In the eighteenth and nineteenth centuries, the links between breastfeeding, maternal health, and child survival were increasingly well understood, with couples enjoined (amongst other things) to practice sexual continence during lactation (van de Walle and van de Walle 1972). More recently, numerous studies have carefully documented the links in modern populations (Wood 1994:338–39) but the most important issue is to determine the dominant cause in people's own minds. The medical community generally stresses the beneficial effects of breastfeeding for children and this is certainly prominent in the literature promoting breastfeeding. The collection of case studies assembled by Page and Lesthaeghe (1981) provides some further information on local practices in Africa (abstinence, both temporary and permanent) but most studies are largely silent on motivation. Caldwell and Caldwell (1981) came closest to exploring past traditions and current changes, pointing to the large role played by sexual desire and the declining ability of women to resist their husband's demands for sex. Notably, it is the better-educated men whose sexual demands were most difficult to rebut, at least in Ibadan (Caldwell and Caldwell 1981:193–94). The role of sexual desire and sexual pleasure *per se* is much neglected in demographic studies but the collection of essays by Abramson and Pinkerton (1995) goes some way to correcting this bias.

While driven by sexual desire and the urge to reproduce, couples everywhere try to organize their patterns of reproduction according to their own convenience and the generally acceptable rules of the society in which they live. Immediately, deliberate avoidance of pregnancy by contraception becomes an issue. Rarely do we have the opportunity to discuss with couples at the beginning of the demographic transition their motives and concerns as they move to manage their fertility patterns in original ways. The issue of contraceptive use throws into high relief the contrast between the explanatory paradigm of fertility analysts and that of the couples and populations actively working with the mechanics of the family building process.

Patterns of Postpartum Behavior

Following a live birth, breast milk is the almost universal source of sustenance for children in The Gambia. In the first year of life, 98 percent of all living children were receiving some milk from the breast. Supplementation with milk from animals or other liquids occurs very early (only 62 percent of the living children under six months were still being fed exclusively at the breast) but complete weaning from breast milk occurs very late. Full severance from the breast commonly occurs around the time of the second birthday—just 36 percent of all children aged 18 to 23 months were fully weaned but for those aged 24 to 29 months, the figure was 90 percent. Given the prolonged period of breastfeeding, albeit accompanied by complementary feeding from an early age, it is well nigh impossible for mothers to shirk their marital responsibilities to husbands until the last child is fully weaned. Furthermore, in polygynous households where wives sleep with their husbands in a strict rota, there are additional responsibilities for the wife whose turn it is to be with her husband. She has responsibilities for preparing meals for the whole compound, for example, and fulfillment of these tasks helps to ensure a man's support. So there are additional reasons why refusing sex whilst breastfeeding, full or partial, is difficult.

Apart from the awareness that breastfeeding is a drain on mothers' physical reserves, many women believe that breastfeeding prevents an early conception. Ideas are mixed on this point since feeding a child at the breast is also good grounds for refusing some of the sexual demands of husbands. In any case, mothers are increasingly unable to resist the pressure from husbands to resume normal marital relations as time elapses since the last pregnancy (fig. 9.1). The outcome of this last pregnancy also has a bearing on subsequent behavior since breastfeeding is of course only initiated following a live birth. The physiological effects of breastfeeding on fertility are clear (as we know from data on the duration of postpartum amenorrhea in the 1992 survey as well as more detailed studies from other Gambian villages; see Lunn 1985), so all women who breastfeed benefit to some extent from several months of "natural" protection although they are unaware of the complex physiological mechanisms involved.

Turning to contraception, we are now in a better position to evaluate the pattern of use by time since the last pregnancy ended. We have divided the women into categories depending on their postpartum status. Thus we have those who used Western contraception (pills, injectables, and the condom) either as a primary or a secondary method of contraception; those who used local methods, including carefully timing acts of intercourse, withdrawal, and belts and charms; those who avoided sex entirely or who had ceased sexual

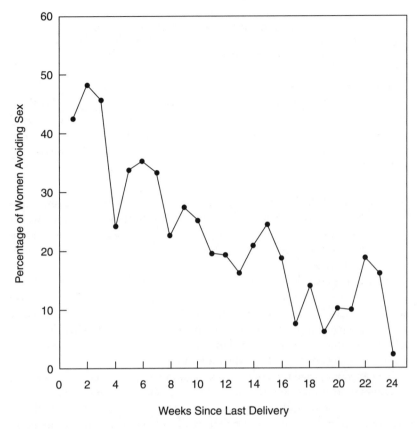

Figure 9.1
Percentage of women who avoided sex for up to eight weeks before interview by weeks since the last delivery.

activity; those who said they were unable to have another child; and those who were pregnant a second time. The balance of the women were in none of these categories.

Several interesting patterns emerge. First, it is clear that contraception of one kind or another begins very soon after delivery. Within six months of the end of the last pregnancy, 4.3 percent (19/440) of all women were practicing local or Western contraception. By six to eleven months, the figure had risen to 8.9 percent. Interviews confirmed this interest in postponing another pregnancy by starting contraception early—in effect, adding to the period of temporary sterility induced by breastfeeding. The close connection between sexual behavior and child development is confirmed by table 9.3. There, we see steadily increasing proportions of women using Western or local contracep-

Table 9.3
Contraceptive Use (Western and Local) by Age of
the Last-Born Child and Feeding Practice: Percentage of Use
by Nonpregnant Women with a Surviving Last Born Child

Age of Child in Months	Full Breastfeeding	Supplemented Breastfeeding	Weaned
0 to 5	4.2% (10/240)	6.3% (6/95)	4.8% (2/42)
6 to 11	6.8% (5/73)	11.3% (17/150)	7.7% (2/26)
12 to 18	5.8% (2/35)	14.7% (29/198)	18.7% (8/59)

SOURCE: 1992 fertility survey, Farafenni area.

tion as the age of the last child increases. The data in table 9.3 are important because they show that even within a single category of infant feeding, we see rising proportions of women using contraception as the age of the child increases. As sex becomes more regular, worries about an early subsequent pregnancy increase.

Some of the complex relationships between breastfeeding and sexual relations are illustrated in table 9.4. The convention to avoid sex soon after a birth (see Fig. 9.1) and whilst still fully breastfeeding is widely flaunted. There may be less regular sex after the postpartum period, but even within the forty-day period of abstinence recommended by Islam, total abstinence is rare except by wives physically separated from their husbands.

We can summarize the complex strategies open to women in the form of an imaginary tree diagram. Down one branch, following a miscarriage, a stillbirth, or a neonatal death, women are still able to postpone full resumption of intercourse even when they continue to reside in their husbands' compounds. Even the use of Western contraceptives for short periods is possible (in the survey, six women with such outcomes were using the injectable contraceptive or pills). For women with a live birth and a surviving child, the strategies are a little different. Breastfeeding provides some natural protection which can be extended by Western or local contraception. Overlaps between different methods are common. A surprising 11.3 percent of women still breastfeeding their last-born children aged 6 to 11 months were using local or modern contraception (see table 9.3). Clearly, it was not concern for the health of the weaned child which might be jeopardized by a subsequent pregnancy, but rather other considerations which were paramount. Interviews suggest that a main reason was the health of the mother.

The linkages between birth interval length and the health of mother and child are complex since we now know from our fieldwork that men and women use the development stage of the last-born child as an index signaling when it is proper to resume sex and to begin a subsequent pregnancy. The pattern of infant feeding is related to these development stages which we have

Table 9.4
Sexual Abstinence and Contraception by Method of Feeding the Last-Born Child

Type of Feeding	No Sex in Preceding 4 weeks	Pill, Condom, or Injection	Other*	All Women
Breast milk alone	343	12	7	362
	95%	3%	2%	100%
Breast milk and liquids	111	3	3	117
	95%	3%	3%	100%
Breast milk and solids	565	44	25	634
	89%	7%	4%	100%
Weaned	354	68	16	438
	81%	7%	4%	100%
Total	1373	127	51	1551

SOURCE: 1992 fertility survey, Farafenni area.
* Including rhythm, withdrawal, and local but excluding abstinence.

classified as "wet infant" (the newborn); "neck straightened" (able to lift its head); sitting; and standing or walking. To our surprise, we see from table 9.4 that even amongst the women practicing exclusive breastfeeding of their last-born child, only 45 percent (155/343) had avoided sex for the four weeks before the interview. There is strong evidence that the rules were flouted or circumvented by different means.

There is additional evidence that modern contraception permits further circumvention of the rules. As table 9.4 shows, there is a little more use of modern contraceptive methods (everywhere quite low overall) by the women who have begun supplementing their children's diet with additional fluids and solid food, this being the preliminary step to fully weaning the child. These numerical results can be readily supplemented by quotations from the women that express their concern about such early pregnancies but for reasons of space, cannot be accommodated here.

The issue here is how differently demographers or anthropologists interpret these key features of reproductive patterns in this population. On the one hand, the rigid, biologically based schema of Bongaarts or others does not adequately deal with the combination of modest use of modern contraception but vigorous practice of avoidance of sex and some temporary and strategic use of a number of methods to achieve the long birth intervals that are a feature of this region. On the other hand, by depending largely on the verbal accounts of the participants, regardless of the number of people interviewed, we risk losing the important capacity to verify the accounts by comparison with some external measure of outcome or process. Further, we need some form of model pattern or reference categories—even a forecast—to know when to be surprised or skeptical about the accounts we are hearing. The discussion of the differences in aims and methods is clearly at source a matter of evidence and proof. Asking questions about private matters—sexual relations, partner exchanges, and ill health, for example—is considered worthless if the aim is to understand the inner workings of society rather than to describe the outer manifestations of such behaviors. But supporters of this classical anthropological position face a real problem in trying to summarize in an orderly way the information painstakingly extracted from many lengthy interviews with men and women, in often difficult conditions. A really revealing quote from an especially interesting case may be persuasive for one school of thought but unacceptable as evidence for most demographers and anthropologists, often for very different reasons. How can the perceptive observer, with good language skills and a long acquaintance with the people under study, convince readers from the demographic epidemiological camp that the interview was typical and not an aberrant case?

Here we see the crux of the problem fully exposed. The sensitive observer is forced into a discussion of averages or typical cases in an effort to meet the particular standards of proof required by those who conduct rigorous studies such as double-blind, placebo-controlled drug intervention trials (to pick an extreme case). There must be a better way to translate field evidence from dense interviews with small numbers of individuals into a more meaningful synopsis of the dynamic processes that are determining birth rates in a particular society. There is, and it involves some overhaul of our theoretical frameworks.

Are We Working with the Wrong Paradigm?

The discordance between the demographic interpretation of our survey data using the proximate determinants schema and the individual-level behaviors, both observed and reported, is striking. Lockwood (1995) draws our attention to other discordances using African examples. It is difficult to dismiss the demographic evidence since it has both its own logic and an external coherence, and yet this is not the way the participants view the processes of fertility determination. The contrasts cannot be dismissed simply as the difference between aggregate-level analysis and individual-level data. It is perfectly possible to construct a new schema to account for both individual and group behavior but it is not the biological model with which we are familiar. Such an account (which we can document from survey data and quotations) might run as follows:[3]

In rural Gambia, the social and economic position of women without formal education depends very largely on a successful marriage. It would be very difficult to remain single and to acquire standing in the community except by extraordinary means, such as becoming a traditional midwife/healer or being a *kafo* (lineage) head. All other routes to advancement—community health nurse, school teacher, etc.—require formal education. Thus almost all women marry (99 percent of women marry at some time in their lives) and 89 percent of women age 20 to 50 were currently married in March–April 1992. At one point in the marriage process, women have to transfer to their husbands' compounds, which involves physically moving to a new home. There may already be children from this marriage and they usually go with her. The woman's first concern in her husband's compound is to establish herself as a good wife and mother, interacting successfully with her mother-in-law and possibly her co-wives. The criteria used to judge her prowess in establishing herself there include hard work, responsiveness to her husband's sexual and other demands, her management of her children, and her ability to control her own budget for food, clothes, and her children's needs. At first she may not be very strongly attached to her husband's compound. If he is much older, she may worry about co-wife competition, widowhood, and divorce as persistent threats. In both circumstances, the number and composition of her family plays a key role. If widowed or divorced without sons, she can be sent away and has no legal rights except to appeal to her husband's family's charity. The more children she has in the compound, the more established she becomes; at one point, women report that "their legs are tied" in their husband's compounds—they are committed to this new home. In the West, there is no exact equivalent of this process but it is tantamount to the new wife being accepted by her in-laws and becoming one of the family.

So marrying and having children quickly is an inevitable strategy if the woman is to make her way as a wife and a mother in her new family. There is another set of conflicting concerns—her own health and the notion that she should plan for the worst—divorce or widowhood, to give just two examples. We hear women's health expressed in an interesting way—the idea of *faaso,* in Mandinka (*faasa* in Bambara, where it indicates the sinews that are responsible for physical movements), meaning literally "sinews" or more figuratively, constitutional strength or "horse power," if we think of mechanical analogies.[4] Whether discussing the proper interval between births, the health costs of frequent childbearing, miscarriages, or the side effects of modern contraception, this notion of a woman's endowment of physical resources keeps cropping up. All the rural women know the concept and explain it in very similar terms. Some cross-checking with observers of other West African ethnic groups suggests that the concept is widespread even beyond The Gambia.[5] Some aspects are still somewhat mysterious but the basic idea is that women have a certain capacity at birth or marriage, that this is depleted steadily as women experience a number of reproductive events (difficult births with much blood loss or miscarriages cost more than simple deliveries), and that once depleted, it cannot be totally replenished although some may be rebuilt through rest and a good diet. Women know a great deal about their own fecundability, distinguishing those who conceive with difficulty ("elephant breeders") from those who conceive very readily ("breed like dogs"). This affects both attitudes to postpartum sex and contraceptive use. Having several "wet infants" (suckling babies) at the same time is seen as undesirable both by wives and

Table 9.5
Terms Used to Describe Physical Condition of Women
in the Three Languages of the North Bank Division, Central Gambia

Meaning of Term	Mandinka	Wollof	Fula
A young woman with no children or one at most	Sukoto	Janka	Surbaajo
A woman at the beginning of her reproductive career: "young spouse"	Foro muso dindingo	Jongoma	Jombaajo
A woman in the middle of her reproductive career: "married woman"	Foro muso	Jegg	Kaaba
A woman at the end of reproductive career: literally "spent"	Sarifo	Sarifo	Dadul taje
A very old woman—all her resources gone	Muso keba	Magette	Nayeejo

SOURCE: Fatou Banja Camara, Adam Thiam, Balla Silla, and Caroline Bledsoe.

husbands. Chronological age or elapsed time in calendar months is thus irrelevant; the key is the stage reached in *faaso* depletion. The stages are well defined, and are set out along with their meanings in table 9.5.

A woman with little *faaso* left is "old." Very few men want women with low *faaso* reserves, so for a woman it may be prudent, if the marriage is rocky or the husband is sickly, to retain or conserve some *faaso* in case a new marriage is imminent. The notion that women are using contraceptives to preserve their *faaso* can inflame some men, who accuse their wives of "spoiling their luck." Altogether, the coherence of these ideas and their logic constitute a strong argument for a radical re-interpretation of the African fertility transition.

Men too understand the *faaso* concept and have a shrewd eye for their wives' fecundity from the date of first marriage onwards. Some men advise close inspection of the bride's mother's reproductive performance before deciding to marry. With several wives, management of the timing and pace of reproduction assumes additional importance. The children's stage of development is crucial, determining the husband's financial responsibilities and the help he can expect from his children as well as his sexual access to his wives. He needs to know the stage of *faaso* depletion for each woman since he may have important decisions to make about taking additional wives if he wants to have more offspring and his current wives are "wearing out." These are very real concerns since the process of depletion and biological aging cannot be reversed and is not amenable to treatment by Western or local medicine. The point of this descriptive analysis (ethnography?) is to show how much calculation and forward planning takes place in such communities. The process can hardly be described as "natural" when so many options and intentions are the subject of daily discourse and of constant negotiation. Note that although the reference framework is still the biological capacity to reproduce as in the classic demographic approach, the stages are not expressed in chronological age or time but in terms of reproductive capacity, consumed or potential.[6]

To social anthropologists, the foregoing account, when properly documented with exact quotes from key informants and additional information from newspapers and official documents such as health cards and marriage certificates, constitutes a solid first step along the road to a fuller cultural interpretation of the processes of reproduction in Gambian society. In this school of thought, the onus is on the researcher to present a coherent view of the workings of the society under study based on often fragmentary evidence gathered from a wide variety of sources, animate and inanimate. The kinds of tests applied to the authenticity of the account will include things such as: Did the researcher speak to respondents in their own language? Was the researcher aware of his or her preconceptions on the subject and have they been honestly presented in the account? Did the investigator, based on past experience on how long this work takes, spend enough time in the field to be an authority on the population studied? And finally, there may be some cross-checking with the accounts of others. This is very different from the standards of accuracy applied to the collection and analysis of the more concrete information which is the stock in trade of the demographers and epidemiologists. For this group, the kind of criteria to be applied would include topics such as sample size and design, accuracy of the translation of the questionnaire, reliability of the results based on re-interviews and comparison with other studies, and conformity to expected patterns based on demographic models. In this latter case, we find major survey programs such as those conducted by the World Fertility Survey or the Demographic and Health Surveys commonly edit the field data in line with expectations to eliminate problems linked to missing or inaccurate dates of birth (Otto and Rattenbury 1987:480–81).

The Concept of a Population

In searching for a resolution of some of these differences, it seems that one of the major stumbling blocks may be the notion of a population. Demographers have a very gross definition of a population—more or less the set of coresident people in a defined geographical area—whereas the tendency in anthropology is to think in terms of societies. Lewis (1976:16) made some helpful comments in this respect, noting that "we study *peoples* rather than *people*. Our primary units of reference are 'societies,' that is distinct and relatively autonomous communities whose members' mutual social relations are embedded in, and expressed through, the medium of a common culture. Culture is the key term here" (1976:16). Once the boundaries of the units of study are drawn on this basis, then the kinds of questions we pose and the approach we adopt are bound to be different from the demographic notion of a population. The choice of the community has more than academic significance as some recent work in epidemiology has shown. There are now numerous studies of high-risk behavior and the distribution of risk in whole populations (David 1995 has a good summary of the issues). Many researchers have shown that, in terms of population-wide public health interventions to reduce premature mortality from cancer or heart disease, the measures that have altered the distribution of say, cigarette smoking or alcohol consumption in the population as a whole have had the most effect not only on the whole distribution but also on the tails of the distribution. We were led to this conclusion by first noting the extreme, "abnormal" cases in the general population, which is the classic approach of clinical practice. We react to observations at the extreme but in practice what happens in the middle of the bell-shaped curve matters most. The parallel with the originally misguided approach to the problem of AIDS in Western countries is very striking.

Within a society, it seems that we often determine our behavior on the basis of extreme cases—avoiding flying after one terrible air crash, staying in after dark following a macabre shooting. In The Gambia, we were eager to find out if mothers have noticed the recent improvements in child mortality and have altered their fertility behavior accordingly. It turns out from interviews that there is some realization that the major epidemics of measles and poliomyelitis have receded but often the one exceptional case is quoted as a basis for concern. Maternal mortality ratios are very high in this area (100 per 10,000 deliveries) but only 100 or so such deaths in many years of surveillance have been recorded among a total resident population of about 17,000 people. A maternal death is so significant socially that even one such death reminds mothers of the risks of having children despite improvements in the overall rate.

Rose (1992) asked many of these questions about population means and exceptional cases in a public health framework and raised the difficult issue of individual variation in human populations. In recent years, the vogue in demographic analysis has been to apply the Cox model and its extension to a variety of problems ranging from mortality and fertility (with their proximate determinants) and to marriage and migration (Trussell, Hankinson, and Tilton 1992). Two separate issues are the subject of current attention. One concerns the problem of "identifying, controlling, and . . . estimating the effects of unobserved variables in demographic analysis" (Manton, Singer, and Woodbury 1992:9). A related issue concerns the problem of heterogeneity, a topic which has gained new prominence from those working in physical anthropology or genetics (see Adams et al. 1990 and Campbell and Wood 1994 for excellent reviews). Both sets of issues arise from the adoption of a particular approach to modeling the interactions we observe in demographic data and the units we select for our analyses.

Bledsoe and her colleagues draw attention to the generally normative framework used in many demographic inquiries (Bledsoe and Hill in press; Bledsoe with Camara 1995; Bledsoe et al. 1994), a point that Lockwood (1995) has developed further. These authors set out to show the malleability of such norms. Indeed, several examples were used to show that norms themselves might be manipulated or re-expressed in different ways in order to justify or render acceptable the comportment of a certain individual. This is more than simply saying there is a variance around any mean; it amounts to asserting that deviations may be conditional upon the mean.

Here, we cannot pursue these ideas further except to indicate that the constant reference to the notion of an idealized, closed, homeostatic, and self-sufficient population may be the stumbling block to a deeper understanding of demographic processes. The aggregate measures we work with do not appear to be the basis for determining human behavior by the individuals involved in the process although they may serve as a basis for negotiating departures from some public norm in certain cases. Individuals require space to pursue their own interests and it is helpful to retain some ambiguity in particular circumstances. In such circumstances, generalizations based on some adaptation of game theory may be more useful than the enforced order and patterns resulting from aggregation of individual data. In an uncertain world, it may be perfectly rational to plan on the basis of extreme cases rather than on the population average.

Divergent Views

Before proceeding to a synthesis, let us remind ourselves of the very polarized positions that confront us. Consider the very clear statement made by an Indian economist familiar with small-scale anthropological studies:

> First, without measurement, any pretense at scientific analysis is impossible; second, even to know what to measure, let alone how to measure, a theoretical framework is necessary; and third, measurement or data collection has to be carefully designed, whether it relates to the design of scientific experiments or to studies of socioeconomic change. (Srinivasan 1989:238)

Compare it with one senior anthropologist's views:

> Social anthropology is not, and should not aim to be, a "science" in the natural sense. . . . Social anthropologists should not see themselves as seekers after objective truth; their purpose is to gain insight into other people's behavior, or for that matter, their own. "Insight" may seem a very vague concept but it is one we admire in other contexts; it is the

> quality of deep understanding which, as critics, we attribute to those
> whom we regard as *great* artists, dramatists, novelists, composers. (Leach
> 1982:53; emphasis in original)

Proof is a slippery concept for all the social sciences and the hard sciences as
well. Whatever the definition, it is nonetheless a key concept since it plays a
central role in the way we formulate our theories and in the process we use to
collect evidence to support or refute our theories. Leaving aside the whole
thorny notion of causality in science, let us take the reasonable approach and
consider proof in the same context we might as jury members in a court of
law. In other words, the accused is assumed innocent until the prosecution can
amass a body of evidence sufficiently persuasive to convince lay people of his
or her guilt beyond any reasonable doubt. This last phrase is important since
it expresses a level of certainty that almost all social scientists would accept.
Regardless of the technical nature of the theory, the evidence, or the analysis,
the conclusions must stand the test of public scrutiny by individuals not pro-
fessionally involved in the work. There may be some academic ostriches who
insist that their theories and conclusions are too complex for lay people to
understand but most of us across a wide variety of disciplines would feel some
sense of failure if we were unable to convince others outside our field of the
correctness and importance of our analyses and conclusions.

There are, however, two major difficulties in adopting this very reasonable
position with reference to proof, both of which arise from our concern in social sciences to mimic our colleagues in the physical and biological sciences.
The first is the pressure to show causality rather than simply stopping at associations. The second follows naturally from this: once we establish a truly
causal set of connections, then of course we should be able to predict the outcomes in circumstances different from the original. Many scientists, social and
otherwise, regard prediction and the testing of predictions against real life
situations as the hallmark of sound research. Let us briefly revisit this well-
worn path with special reference to the interface between demography and
anthropology.

Causality and Its Implications

As graduate students, we made the belated discovery of Heisenberg's Uncertainty Principle and with this came the realization that even at the atomic and
the subatomic level relationships between different particles or elements in
physical systems were associated with probability distributions rather than
being linked by discrete, closed form equations. We lifted our heads a little
and reviewed equations with our physical and biological friends (not the
chemists—they were beyond the pale) since for a while we felt on an equal
footing. Popular science was blossoming on radio and television as well as in
publications such as *The New Scientist* and *Scientific American.* All science

could be understood through basic intelligence and some careful reading. The essential wholeness of the social and the physical sciences seemed assured; as budding population scientists, we thought of people as particles; surveys, censuses and vital statistics were the meter readings needed to quantify the relations between the particles and hence formed the basis of theory. Perhaps nothing as grand as a General Theory of Relativity was in our minds but nonetheless we felt that some general principles could be evolved to provide an orderly framework for interpreting the chaos we saw around us.[7] Jacob Bronowski provided lucid support for these fancies (1960). In geography and regional science, Ravenstein's Laws on migration were dusted off to provide new insights into population movements; the work of Lotka and Coale provided a basis for understanding how birth rates, deaths rates, and the age structure of all human populations were inextricably linked; and we took in our stride the work of political economists such as Marx, Rostow, and Schultz to understand the links between population and development.

All of these developments seemed to be adding flesh to the skeleton of population studies—the demographic transition model. There have been ripples of dissent in the past to this very normative approach to the description of demographic development: Simon (1992) asks awkward questions about the economic consequences of rapid population growth, while Boserup (1965) queries the circumstances in which agricultural innovation is most likely. But these are minor waves in a sea of extraordinary orthodoxy. In retrospect, the isolation of demographers seems shocking given the intellectual ferment in the main disciplines encompassing population studies. This is not the place to analyze the reasons for demography's isolation but the result was that, due to the very success of its central tenets (mortality has improved as a result of health interventions, fertility has fallen in part due to family planning programs, and population projections have produced some quite accurate forecasts of the numbers which eventually materialized) demography has been left behind by the medical and biological sciences and by sociology, economics, and anthropology in two quite different ways. First, the medical and biological sciences have developed new tests, new statistical methods, and new field methods which have allowed them to increase the accuracy of their predictions in nonlaboratory situations. Modern epidemiology is a treasure trove of methods to simplify the real world so that the "true" effects of a factor can be isolated amidst myriad other effects. Although not causal at the molecular level but certainly reductionist in approach, these statistical associations between input variables and selected outcomes have proved solid enough to form the basis of successful, population-wide interventions which have greatly contributed to raising the quality and the length of life. Meanwhile the mainstream social sciences, many of which eschew prediction as a goal, have developed new criteria to successfully demonstrate the connection between one set of observations and another. Developments in theory and logic have to-

gether lifted the level of discourse beyond the description of patterns and con-
sistencies to the point where much of social welfare policy is based on the
results of this work. There is some general agreement about evidence and the
nature of the explanation, albeit at a very different level from conventions in
the medical and biological sciences.

Issues of prediction have also created major divisions in the various human
sciences. Surely the good ethnographer or anthropologist should have some
views about the direction of future change in the population under study.
These views are not likely to be as exact as a prediction in the physical sciences
but looking backwards and forwards is also a way to know when to be surprised. Impressions alone without some rigorous testing can be quite misleading. My own predictions about mortality differentials in the work in central
Mali in the 1980s were proved quite wrong by later events (Hill 1985). The
surprise sent me back to the field with new questions and a realization that I
had missed something important. Shying away from constructing future sce-
narios (or current ones from historical studies) is reneging on some responsibilities to be rigorous. There is certainly a case for declaring more carefully
our predispositions and hunches at the outset. One advantage of model building is that it forces us to be explicit about assumptions.

Final Remarks

The conclusion from this essay is that demography and anthropology are
passing like ships in the night since neither group feels the need to embark an
on open discussion about the nature of evidence and the prerequisites for what
might amount to convincing proof. Demography in particular has fallen between two stools, missing out on developments in both the physical and the
social sciences and not realizing that other approaches are possible. Two reasons for this oversight stand out. One is that demographic data are abundant,
discrete, and accessible. With such a wealth of this kind of material, demographers can become arch-empiricists without much need for bridging theory
or even crude speculation. The other is that the easy definition of a population
has blinded us to more complex thoughts about what holds people together
and what divides them.

On the other hand, anthropology, and to a lesser extent all the related social sciences, have been riven by postmodern uncertainties about subjectivity
and objectivity. The attack on structural functionalism has not produced any
satisfactory synthesis, simply scorn by one camp for the others. Bourdieu for
once concisely explained the crossroads we face in this subjectivist/objectivist
dichotomy: "the analysis of objective structures . . . is inseparable from the
analysis of the genesis, within biological individuals, of the mental structures
which are to some extent the product of the incorporation of social structures;
inseparable too, from the analysis of the genesis of these social structures themselves" (1990:14).

In case we might think that understanding both objective and subjective structures and processes might produce a masterly synthesis, Bourdieu went on to criticize this "synoptic illusion" since the coherence generated was necessarily imposed rather than *sui generis* (1984, 1990). There is a rocky road ahead until we can develop the "communal consensus" which philosophers such as Wittgenstein and Kripke invoke to help us understand how relatively simple concepts such as addition are dependent less on understanding the underlying principles and more on a collective agreement to accept that twelve plus seven equals nineteen. And it appears that the proper beginning for the development of this consensus must be a frank discussion of what all of us, regardless of disciplinary origins, will accept as evidence in the first instance and as convincing proof (or disproof) later on.

NOTES

The field project in The Gambia conducted jointly with Caroline Bledsoe provided much of the raw materials for this chapter. Caroline's willingness to share her field notes is much appreciated. In addition to the people directly linked to this project such as Fatou Banja Camara, Ousman Cham, and Tanya Marchant, I would like to acknowledge the suggestions and insights contributed by Margaret Luck, Balla Silla, and Adam Thiam. The project was run in The Gambia under the auspices of the U.K. Medical Research Council with financial support from both the Rockefeller and the Mellon Foundations.

1. Tom Fricke was the source of this suggestion.

2. In Mandinka, the adjective is *sere*, meaning close, growth arrested; in Wollof *neff*, implying deprived; and in Fula *kodaado*, meaning prevented, also deprived.

3. I would like to thank Caroline Bledsoe for allowing access to her field notes on which much of this section is based. Some of her recent work is summarized in Bledsoe with Camara (1995). The rest of the material is taken from the "Rounds" interviews conducted by Fatou Banja Camara in 1993–95, during which a separate topic was examined in depth each month for a total of fifteen months.

4. I thank Fatou Banja Camara and Adam Thiam for a revealing discussion of this concept.

5. Personal communications from Balla Silla (The Gambia); Adam Thiam (Mali) and Jacob Adetunji (Nigeria-Yorubaland).

6. Bourdieu explores this idea of relative time in his essay on Algerian peasants (1963); some similar ideas appear in Hill 1993.

7. Many of these ideas are wittily presented in Gellner 1985.

REFERENCES

Abramson, Paul R., and Steven D. Pinkerton. 1995. *Sexual Nature Sexual Culture*. Chicago: University of Chicago Press.

Adams, Julian, David A. Lam, Albert I. Hermalin, and Peter E. Smouse. 1990. *Convergent Issues in Genetics and Demography*. Oxford: Oxford University Press.

Bledsoe, Caroline H., with Fatou Banja Camara. 1995. "Numerators and Denominators in the Study of High Fertility Populations: Past and Potential Contributions from Cultural Anthropology." Paper for the seminar on The Continuing Demographic Transition, organized in honor of John C. Caldwell, August, 14–17. Australian National University, Canberra.

Bledsoe, Caroline H., and Allan G. Hill. In press. "Social Norms, Natural Fertility, and the Resumption of Post-Partum 'Contact' in The Gambia." In *New Approaches to Anthropological Demography*, ed. Alaka Basu. Oxford: Oxford University Press.

Bledsoe, Caroline H., Allan G. Hill, Patricia Langerock, and Umberto D'Allesandro. 1994. "Constructing Natural Fertility: The Use of Western Contraceptive Technologies in Rural Gambia." *Population and Development Review* 20(1):81–113.

Bongaarts, John. 1982. "The Fertility-Inhibiting Effects of the Intermediate Fertility Variables." *Studies in Family Planning* 13(6/7):179–89.

Bongaarts, John, and Robert G. Potter. 1983. *Fertility, Biology, and Behavior*. New York: Academic Press.

Boserup, Esther. 1965. The Conditions of Agricultural Growth. Chicago: Aldine.

Bourdieu, Pierre. 1963. "The Attitude of the Algerian Peasant towards Time." In *Mediterranean Countrymen*, ed. Julian Pitt-Rivers. 55–72. Paris: Mouton.

———. 1984. *Distinction*, trans. Richard Nice. Cambridge: Harvard University Press.

———. 1990. *In Other Words: Essays Towards a Reflexive Sociology*. Cambridge: Polity Press.

Bronowski, Jacob. 1960. *The Common Sense of Science*. London: Pelican Books.

Caldwell, John C., and Pat Caldwell. 1981. "Cause and Sequence in the Reduction of Post-Natal Abstinence in Ibadan City, Nigeria." In *Child-Spacing in Tropical Africa*, ed. Hillary J. Page and Ron Lesthaeghe. 181–99. London: Academic Press.

Campbell, Kenneth L., and James W. Wood, eds. 1994. *Human Reproductive Ecology: Interactions of Environment, Fertility, and Behavior*. Annals of the New York Academy of Sciences, vol. 709. New York: New York Academy of Sciences.

Coale, Ansley J., and Susan C. Watkins. 1986. *The Decline of Fertility in Europe*. Princeton: Princeton University Press.

David, Patricia H. 1995. "High Fertility and Short Birth Spacing: The Poverty Consequences of Family Building Patterns." Paper for the IUSSP Seminar on Demography and Poverty, Florence, March 2–4.

Davis, Kingsley, and Judith Blake. 1956. "Social Structure and Fertility: An Analytic Framework." *Economic Development and Cultural Change* 4(4):211–35.

Gellner, Ernest. 1985. *Relativism and the Social Sciences*. Cambridge: Cambridge University Press.

Greenwood, Brian M., and John R. Baker, eds. 1993. "A Malaria-Control Trial Using Insecticide Treated Bed Nets and Targeted Chemoprophylaxis in a Rural Area of The Gambia, West Africa." *Transactions of the Royal Society of Tropical Medicine and Hygiene* 87 (June), suppl. 2.

Hill, Allan G. 1993. "Breaking Free: Alternatives to the Lexis Diagram." Paper given at IUSSP meeting, New Approaches to Anthropological Demography, Barcelona, November 10–13.

———, ed. 1985. *Population, Health, and Nutrition in the Sahel*. London: Kegan Paul.

Hobcraft, John, and Roderick Little. 1984. "Fertility Exposure Analysis." *Population Studies* 38:21–45.

Leach, Edmund. 1982. *Social Anthropology*. London: Fontana Paperbacks.

Lewis, Ioan M. 1976. *Social Anthropology in Perspective*. London: Penguin.

Lockwood, Matthew. 1995. "Structure and Behavior in the Demography of Africa." *Population and Development Review* 21(1):1–32.

Lunn, Peter G. 1985. "Maternal Nutrition and Lactational Infertility: The Baby in the

Driving Seat." In *Maternal Nutrition and Lactational Infertility*, ed. John Dobbing, 41–64. New York: Raven Press.

Manton, Kenneth, G. Burton Singer, and Max A. Woodbury. 1992. "Some Issues in the Quantitative Characterization of Heterogeneous Populations." In *Demographic Applications of Event History Analysis*, ed. James T. Trussell, Richard Hankinson, and Judith Tilton, 8–37. Oxford: Clarendon Press.

Otto, James, and Judith Rattenbury. 1987. "WFS Data Processing Strategy." In *The World Fertility Survey: An Assessment*, ed. John Cleland and Chris Scott, 477ñ514. Oxford: Clarendon Press.

Page, Hilary J., and Ron Lesthaeghe, eds. 1981. *Child-Spacing in Tropical Africa*. London: Academic Press.

Popper, Karl. 1961. *The Poverty of Historicism*. London: Routledge and Kegan Paul.

Rose, Geoffrey. 1992. *The Strategy of Preventive Medicine*. Oxford: Oxford University Press.

Simon, Julian. 1992. *Population and Development in Poor Countries: Selected Essays*. Princeton: Princeton University Press.

Srinivasan, T. N. 1989. "On Studying Socio-Economic Change in Rural India." In *Conversations between Economists and Anthropologists*, ed. Pranah Bardhan, 238–49. Delhi: Oxford University Press.

Taeuber, Irene B., and Carl Taeuber. 1971. *People of the United States in the Twentieth Century*. Washington, D.C.: Bureau of the Census, U.S. Government Printing Office.

Trussell, James T., Richard Hankinson, and Judith Tilton, eds. 1992. *Demographic Applications of Event History Analysis*. Oxford: Clarendon Press.

United Nations. 1983. *Indirect Techniques of Demographic Estimation*. New York: United Nations.

Vallin, Jaques. 1985. "Présentation et analyse critique des sources statistiques." In *Manuel d'Analyse de la Mortalité*, ed. Roland Pressat. Paris: Institut National d'Etudes Démographiques.

van de Walle, Etienne, and Helmut V. Muhsam. 1995. "Fatal Secrets and the French Fertility Transition." *Population and Development Review* 21(2):261–79.

van de Walle, Etienne, and Francine van de Walle. 1972. "Allaitement, Sterilité et Contraception: les Opinions Jusqu'au 19e. Siècle." *Population* 27(4–5):685–701.

Westoff, Charles, and Luis H. Ochoa. 1991. *Unmet Need and the Demand for Family Planning*. Comparative Studies 5. Columbia, Md.: Demographic and Health Surveys.

Wood, James. 1994. *Dynamics of Human Reproduction*. New York: Aldine de Gruyter.

Chapter Ten

Culture Theory and Demographic Process: Toward a Thicker Demography

Tom Fricke

Research traditions are strengthened by their encounters with new problems and the incorporation of concepts from other disciplines. A corollary is that a discipline which avoids new problem areas or which does a bad job of developing new concepts will soon be confronted by its own irrelevance. Within anthropology, Clifford Geertz noted the torpor settling over studies of religion after World War II and attributed some of this to the "narrowly defined intellectual tradition" from which its concepts were increasingly drawn (1973:87). His subsequent merging of concepts from the philosophy of symbolism with the sociology of Parsons and Shils breathed new life into these studies (1973). In demography, too, the vigor of interdisciplinary borrowing is well illustrated by John Caldwell's turn to quasi-anthropological techniques in the early 1960s as a precursor to a subfield—microdemography—that is still coming into its own (1982).

Alasdair MacIntyre (1988:355) suggests more generally that all traditions are characterized by a recurrent developmental trajectory across three phases: (1) in periods of stability, authority, texts, and beliefs have not yet been put to question; (2) eventually, however, inadequacies are identified but not yet remedied; (3) finally, reformulations are identified. For MacIntyre, the success or failure of these reformulations mark a discipline's intellectual maturity. He refers to that period in which practitioners grapple with their tradition's inadequacies as one of "epistemological crisis" (1988:361).

In this chapter, I suggest that demography is in the midst of its own epistemological crisis, the seeds of which have been recognized since at least Caldwell's turn to anthropological concepts and methods some thirty years ago.[1] Rather than leading to a stable reformulation of the demographic tradition, however, the borrowing from anthropology has had a more piecemeal effect. This is because direct borrowing has tended, until recently, to be confined to methodological innovations leading to the subfield of microdemography or to a small range of theoretical contributions from British social anthropology most amenable to the emphasis on family and kin relations. All of these areas lend themselves well to demography's quantitative orientation, focusing on individual-level variation, but they are less adequate to the needs of researchers interested in meaning and motivation.

The parameters of what I, following MacIntyre, will call demography's epistemological crisis are quite straightforward and widely agreed upon. First, many demographers recognize that reductionist explanations in terms of economic variables alone cannot adequately explain demographic processes. Second, they have rightly searched within other social science traditions, notably anthropology, for conceptual tools that will allow them to incorporate meaning and motivation into analysis. Finally, demographers' appeal to the culture concept without attention to its uses in anthropology often causes either confusion or misapplication.

As outlined in chapter 1 of this volume and elsewhere (Kertzer 1995; Greenhalgh 1990, 1995, 1996), the problem derives from demography's historical inattention to debates in culture theory, long a special province of anthropology but with increasing participation from the other social sciences (Ortner 1984; Wuthnow 1987; Alexander 1988; Strauss 1992). Nevertheless, to the extent that a connection exists between individual behavior and the cultural and social contexts of its occurrence, the issues raised by culture theory are central to our consideration of demographic outcomes. While some have begun to tie these broader theoretical formulations to the understanding of demographic events (Kertzer 1984; Greenhalgh 1990, 1995; Hammel 1991), the work of fleshing out a complete theory linking these analytic levels is only beginning. It is this linkage that will require a fundamental rethinking of demography's place within the larger social science enterprise. The outcomes which demography seeks to explain and understand will always be behavioral and subject to forms of analysis in the tradition of the natural sciences, but they are also the products of human action and thus susceptible to further analysis from the full range of approaches in the human sciences.[2]

In what follows, I explore the nature of demography's crisis and its potential solution in cultural theories which link multiple analytic levels of culture, society, and the individual. I draw out some of the implications of this theoretical solution for method in demography and provide examples of my reasoning from empirical research into demographic and family transitions in Nepal.

Demography's Crisis

MacIntyre's account of epistemological crisis describes both its form and the nature of adequate resolution.[3] A key to the dynamism of all traditions of inquiry is the existence of unsolved problems; at any moment, these problems have the potential to remain insoluble through a tradition's standard concepts and methods. In the perpetual encounter between tradition and the world, the indications of crisis are clear: "Hitherto trusted methods of enquiry have become sterile. . . . Moreover, it may indeed happen that the use of methods of enquiry and of the forms of argument, by means of which rational progress has been achieved so far, begins to have the effect of increasingly disclosing new inadequacies, hitherto unrecognized incoherences, and new problems for the solution of which there seem to be insufficient or no resources within the established fabric of belief" (MacIntyre 1988:362–63). Resolving this condition involves new conceptual developments that can clarify the reasons for past inadequacies while maintaining the overall continuity between old and new theoretical structures. Resolutions lacking these attributes indicate a tradition's demise rather than its further development.

My claim that demography is in the midst of an epistemological crisis is predicated on demographers' recognition of key inadequacies within this tradition of inquiry. These inadequacies bear a family resemblance even though they have been encountered by single researchers across thirty years of work in strikingly different settings. An early indicator of the need for conceptual development was the recognition that reductive economic explanation left a substantial portion of demographic variation unaccounted for and that more complete explanation needed reference to normative and cultural systems of meaning (Anderson 1986; Lesthaeghe and Wilson 1986). Caldwell's turn to microdemography outside of Euro-American settings was motivated by a similar recognition of the need to make room for local systems of meaning in demographic theory. On the one hand, Caldwell's insights enlarged the scope of relevant dimensions for analyzing demographic regimes. At the very least, microdemographic techniques allow for new attention to the complexity of local contexts and highlight the mediating role of family and kinship relations in demographic events (Caldwell 1982; Caldwell, Reddy, and Caldwell 1988). A potentially more far-reaching insight was Caldwell's attention to the changing institutional regimes that formed a social context for individual fertility strategies. This familial and institutional matrix for demographic transition continues to motivate much theoretical and empirical work, drawing attention to the consideration of demographic behavior within relatively localized institutional contexts (Kertzer and Hogan 1989; McNicoll 1980; Thornton and Fricke 1987; Thornton and Lin 1994).

Notwithstanding this pervasive recognition of inadequacy in past demographic accounts, the search for a remedy seldom approaches the reformulation of fundamentals required in a living research tradition. As a result, researchers concerned with the problem of meaning and its connection to demographic events look for meanings at strikingly different levels, with little attention to their integration or location within an overall scheme. One outcome of this is a creative anarchy of methods and measures. On the methodological side, microdemography and more clearly ethnographic approaches contend against focus group approaches with little sense of their relative merits for gathering information at various levels. Indeed, the very act of contrasting focus groups to ethnography betrays a misunderstanding of both ethnography, which is a general approach encompassing a variety of particular methods, and the multiple levels at which meaning is found.[4]

At the conceptual level, the locus of meaning seems to vary considerably from study to study. One approach fixes on subjective measures of value at the individual level (Arnold et al. 1975; Lesthaeghe and Surkyn 1988). Another fixes on elements of social structure and social organization (Dyson and Moore 1983; Caldwell, Reddy, and Caldwell 1988). Others approach cultural and social systems as rule-based or normative systems (Mason 1987; Mason and Taj 1987). In the end, with all the unprecedented methodological and conceptual borrowing, much of the excitement derives from the search for a quick technical fix to perceived inadequacy rather than rethinking the position of demography within larger social theory. This is evident in the demographic treatment of culture.

Culture, Meaning, and Motivation

As members of a research tradition in the social sciences, demographers are likely to stay closer to their data than many others. Still, they recognize a wide range of variables, many from well beyond the proximate determinants of population processes, as being worthy of consideration.[5] Thus while a narrow view of the demographic enterprise relegates it to an important but relatively sterile series of proximate determinant analyses of fertility, mortality, and migration, the importance of wider dimensions of individual experience, such as those influencing marriage timing and fertility, is itself implicit in Davis and Blake's original formulation (1956) and is so well-established as to need no defense. Demographic attention has quite naturally been drawn to the determinants of these other experiences. Similarly, the relevance of contextual factors at the levels of community and social organization is widely accepted. Many analysts are comfortable moving back and forth between individual-level experience and institutional context, in part because these dimensions have intuitively clear empirical referents in the environment or in behavior. For most scholars, the presence of a particularly sanctioned relationship for parental authority, set of household labor and resource contributions, or form of consanguineous marriage are as concretely verifiable as the presence of a school or family planning clinic (Caldwell 1982; Dyson and Moore 1983; McNicoll 1980; Entwisle, Casterline, and Sayed 1989).

Institutional analyses, however, are notably deficient at uncovering the locale-specific meanings of behaviors or of the motivations driving actors toward particular strategies of behavior. Analyses that take social organizational features as the ultimate level of context, while ignoring local contexts of meaning, implicitly assume that people's motivations are universal; this can lead to untested suppositions such as ascribing the childbearing behavior and desires of non-European women to oppressive patriarchal constraints, the absence of which would free women to behave exactly as they would in Europe or North America. Culture, if referred to at all, exists in highly normative formulations that assume a law-like authority in behavior. Its measurement is often confined to categorical measures within which normative regimes are felt to apply.

I avoid singling out any particular studies here, but readers are probably familiar with references in the literature to "Muslim cultures," "Confucian cultures," "cross-cousin marriage cultures," and the like. In the former two cases, the categories are so broad and include so many distinct local histories and symbolic systems as to be nearly worthless in identifying cultural attributes. Such categories virtually ensure an approach to culture which stresses what Malinowski called "that lifeless body of laws, regulations, morals, and conventionalities which *ought* to be obeyed, but in reality are often only evaded" (quoted in MacIntyre 1971:212). The danger of this approach is that any behavioral divergence from these normative statements could be taken as culture change. In the case of referring to cross-cousin marriage as a cultural pattern, cultural and institutional levels are conflated. This has the effect of seriously undermining the potential for analyzing meaning and motivation while sharing the problem of how to evaluate behavioral divergences from the rule.[6] Within anthropology, the importance of distinguishing terminological kinship categories, institutional preferences, and strategically variable behaviors has been clarified through complex, often tedious, debate (Levi-Strauss 1969: xxx–xxxv; Needham 1971: xci–xcv; Barnard and Good 1984:100–104). When demographers incorporate anthropological concepts without a sense of their history, they tend to repeat the earlier anthropological sins hashed out in these clarifying discussions.

Such has been the case with culture theory where, as Eugene Hammel notes: "anthropological theory has moved away from the institutional, structural-functional approach it has long presented to its sister social sciences, toward the elucidation of local, culture-specific rationalities, in the building of which actors are important perceiving, interpreting, and constructing agents" (1990:456). But if anthropological conceptions of culture have moved beyond these earlier notions of behavioral prescription and institutions, their measurement becomes much more problematic and their uses to demography less evident. What then is a more current view and what does it offer to demography?

Culture as Context

Cultural theorists are especially insistent on the complexity and partial autonomy of cultural processes (Alexander 1988, 1990),[7] but a useful starting place for arguing the relevance of culture to demography is to treat it as yet another contextual level with parallels to social and institutional contexts. As context, culture is a part of the shared background against which and in terms of which social life is carried out. Culture is not simply a summation of individual preferences or overlapping values; it is an underlying framework for these individual characteristics (Taylor 1985). From this point of view, it is difficult to top the clarity of Geertz's formulation: "[Culture] denotes an historically transmitted pattern of meanings embodied in symbols, a system of inherited conceptions expressed in symbolic forms by means of which men [and women] communicate, perpetuate, and develop their knowledge about and attitudes toward life" (1973:89).

Models of Reality

In that same essay, Geertz developed the notion, important to theories of meaning and motivation, of cultural patterns as both models *of* and models *for* reality. As models of reality, cultural patterns constitute the perceived worlds of human actors and define the significance of behaviors and institutions for the analyst. A question confronting any demographer seeking to go beyond the proximate determinants of phenomena is: What variables do I measure in this society? We proceed from various empirical clues and theoretical understandings of causal processes. We now commonly measure individual experiences such as wage labor experience, schooling, and a range of marriage attributes that have demonstrated significance across populations. But our tendency to pull these variables out of theory simultaneously evades the localized meaning these behaviors may have and blinds us to other potential variables of local significance.

Caldwell's discovery, and the discovery of all social scientists who have experienced life in the communities we study, is that actual contact with people will open analysis to important new causal variables. At the same time, his method also illustrates the larger weakness of ignoring the place of demographic research within broader social and cultural theory. A data-collection method that takes culture seriously would allow for an interplay between locale-specific definitions of significant variables and *a priori* causal models. Caldwell's south Indian research (Caldwell, Reddy, and Caldwell 1988) proceeded more directly from his interest in concrete determinants of demographic variables—a movement outward from the dependent variables of interest—rather than from an understanding of cultural context. As a result of his earlier work in Africa (1982), his theoretical model emphasizes intergenerational relationships within patrilineal systems and his analysis of the South Indian fertility and marriage transition is largely concerned with relationships within patrilines. Important as these relationships are, Caldwell's analysis gives far less attention to the interpatriline relationships organized between members of senior generations through the marriages of their children even though anthropological work suggests the importance of these processes.[8]

Beginning with cultural models of reality allows demographers to discover what is significant from the point of view of the actors themselves. Another way of making the point is to use Taylor's language: we cannot know what behaviors actors find significant in making choices of potential demographic importance without attention to the background horizons which give them meaning (1991:36–40). Behaviors that are trivial in one setting may take on significant meanings in another and these meanings may have demographic relevance. In research among the Tamang, for example, my colleagues and I discovered exactly this with the pattern of natal home visits by newly married women. We found that these visits among the virilocal Tamang varied with marriage form and that the visits were themselves a significant factor in the timing of first births. Our procedure began with cultural models and moved toward hypotheses concerning fertility outcomes (Fricke, Axinn, and Thornton 1993; Fricke and Teachman 1993).

Models for Reality

Taken as models for reality, cultural patterns offer a partial resolution to the problem of establishing motivation for actors within a common cultural context. Actors are necessarily aware that their actions have meaning for those around them. Apart from their implications for demographic outcomes, behaviors are also statements or symbols of relationship and subject to interpretation. The analogy is with language. In any culture, there are limits to the range of acceptable statements and actors can be assumed to want to convey meanings from the range of values available to them. Key values, or goods (MacIntyre 1981, 1988), come to define that culture and to form an overall motivation for actors within it. As with the elements that define a cultural model of reality, these motivations are held in common and define the bounds of the community within which a culture is shared. Subjective motivations exist within the range of the culturally possible.[9]

For demography, an important implication of this is that demographically relevant behavior need not be motivated by any explicit consideration of the demographic outcome. Marriage practices are, again, a useful illustration since marriage timing in populations not using contraception is so closely linked to fertility. Among the Tamang of Nepal, for example, marriages signify the entry into multiple exchange relationships between families and are interpreted in terms of the superordinate ethic of reciprocity. Relationships between families are manipulated through the marriage of daughters and hypotheses about the timing of marriage need to consider its cultural meaning in those terms (Dahal, Fricke, and Thornton 1993; Fricke 1995). These cultural motivations, which take the form of common notions of the good, cannot be discovered through analyzing institutionalized behaviors or individual preferences alone (MacIntyre 1971; Barnes 1971). Although cross-cousin marriages are often consistent with a cultural emphasis on reciprocity, there are no verified examples of societies in which all marriages are between even categorical cross-cousins (defined as such before marriage). If culturally acceptable marriage alternatives exist, then the simple prevalence of a particular marriage behavior in a population cannot by itself indicate common motivation even though it is a partial outcome of an underlying cultural model for reality.

This suggests that cultural motivations are not easily discovered by beginning with proximate determinants of demographic outcomes and working back from behavior toward antecedent cultural patterns. Again, as with cultural patterns as models of reality, culture must be analyzed in its own terms before its implications for demographic phenomena can be hypothesized. The form of that analysis is fundamentally different from the causal analyses more familiar to demographers since there is no variance to be explained in the same sense that there is at the level of individual behavior or preferences. This suggests that even the format for presenting a culturally sensitive demography would be altered so that the development of expectations followed some discussion of cultural meaning and context.

Analytic Levels and a Thicker Demography

Although cultural patterns can be analyzed separately and in their own terms, their links with other analytic levels are a central issue for demographers. Geertz developed the approach to culture sketched above while still acknowledging the Parsonian framework emphasizing the three analytic dimensions of culture, society, and the individual (Alexander 1987:302–29). He moved away from that position toward one that established culture as prime mover in social analysis in subsequent work. Just as Parsons never seriously developed the mechanisms by which context and behavior were connected, Geertz's own later development had the effect of disconnecting culture from mechanisms which recognize its reciprocal relations with individual behavior and subjective experience. This model left little room for the demographic interest in dynamic causal analyses (Kertzer 1984; Hammel 1990). Since then, culture theory has returned to linking culture with behavior, although important works in this area have been shielded from demographic eyes by their exotic titles and apparent lack of demographic relevance.[10]

One set of explicit discussions linking these levels is in a series of works by Jeffrey Alexander (1988, 1990), who views behaviors as strategies carried out within constraints and with resources that are culturally and materially defined. This analytic model shows great promise for reconceiving analyses of demographic outcomes by striving to link levels of analysis without asserting the priority of one over the other. The cultural level both constructs and provides evaluative meaning for the social reality of actors. The social system level provides normative constraints and guidelines and allocates social resources. Individuals pursue strategies in terms of these larger contexts and in terms of their own life-course experiences within these contexts.

Recent work in cultural psychology has also modified earlier failures in cultural theory to accommodate variation among individual actors. For example, while continuing to recognize that cultural models may have motivational force, Strauss (1992) and D'Andrade (1992) argue that knowing the "dominant ideologies, discourses, and symbols of a society" constitutes a first step in analysis that must be followed by attempts to link these intersubjective symbols or meanings to individuals (Strauss 1992:1). They suggest that actors vary with respect to their internalization of culturally defined motivations and that the differential experience of buttressing events throughout the life course may explain some of that variation. This is similar to MacIntyre's discussion of the importance of actual practice to the internalization of culturally defined goods or virtues (1981:187–96). It follows that we might expect those individuals who engage in practices closely linked to cultural models of the good or the moral will be more likely to have internalized cultural motivations than those who do not (D'Andrade 1992).

The pursuit of analyses in these terms implies different research styles appropriate to each level. Selection of appropriate variables aside, much demographic analysis would proceed as it has up to now, but the placement of levels of analysis within an overall framework would resolve the demographic crisis in incorporating meaning into analysis. At the very least, cultural analysis would not be straitjacketed into the formal causal models of individual-level analyses. Insofar as cultural patterns provide a necessary context for understanding meaning and motivation, we are calling for another level of analysis in addition to those that already incorporate social and community contexts into individual-level analyses—a thicker, cultural demography to match interpretive analyses of culture (Geertz 1973).

Descriptions of culture necessarily describe systems of meaning and require different criteria of validity than the causal explanations appropriate to individual variation. The primary criterion of an adequate description is its coherence, as Taylor points out: "A successful interpretation is one which makes clear the meaning originally present in a confused, fragmentary, cloudy form. . . . [W]hat is strange, mystifying, puzzling, contradictory is no longer so, is accounted for. . . . What we are trying to establish is a certain reading of text or expressions, and what we appeal to as our grounds for this reading can only be other readings. The circle can also be put in terms of part-whole relations: we are trying to establish a reading for the whole text, and for this we appeal to the readings of its partial expressions" (Taylor 1985:17–18). This may be the most difficult characteristic of this approach for demographers to accept. It requires a different form of argument and greater openness to reformulation than is typical for the usual analytic verifications of quantitative analyses. Its rewards are found in more nuanced and contextualized discussions of meaning based on local criteria.

An Empirical Example

A thicker demography will necessarily open up presentations of empirical analyses to forms that go beyond the natural science models of much of the literature. At the same time, it will continue to recognize the value of many of the currently prevalent individual-level analyses, although that value will be transformed by assigning them a place within a larger model of human action. Existing examples of studies that invoke cultural meaning include a broad spectrum ranging from those that closely resemble more traditional ethnography in communities (Ahearn 1994; Fricke 1994), to characterizations of cultural models in complex societies (Martin 1987; Scheper-Hughes 1992; Kertzer 1993), to more focused examinations of a single motivational idea (Santow and Bracher 1994). In our own work, my colleagues and I have used cultural models to develop hypotheses for testing in multivariate models which, except for the culturally informed selection of particular independent variables, are very similar to standard demographic analyses (Fricke, Axinn, and Thornton 1993; Fricke and Teachman 1993; Dahal, Fricke, and Thornton 1993). Analyses from our research have also been generated in terms of models that make more use of social, rather than cultural, context (Axinn 1992a, 1992b). The resolution of demography's crisis that I propose here is intended to broaden rather than restrict the bounds of acceptable demographic analyses. In the remainder of this chapter, I present an example of an analysis which integrates the several levels described above. I have intentionally chosen to analyze a demographic watershed involving few cases, not because quantitative analyses are inappropriate to the cultural demography advocated here, but in order to illustrate more concretely some of the new dimensions drawn into analysis.

The Research Problem

In 1985, four years after my first research visit to Timling, a remote Himalayan community in central Nepal, and two years before a second data collection visit, the first men in the village's history obtained vasectomies. What follows here is a case study of that watershed event in community demographic history: the transition from a society in which no person had used contraception to limit marital fertility to one in which a small number had begun to do so. The theme is demographic, but the approach self-consciously differs from orthodox presentations in demographic forums. Where the normal course of analysis begins with a theoretical introduction and develops expectations which are then tested against a set of empirical data, this example begins with the event itself and explores the multiple contexts of its occurrence.

I approach these issues by proceeding inductively from the nascent arrival of family planning in Timling. My procedure, following more interpretive anthropological styles (Geertz 1973; Ortner 1989), is to successively explore the multiple contexts in which these vasectomies occurred and to attempt to tease out the motivation of these five men within cultural structures. Attention to motivation implies a concern with indigenous meaning; cultural theorists argue that it is in terms of antecedent meaning systems that individuals survey their social world and attempt to weigh action strategies based on conflicting goods. As argued above, a procedure intended to explore the culturally informed motivations of actors cannot work backwards from the event requiring explanation, uncovering a rationalized decision-making process. The key interpretive frames in a culture may appear quite distant from demographically relevant action, but more importantly, they are features of context that are simply assumed and not easily available to the actors themselves. The purpose of this extended case study is to suggest the interpretive processes that these five men were likely to have employed as a way of sketching the issues we as analysts need to consider in linking moral change and fertility behavior.

A Himalayan Village and the Onset of Family Planning

Timling was, in 1987–88, a nucleated settlement of 142 households and 609 people located in the strikingly rugged terrain of central Nepal some five days' walk from the nearest roadhead. Its residents, members of an ethnic group known as Tamang, are aware of their marginal involvement in national affairs and have until recently obtained most of their livelihood through subsistence agriculture and pastoralism within a cul de sac formed by the ridges of higher Himalayan peaks. At the same time their economy is also marked by increasing involvement in migratory wage labor since the closing of the Tibet-Nepal border in 1960. Lying on a narrow shelf of land between 7,000 and 7,600 feet above sea level, the village is centrally located for exploitation of vertical climatic zones appropriate to growing millet, maize, wheat, barley, and potatoes. Until recently, Timling's social organization of labor exchanges through marital alliance and family-organized work admirably suited the subsistence requirements of domestic groups in the local setting (Fricke 1994).

The Tamang, who speak a Tibeto-Burmese language, inhabit much of the central Himalaya around the Kathmandu Valley. Their ancestors arrived in the country from Tibet and today's widely dispersed Tamang share many characteristics including the practice of Tibetan forms of Buddhism in daily ritual life, common preferences for bilateral cross-cousin marriage,[11] and an emphasis on the exchange and alliance values of marriage. Tamang social organization includes patrilineal clan structure and the practice of virilocal residence after marriage. Marriage itself organizes relationships involving interfamilial labor cooperation and, in the past, was crucial to the re-creation of political alliances between families and lineages. Marriage among the Tamang organizes cooperative relations between families in which wife-receiving groups are expected to provide services to their in-laws.

Timling's ethnographic and demographic character were first systematically described from 1981–82 fieldwork (Fricke 1994). Marriage and fertility histories gathered at this time from all married women in the village established that no person used nonindigenous methods of family planning.[12] Lack of use was not due to a lack of availability since mobile family planning clinics and fieldworkers had been coming to the village area for some years before 1981. The consensus in that first research period was that Timling men and women didn't use the services because they didn't feel a need to use them. Indeed, once it became known that the ethnographer was asking questions about the uses of and desires for children, he was often spontaneously approached at the village spring or on the trail by men who wanted to explain why Timling people needed as many children as god would give them. Subsequent data collection in 1987 (Axinn, Fricke, and Thornton 1991) revealed that five Timling men had received vasectomies in the intervening years, two in 1985 and three in 1986.[13] Among these men was one who had approached the ethnographer in 1981 to argue that it was sinful to limit fertility.

The Arrival of Family Planning

The first news that a mobile family planning clinic would be available to perform vasectomies spread by word of mouth when three men were returning from the market at the nearest roadhead with loads of salt and oil. They passed through the neighboring village of Sertung where the regional health post had been established and were asked to pass the word on to Timling. One of these men (YT)[14] was among the first two to receive a vasectomy, bringing with him a village Lama (GL) who was related to him as the father of his younger brother's wife and also connected by labor exchanges. Most people agreed that, although YT brought the news, he was convinced to actually obtain a vasectomy by GL, who already had seven living children. People also pointed out the special ranked relationship between the two men—GL held a socially higher standing in their system because his family provided a daughter in marriage to YT's family. The two men were closely watched by others in the village and, when nothing untoward occurred, were followed the next year by a group of three men (BG, SG, and CT). These men were led by BG, who himself had six living children and who was married to YT's sister. CT had no close kin connection to the others, but had seven living children.

While these five men brought Timling across the threshold into what Caldwell has characterized as a transitional society,[15] they were not followed by other vasectomies through the fall of 1993, an indication of how tentative innovative behaviors may be before widespread acceptance. The explanations for why others have not followed focus on the complaints of CT and GL, both of whom have claimed that they lost their strength as a result of the operation.[16] GL's complaints were delayed long enough for the three others to obtain operations the following year, but CT's were more immediate since he suffered a severe infection of the groin after his operation.

A Difference in Values?

The novel behavior of permanent sterilization was met in Timling with differing degrees of enthusiasm, illustrated by a central rite of passage performed for SG's son in early December 1987. The ritual, a haircutting ceremony for boys, involves the invocation of family connections established by marriage as well as ritual purifications in the families of the boys receiving these haircuts. Patriline elders sit around the fire the night before the interfamilial rituals to burn juniper incense and chant the transmission of lineage histories, mixing the names of religious teachers and important ancestors from whom the boy is descended in an unbroken lineage. In the case of SG's son, the patriline ritual was to be performed by the sixty-two-year-old former village headman, SG's paternal uncle, who disapproved of the vasectomy. At one point in the ceremony, he stopped his chanting long enough to remonstrate his nephew for stopping the lineage names by making this the last son he would have.

From the perspective of contemporary demographic analysis, this might constitute the starting place for an explanation since the statement of lineage continuity is clearly and proximately related to the desire to have children. The difference of opinion between the uncle and nephew could be taken as consistent with a value shift across generations. If this were the case, we might expect that those men who had obtained vasectomies were acting on new values acquired through contact with nonfamilial or other novel experiences in their past. Such a view, while plausible in many respects and consistent with a number of models of life-course and family transition, draws attention away from an analysis of culture and toward a set of variables easily measured across settings. Its problem is not that it is necessarily wrong in any simple way, but that it is incomplete in its inability to consider culturally shaped motivations and actors' strategic attempts to achieve ends consistent with these motivations.

To make this more clear, table 10.1 displays selected characteristics of these five men. Were there a fairly consistent linkage among prior novel experience, new values, and subsequent behavior at the individual level, we might expect these men to appear unusual in other dimensions related to their life-course experience and family relationships. Literacy is one source of exposure to new ideas, for example, yet only one man claims to be able to read a letter in Nepali. Similarly, only one man has lived away from the village for a month or longer before marriage. Furthermore, in a set of characteristics that directly reflect an individual's commitment to family relationships organized by marriage, we find a prevalence of behaviors that seem to reflect values that we might associate with the disapproving headman instead of his nephew SG. Four of the five men have married women classified as cross-cousins, a form of marriage consistent with highly-regarded family alliances and labor exchange in Timling. All of these men had their first marriages entirely arranged by a senior family member. Four of the five contributed expected labor services to their in-laws' families after their marriages. These do not seem to be the characteristics of innovators across all dimensions.

Nor is it that alternative behaviors were unavailable to these men. There has been a lot of change in Timling and yet these men are not involved in the most dramatic dimensions of this change. Restricting ourselves to the forty-

Table 10.1
Selected Characteristics of People Reporting Vasectomies in Timling

Person	Age	Number of Living Children		Reads Nepali	Lived Away	Wife First Cross-Cousin	Marriage Arranged	Performed Brideservice	Year of Vasectomy
		Sons	Daughters						
GL	42	2	5	N	N	Y	Y	Y	1985
YT	36	2	1	Y	Y	Y	Y	Y	1985
BG	45	4	2	N	N	N	Y	Y	1986
SG	36	2	2	N	N	Y	Y	N	1986
CT	40	4	3	N	N	Y	Y	Y	1986

four men who were currently married and aged thirty-one to forty-five in 1987 (a group which includes the five men who obtained vasectomies), we find that 23 percent were literate, 34 percent lived out of the village for a month or longer before marriage, 25 percent married nonrelatives, 52 percent participated in the choice of their first spouse, and 20 percent did not perform brideservice duties for their in-laws.

A quantitative analysis would be futile if we hoped to relate the behaviors of these men to their other individual characteristics, but ethnographic analysis has a long tradition of exploring apparently aberrant behaviors or events to cast light on systems of meaning. Where the goal is to understand action in cultural and social context, the actions of these five men offer analytical possibility through a successive detailing of the contexts in which they occurred (Ortner 1989; Alexander 1988).

Cultural and Societal Contexts

Culture and society form the two contextual levels within which individuals with their own contingent histories and circumstances pursue goals (Alexander 1988). By referring to cultural context, we are appealing to specific meanings of behavior while also developing a distinct, culture-bound theory of motivation for individuals. Society, on the other hand, refers to the context of interpersonal relations within which individuals are concretely located. Its scope may differ in the degree to which communities are integrated into large state systems (Alexander 1988; Greenhalgh 1990), but in populations that organize most social activities locally, the effective societal context is often at the community level.[17]

Cultural Goods: An Ethos of Reciprocity

If culture can be taken heuristically as distinctive models of and for reality, both constituting individual perceptions and providing sources of motivation, then the core of Tamang culture centers on an ethos of exchange and reciprocity which has been described in detail and related to various social strategies in earlier analyses (Fricke, Axinn, and Thornton 1993; Fricke 1990). This ethos is played out in every domain of Tamang social life, from myth and ritual to the organization of marriage and other relationships such as the exchange of work or the distribution of food. While I am here concerned with those proximate dimensions implicated in fertility, the demand for children, and interfamilial relations, the demands of reciprocity provide cultural motivation and meaning for these secondary, or instrumental, values. Thus, the overall cultural context within which the Tamang pursue their ends is one predicated on an ethos of reciprocity and exchange; this ethos provides Timling actors with an interpretive model for their own actions and the actions of others.

Evidence for the primacy of reciprocity is found in the extent to which it is appealed to as a justification of many disparate actions. One man, for example, who had subverted the marital arrangements made for him by his parents explained that he did so because the woman violated Tamang standards of reciprocity. He refused to marry her because "she had bad habits." When pressed, he elaborated that these bad habits were seen in her refusal to offer food and drink to visitors, an essential marker of Tamang hospitality (Fricke 1990). Paradoxically, his parents justified the marriage arrangement itself as a part of reciprocal obligations in the exchange of women between clans in cross-cousin marriage.

That two very different actions can be justified with appeals to the same superordinate good suggests that a cultural ethos may have some staying power in the face of the gradual shifts in individual behaviors that constitute social change. The staying power is illustrated by the comment of a woman who had herself, against great pressure from her family, refused to stay in a marriage arranged by her parents.[18] In spite of her own history, when asked in 1991 if she would give her own daughter away in an arranged marriage, she replied that she would if the request was on behalf of her brother's son: "How can I be so self-important as to deny my own brother?" A brother's right to a sister's daughter for his son is a linchpin of the Tamang reciprocal marriage system.

Violations of expectations in familial relationships elicit great emotion when they cut against the obligations of reciprocity. One man, who had himself lost his parents at an early age, spoke of the care he gave his eldest son from early on and his bitterness at not having it reciprocated:

> [A]fter he brought in this daughter-in-law, he began to listen to her words and his good habits were ruined. Ohhh. . . . But after he was spoiled it was made right. It was made right. He has not had a son. My son who just split off from my house has not had a son of his own.
>
> I damned him with a powerful curse [and] he has not had a single child. None at all. . . . And he won't have any in the future either. . . .
>
> When I gave that parents' curse. . . . Oh, but who is really afflicted? It's the parents who are cursed! . . .

> ... A father's own son gives him how much suffering by being born
> and if he doesn't do well by his father then it is the father's curse.... [F]or
> a mother and father the curse is like a long road surrounding them.[19]

Proximate values and their implications for behavior need to be seen against the overarching interpretive framework that gives them meaning. Thus, the reports of informants concerning the advantages and disadvantages of having children take on additional relevance in this context. Among the Tamang, children confer numerous advantages to their parents, many of which are common to subsistence economies. Children contribute to the continuity of families and to the economic activities of discrete households, for example. Timling informants recounted the need for children in terms of the essential household tasks in an undifferentiated agricultural subsistence economy. Many informants spoke of their desire for children in terms of the need to have labor for plowing fields, hauling firewood, and watching cattle, sheep, and goats. Parents spoke of the future security that children would provide by supporting them in old age (Fricke 1994).

A distinctively Tamang desire, however, places children into the context of the exchange ethos. Children "tie us to other households" as one informant put it (Fricke 1994:182). They do so by organizing interfamilial exchange relations through their marriages. That is, cross-cousin marriages in subsequent generations maintain the links between families over time. The centrality of these relationships for Tamang social life draws the desire for children out of individual household needs alone and places it within the context of wider social requirements.

At the same time, the interpretation of interpersonal relationships in terms of reciprocal obligation extends to those between parents and children. While every informant spoken to in 1981 mentioned the advantages of having many children because of their contribution to the family economy, social support, and connections to households, they also viewed the disadvantages of children in terms that suggest reciprocal obligations between parents and children: "Too many children reduce the inheritance share." The inheritance share is a kind of establishment fund which parents are expected to supply to their children—land for sons and moveable goods for daughters—when they leave the household. The provision of an inheritance is part of a cycle of reciprocity between parents and children which begins at birth. Parents support young children who, as they themselves age, contribute increasingly to the household. Later, children receive their inheritance, part of which is contingent on their own contributions to the household.

In 1981, every person asked about the potential disadvantages of a large family referred to the reduction in inheritance shares for their children. In 1987 each of the men who received a vasectomy justified it in terms of protecting the inheritance portion of their children. The discussion above suggests that this responsibility to provide such an establishment fund was not in itself a novel value. Rather it was already part of an existing array of values joined under the ethos of reciprocity.[20]

The previous coexistence and apparent complementary nature of these values direct attention to a shift in their relative weight in motivating behavior. At some point we can assume that bearing many children for the good of the household and for marriage exchange became incompatible with the simultaneous responsibility to reciprocally provide for the children themselves. Put another way, the change is not in the prevalence of one disposition over another in this population. These multiple ends have always, in living memory, coexisted and they continue to coexist. What has changed is their integration with other values in the context of a changed material environment.

Many social theorists recognize the need to integrate culture and values with the material conditions in which individuals pursue their strategies if we are to truly understand actual behavior. This attention to individuals as creative, active participants in their lives represents an advance over antiquated cultural analyses that seemed to treat people as automatons hopelessly caught in the gears of a giant culture machine. As people pursue their goals they consider information about the world as they experience it, however filtered their perceptions are by their culture itself. For Timling, that world is embodied in the concrete relationships in which the demands of reciprocity are realized.

Thus while the first step in the cultural demography I advocate establishes motivations by beginning with the interpretive frame used by the actors themselves, it quickly moves to second-order obligations concerning how people should act in many different situations and relationships. The multiplicity of those situations introduces the potential for conflict in the satisfaction of obligation and requires consideration of the actual material and social world of our actors since diverse goods can come into conflict (Taylor 1985). I turn next to changes in that social context of decision-making.

Societal and Material Contexts of Decisions

The changes in material context and individual experience for Timling's people has reached into nearly every element of their lives. From shortages of new arable land to new experiences of work and other relations with the outside world, the evaluative environment has been radically transformed. Timling's people are strikingly aware of these transformations in their social world. In a conversation with the ethnographer, the former headman reflected on changes occurring within his own lifetime:

> When I was young, Calcutta was only a name. Now many of our people have been there. Trains, buses, cars . . . only things heard about. Now a road goes to Lari. Slowly, people here will change. The school will get bigger. Someday a road will come to the village—first across Pang Sang

[the high pass to the east], then from Dhading [the district headquarters to the south]. . . . We will be able to take our things to Kathmandu to sell and we will have Kathmandu things here. It will only take a day instead of four or five. (Fricke 1994:205)

The changes recounted in that fireside conversation are precisely those areas marked by theoretical discussions as central to the link between individual experience, the structure and content of authority in kin relations, and their implications for larger social transition (Caldwell 1982; Thornton and Fricke 1987). Their implications for once-assumed transactions in reciprocity networks have destabilized many of the links based on cross-patriline marriage alliance.

Most central and compelling are the transformations in individual activities that have taken men and women outside of the village and into non–kin-organized relationships with elites in Kathmandu and beyond. Their participation in wage labor, motivated at least partially by a need to supplement subsistence from the local environment, is the single most dramatic transformation in individual experience in the village. The motivation for participating in these external work opportunities is, in part, the widespread recognition that Timling's population has expanded to the limits of its land base. Little high quality arable land remains to be extracted from the forest as new expansion is hemmed in on the one side by a wall of snow peaks forming the border with Tibet and on the other by already established Tamang settlements facing similar problems (Fricke 1994). The outcome, recognized explicitly by Timling people, is a slow process of decline in average household land and a need to go beyond the community to supplement subsistence.

If we look at the different experience of men and women across birth cohorts we can see some of the extent of transformation in individual activities across time. In early analyses I broke the population of Timling into birth cohorts and examined the proportions of men and women who had, by given ages, experienced wage labor organized outside the village. Table 10.2 repli-

Table 10.2

Life Table Estimates of Cumulative Proportions Working for Wages Outside of Family Enterprises for One Month or More through Age X by Sex and by Ten-Year Birth Cohort

	Males					Females				
AGE (N)	<1936 45	36–45 37	46–55 31	56–65 51	66–75 82	<1936 43	36–45 30	46–55 32	56–65 57	66–75 72
6	.000	.000	.000	.000	.000	.000	.000	.000	.000	.000
12	.044	.027	.032	.059	.065	.023	.000	.031	.000	.061
18	.267	.135	.290	.471	—	.116	.133	.313	.228	—
24	.444	.378	.484	.784	—	.233	.200	.500	.507	—
30	.533	.459	.677	—	—	.233	.233	.531	—	—

Table 10.3
Living Arrangements, Work, and First Marriage Processes
in Selected Birth Cohorts of Timling Women

Birth Cohort	<1946	46–65	66–75	Total
Number of Women	76	82	26	184
	%	%	%	%
A. Parental Background and Premarital Life-Course Experience				
Parental work before R's marriage				
Neither parent	83	56	35	64
Mother only	4	5	4	4
Both	3	17	35	14
Father only	11	22	27	18
R lived out of Natal village before marriage				
Never	99	79	69	82
Yes	11	21	31	18
R lived away from parents before marriage				
Never	86	68	39	71
Supervised	3	10	15	8
Unsupervised	12	22	46	21
Monetary income work before marriage				
None	80	63	35	66
Family only	4	11	8	8
Fam. & nonfamily	8	7	12	8
Nonfamily only	8	18	46	18
B. Marital Autonomy and Indicators of Reciprocal Marriage Alliance				
Choice of spouse				
Entirely senior	51	33	27	40
Together	31	30	31	30
R alone	18	37	42	30
Marriage type				
Cross-cousin	72	70	69	71
Unrelated	28	30	31	29
Husband provided brideservice				
No	18	37	50	31
Yes	82	63	50	69

SOURCE: Fricke et al. n.d.

cates this cohort analysis to show that, of men born in the decade between 1936 and 1945, only 14 percent reported having worked for a month or more at wage labor by age 18. The percentage more than doubled to 29 percent for men born in the next decade, 1946–55. It increased to 47 percent for men born in the next decade. Percentages for women show a similar rise followed with a slight decline with 13 percent, 31 percent, and 23 percent reporting wage labor by age 18 for these same periods.

Table 10.3 also indicates dramatic transformations in individual lives by comparing the reports of successive birth cohorts of women for key experiences relating to the familial organization of work, living arrangements, and marriage. The story is quite similar for men and parallels the transformations described above. The trends for family background and life-course transitions show that Timling women are increasingly likely to have some involvement in their choice of spouse, to come from families in which one or both parents work at wage labor, to live out of the village for a month or longer before marriage, and to engage in wage labor before their marriages.

When coupled with life-course theories of socialization that link processes of individual experience with other dimensions of social life and cultural transformation, these cohort differences become provocative hints of the larger changes in social relationships which structure demographic process in Timling. The changing experiences of men and women implicate relations between the generations and genders in ways recognized by the people themselves. In Part B of table 10.3, indicators of these authority relations between generations and the reciprocity relations between families joined in marriage show that women are increasingly likely to choose spouses themselves, that there has been a small increase in marriages outside of relational networks, and that the provision of brideservice labor has dramatically declined. PG, a sixty-two-year-old man, reflected during 1987–88 fieldwork on these changes:

> Before when we went together traveling across country [paradesh] they [women] didn't travel without the company of men from their own families, not even as far as Trisuli, certainly not to Kathmandu. And if they needed to go to the bazaar for supplies or to buy anything at all, they didn't buy it themselves but we [patriline men] bought it and gave it to them. Nowadays they buy it themselves and give it to us. . . . Now they have no fear, no respect for the unknown. They go about completely by themselves.

Consequent changes in authority relations have further transformed the village even as exposure to outside influences in the work camps and in Kathmandu offer contrasting visions of life to young people. As the conversation continued, PG mentioned the changes in intergenerational power and drew out the contrasts:

> Now those old habits are gone and finished. The habit of farming . . . gone and finished. You need to cut hay; you need to cut firewood; you need to do farm work at the house. In the morning, you wake and do farm work. Then you come back at mealtime. Then in the afternoon you need to go and cut hay or have to go and work the furrows in your garden plots. You need to go for that. So you do that and then in the evening you need to roast corn, or millet, and you need to grind grain for flour. And

doing this means that you don't get any sleep. After your evening meal
then you need to get things ready for the next day. . . .

Now there [at the work camps for road construction] they don't have
to do that. In the afternoon, their meal is given to them and in the evening
they can play and have a good time. Oh there is a little bit of work but it
is swiftly completed. And after that they can return [to their quarters] to
cook and eat good, filling rice. . . . In the evening at 5 or 6 o'clock, they
can sleep. Sleep or sing songs or have a party. At home they can't have this
kind of constant fair.

Paradoxically, the initial motivation for sending children out to work in these
camps derived from household strategies largely determined by the interests
of the senior generation. Among the many values of children outlined earlier
were the diversification of the household economy and the reduction of drudgery. One woman also mentioned the role of children in tying households together through cooperative labor and exchange relationships in marriage. The
value of children as social support for the aged was a universal refrain during
1981 fieldwork. PG's reflections on change in Timling suggest a transformation even in this arena by drawing out the further implications of exposure to
life outside of Timling.

In the village, everybody is joined. But there [in the work camps and in
Kathmandu] a person makes his own way, his own provisions for tomorrow's food; he's alone. He builds one house for himself. And then another
builds one for himself and so on . . . everybody for himself. And with that
kind of process the old habits are gone, finished.

Survey data from 1987–88 support many of PG's statements. We have already
seen figures that show the differential exposure of young people to life outside
of Timling and evidence of decline in interfamilial forms of reciprocity. Analyses exploring the relationship of these changing experiences with other central
components of Timling's organization—notably marriage and the relations
organized by it—clarify their immediate impact (Fricke et al. n.d.). These results indicate that social transformations in family and individual life-course
experience affect the likelihood of interfamilial exchanges. Marriage to non-
kin is associated with a significant reduction in brideservice and non-kin marriages themselves are more likely in cases where women have some say in the
choice of spouse.

Changes at this level represent a real threat to the stable coexistence of
goods recounted above. The coexisting interfamilial obligations to exchange
women and labor along networks organized by marriage begin to slip in a
world where, as PG commented, "a person makes his own way, his own provisions for tomorrow's food." Analytically, these characteristics constitute yet
another contextual level. Although the transformations in life-course experience and in the practice of institutionalized behaviors such as brideservice oc-

cur at the level of individuals, they form a perceptual context for the people of Timling. Extended comments by informants illustrate how those behaviors can be regarded as a general contextual feature of the social environment.

Culture, Values, and Strategy

In the other Tamang Family Research Project setting of Sangila, these changes toward nonfamilial organization of activities are positively correlated with the acceptance of contraception at the individual level (Axinn 1992a), although even there contraception is largely used to terminate childbearing rather than to delay births or extend intervals. The five innovators from Timling, on the other hand, were generally characterized by behaviors that seemed to show a commitment to declining practices. Most entered into marriages regarded as classic examples of reciprocal exchange; all had their marriages arranged by seniors; most engaged in interfamilial labor exchanges organized by marriage. All of these activities are quite consistent with the ethos of reciprocity. Moreover, when asked about the rationale for their vasectomies, each replied in terms of that ethos: to provide their children with an adequate inheritance share.

Sangila differs from Timling in numerous ways, including longer histories of immersion into a wage labor economy, proximity to roads, and family planning services (Axinn 1992b, 1993). I suggest that in Timling, where levels of cross-cousin marriage, brideservice, and the like have always been higher in the lifetimes of these respondents (Fricke, Axinn, and Thornton 1993), that the earliest stages of processes in their fertility transition proceed from conservative values. I also suggest that these values are ordered into different levels of specificity, implied here in the distinction between a general Tamang ethos of reciprocity and second-order values such as "having as many children as god gives," "providing children with an inheritance share," or "a sister giving her daughter to her brother's son if asked." All of these second-order values are defended in terms of the more general antecedent value, which because of its less specific phrasing is more likely to be compatible with simultaneously held indigenous values. This last feature argues for its stability in the face of change.

Timling society was stable until roughly 1960 (Fricke 1990, 1994); during this period there was no incompatibility between having as large a family as possible and the need to provide for children. Having many children provided the possibility of returning children in marriage exchanges, diversifying labor tasks in the household economy, opening new land from the forest for provisioning the family (and providing an inheritance share to sons), and expanding the social support network for parents in their old age. That stability was threatened by a number of contextual developments occurring at roughly the same time, each of which limited the resources on which the system depended.

In recent years, Timling's population has experienced a general tightening of resources, including time, which have affected virtually every family. Ritual activities that buttressed small reciprocities between families at village festivals, harvest festivals, and the like are increasingly discarded as men and women to seek to supplement their household economies through outside wage labor. The clan fairs of 1987–88 were a pale reflection of those witnessed in 1981 in part because so many villagers had left Timling right after the harvest to seek other employment.

I suggest that the general transformation of their material conditions has brought once compatible secondary values into potential conflict, most obviously between the value of having many children for reproducing broader social exchange and support networks and the value of providing for one's children with an establishment fund. The conflict forces individuals to make new kinds of decisions, to strategize by weighing the potential benefits of one course of action (favoring maximally extensive relationship networks) over another (favoring provisioning children). This suggests that the early stages of change in this setting, which may well lead ultimately to far-reaching transformations of ethos, do not bring new values into play but involve a reconfiguration of existing and not previously incompatible ones. The increasing incompatibility between values and circumstances forces their reintegration into a new form.

None of this discussion suggests that an individual-level analysis, given a large enough number of cases, is unwarranted. Turning again to the characteristics of the men listed in Table 10.1, we can see that all of them had at least two living sons at the time of their vasectomies and at least three living children. The average number of living children for those thirty-nine men aged 31 to 45 who did not get vasectomies is, as one would expect, less (1.2 sons and 2.3 total children). The point here is that attention to culture and values explores the indigenous meaning of decisions in terms that the actors themselves might use. Making clear associations such as the apparent conservatism of these innovators adds texture to our theoretical understanding of fertility transitions.

Conclusion: Demographic Process in Context

I opened my discussion by suggesting that demography is in the midst of an epistemological crisis centering around its recognition of the need to incorporate localized notions of meaningfulness and culturally shaped motivations into analyses. The terminology of crisis has raised the eyebrows of more than a few demographic colleagues; as MacIntyre insists, however, periodic crisis is essential to development in any tradition of inquiry. Rather than being pejorative comment, this assessment is evidence of intellectual vigor in the demographic tradition, especially since the steady movement toward incorporating new concepts has been initiated by the practitioners themselves (Caldwell 1982; Anderson 1986; Lesthaeghe and Wilson 1986).

The suggestion that culture be taken as yet another contextual level, the characteristics of which are essential to the logic of behavioral strategies, is partially an extension of the already well-developed demographic interest in the familial, community, and institutional contexts of population processes (McNicoll 1980; Caldwell 1982, Entwisle, Casterline, and Sayed 1989; Thornton and Lin 1994). The integration of proximate demographic analyses into these social contexts has brought the demographic tradition into a closer relationship with more general social theory. Taking culture as context continues that movement toward engaging central theoretical issues in the social sciences.

The outcome for demography, I suggest, will include a new openness to novel forms of research presentation and multiple standards of validity. While the types of analysis—this empirical example represents only one of a broad range—do not supplant the individual-level, quantitative analyses now characteristic of demographic practice, the claims for explanatory completeness for these prevalent analytic treatments will necessarily be modified with an eye to their location within a total theory of social meaning and behavior.

Nor is this proposed use of a framework, which derives from Geertz (1973), Alexander (1988), and recent discussion in cultural psychology (D'Andrade and Strauss 1992), the last word on integrating demography into contemporary culture theory.[21] On the one hand, if we take MacIntyre's discussion of developmental trajectories seriously, there can be no final word. On the other hand, we need to recognize that the area of culture theory is itself in such ferment that this framework will appear hopelessly out of date to some and radically novel to others. Further, in the limited space of this chapter I have avoided the essential complexities of political economic and gender issues that receive important treatment in other contributions to this volume and elsewhere (Kertzer and Hogan 1989; Greenhalgh 1990, 1995; Kertzer 1995; Fricke 1995; Nancy Riley, chapter 5 in this volume). Furthermore, because of the empirical nature of my case study, I have not highlighted the important dynamics of culture transformation developed by others (Hammel 1990).[22] This is, of course, part of the larger point here: theoretical sophistication brings with it an awareness that no single analysis will tell the whole story. Nevertheless, while there can never be an absolute standard for a thick demography, it is still certain that attention to demography's place within more general cultural and social theory will inevitably leave it thicker.

NOTES

Portions of this chapter appeared in an earlier form in a paper presented at the IUSSP Seminar on Values and Fertility Change, Sion, Switzerland, February 16–19, 1994. Thanks to Gigi Santow, Michael Bracher, Susan Watkins, John Casterline, and Philip Kreager for comments on that earlier material. Special thanks to Philip for pointing out that Geertz would never find my demography "thick enough." Thanks to Julia Adams,

Bill Axinn, Jennifer Cornman, Dilli R. Dahal, Susan Greenhalgh, Brian Hoey, Dennis Hogan, David Kertzer, Phil Morgan, Sarah Munro, and Nancy Riley for comments on more recent versions. As always, discussions with Arland Thornton have been enormously helpful in thinking through the issues raised here.

1. Readers may object to the idea that participants in any tradition could tough it out through 30 years of crisis. As MacIntyre argues, however, "an epistemological crisis may only be recognized for what it was in retrospect" (1988:363), so it's not necessary to imagine that demographers labored under some overarching sense of crisis throughout this period.

2. See Greenhalgh 1990 for a discussion of the nature of demography's dependent variables within an anthropological framework and Taylor 1985 for a discussion of interpretive versus natural science approaches to human action.

3. Most will recognize the resemblance between MacIntyre's account of developmental trajectories in research traditions and Thomas Kuhn's account of normal science, the emergence of anomalies, and scientific revolution (Kuhn 1970). One difference between the two is that MacIntyre's scheme more explicitly addresses the notion of progress within a research tradition; Kuhn's account implies, for some, a greater relativism.

4. For examples of microdemographic studies, see Caldwell, Hill, and Hull 1988 and Axinn, Fricke, and Thornton 1991. Knodel, Chamratrithirong, and Debavalya (1987) provide a useful empirical example of focus group analysis.

5. The list of work by demographers who have gone beyond formal demographic concerns is huge. See, for example, Dyson and Moore 1983, Rindfuss and Morgan 1983, Morgan and Rindfuss 1984, Lesthaeghe and Surkyn 1988, Watkins 1990, Santow and Bracher 1994, and Thornton and Lin 1994.

6. See Barnes 1971 and Leach 1961 for criticisms of these behavioral approaches to culture, which were often concentrated in the area of kinship and which are therefore especially relevant to demography.

7. It's important to emphasize that this autonomy is partial. Wuthnow (1987) and many others (Alexander 1990; Geertz 1973) make convincingly strong cases for analyzing culture in nonreductive terms, but it is also clear that culture is linked to subjective individual experience in complex ways and indeed must be considered in this context if any dynamic analysis is to make sense (Ortner 1984; Alexander 1990; Strauss 1992; D'Andrade 1992).

8. The contrast between north and south India at the level of social structure is key to Dyson and Moore's analysis (1983). These notions of exchange and hierarchy motivating South Indian relationships are classics of anthropology (Dumont 1983). In many respects, Caldwell's transfer of lineage models from his earlier work in Africa parallels the processes leading to earlier debates about descent and alliance as models of social organization by anthropologists (Leach 1961; Barnes 1971).

9. James Turner provides a useful example from outside of demography in his historical study of atheism in America (1985). As he makes clear, his analysis is not of an increasing proportion of the population professing no belief in God. Rather, he documents the shift in the field of meaning that makes unbelief a possibility in the first place. See also Taylor 1989.

10. Among the important studies redefining the relationship between culture and behavior are Renato Rosaldo's *Ilongot Headhunting* (1980), which uses Norman Ryder's (1965) discussion of cohort and social change to good effect, and Sherry Ortner's *High Religion* (1989).

11. In classic systems of bilateral cross-cousin marriage, women move back and forth between the exchanging groups, which may be clans or lineages; these systems differ from unilateral cross-cousin marriage systems in which women move in only one direction between any two exchange groups. Where the acceptance of a woman implies obligations, bilateral systems organize more egalitarian relations between groups (Barnard and Good 1984; Leach 1961; Fricke 1990).

12. Fricke and Teachman (1993) recount two cases of abortion induced through severe blows to the body, but the circumstances of these were unique, involving unmarried women who had become pregnant by men who refused to take them as junior wives in spite of the acceptability of polygyny among the Tamang.

13. Plus an additional man from within the Timling administrative boundaries but outside the study area.

14. I have preserved informants' confidentiality by creating pseudonyms and using the initials of these pseudonyms in the discussion.

15. This was reported by Timling residents visited in Kathmandu in 1993. As of the summer of 1991, I have first-hand verification of this lack of subsequent vasectomies from a visit to Timling.

16. GL was explicit. Where once he could carry the equivalent of 120 pounds of rice on his back, after his operation he could only carry half that weight. He also complained about sickness serious enough to require the sacrifice of a goat.

17. See Fricke 1995 for a detailing of the relationship between the histories of Timling and Nepali state formation. Ortner (1989) addresses the issue of state and indigenous Sherpa cultural interaction in another Nepali setting.

18. Her case is described in Fricke 1994:136–37.

19. Unless otherwise indicated, lengthy quotations from Timling residents are from translations of Nepali-language transcripts of taped interviews collected in 1987–88.

20. In the other Tamang Family Research Project setting (Sangila), separated from Timling by distance and degree of immersion into the monetary economy of the Kathmandu Valley, Bill Axinn finds a strong positive relationship between practicing contraception and enrolling one's children in school (Axinn 1993). In the context of the shared Tamang ethos of reciprocity across these settings, the schooling of children in Sangila is as much a provision of inheritance share as the giving of land or moveable goods in Timling.

21. See Hammel and Friou, chapter 7 in this volume, and Hammel 1990 for a strongly stated argument against the kind of interpretive framework I propose here.

22. I take up the issue of culture change more explicitly in Fricke (in press).

REFERENCES

Ahearn, Laura Marie. 1994. *Consent and Coercion: Changing Marriage Practices among Magars in Nepal.* Ph.D. diss., University of Michigan.

Alexander, Jeffrey C. 1987. *Twenty Lectures: Sociological Theory Since World War II.* New York: Columbia University Press.

———. 1988. *Action and Its Environments: Toward a New Synthesis.* New York: Columbia University Press.

———. 1990. "Analytic Debates: Understanding the Relative Autonomy of Culture." In *Culture and Society: Contemporary Debates,* ed. Jeffrey C. Alexander and Steven Seidman, 1–27. New York: Cambridge University Press.

Anderson, Barbara A. 1986. "Regional and Cultural Factors in the Decline of Marital Fertility in Europe." In *The Decline of Fertility in Europe,* ed. Ansley Coale and Susan Watkins, 293–313. Princeton: Princeton University Press.

Arnold, Fred, Rodolfo Bulatao, Chalio Buripakdi, Betty Jamie Chung, James T. Fawcett, Toshio Iritani, Sung Jin Lee, and Tsong-Shien Wu. 1975. *The Value of Children: A Cross-National Study.* Honolulu: East-West Population Institute.

Axinn, William G. 1992a. "Family Organization and Fertility Limitation in Nepal." *Demography* 29:503–21.

———. 1992b. "Rural Income-Generating Programs and Fertility Limitation: Evidence from a Microdemographic Study in Nepal." *Rural Sociology* 57(3):396–413.

———. 1993. "The Effects of Children's Schooling on Fertility Limitation." *Population Studies* 47(3):481–93.

Axinn, William G., Tom Fricke, and Arland Thornton. 1991. "The Microdemographic Community Study Approach: Improving Data Quality by Integrating the Ethnographic Method." *Sociological Methods and Research* 20(2):187–217.

Barnard, Alan, and Anthony Good. 1984. *Research Practices in the Study of Kinship.* Orlando: Academic Press.

Barnes, John A. 1971. *Three Styles in the Study of Kinship.* Berkeley: University of California Press.

Caldwell, John C. 1982. *Theory of Fertility Decline.* New York: Academic Press.

Caldwell, John C., Allan G. Hill, and Valerie J. Hull, eds. 1988. *Micro-Approaches to Demographic Research.* London: Kegan Paul International.

Caldwell, John C., P. H. Reddy, and Pat Caldwell. 1988. *The Causes of Demographic Change: Experimental Research in South India.* Madison: University of Wisconsin Press.

Dahal, Dilli R., Tom Fricke, and Arland Thornton. 1993. "The Family Contexts of Marriage Timing in Nepal." *Ethnology* 32(4):305–23.

D'Andrade, Roy G. 1992. "Schemas and Motivation." In *Human Motives and Cultural Models,* ed. Roy G. D'Andrade and Claudia Strauss, 23–44. Cambridge: Cambridge University Press.

D'Andrade, Roy G., and Claudia Strauss, eds. 1992. *Human Motives and Cultural Models.* Cambridge: Cambridge University Press.

Davis, Kingsley, and Judith Blake. 1956. "Social Structure and Fertility: An Analytic Framework." *Economic Development and Cultural Change* 4:211–35.

Dumont, Louis. 1983. *Affinity as a Value: Marriage Alliance in South India.* Chicago: University of Chicago Press.

Dyson, Tim, and Mick Moore. 1983. "On Kinship Structure, Female Autonomy, and Demographic Behavior in India." *Population and Development Review* 9(1): 35–60.

Entwisle, Barbara, John B. Casterline, and Hussein A.-A. Sayed. 1989. "Villages as Contexts for Contraceptive Behavior in Rural Egypt." *American Sociological Review* 54(6):1019–34.

Fricke, Tom. 1990. "Elementary Structures in the Nepal Himalaya: Reciprocity and the Politics of Hierarchy in Ghale-Tamang Marriage." *Ethnology* 29(2):135–58.

———. 1994. *Himalayan Households: Tamang Demography and Domestic Processes.* Enlarged Edition. New York: Columbia University Press.

———. 1995. "History, Marriage Politics, and Demographic Events in the Central

Himalaya." In *Situating Fertility: Anthropology and Demographic Inquiry*, ed. Susan Greenhalgh, 202–24. Cambridge: Cambridge University Press.

———. In press. "Marriage Change as Moral Change: Culture, Virtue, and Demographic Transition." In *The Continuing Demographic Transition*, ed. Gavin W. Jones, John C. Caldwell, Robert M. Douglas, and Rennie D'Souza. London: Oxford University Press.

Fricke, Tom, William G. Axinn, and Arland Thornton. 1993. "Marriage, Social Inequality, and Women's Contact with Their Natal Families in Alliance Societies: Two Tamang Examples." *American Anthropologist* 95(2):395–419.

Fricke, Tom, and Jay D. Teachman. 1993. "Writing the Names: Marriage Style, Living Arrangements, and Family Building in a Nepali Society." *Demography* 30(2): 175–88.

Fricke, Tom, Arland Thornton, Dilli R. Dahal, and Rajendra K. Lama. n.d. "Community Context and the Practice of Brideservice Among the Tamang of Nepal." Unpublished manuscript. Institute for Social Research, University of Michigan.

Geertz, Clifford. 1973. *The Interpretation of Cultures*. New York: Basic Books.

Greenhalgh, Susan. 1990. "Toward a Political Economy of Fertility: Anthropological Contributions." *Population and Development Review* 16(1):85–106.

———. 1995. "Anthropology Theorizes Reproduction: Integrating Practice, Political Economic, and Feminist Perspectives." In *Situating Fertility: Anthropology and Demographic Inquiry*, ed. Susan Greenhalgh, 3–28. Cambridge: Cambridge University Press.

———. 1996. "The Social Construction of Population Science: An Intellectual, Institutional, and Political History of Twentieth-Century Demography." *Comparative Studies in Society and History* 38(1):26–66.

Hammel, Eugene. 1991. "A Theory of Culture for Demography." *Population and Development Review* 16(3):455–85.

Kertzer, David I. 1984. "Anthropology and Family History." *Journal of Family History* 9(3):201–16.

———. 1993. *Sacrificed for Honor: Italian Infant Abandonment and the Politics of Reproductive Control*. Boston: Beacon Press.

———. 1995. "Political Economic and Cultural Explanations of Demographic Behavior." In *Situating Fertility: Anthropology and Demographic Inquiry*, ed. Susan Greenhalgh, 29–52. Cambridge: Cambridge University Press.

Kertzer, David I., and Dennis P. Hogan. 1989. *Family, Political Economy, and Demographic Change: The Transformation of Life in Casalecchio, Italy, 1861–1921*. Madison: University of Wisconsin Press.

Knodel, John, Aphichat Chamratrithirong, and Nibhon Debavalya. 1987. *Thailand's Reproductive Revolution: Rapid Fertility Decline in a Third World Setting*. Madison: University of Wisconsin Press.

Kuhn, Thomas S. 1970. *The Structure of Scientific Revolutions*. Enlarged Edition. Chicago: University of Chicago Press.

Leach, Edmund R. 1961. *Rethinking Anthropology*. London School of Economics Monographs on Social Anthropology No. 22. London: The Athlone Press.

Lesthaeghe, Ron, and Johan Surkyn. 1988. "Cultural Dynamics and Economic Theories of Fertility Change." *Population and Development Review* 14(1):1–45.

Lesthaeghe, Ron, and Chris Wilson. 1986. "Modes of Production, Secularization, and the Pace of Fertility Decline in Western Europe, 1870–1930." In *The Decline of Fertility in Europe,* ed. Ansley Coale and Susan Watkins, 261–92. Princeton: Princeton University Press.

Levi-Strauss, Claude. 1969. *The Elementary Structures of Kinship.* Boston: Beacon Press.

MacIntyre, Alasdair. 1971. *Against the Self-Images of the Age.* New York: Schocken Books.

———. 1981. *After Virtue: A Study in Moral Theory.* Notre Dame: University of Notre Dame Press.

———. 1988. *Whose Justice? Which Rationality?* Notre Dame: University of Notre Dame Press.

McNicoll, Geoffrey. 1980. "Institutional Determinants of Fertility Change." *Population and Development Review* 6:441–62.

Martin, Emily. 1987. *The Woman in the Body: A Cultural Analysis of Reproduction.* Boston: Beacon Press.

Mason, Karen Oppenheim. 1987. "The Impact of Women's Social Position on Fertility in Developing Countries." *Sociological Forum* 2(4):718–45.

Mason, Karen Oppenheim, and Anju M. Taj. 1987. "Differences between Women's and Men's Reproductive Goals in Developing Countries." *Population and Development Review* 13(4):611–38.

Morgan, S. Philip, and Ronald R. Rindfuss. 1984. "Household Formation and the Tempo of Family Formation in Comparative Perspective." *Population Studies* 38: 129–39.

Needham, Rodney. 1971. Introduction to *Rethinking Kinship and Marriage,* ed. Rodney Needham, xiii–cxvii. London: Tavistock.

Ortner, Sherry B. 1984. "Theory in Anthropology Since the Sixties." *Comparative Studies in Society and History* 26(1):126–66.

———. 1989. *High Religion: A Cultural and Political History of Sherpa Buddhism.* Princeton: Princeton University Press.

Rindfuss, Ronald R., and S. Philip Morgan. 1983. "Marriage, Sex, and the First Birth Interval: The Quiet Revolution in Asia." *Population and Development Review* 9: 259–78.

Rosaldo, Renato. 1980. *Ilongot Headhunting, 1883–1974: A Study in Society and History.* Stanford: Stanford University Press.

Ryder, Norman. 1965. "The Cohort as a Concept in the Study of Social Change." *American Sociological Review* 30:843–61.

Santow, Gigi, and Michael Bracher. 1994. "Traditional Families and Fertility Decline: Lessons from Australia's Southern Europeans." Paper presented at the IUSSP Seminar on Values and Fertility Change, Sion, Switzerland, February 16–19.

Scheper-Hughes, Nancy. 1992. *Death without Weeping: The Violence of Everyday Life in Brazil.* Berkeley: University of California Press.

Strauss, Claudia. 1992. "Models and Motives." In *Human Motives and Cultural Models,* ed. Roy G. D'Andrade and Claudia Strauss, 1–20. Cambridge: Cambridge University Press.

Taylor, Charles. 1985. *Philosophy and the Human Sciences.* Cambridge: Cambridge University Press.

———. 1989. *Sources of the Self: The Making of the Modern Identity.* Cambridge: Harvard University Press.

———. 1991. *The Ethics of Authenticity.* Cambridge: Harvard University Press.

Thornton, Arland, and Tom Fricke. 1987. "Social Change and the Family: Comparative Perspectives from the West, China, and South Asia." *Sociological Forum* 2(4): 746–79.

Thornton, Arland, and Hui Sheng Lin. 1994. *Social Change and the Family in Taiwan.* Chicago: University of Chicago Press.

Turner, James. 1985. *Without God, without Creed: The Origins of Unbelief in America.* Baltimore: Johns Hopkins University Press.

Watkins, Susan C. 1990. *From Provinces into Nations: Demographic Integration in Western Europe, 1870–1960.* Princeton: Princeton University Press.

Wuthnow, Robert. 1987. *Meaning and Moral Order: Explorations in Cultural Analysis.* Berkeley: University of California Press.

Contributors

Monica Das Gupta is senior fellow at the Center for Population and Development Studies, Harvard University and, at the time of writing was a Mellon fellow at the Population Studies and Training Center, Brown University.

Tom Fricke is associate professor of anthropology at the University of Michigan, where he is also associate research scientist at the Institute for Social Research and research associate at the Population Studies Center.

Diana S. Friou is a doctoral student in Anthropology and Demography at the University of California, Berkeley.

E. A. Hammel is professor of anthropology and demography emeritus at the University of California, Berkeley.

Allan G. Hill is Andelot Professor of Demography at the School of Public Health, Harvard University.

David I. Kertzer is the Paul Dupee University Professor of Social Science at Brown University, where he is also professor of anthropology and history, and associate of the Population Studies and Training Center.

Philip Kreager is lecturer in human sciences, Somerville College, and tutor in demography and anthropology, Pauling Centre for Human Sciences, Oxford University.

Nancy E. Riley is assistant professor of sociology at the Department of Sociology and Anthropology, Bowdoin College.

Nancy Scheper-Hughes is professor of anthropology and chair of the Department of Anthropology at the University of California, Berkeley, where she also directs graduate training in critical medical anthropology.

G. William Skinner is professor of anthropology at the University of California, Davis, where he holds a joint appointment in the Center for Comparative Research in History, Society and Culture.

Nicholas Townsend is assistant professor of anthropology and associate of the Population Studies and Training Center at Brown University.

Index